CROSSROADS CUTOFFS & CONFLUENCES

CROSSROADS CUTOFFS & CONFLUENCES

Origins of Louisiana Cities, Towns, and Villages

RICHARD CAMPANELLA

LOUISIANA STATE UNIVERSITY PRESS BATON ROUGE

Published with the support of the Jean and Saul A. Mintz Professorship at the Tulane School of Architecture, and the Carol Lavin Bernick Faculty Grant Program at Tulane University

Published by Louisiana State University Press
lsupress.org

Manufactured in Canada
First printing

Designer: Barbara Neely Bourgoyne
Typeface: Calluna
Printer and binder: Friesens Books

Cover illustration created by Barbara Neely Bourgoyne, base image from AdobeStock/Naya Na

Cataloging-in-Publication Data are available from the Library of Congress.
ISBN 978-0-8071-8368-7 (cloth: alk. paper) — ISBN 978-0-8071-8510-0 (pbk.: alk. paper)

TO

Marina and Jason Campanella,

and to the people of Louisiana—

past, present, and future

CONTENTS

CROSSROADS CUTOFFS & CONFLUENCES

INTRODUCTION

This book answers the question *Why are we here?* for most of the 4.6 million people who call Louisiana home. It engages geography's most rudimentary inquiry—the *where* and *why* of human settlement—unearthing the initial siting rationales, and the people and impetuses behind them, for cities, towns, villages, and other populated sites statewide.

"Site" can mean many things. To a director, it is setting and scenography; to an archaeologist, it is an excavation; to an architect, it is the context of a design; in real estate, it is location, location, location. To a geographer, site means the absolute location and underlying geophysical characteristics of a human settlement. It is best understood vis-à-vis "situation," which means relative location—the broader regional ambit of a site, and how strategically it connects with the rest of the world.

"The first task of the geographer," wrote Robert E. Dickinson, "is to determine exactly the characteristics of the site and situation of a settlement."[1] Doing so can elucidate the community's morphology, history, economy, culture, and destiny. A good site in a mediocre situation may never become more than an enclave or hamlet, and Louisiana has lots of those. A good site in a decent situation may yield a sizeable town or city, of which we have many examples. A bad site in a lousy situation usually ends up a ghost town: try visiting Sparta, Louisiana. A lousy site in a fantastic situation is a particularly spirited combination, as New Orleans can attest like few other cities on Earth. Infinite are the gradations therein, and relentless are their changes, as political powers rise and fall, hinterlands develop, markets shift, jurisdictions morph, technologies advance, climate changes, and new opportunities arise. Yesterday's Venice can become, well, today's Venice, just as a desert oasis can become Las Vegas, a railroad junction can become an airline hub (Atlanta), and a bayou confluence may become the petrol capital of the world (Houston). And then there are "Zoom towns."

The siting of settlements is an exercise in hope, a reasoned forecast of the destiny of place and people. Though their fates vary widely, most settlements begin with that spatial reckoning. Writing in 1903, economist Richard Hurd expounded on the resulting site typologies in "Locations of Cities":

> Cities originate at their most convenient point of contact with the outer world and grow in the lines of least resistance or greatest attraction. . . .
>
> Trade routes, the lines of least resistance between the sources of products and their final markets, have in all ages located commercial cities at the points where a break in transportation occurs. . . .
>
> Where a trade route traverses an ocean or lake, cities arise at the harbors which have easy topographical approach from productive regions [and] markets. . . .
>
> Where the trade route follows a river, cities arise either near the mouth where ocean and river navigation meet[,] at the head of rivers[,] the confluence of two or more rivers, [or] at an obstruction in the river requiring unloading. . . .
>
> Land trade routes, prior to the time of railroads, created cities at their intersections, commonly in the centre of great plains. [But] when railroads were invented, they superseded all other land trade routes, and owing to the greater economy[,] their influence has in most cases strengthened existing cities located by water routes.[2]

Geographers have identified scores of siting drivers worldwide, and usually make a distinction between unplanned versus planned settlements. Because this study examines location decisions, it focuses on the process of initial site selection rather than subsequent urban design, be it unplanned or planned. I therefore distinguish between settlements that *emerged* from the bottom up versus those that were *ordained* from the top down.

Emergent sites describe settlements that arise spontaneously from people on the move—from their arrivals, overnighting, circumventions, departures, transshipments, or their quest for game, fertile soil, water, or valued resources. Be they colonists, migrants, or travelers, they moved in sufficient numbers through varyingly strategic spaces (that is, what geographers call *situations*) for some to see opportunities, build houses, open stores or inns, or launch ferries at specific *sites*. Those reasons to pause might attract more foot traffic and cash flow, thus motivating the construction of additional houses, stores, and inns.

Eventually the settlement reaches a critical mass to attain a name, a church, a school, a post office, governance, and an urban layout.

Sites that emerge in this organic manner tend to have no famous founder or official charter; rather, they materialize through the collective action of ordinary people seeking to minimize exertions in the pursuit of better lives. The coin of the realm is *access,* defined as the "relative quality accruing to a piece of land by virtue of its relationship to a system of transport [or] centrality or nearness to other functions and locations."[3] Such settlement sites often entail where cargo must be carried, repackaged, or stored before proceeding to its destination, called break-of-bulk points. They include portages, shortcuts, cutoffs, minimum distances ("perigees"), ports and harbors, forks and confluences, fords, ferry landings, river mouths, and heads of navigation—that is, the farthest point up a waterbody reachable by contemporary vessels before encountering shallow drafts, shoals, logjams, or waterfalls. Settlements may also emerge wherever humans pause, funnel, or linger: at crossroads, bridgeheads, springs, or nighttime stopovers; at grist mills or resource sites; at topographical passes ("gap towns," of which Louisiana has one example); or just above the head of tides, meaning the lowermost freshwater before salinity becomes detectable.

Heads of navigation were frequent town sites in the thirteen colonies, and many occurred where rivers plunged over rocky outcroppings. "'Fall towns' are legion in the regions of good rainfall throughout the east of North America," wrote geographer Griffith Taylor, pointing to waterfalls' utility for powering mills as well as their hindrance to navigation as triggers for settlement. Heads-of-navigation sites may be found all along the geological escarpment known as the Atlantic Seaboard Fall Line, among them Trenton on the Delaware River in New Jersey, Philadelphia on the Schuylkill in Pennsylvania, Georgetown on the Potomac in Washington, D.C., Richmond on the James in Virginia, Raleigh on the Neuse in North Carolina, Augusta on the Savannah in Georgia, and Tuscaloosa on the Warrior in Alabama. Louisiana's best example of a fall town is Alexandria, and depending on Red River conditions, it was also sometimes the head of navigation.[4]

If an attractive situation offers no habitable site, the nearest viable site gets the settlement. In the face of flood risk, such places are known as dry-point sites (or "first high ground"), of which Natchitoches, St. Francisville, and Opelousas are examples. If lack of potable water is the limitation, the nearest alternative is called a wet-point site, which describes Louisiana's spring-based settlements, some of which went on to become resorts. At the coastal fringes or the edges of swamp basins, settlements may emerge at island sites or land's end sites, which served as jumping-off points into adjacent spaces with resources but without habitability, such as swamps, bays, or gulfs. Venice, Grand Isle, and Cocodrie are examples.

Sites may also emerge in response to the spatial distribution of neighbors. What result are settlements occurring at regular increments along arteries—the so-called "five-mile" or "ten-mile towns"—or in array-like patterns, in which each node aggregates rural denizens needing services, supplies, capital, post offices, schools, courts, or religious services ("Sunday towns"). This spatial dynamic reflects German geographer Walter Christaller's Central Place Theory, which posited that, given a flat plain with evenly distributed resources, a checkerboard pattern of hierarchical towns would form.[5] Some prairies in southwestern Louisiana come close to Christaller's isotropic surface, and to be sure, they exhibit a regularized array of settlements. In this volume, we will refer to the linear equivalents of Christaller's centralized places as "arterial increment" or "five-mile/ten-mile towns."

Ordained settlements grow similarly to emergent settlements, but they start differently, originating from the top down by an empowered authority. Picture Brigham Young proclaiming "This is the place" to Mormon pioneers as they first viewed what would become Salt Lake City—an ordained site if ever there was one. In Louisiana, ordained siting occurred during the imperial and colonial phase of settlement, starting in the 1710s, when those doing the ordaining tended to be governing officials and military leaders. Their first tactic was to ally themselves, however duplicitously, with Natives for their valuable field knowledge. "The greatest benefit that the Europeans acquired from their Indian predecessors was a landscape that had already been used," wrote Louisiana geographer Milton B. Newton. "Indian humanization of the landscape greatly softened the wilderness[;] Indians had already discovered and marked trails to most important places," and colonials often "found that their choice sites of settlement, though by then usually abandoned, had been occupied and identified by the natives."[6] St. Denis's establishment of Natchitoches and Bienville's founding of New Orleans exemplify ordained sites of this period. Both men were under orders traceable to the French crown, and both selected sites initially pointed out by indigenous informants. They raise questions of who really did the ordaining, and who ought to be credited for the siting.

Ordained siting continued through the mid-1800s under new agents and rationales. As American political authorities divvied Louisiana into civil jurisdictions, they aimed to position administrative centers for maximum convenience, such that most residents could ride horseback to the courthouse and return home within a day. While that left a lot of wiggle room, it usually meant the geographical center of the jurisdiction or its population distribution. This convention was practiced nationwide, and it produced a key element of American political geography: the centralized county seat—the courthouse town or shire town. Louisiana's version had a distinct nomenclature—*paroisses* in French, *parroquias* in Spanish, parishes in English—and in colonial times they served as ecclesiastic units that also had some civic functions. But in 1805, incoming American authorities introduced counties as civic jurisdictions, and for the next forty years Louisiana had both counties and parishes, each with different governmental uses. Confusing and unpopular, counties were finally eliminated in 1845. But the centrality intent was the same in positioning courthouses in Louisiana parishes as it was for counties elsewhere in the nation. Because the state legislature often reconfigured parishes, shrinking the nineteen original super-sized units designated in 1807 by carving out an additional forty-five parishes by 1912, seats of justices changed as well. Winning that designation brought with it civic pride, an iconic courthouse, and a slew of good jobs—a justice of the peace, clerk of court, tax assessors, a school board, a sheriff and jail keepers, and maintenance workers, as well as spillover support services. All that bureaucracy generated foot traffic, as citizens trekked in to serve on juries, sign paperwork, pay taxes, file lawsuits, or get married. The traffic, in turn, invigorated cash flow—lunch at a diner, a deposit at the bank, a purchase at the store, a beer at the tavern. For many seats of justice in rural Louisiana, parish administration *is* the local economy, and spatial centrality was the sole rationale behind the ordaining. Conversely, getting deordained as a parish seat could kill a courthouse town, because beyond administrative centrality, its site probably had no other reason for getting selected.[7]

Ordained sites surged in Louisiana during the late 1800s through early 1900s. The ordainers this time were not wearing epaulettes or legislating from the state capitol; now they donned cutaway frocks and pored over maps in paneled offices. Capitalists in this era built railroads, timber mills, sugar mills, cotton gins, mines, oil derricks, factories, and real estate developments, and what resulted were hundreds of train-stop towns, company towns, gin towns, mining towns, mill towns, and residential subdivisions.

Ordained sites in general tend to have succinct siting stories and fixed establishment dates, with documents to back them up. But despite the lordly air of those who selected the sites, the rationales at play were usually just as geographically pragmatic as those that emerged from pioneers guiding ox carts or paddling pirogues. St. Denis's Natchitoches and Bouligny's New Iberia, for example were both ordained at heads-of-navigation sites, Bienville's New Orleans was ordained at an ancient indigenous portage, and every lumber or oil town was ultimately predestined for wherever nature put the pines or petrol.

Emergent and ordained processes can occur sequentially or entwine intricately. Some emergent settlements later got "nudged" to nearby ordained railroad stations (examples include Kinder, Mermentau, and West Monroe) or wood mills (Krotz Springs, for instance). Some ordained sites managed to secure the sort of natural advantages typically associated with emergent sites; witness how Bastrop began as an administrative center but became an industrial hub, or how Baton Rouge began as a fort but became a port and administrative center. A few sites emerged from natural advantages but happened to fit the bill as administrative sites, such as Franklin on Bayou Teche. Still others gained traction thanks to the synergy of multiple factors, with no one reason prevailing: to wit, the stopover that gained a store and a church and then attracted settlers; the landing that attained a cotton gin and became a trade center; the crossroads that got a school and became a locus. One interesting rural settlement factor may involve "Sixteenth Sections"—those one-mile squares within Thomas Jefferson's Public Lands System township grid that the Land Ordinance of 1785 reserved "for the maintenance of public schools[,] being necessary to good government and the happiness of mankind."[8] Congress later granted states the right to sell these "school lands" so long as the revenue went to fund public education. Schoolhouses being key elements of community, Sixteenth Sections have supported the growth of numerous Louisiana settlements, and possibly informed some siting decisions.[9]

Myriad phenomena get enmeshed in settlement siting, from the quotidian to the polemical. The prologue to most Louisiana siting stories was the *un*-siting—that is, the violent removal or gradual displacement—of Native settlements, whose places and paths often foretold where colonials would select their sites. The subtext of many Louisiana siting stories, meanwhile, was the expectation that enslaved labor would power the agricultural economy on which settlements would be based. At work in all of Louisiana's siting stories were forces ranging from imperialism and racism to capitalism, individualism, and civic spirit; at play were greed and exploitation as well as courage and ingenuity. What resulted was a modern-day landscape redolent of beauty, blight, affluence, poverty, and sheer perseverance. Those stories began with settlements, and those settlements began at sites. Indeed, one might trace Louisiana siting stories to April 9, 1682, when René-Robert Cavelier, Sieur de La Salle, standing beside the lower Mississippi near the sea and with a notary at his side, spelled out France's claim to all the geographies examined in this book: "the seas, harbors, ports, bays, adjacent straits, and all the nations, peoples, provinces, cities, towns, villages, mines, minerals, fisheries, streams, and rivers . . . which discharge themselves [into the] Gulf of Mexico."[10]

As fundamental as settlement siting is to the human story, articulating why we live where we live seems to elude our discourse. Folks feel more obliged to memorize hometown trivia than to understand the provenance of their own inhabitation.[11] It does not help that the subject lacks a clear, consistent lexicon. Shall we call it "siting geography," or "settlement geography?" "Spatial rationale," "geographical etiology," or, as Hurst put it, "the location of cities"? Should we speak of "town types," as did Newton, or use awkward phrases like "why cities arise where they do," or "why cites form at their locales"? Many geography texts speak of "urban functions" (market centers, transportation centers, service centers, etc.), but such functionality is more often an economic outcome, while our focus here is on the initial impetus.[12] Sensing an inquiry in need of a vocabulary, I coined the term "siting stories" in the hope of encouraging more talk about this fascinating subject—one shared by every human being who has ever had a neighbor, but also one prone to seeming arcane and even unfathomable. For example, people no longer reside in Alexandria because they could not row their keelboat past the Red River rapids; nor do they reside in Breaux Bridge on account of Breaux's bridge, or in Cut Off because its canal cut off days of travel. Yet every resident of those communities can trace *every movement of their everyday lives* to those forgotten reckonings, made at a time when history cast those geographies as critical to the comings and goings of their forebears.

Regions of Louisiana used in this book. Map by Richard Campanella.

There is no perfect way to organize a book like this. I ruled out a cyclopedic format in favor of a flowing narrative, beginning with greater New Orleans and the lower Mississippi and continuing with Bayou Lafourche, Bayou Terrebonne, greater Baton Rouge, and the Pointe Coupée region. We then head east along Bayou Manchac into the Maurepas Basin, and across the Florida parishes, west and east of the Amite River. Next come the Atchafalaya Basin, Bayou Teche, the Vermilion River, and the Opelousas and Attakapas districts, through southwestern Louisiana and the Chenier Plain. We then head up the Red River to the hill country in the western and northern parts of the state, then east to the Ouachita River Valley, and circle back down the upper delta country of the lower Mississippi Valley.

The fifteen regions organized themselves rather innately, thanks to their unifying geographies and intertwined siting stories. I did not use hard lines or official boundaries in demarcating the regions, placing more emphasis on their cores than their perimeters. All Louisiana cities are covered, as are most towns and villages (state law defines a "city" as an incorporated municipality with a population of over 5,000, a "town" as having 1,000 to 5,000 residents, and a "village" as being under 1,000), as well as many unincorporated Census-Designated Places, enclaves, and hamlets, so long as they had a nucleus or downtown. The book even covers some ghost towns—that is, sites where the reckoning went awry.[13]

Siting stories usually have to be teased out from local historical accounts, and when they come to light, they are sometimes messy, sporadic, and occasionally idiosyncratic. Yet *in toto,* they have a regularity that may be categorized and generalized for our greater understanding of life on earth. To this end, the book concludes with a meta-analysis of 418 Louisiana siting stories, identifying trends and patterns addressing our guiding question—*Why are we here?*

Near Farmerville, in Union Parish. Photograph by Richard Campanella.

1

GREATER NEW ORLEANS

To European eyes, the lower Mississippi River presented something altogether new, and hardly enticing. Its volume, power, swirling eddies, and hairpin meanders intimidated navigators, and its meager banks dense with jungle-like woods dispirited those charged with settlement. More so, the current did not emerge from a valley, as one might expect to see in Europe, but from a broad deltaic plain splayed out upon what the Natives called *Ouquódky,* the Gulf of Mexico.[1] Geography worked differently on this sodden mudflat, wrought by the avulsing river's deposition of alluvium over seven millennia. Those sediments were dispersed as far west as Vermilion Bay and as far east as the Chandeleur Sound, building up thin soils just above the sea surface, which thence captured more sediment. Slivers of land fronting the river would rise high enough to support human habitation, on features known as natural levees, while farther back the terrain tapered downward to swamp and marsh. It all seemed very strange to newcomers. "Drainage is in the opposite direction from what we see in Europe," reported a perplexed Frenchman of "this reversal of the usual order of things."[2]

Contrast this deltaic disorder with the more familiar riverine environs of the Red, Sabine, Tensas, Ouachita, Tangipahoa, Tchefuncte, Pearl, and upper Mississippi, which flow through valleys (however broad) bounded by terraces or bluffs (however modest). Terrain slopes downward to the river, into which runoff collects via tributaries (influxes). On the delta, however, there are neither bluffs nor terraces nor tributaries; being the highest feature around, the river has distributaries (effluxes), and local runoff drains backward into the swamp.[3] To European eyes, this amorphous land of "watery in-betweenness," as one geographer put it, with "a sense of disorder and otherworldliness," offered no sites for settlement except those natural levees, slender and scant as

Murals on the Tchoupitoulas Street floodwall in New Orleans. Photograph by Richard Campanella.

they were.[4] And yet the region as a whole represented a fantastic geographical situation, replete with opportunities for ingress and egress, fertile in soil, rich in ecology, and verdant in its subtropical climate. Here might arise a great entrepôt (transshipment port), a break-of-bulk point like no other, at the gateway to a million square miles of hinterland, with a foreland that opened to the Gulf, Caribbean, and Atlantic basins and beyond.

Robert La Salle intuited as much upon first sailing down from French Canada in 1682 and claiming La Louisiane for his king, Louis XIV. "A port or two here would make us masters of the whole of this continent," La Salle proclaimed of the lower "Mississippy," his spelling of Michi Sepe (meaning "Big River," or "Father of Waters"), a name he had heard upriver from the Ojibway tribe.[5] While other colonies may lay prone to "as many points as their coasts are washed by the sea," here, La Salle explicated, "one single post, established towards the lower part of the river, will be sufficient to protect a territory extending more than 800 leagues from north to south, and still farther from east to west, because its banks are only accessible from the sea through the mouth of the river."[6]

Natives understood the strategic nature of the Mississippi Delta. It formed the nexus of trade networks spanning thousands of square miles, from local bays and bayous out to the salty littoral of the Gulf Coast and up to hilly interior woodlands. So many languages were heard here that the Choctaw called this realm *Balbancha,* "land of many tongues" in Mobilian Jargon, a pidgin language spoken among what the French referred to as *petites nations.* They included the Mugulasha, Quinapisa, Oachas (Washa), Chaouachas (Chawasha), and Chitimacha bands or tribes in what is now metro New Orleans; the Tangipahoa, Acolapissa, and Choctaw across *Okwa-ta* (Lake Pontchartrain) to the north; the Annochy, Biloxi, and Mobile to the east; and the Bayougoula, Houma, Atakapa, Opelousas, Natchez, and Tunica tribes to the west.[7]

Those *petites nations* living upon the natural levees built villages of circular palmetto dwellings and raised maize and millet, relocating when floods occurred, when resources grew scarce, or when inter-tribal conflicts arose. Those on the coastal plain lived on interbasin ridges or relict beaches, and in addition to fish and game, subsisted on bivalves such as oysters and clams. Shells were discarded in middens that grew so high they became "an entirely new ecozone in the marsh," according to anthropologist Tristan Kidder, creating living as well as ceremonial space.[8] Some middens, like Little Temple and Grand Temple on Lake Salvador, rose dozens of feet high. "The shellfish is so abundant," marveled one colonist, "that the different tribes that inhabit these lakes make it their principal diet [and] pile them up [around] their villages, [creating] pyramidal forms that still grow."[9] Native middens represent an early case of humans in Louisiana building their own settlement sites where no natural option existed. Indigenous people of the deltaic plain were fonts of local knowledge, and that intelligence made the next generation of French colonials—La Salle having perished on his return trip—better attuned to how and where they might occupy this *aquatique* land.

That next generation arrived in 1699, when thirty-six-year-old Pierre Le Moyne, Sieur d'Iberville, and his nineteen-year-old brother, Jean Baptiste Le Moyne, Sieur de Bienville, led an expedition across the Caribbean and into the Gulf of Mexico, seeking to re-find La Salle's Mississippi River. A seasoned naval commander who had repelled the English from the Hudson Bay, Iberville shared La Salle's appreciation of the importance—and vulnerability—of the lower Mississippi region. "If France does not seize this most beautiful part of America and set up a colony," he had written in 1697, "the English [presence] will increase to such a degree that, in less than one hundred years, it will be strong enough to take over all of America and chase away all other nations."[10] Now, in the late winter of 1699, Iberville could make good on that admonition. Leaving his oceangoing vessels anchored in the Mississippi Sound, he and his

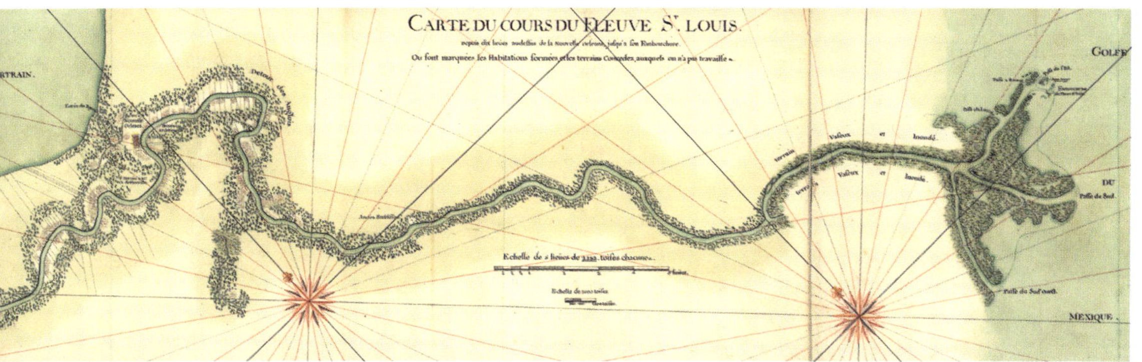

Detail of *Carte du cours du fleuve St. Louis depuis dix lieues audessus de la Nouvelle Orleans*, circa 1732, showing the progradeded nature of this fluvial delta, with Lake Pontchartrain at left and the mouth of the Mississippi at right, discharging into the Golfe du Mexique. Library of Congress.

crew rowed sail-mounted longboats up a strong current he deduced to be the same river La Salle had sailed down seventeen years earlier. Any elation at the rediscovery soon fell to anxiety as dissipating fog revealed nothing but "reeds and brambles and very tall grass" amid "canes and bushes," much of it inundated during high water and strewn with "an abundance of driftwood." Lacking any discernible landmark, Iberville used bends, forks, points (promontories), and other river peculiarities to mark his progress, measuring distances with the unit *liga* (league), which equals roughly three miles.[11]

"Two leagues and a half above the mouth it forks into three branches," wrote Iberville of the bird foot-shaped mouth of the Mississippi. "From the forks up to 6 leagues inland," he continued, "the river is rather straight, running northwest 5° north"—that's the section by present-day Venice—"then it winds west for 2 leagues and again runs northwest," meaning the bends from Boothville to Triumph to Buras. There on the evening of March 3 the expedition camped "at a bend it makes to the west . . . to which we have given the name Mardy Gras," a fortuitous first mention of the pre-Lenten feast that would become a hallmark of Louisiana culture. On Ash Wednesday, Iberville progressed "8½ leagues, coming to several bends . . . to the west-northwest and north-northwest," meaning Jesuit Bend, past today's Empire and Port Sulphur. Fog slowed the expedition on Thursday, March 5, by which time Iberville noted how meanders that had previously "shifted from west to southwest" were now leaning "northwest and north"—today's upper Plaquemines Parish, approaching Belle Chasse. Conditions worsened on Friday, when "all morning there was fog and no wind," as the longboats dodged snags and strong currents. The expedition progressed up "the first bend the river makes east-northeast," now the Braithwaite area, then tacked six and a half leagues east to camp for the night near today's Caernarvon. Saturday morning's sailing brought more meanders, the river curving "a great deal from northeast to southwest, through the north and the west. Over a distance of 2 leagues it will make two and three bends." This is clearly a reference to English Turn, a name ascribed to this sharp meander in September 1699, when Bienville bluffed an enemy English corvette into retreating. Strong headwinds on Sunday, March 8, again slowed progress, such that the expedition "made only 4½ leagues and camped on the right side of the river. My men are getting very tired." If we assume a Chalmette-area encampment for the previous night, that puts Iberville in today's Uptown New Orleans on Sunday evening.

Progress on Monday, March 9, got the expedition to today's Elmwood/Harahan area, where Iberville dropped anchor and interacted with curious Natives who had been furtively tracking the intruders. It was at this moment that Iber-

Detail of *Carte de la rivière de Mississippi, sur les mémoires de Mr. Le Sueur*, by Guillaume L'Isle (1702), showing the future sites of New Orleans (at Portage des égarez, *center*), Donaldsonville (la Fourche, *left center*), and White Castle (Village des Bayogoula). Note Bayou Manchac at upper left, labeled as Rivière d'Iberville. Library of Congress.

ville recorded what would become the most crucial siting story in Louisiana history. "The Indian," he wrote, "pointed out to me the place through which the Indians make their portage to this river from the back of the bay where the ships are anchored. They drag their canoes over a rather good road [whose] distance . . . was slight." A portage (from *porter,* "to carry cargo") along a good road, of slight distance, connecting river and bay, would eliminate days of arduous river navigation. After noting the "several pieces of baggage owned by men that were going there or were returning"—literally a break-of-bulk point—Iberville noted this key learning, and as time would tell, so would his brother Bienville.[12]

Onward they pressed, seeking the rumored encampment of the Bayougoula Indians—which they found near present-day White Castle, their first close-up view of an indigenous settlement in Balbancha. Afterward, Iberville continued upriver, past the *bâton* (pole) painted *rouge* (red) on a bluff called Istrouma—future Baton Rouge—and nearly up to the Red River confluence. There he turned around and returned via another newly learned shortcut, the Bayou Manchac distributary (from *imashaka,* or "rear entrance" in the Mugulasha tongue) to the lakes he named Maurepas and Pontchartrain, to honor the French naval minister and his son. Those tidal lagoons provided egress to the Mississippi Sound, that same "back bay" where the ships had been anchored. With enormous help from Native informants, Iberville had demystified the amorphous delta, and now began to assess it for settlement sites.[13]

Historians have reasonably surmised that the portage Iberville saw on

March 9, 1699, was New Orleans's Bayou Road/Governor Nicholls Street corridor. This trail followed a slight topographical ridge extending from today's French Quarter to Bayou St. John, a navigable rivulet discharging into Lake Pontchartrain, which in turn accessed the Mississippi Sound. A close reading of Iberville's journals, however, leads me to conclude that what Iberville reported on March 9 was a trailhead farther upriver, in today's Jefferson Parish, whereby one could cut across to the Metairie Ridge (today's Metairie Road and City Park Avenue) and still arrive at the juncture of Bayou St. John and Bayou Road.

Iberville was able to ascertain that portage from the reverse direction when he returned in early 1700 by sailing into Lake Pontchartrain on the *Renommee.* "I got to the mouth of the stream that leads to the portage," he wrote of Bayou St. John on January 17; "it is 20 yards wide, 10 feet deep, and 1 league long." The next day he "went to the portage, which I found to be 1 league long, about half the distance being full of water and mud up to the knee, the other half fairly good, part of it being a country of canes and fine woods, suitable to live in." He had his men carry three canoes over the portage and arrived "at a spot where the Quinipissas once had a village, 1½ leagues above this portage."[14]

The importance of such a portage was that it enabled one to get *to* the river faster and easier than going *up* the river. Wouldn't that make an optimal site for a settlement? Perhaps, but Iberville nevertheless came away shuddering at "this empire of mud," as historian Joseph Tregle wrote of the perspective at that time, "too recently spewed from the maw of the river to support huts or the foot of man."[15] Iberville ended up establishing the Louisiana colony's first settlement at Fort Maurepas (1699) at what is now Ocean Springs, Mississippi—a better site, one could argue, but in a mediocre situation, with nothing but piney woods on hard clays. In 1702, his younger brother Bienville founded the next settlement farther east, on the Mobile River—a better situation, but a worse site, as it later flooded out, forcing him to relocate the outpost to present-day Mobile, Alabama, in 1711.

By that time, with Iberville deceased and the Louisiana project moribund, the French crown sought a way to unburden itself of operating the unwieldy colony. It found one in the person of Antoine Crozat, a Parisian financier who thought he could turn remote Louisiana into a private commercial venture raising tobacco, mining metals, and trading with the Spanish in Mexico. Within five years, all three schemes failed utterly, the only progress being the establishment of four isolated forts in the interior. Louisiana seemed doomed, with few good sites and no compelling reason to settle them.

What changed Louisiana's destiny was another scheming financier, this one a Scotsman named John Law, who also sought a charter to run Louisiana as a business. But unlike Crozat, Law had charisma, connections, a persuasive personality, and a gambler's vision of riches. An early theoretician of monetary policy, Law argued for the use of paper currency to represent wealth—both real wealth (that is, gold, of which France had next to nothing) and commercial wealth (of which, Law ingenuously pointed out, France had Louisiana).

Law's argument found a receptive audience in Philippe II, Duc d'Orléans, who, as the regent of France, wrestled with the paralyzing national debt left behind by the late King Louis XIV. Law's plan seemed to cover all the bases: his proposed company would grow tobacco and extract valuable raw materials for shipment to France, in exchange for the mother country's technical support and protection from competitors. The company's financing would be raised from the sale of stock; its settlers would comprise 6,000 Europeans recruited or forced to emigrate; its labor would come from 3,000 enslaved West Africans; and the ensuing profits would enrich all shareholders, including Law and Philippe, while equity in the company would help pay off the national debt. Better yet, Louisiana-grown tobacco would undercut enemy English growers in the Chesapeake, while new French settlements could defend Louisiana from both the English and the Spanish. "The beguiling inclusiveness of Law's plan," wrote historian Lawrence N. Powell, "—its promise to retire the national debt, revive the French domestic and overseas economy, and establish an autarkic source of tobacco—is what drew [Philippe] to Law's theories."[16] On September 6, 1717, the French crown granted John Law's Company of the West a twenty-five-year monopoly charter to develop Louisiana. Nearly all subsequent siting stories are traceable, directly or indirectly, to that act.

Company officials got to work launching a continent-wide marketing campaign to recruit investors and settlers, and raced to dispatch personnel and supplies to Louisiana. But first they would have to designate a headquarters, the siting of which they reckoned from reports, and the naming of which they savvily used to flatter their royal patron, the Duke of Orleans. On September 9, 1717, a clerk wrote into the company register, "Resolved to establish, thirty leagues up the river, a burg which should be called La Nouvelle Orléans, where landing would be possible from either the river or Lake Pontchartrain."[17]

And that's what turned that sighting of the Indian portage back in 1699 into the siting story of Louisiana's greatest city, New Orleans. When the company's resolution landed in Bienville's hands, he knew where to go, drawing upon nineteen years of regional reconnaissance. In February 1718, he scouted for an ideal site roughly thirty leagues (ninety miles) up the river, and selected a particularly sharp meander (good for confronting approaching enemy ships) on the natural levee (higher ground) on the east bank of the river, because

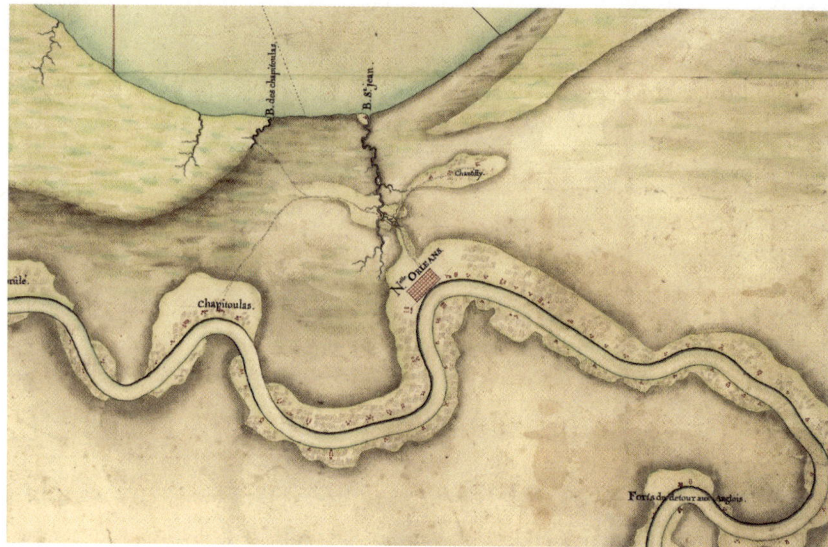

Detail of *Carte particulière du cours du fleuve St. Louis*, by F. Saucier (1749), showing Bayou St. John (B. St. Jean) and the Bayou Road portage connecting Lake Pontchartrain with New Orleans. Library of Congress.

The portage retains its original name, Bayou Road, through the Sixth and Seventh Wards of New Orleans. Photograph by Richard Campanella.

that's where that portage (today's Bayou Road) led to Bayou St. John and Lake Pontchartrain, fulfilling all the siting criteria in the company's resolution.

In early spring 1718, Bienville returned "with six vessels, loaded with provisions and . . . thirty workmen, all convicts; six carpenters and four Canadians," recalled colonist Jonathan Darby. "The whole locality was a dense canebrake, with only a small pathway [Bayou Road] leading from the Mississippi to the Bayou [St. John] communicating with Lake Pontchartrain." Darby recalled that "M. de Bienville cut the first cane" followed by "MM. Pradel and Dreux," after which the men got to work clearing thicket, draining puddles, and building shelters "made of standing boards and posts, with walls and chimneys of dirt and covered with cypress bark."[18]

So began New Orleans, ever so tenuously. Even as work progressed at today's French Quarter, company officials in Paris suggested siting New Orleans at Bayou Manchac near Baton Rouge, and dispatched an engineer to make that recommendation to Bienville. Alas, the engineer died en route, the message never arrived, and Bienville, perhaps unknowingly, gained precious time to advance in his city-building before another Parisian dilettante could interfere.[19]

Instead, the Mississippi River interfered, flooding New Orleans in April 1719. Skeptics took the occasion to argue Bienville's site was not viable, and that the company headquarters ought to go elsewhere, such as the colonial capital of Mobile. Combined with reports of navigational difficulties at the river's mouth, the 1719 flood convinced officials in Paris in late 1720 to relocate the capital from Mobile to New Biloxi (today's Biloxi, Mississippi), which could serve as a coastal transshipment port for oceangoing vessels to transfer cargo to smaller longboats to proceed inland. It was a major setback for Bienville's New Orleans, though his men continued to work on the company headquarters there.[20]

The year 1720 brought more bad news, this time from Paris, where rumors of difficulties in Louisiana put the lie to John Law's promises. Company shares plunged in value, panic erupted among shareholders, and frantic company officials focused on damage control. Distant New Orleans, conceived during the halcyon days of 1717, became a low priority of a volatile company chartered by an overextended empire.

Ironically, the Company of the West's financial turmoil gave New Orleans an opportunity to rise in contrast. That is, any progress the struggling outpost could make at this moment would cast it in a better light, and demonstrate that Law's project was beginning to recover. One glint of progress came from the two men assigned to replace the engineer who had died, Le Blond de La Tour and his assistant, Adrien de Pauger. Starting in March 1721, Pauger carefully analyzed New Orleans's site conditions, made some key decisions, and designed a magnificent urban plan. Approved by La Tour, Pauger's plat made its way back to officials in Paris. La Tour also made a point of corroborating Bienville's siting decision, specifically referring to the shortcut portage: "In ascending the river," he wrote, "I have examined the most suitable sites for placing New Orleans and have not found a better situation than the spot where it is. The land is highest here and it is located at a portage of a bayou, a small river that flows into Lake Pontchartrain by which one can at all times communicate with New Biloxi, Mobile and the other posts more easily than by the lower river."[21]

What also got sent back to Paris were Pauger's reports on the navigational potential of the lower Mississippi. Well-schooled in hydrology, Pauger determined the river's shoals and currents could be surmounted, and rebuked the "stubbornness" and "arrogance" of company officials who forced "ships from France to be stopped at Biloxi, rather than enter the Mississippi . . . keystone of the country's establishment."[22] Stronger grew the argument that the company's headquarters *and* the colony's capital ought to be at Bienville's site on the lower Mississippi, and not some coastal or interior site.

During this time, Philippe II, Duc d'Orléans, had taken a more proactive role in managing Louisiana affairs while company officials rectified financial matters. The regent's involvement may have made military defensibility more of a priority, and it was plain to see that New Orleans did the best job among all of the outposts of guarding the lower river. Pauger's plat also did well in impressing Philippe, with its orderly street grid and stout fortifications, all emblazoned with his royal title, La Nouvelle Orléans. According to historian Marc de Villiers du Terrage, "the regent, god-father to the new capital, was necessarily flattered to see the project put into effect," the first good news coming out of Louisiana in a long time. "The year 1721 had been generally favourable to New Orleans. . . . From a military post, a sales-counter, and a camping-ground for travellers, it had become, in November, a small town, and the number of its irreconcilable enemies began to decrease."[23]

It took one more ordeal to get New Orleans past its perilous infancy. On September 11, 1722, a hurricane destroyed over four years of development, greatly setting the project back. But it also cleared the way for Pauger to finally lay out his orderly plan, creating today's French Quarter. For a site that had been selected in 1717–1718 at a shortcut portage first seen by Iberville in 1699—which during 1719–1722 had been flooded, demoted, bankrupted, effaced, and nearly relocated—New Orleans had defied all odds to become the company headquarters and, finally, the colony capital. "His Royal Highness having thought it advisable to make the principal establishment of the colony at New Orleans on the Mississippi River," Bienville beamed on February 1, 1723, "we have accordingly transported here all the goods that were at Biloxi," the previous capital. "It appears to me that a better decision could not have been made, in view of the good quality of the soil along the river [and the] considerable advantage for . . . the unloading of the vessels."[24]

Within a few years, New Orleans became the largest settlement in the Louisiana colony; a century later it was the largest city in the South; and in 1840 it ranked as the third-largest city in the United States. Its population peaked at 627,000 in 1960, and the city remains the state's largest municipality in terms of population, with 364,000 residents in a conurbation of over 800,000.[25]

Bienville's siting decision has evoked criticism and even incredulity ever since he made it in 1718. But consider the circumstances of the period. The decision resolved for Bienville a high-stakes dilemma, one that is inherent in many siting stories: should a settlement be built on the safest site, despite its inconvenience? Or should it exploit the most strategic situation, despite its risk? Bienville chose the latter, confident that his engineers could fix the risky site. That decision enabled New Orleans to become a great city by the early 1800s, but it also set it on a path toward environmental precarity by the late 1900s. Had he sited New Orleans anywhere else along the lower Mississippi,

Bienville's site for New Orleans. Photograph by Richard Campanella.

the outcome would have been worse in either regard. French visitor François Marie Perrin Du Lac said as much in 1803, when he wrote of New Orleans, "there is not for a great distance a finer, more elevated, or healthier position," adding with an asterisk, "If higher, it would be too distant from the sea; if lower, subject to inundations."[26] German geographer Friedrich Ratzel contemplated New Orleans's site-versus-situation dilemma and came away equally judicious. "New Orleans," he wrote in 1876, "is just as poorly located as a city, or more precisely as a dwelling place, as it is excellently located as a commercial site." He then added: "*This last-mentioned advantage has made up for all disadvantages.*"[27]

Siting decisions beget derivative settlements with their own spatial logics. One example is the cross-river subsidiary, a site activated for no other reason than propinquity to the parent across the water. As early as 1719, New Orleans spawned a cross-river subsidiary on a promontory of what colonials called the left bank, what nineteenth-century residents called the right bank, and New Orleanians today call the west bank. The settlement was initially known as the Company Plantation, a multipurpose bunkhouse, depot, workshop, mill, and farm serving the larger colony. It was also a temporary encampment for Africans who survived the Middle Passage, and at one point it held 154 people, "the largest single group of enslaved men, women, and children living in Louisiana."[28] After the Company of the Indies (successor to Law's Company of the West) finally went bankrupt and the French crown assumed responsibility for Louisiana, the operation became known as the King's Plantation or King's Domain. When Spanish officials took full control of Louisiana in 1769, they divested of the operation and sold off the land as a series of plantations. One parcel came into the hands of Barthélémy Duverjé, whose heirs had it subdivided as Duverjéville. Along with adjacent subdivisions, Duverjéville eventually

Dry dock and ferry at Algiers Point, operations that are typical of cross-river subsidiaries. Photograph by Richard Campanella.

gained the nickname Algiers, likely a real estate marketing term referencing France's 1830 colonization of Algeria. Soon, Algiers developed an economy based on shipbuilding, dry docks, ironworks, railroads, and light industry, with ferry connections tying it to New Orleans—even as the unbridged river ensured that Algiers would retain its independent identity. Though the city finally annexed Algiers in 1870, residents have long taken pride in their community's village-like sense of distinction, while rebuking treatment as "the red-headed stepsister of New Orleans"—a familiar grievance of cross-river subsidiaries.[29] Today, historic Algiers Point is home to 2,600 people, while the west bank of Orleans Parish has just over 50,000 residents, or 13 percent of the city's total population.[30]

Siting stories elsewhere in greater New Orleans showcase canals, ferries, and railroads as settlement instigators. The communities they spurred may be categorized as arterial variations on the theme of heads of navigation, confluences, and crossings, in that they emerged (1) where canals adjoined natural waterbodies, (2) where ferries landed, (3) where railroads established stations, (4) where tracks merged, crossed, or terminated, or (5) where any of the above intersected with roads. The resulting settlements endure today either as city neighborhoods or as municipalities or nucleated suburbs in adjacent parishes.

In 1794, for example, Spanish authorities began excavating a canal to connect the city directly with Bayou St. John, superseding Bayou Road and speeding access to Lake Pontchartrain. That artery, known as the Carondelet Canal and later the Old Basin Canal (today's Lafitte Greenway), actuated the mouth of the bayou, giving rise to Spanish Fort—initially a military site, later a resort, and now a residential neighborhood in the Lakeview/Lake Vista section of New Orleans.

Similarly, investors starting in 1832 had another canal dug from New Orleans to a spot farther west on the Lake Pontchartrain shore, giving rise to the port-turned-resort-turned-neighborhood called West End. Known as the New Basin Canal, its now-filled bed underlays part of the Interstate 10 corridor.[31]

Across the river, the Barataria & Lafourche Company began excavating a navigation canal to connect the Mississippi River with Bayou Lafourche. Its riverside segment, opened in 1834, impelled settlement that would later become the Salaville neighborhood in Westwego, while its bayou terminus, completed by 1841, gave rise to Lockport in Lafourche Parish, named for the lock built to reconcile the differing water stages. Later known as the Company Canal, its surviving portion in modern Westwego still hosts a fishing fleet and seafood market, while ruins of the old lock may still be seen in Lockport.[32]

Around that time, the owner of a nearby plantation, Nicolas Noël Destréhan, oversaw the excavation of his own channel to tap the resources of the Barataria Bay. Now known as the Harvey Canal, Destréhan's waterway spawned an enlightened vision for a place named Cosmopolite City at its juncture with the Mississippi. Initially designed with a Savannah-style Oglethorpe Plan, Destréhan's Cosmopolite City never quite got off the ground, but later came into fruition as Harvey, an unincorporated area abutting the still-busy Harvey Canal and now home to 21,000 people. As for its coastal connection, the Harvey Canal stimulated economic activity on Bayou Barataria and helped give rise to the Jefferson Parish communities of Estelle down to Crown Point and Lafitte, today with a combined population of 4,500 inhabitants.[33]

In an unbridged metropolis like New Orleans, ferries became cross-river settlement triggers. "Ferryboat connections with the east bank were the strongest determinants of how isolated from, or integrated with, the outside world, [the west bank] was," wrote historians David Fritz and Sally K. Reeves. "Without them [it] would have been ten times more provincial."[34] A prime example of a ferry landing settlement site is Gretna, which originated as Mechanickham on the former plantation of Nicolas Noël Destréhan, the same man behind the Harvey Canal and Cosmopolite City. The moniker aimed to attract German immigrants recently settled in New Orleans, many of whom were skilled workers (*mechanic*). With the help of engineer Benjamin Buisson, Destréhan planned for Mechanickham a scenic commons framed by twin boulevards (now Huey P. Long Avenue) with space for religious and civil structures (today's Gretna City Hall), and provisions for a future railroad, a foundry, and most importantly a ferry landing. Service became available courtesy of the St. Mary's Market

Steam Ferry Company, which in 1838 expanded Mechanickham with an adjacent subdivision dubbed Gretna—likely a reference to Gretna Green, a Scottish village known for runaway weddings, and the title of a theatrical farce playing in New Orleans. Key to Gretna's siting story is the symbiotic relationship between transportation and real estate: the ferry company would profit from riders paying fares to cross the river, while the daily access would increase demand for parcels in bucolic Gretna. "Persons wishing delightful country residences, and to be near the centre of business," read a Gretna real estate ad, will enjoy "advantages too obvious to require description," to which was appended the note, "The St. Mary's Market Steam Ferry Co. will also grant to all persons purchasing property at the above sale a free ticket . . . to cross in the ferry boat for one year." The strategy worked, and after another ferry began launching from Jackson Avenue, Gretna expanded in each direction, its pithy name eventually supplanting the clunky "Mechanickham."[35] We may conclude that while the ferry was the proximate cause for the creation of Gretna, its siting story is ultimately that of a cross-river subsidiary: no New Orleans, no Gretna.

Starting in the 1850s, railroads interconnected the string of ferry-spawned villages of the west bank, fostering the eventual convergence of the street grids of Algiers, McDonoghville, Gretna, Harvey, Amesville (now Marrero), and finally Westwego. By 1858, each of New Orleans's four municipal districts on the east bank had its own ferry service to their cross-river counterparts, enabling hundreds of people to commute daily. One ferry ran from Elysian Fields Avenue to the Belleville area of Algiers, a second connected St. Ann Street by Jackson Square to Powder Street in Algiers, a third linked Canal Street with McDonoghville, and the fourth connected Jackson Avenue to Gretna.[36] Ferries remained vital even after the 1935 opening of the Huey P. Long Bridge, which gave rise to Bridge City as a bridgehead site. But ferries declined precipitously following the 1958 opening of the Greater New Orleans Mississippi River Bridge. By then, Gretna had long since become an administrative center, seat of Jefferson Parish, having incorporated as a town in 1913 and a city in 1916. Today, the city of Gretna is home to 17,200 people, and while regular ferry service to Jackson Avenue ended in 2008, the terminal resumes service for the annual Gretna Heritage Festival—a last vestige of Gretna's siting story.

Railroads became premier settlement makers statewide in the late 1800s and early 1900s. But they began in New Orleans a half-century earlier, when the Pontchartrain Railroad opened in 1831 to connect the city to Lake Pontchartrain, becoming the first line to complete its charter west of the Appalachian Mountains. The Pontchartrain Railroad turned a featureless saline marsh into a vital port and resort known as Milneburg, now a neighborhood in greater

Gentilly—which itself emanated from where the tracks crossed an old Indian trail following the Gentilly Ridge, making it a dry-point crossroads site. The surrounding swamps have since been drained, and the Pontchartrain Railroad ceased service in 1932, but that old crossroads—now Elysian Fields Avenue at Gentilly Boulevard—remains the heart of Gentilly, while a circa 1855 lighthouse marking the lake-end terminus of the old Pontchartrain Railroad still stands in Milneburg.[37]

Investors at the opposite end of New Orleans devised a similar passenger line to cross five miles of plantations in today's Uptown, many of which had already undergone subdivision. Opened in 1835, the New Orleans & Carrollton Railroad accelerated this agrarian-to-urban transformation by instilling three sites where populations would soon agglomerate. One began as a river landing and became the city of Lafayette in 1833, the next became Jefferson City in 1850, and the terminal station became the city of Carrollton in 1845. In the decades ahead, specifically 1852 to 1874, New Orleans forcibly annexed all three cities. Former Lafayette is today's Irish Channel, Garden District, and Central City neighborhoods, old Jefferson City is now the heart of Uptown, and former Carrollton City is today's Riverbend and Carrollton neighborhoods, still home to the circa 1855 former Jefferson Parish courthouse. Now home to over 100,000 people, roughly a quarter the city's population, the three erstwhile cities share siting stories of river landings and stops on that 1835 railroad—now the St. Charles Avenue Streetcar, described as the oldest continually operating urban railroad in the world.

Later railroads emanating from New Orleans seeded station-stop communities throughout the future metropolis. Investors in 1837, for example, launched the Mexican Gulf Railroad to points east. Soon, the line spurred new subdivisions along today's St. Claude Avenue through Bywater and the Lower Ninth Ward, and by the late 1840s to Abattoir (now Arabi), Versailles (Chalmette), Poydras Junction, and Proctorsville (Proctor's Point, now Shell Beach). The former track bed of that antebellum railroad is now Highway 46, still the main artery through eastern St. Bernard Parish.[38]

Two other railroads dating to the 1870s and 1880s, the New Orleans, Mobile & Texas (later Louisville & Nashville) and the New Orleans & North Eastern (later Southern), established a similar string of stations and flag stops toward the east—Lee, Michoud, and Chef Menteur, each of which attracted settlements. The stations are gone, but their sites trace the trajectory of today's Chef Menteur Highway through eastern New Orleans, where, with a gigantic boost from Interstate 10 in the 1970s, modern subdivisions were laid out to become home today to over 70,000 people.[39]

In emphasizing waterways and railroads, this 1884 *Bird's-Eye View of the Mississippi River* detail illustrates siting stories throughout greater New Orleans. Library of Congress.

At the opposite end of the metropolis, investors in 1853 opened the Jefferson & Pontchartrain Railroad to link the city of Carrollton with Lake Pontchartrain, where they erected a pier for steamers to transfer cargo. The port came to be known as Jefferson Lake End, later East End (despite being west of West End). Like Milneburg, Spanish Fort, and West End, this lakeside terminus developed a fishing and recreational economy. It was likely in this resort capacity that East End gained the sobriquet Bucktown and became Jefferson Parish's premier lakefront community. To this day, scenic Bucktown retains a village-like feel, with a small fishing fleet and seafood economy. Its siting story may be classified as a head-of-rails site, akin to the head-of-canal rationale of West End, Spanish Fort, Westwego, and Harvey. It wasn't the only settlement triggered by the Jefferson & Pontchartrain Railroad; to the south, those tracks intersected an old Indian path atop the Metairie Ridge, and just as the Pontchartrain Railroad had done for Gentilly, that crossroads became the nucleus of today's Old Metairie.[40]

Jefferson Parish soon became a railroad frontier, with siting stories to match. In 1854, the New Orleans, Jackson & Great Northern Railroad Company commenced the city's first interstate railroad leading to Mississippi and Tennessee. Later taken over by the Illinois Central, its gently curving track bed is today's Earhart Expressway, an alternative artery to Interstate 10 framing the Metairie suburbs. Competing lines established tracks nearby, among them the Louisiana Railway & Navigation Company and the Yazoo & Mississippi Valley Railroad, each with its own spurs. Through the same station-stop siting impetus seen in the east, these railroads activated settlements to the west and north. Some have gotten subsumed into suburbia, like Southport Junction; others have faded away, like Frenier and DeSair on the western shore of Lake Pontchartrain; and still others endure—like Harahan (1914), where the Illinois Central established its rail yards, roundhouses, and a transfer ferry to the west bank (today's Avondale and Waggaman). A worker settlement formed adjacently, practically a company town, and it gained the name of the company president, James Harahan. The village of Harahan incorporated in 1920 and became the city of Harahan in 1953, now home to 9,200 residents.[41]

What is now Kenner began as two French land concessions at Cannes Brûlées (Burnt Canes) followed by a sequence of plantations, including Oakland, Belle Grove, and Pasture. What made this particular bend salient was the routing of the circa 1854 New Orleans, Jackson & Great Northern, which, after crossing the backswamp on berms and trestles, clipped lands owned by the Kenner family. Recognizing the real estate opportunity, the Kenners donated a right-of-way so the railroad company could build a station for passengers, a depot for cargo, and water and firewood facilities. The station motivated family patriarch Minor Kenner to develop the adjacent land, and in 1855 he hired W. T. Thompson to lay out Kennerville, now Old Town Kenner. Far enough from New Orleans to keep land values cheap yet close enough to serve the urban market, Kenner became a center for truck farming (from the French *troc,* "to exchange or barter"), where produce was raised for regional consumption. Kenner incorporated as a town in 1866 and a city in 1873. "By 1900 the once sluggish and troubled little town had turned into one of the richest and busiest produce-generating areas in Louisiana," wrote historian Craig A. Bauer. "Over sixty refrigerated carloads of locally grown produce left Kenner every month."[42] Truck farming became an impetus for swamp reclamation—in eastern New Orleans, on the west bank, and here in Kenner, where Chicago investor L. B. Langworthy, "one of the most enthusiastic believers in the future of the drained wet lands of Louisiana," aimed in 1910 to "cut up [the Kenner backswamp] into small farms and truck gardens" and eventually build "attractive suburban homes for people doing business in New Orleans."[43] By the 1920s, Kenner's bogs became farms, and by the 1960s those farms had become subdivisions. No one thereafter thought of Kenner—the sixth-largest city in Louisiana, home to 64,000 people—as a rural railroad stop for farmers.

Despite the fact that most people lived on the east bank, railroad interests gravitated to the west bank, for its terrestrial connections to points west. They made it a premier jumping-off point to Texas and the frontier, home to vast rail yards, train car plants, and intermodal facilities. If you wanted to get from the Gulf Coast to the Pacific Coast in the late 1800s—or to send cotton or cattle or lumber back—you had to go through the west bank of greater New Orleans.

Kenner's historical value came from its landing on the Mississippi River (*top*), but what triggered its transformation into a town was a station along the New Orleans, Jackson & Great Northern Railroad, opened in 1854 (*modern site at bottom*). Photographs by Richard Campanella.

A key moment in that westward reach came with the late 1860s formation of the New Orleans, Mobile & Texas Railroad, connecting with Fort Worth and calling for a major terminal with a transfer (train) ferry across the Mississippi. Algiers and Gretna proved too congested, so company officials looked to the head of the circa 1830s Company Canal, where they found sufficiently elevated open land that was conveniently positioned and reasonably priced. To advertise its strategic advantage, they named the site "West-We-Go," which got truncated to Westwego and applied to surrounding areas. The terminal facility was constructed in 1870, followed by forty miles of track in 1871, after which the company became known as the Texas & Pacific Railroad.[44] Together with the nearby Company Canal, the terminal and affiliated industries spawned a worker community that incorporated as the town of Westwego in 1919 and became the city of Westwego in 1951. Locals claim Westwego, now home to 8,200 people, is the only city in the United States whose name forms a complete sentence. Westwego's siting story is equally pat, born at the head of a navigation canal and later as a railroad terminal and jumping-off point to the western frontier, a geographical advantage for which it was cleverly named.

Of the fourteen cities, towns, villages, and other communities in greater New Orleans analyzed in this study, 43 percent had riverine- or water-based primary siting stories (above the state average of 29 percent), while 29 percent were railroad sites, 21 percent were resource extraction or processing sites, and 7 percent were crossroads (compared to state averages of 33 percent, 10 percent, and 13 percent, respectively). Settlements began forming in this region in the late 1710s, crested in the 1860s–1870s, and ended by the 1930s—though suburban expansion would continue for another fifty years. Only 12 percent of greater New Orleans-area settlements emerged organically, the other 88 percent having been ordained by a founder, including New Orleans itself—an unusually high proportion, as the statewide split is 49 percent emergent and 51 percent ordained. The 88 percent figure indicates the central role played by this region in the earliest days of the Louisiana colony, in which leaders rather than settlers spearheaded settlement formation.

2

THE LOWER MISSISSIPPI RIVER

La Salle had been right, and so had Bienville. New Orleans by the early 1800s became a major river/sea port, second nationally only to New York, and "the dominant metropolis of the antebellum South; it had no rivals."[1] So rigorously did the Crescent City drain tribute from its hinterland, supplying planters with everything from capital to slaves and collecting their commodities for export, that it left very little action for its neighbors. As a result, few other substantial cities formed in antebellum Louisiana, particularly along the lower Mississippi. To this day, there is not a single incorporated city, town, or village downriver of the city of New Orleans.

There is another reason for the paucity of urban centers. Plantations were not just farms, and plantation regimes did not develop willy-nilly. They arose where large landholdings of fertile soil could be amassed; where capital could be attained for equipment, facilities, and expert management; and where "an abundant, rural, landless labor source" could be secured—"abundant so as to remain cheap," wrote geographer Milton Newton, "rural so as to be hardened to the strains of agricultural labor, and landless so as to be willing to submit to the alienation of plantation life."[2] To French colonials, Louisiana offered all the conditions for plantations except labor—until they began importing enslaved Africans in 1718–1719, concurrent with the founding of New Orleans.

The resulting regime comprised multiuse agricultural operations largely dedicated to raising export commodities, with on-site owners and managers overseeing a resident enslaved workforce. Parcels were surveyed in an elongated shape attuned to local geography, each having river or bayou frontage and transecting the natural levee until it petered out in the backswamp. Boundaries of these long lots converged on the concave side of meanders and diverged on the convex side. The unit of measure was the arpent, the French equivalent of the acre, except that it was used for either areal or linear measurement (approximately 192 U.S. feet). *Arpenteurs* (surveyors) usually laid out long lots that were eight to twelve arpents in frontage and forty to eighty arpents in depth, typical widths of the natural levee.[3]

Water frontage was vital for transportation, so nearly every plantation had a landing, where boatmen and passengers intermingled with locals and travelers on the public road, and where planters built stores, depots, and light industry, such as sawmills and brick kilns. Landings became portals to the world, and their adjoining plantations, with scores or hundreds of people, were sort of like villages or towns. "Splendid old homesteads dot the road at the distance of a quarter of a mile apart," wrote J. W. Dorr in 1860, "the out-buildings, negro quarters, etc., forming at each a considerable village, so that the road up the coast is almost like a street of a vast, thinly built city."[4]

This dynamic tended to undercut the emergence of nucleated settlements with traditional siting rationales. That is to say, if large numbers of people dwell within the plantation complex and obtain their sustenance thereupon—and most are denied the freedom to choose their own destiny anyway—then who's left to found villages and towns? With so many basic trade-and-transport functions already performed at plantation landings, what's to be gained by establishing towns? River traders sailed from wharf to wharf "to linger and trade along the Sugar coast," as one former flatboatman put it, turning landings into commercial centers, and the sugarcane plantations behind them into de facto settlements.[5] We may go so far to say that the plantation system in and of itself constituted a settlement geography—*forced* settlement, for most of its populace—with its main siting story being fertile soil and a landing on a navigable river.

As a result, the lowermost Mississippi River, below Baton Rouge and excluding metro New Orleans, was historically bereft of substantial nucleated settlements. Period maps show very little consensus of what deserved cartographic depiction as an enduring community. The 1814 Matthew Carey map, for example, labeled only military forts and parish churches; the 1820 John Melish map shows a smattering of communities largely inconsistent with the few depicted on H. S. Tanner's 1851 map, or J. H. Colton's maps from 1855 and 1863.[6] Those lower river settlements that did manage to materialize outside of the plantation regime tended to have three siting stories. Some were centralized service or administrative nodes, others had salient geographical advantages, and the rest formed as resource extraction and processing sites.

Centralized service and administration sites arose from dovetailing religious and political imperatives. To serve the faithful in this Catholic society, leaders established *paroisses* centered around sanctioned churches for the celebration of Mass and sacramental rituals. That charge had been written into the original 1717 commercial charter for Louisiana, stipulating that the Company of the West "shall be obliged to build at its expense churches at the places where it forms settlements, [and] to maintain there the necessary number of approved ecclesiastics [priests], all under the authority of the Bishop of Quebec."[7]

Where to site the churches? In the case of ordained places like Mobile, Natchitoches, or New Orleans, their urban siting decisions naturally determined their church locations. But in rural areas, the opposite was the case: church siting decisions informed where settlements would occur. Authorities positioned churches to be maximally convenient, such that most congregants would have to travel some distance on Sunday, but few would have to trek far. One French colonial recalled how congregants gravitated to a particular church to attend "mass, some in boats which ferried them across the river [because the] parish includes both river banks for five leagues around," meaning a fifteen-mile radius.[8] Given their importance, churches seeded community formation under the system of French *paroisses* overseen from Quebec, and later as Spanish *parroquias* administered from Havana until 1793, after which New Orleans became its own diocese. Parish churches in south Louisiana gave rise to the regional version of what geographers have called "Sunday towns," enclaves nourished by their weekly congregational surge. Comparable agglomerations tended to occur around post offices, courthouses, schools, academies, mills, and other key services.

"Coming from church—scene on the Bayou Lafourche," by Alfred Rudolph Waud (1867). Library of Congress.

After the Louisiana Purchase, incoming American administrators, being mostly Protestant, found themselves bemused by the weighty role of ecclesiastical parishes in Creole society. Not only were parish churches vital cultural hearths, they also informed regional identity. Clumsily, the Americans imposed their own jurisdictions on top of the local religious units. Each had different borders and purposes, the American "counties" for electoral and judicial uses, and the Louisiana "parishes" for ecclesiastic services and now also for civil governance—which called for new seats of justice.[9]

Where to put the parish seats? The same centrality exigency that had informed church locations, maximizing convenience by minimizing distances, also got applied to siting courthouses. Whenever lawmakers created new parishes or resized existing ones, they called for seats to be centrally located, and left it to local leaders to work out the details. In central and northern Louisiana, where parish centers often ended up in wilderness, landholders might donate space, knowing the value a courthouse would impart to their holding. In other cases, the selection went to a riverbank, spring, or crossroads nearest the center. But in Catholic southern Louisiana, parish courthouses often ended up right by parish churches, for the same spatial logic of centralization. In this manner, political geography iterated religious geography, and for all those who needed to pay a tax, obtain a license, or appear in court, Sunday towns now became Monday-Tuesday-Wednesday-Thursday-Friday towns.

One example is Pointe à la Hache, whose location on the east bank of lower Plaquemines Parish had no particular geographical attribute aside from occupying the natural levee. But it happened to be halfway up the river to New Orleans, nicely centralized amid a large catchment area of fruit farmers and sugar planters. Serving their needs, Pointe à la Hache managed to become "one of the largest settlements between English Turn and the mouth of the river," wrote historian Alcée Fortier in 1914, "and was chosen as the seat of parochial government. The first church in the town was built in 1820, the jail was built in 1835, and the present courthouse in 1890." Pointe à la Hache also furnished the services of "rice mills, fruit houses, a money order post office, telegraph station, commercial houses and hotel," along with two newspapers, giving it an early 1900s population of 400 and making it "the shipping and supply town for a large stretch of farming lands" with a few thousand residents.[10]

But when the plantation regime declined, rural Plaquemines's populations shifted closer to metro New Orleans. The parish's largest community formed at Belle Chasse, sited on the west bank by virtue of its terrestrial shortcut to Gretna—a sort of modern portage, today's Belle Chasse Highway—and catalyzed by the New Orleans, Fort Jackson & Grand Isle Railroad (1888). Those

All that remains of the historic Plaquemines Parish Courthouse in Pointe à la Hache, an exemplar of administrative centrality as a siting rationale, and of what happens when it disappears. Photograph by Richard Campanella.

folks who remained in lower Plaquemines increasingly depended on resource extraction economies, such as fishing, petroleum, and sulfur, each of which gave rise to new settlement sites. It didn't help that both the River Road and the levee terminated at Pointe à la Hache, whereas across the Mississippi the road continued downriver another thirty miles closer to fishing areas and oil fields. Pointe à la Hache thus found itself at land's end, ill-positioned for modernity, the only two things keeping it relevant being the courthouse and the ferry. In 2002, the historic circa 1890 Plaquemines Parish Courthouse burned in a bizarre arson plot, sending parish government packing for—where else?—Belle Chasse, thirty miles upriver, and the closest thing Plaquemines Parish has to a city. Even the Croatian House cultural center is now located in Belle Chasse, despite the fact that immigrants from Croatia had established fishing settlements in the far lower reaches of the parish. Today only the ferry, a district court, some administrative offices, and 180 inhabitants keep Pointe à la Hache on the map—its coast eroding, its marshes sinking, and its siting story as a service and administrative center being unwritten by steadfast depopulation.[11]

Other settlements originating from church/courthouse pairings occur in St. John the Baptist and St. Charles parishes, where German and Swiss *engagés* (indentured workers) settled during 1720–1721 "on the right bank of the Mississippi between . . . Bustard Bend and the Lac des Ouaches," today's Edgard and Hahnville. The siting rationales for their settlements of Hoffen, Augsburg, Karlstein, and Mariental—roughly today's Killona, Waterford, and Taft—included a distributary ridge accessing Lac des Allemands to the south, and the fact that, according to historian Ellen C. Merrill, this river bend "had already been partially cleared and cultivated by two Indian tribes." Settlers of the Côte des Allemands (German Coast) were soon joined by French colonists and African slaves, who established river-fronting plantations along both banks. As most Germans were or became Catholics and assimilated into French Creole society, a need arose to replace provisional chapels with sanctioned parish churches.[12]

One such chapel had initially been built in 1723 at an unremembered site on the west bank, and in 1770 became St. John the Baptist Parish Church. While centralization explains its general placement, its exact siting came from headstrong neighbors. Archival documents indicate members of the community, led by Michel Poché, concluded a neighbor named Jacques Dubroc had too much land (twelve arpents) and too few responsibilities ("a single man . . . having no family to support"). Poché petitioned Spanish governor Alejandro O'Reilly to expropriate "four arpents . . . for the church" and compensate Dubroc by giving him "new pickets" for the fence he'd have to reconfigure. O'Reilly agreed, and those four arpents have been home to St. John the Baptist Parish Church ever since, centerpiece of the community it helped spawn.[13]

The ecclesiastic parish soon became the namesake for the new civil parish established in 1807, and the affiliated community of St. John became the parish seat in 1848 (the prior courthouse having been at Lucy, three miles downriver.) By now boasting a post office, stores, houses, and a river landing, St. John was renamed in 1850 for postmaster Edgar Perret (but spelled "Edgard" to distinguish it from another town named Edgar), and later connected with a rail line. A visitor in 1860 described Edgard as "some ninety or a hundred buildings, scattered along the levee road, two or three pretty nice stores, and parish buildings, well built of brick, a neat Catholic church, and a graveyard of considerable extent." Home to the courthouse and affiliated administrative offices, Edgard in 1860 presided over a parish with eight public schools ("four on each bank"), two French-language newspapers, and a total property value of $4.5 million, "half of which is the value of slaves." While Edgard never incorporated, its siting story as a Sunday town and service/administrative node has kept it relevant. It remains home to the parish's oldest church as well as its government, judiciary, and around 1,900 people, despite the fact that most parish residents live across the river.[14]

In light of that centralization mandate, it might seem counterintuitive that an administrative node might be inconveniently positioned for most parish residents. Such lopsided emplacements often were intended to keep rural areas relevant—until pragmatism prevailed. Case in point: the St. Bernard Parish

Edgard abounds in siting stories—Sunday town, administrative center, trade hub, and river landing, among others. Home to both the parish church and seat of the civic parish of St. John the Baptist, it is nonetheless unincorporated, and across the Mississippi from most parish residents. Photograph by Richard Campanella.

Courthouse, which was sited in 1848 east of Poydras, at the geographical center of the parish's landmass. But as urbanized areas grew in Arabi and Chalmette, pressure mounted to move the courthouse toward the parish's population. That argument prevailed in 1939, when the parish seat was relocated to a new courthouse in Chalmette—good for the many who lived near the metropolis, but a lasting blow to the few living in the eastern marshes.[15]

The other German Coast church, originally a chapel built in 1740 on the east bank, became St. Charles Borromeo Church by 1770. A classic Sunday town for its eponymous civil parish, the service center that developed adjacently became known as Red Church for the house of worship's vibrant coloring, a landmark for river travelers. (Wrote one flatboatman marking his long journey down the Mississippi in 1839, "Bonnet Quarre Church . . . Destrehan Point . . . the Red Church . . . Landed at the fair famed City of New Orleans . . . Here at last!)"[16] Still attracting the faithful, that red-roofed house of worship marks the heart of Destrehan, a community named for the nearby plantation whose circa 1787 main house still stands. Although it never incorporated, Destrehan got reinvigorated in 1983 as a bridgehead site for the Hale Boggs Memorial (Luling) Bridge, and is now practically a suburb of metro New Orleans, home to 12,000 people.

Despite its size, Destrehan is not the seat of St. Charles Parish. That designation initially went to an early colonial German farming settlement on the west bank where there had been a Quinnitassa Indian village. The resulting administrative and service center became known as St. Charles Courthouse; it gained a post office in 1843 and by 1860 boasted a half-dozen houses, a store, a jail, and a ferry. Then came a railroad station in 1870, which motivated the surveying of two small subdivisions, one a mile upriver on a property owned by former governor Michael Hahn, and another in 1872 near the courthouse itself,

St. Charles Parish Courthouse near Hahnville. Photograph by Richard Campanella.

named for District Judge Othelle Flagg. In time, the name "Flaggville" fell out of use, and today "Hahnville," population 3,700, remains the seat of St. Charles Parish, despite being a mile from the modern courthouse.[17]

As colonial tensions erupted into the French and Indian War, the British in 1755 began expelling French Canadians from the Acadie region of what is now Nova Scotia. After years adrift, some *Acadiens* made their way to French Louisiana, only to learn that the colony was transitioning to Spanish rule. For many, the regime change worked in their favor, because Spanish policy aimed to populate Louisiana as a *barrera* (barrier) between enemy British to the east and the Spanish Main to the west. Thus began one of the most impactful siting stories in Louisiana history: Spanish land grants made to officials, immigrants, refugees, and locals, often in parallel with the siting of military *postes,* or garrisons.

Over the next twenty years, French Canadians received land grants to settle what became known as la Côte des Acadiens, and later spread westward into the prairies and bayous of the Attakapas region. In time, *Acadiens* got corrupted to *'Cadiens,* which got anglicized to *Cajuns,* a slur that has since been proudly reappropriated. Their settlement region became known as "Arcady" in the late 1800s, and by the mid-1900s as Acadiana, the Acadian Triangle, or Cajun Country, reaching as far north as Marksville—itself originally a Spanish military post and land grant.[18]

The original Côte des Acadiens, which formed around the Native village of Cabahanoce, spread from Vacherie westward to the hamlet of St. James in the parish of the same name. What made this site advantageous was a distributary ridge (today's South Vacherie) that adjoined another ridge to the southwest (today's Chackbay), thus forming a shortcut to Bayou Lafourche at Thibodaux. Fused with the natural levee of the Mississippi, the South Vacherie ridge also had fine pasturelands, possibly accounting for its name, meaning "cattle ranch." As populations grew, the St. James/Vacherie community landed St. James Catholic Church (originally St. Jacques de Cabahanoce, 1770), and later the St. James Parish Courthouse. Borne as a crossroads and shortcut site, the Vacherie area is now home to over 6,000 people across two Census-Designated Places.

But no longer is Vacherie the seat of St. James Parish. In 1869, the courthouse was relocated across the river to Convent. That locale had garnered its own spatial momentum, being centralized, ferry-accessed, home to St. Michael's Church since 1809, to the Sacred Heart Convent since 1825 (for which it was renamed from its previous moniker, St. Michael), and to Jefferson College (today's Manresa Retreat House) since 1834. In effect, Convent had supplanted Vacherie as the parish's main service node, and the 1869 courthouse shift made it an administrative center as well. One writer in 1892 described "Convent Town, with its horde of stores, its many sweet homes, its parish church and presbytery and convent and college," as "one of the most important commercial centers on the river front, [and] the only town on the left bank between New Orleans and Baton Rouge."[19] Convent attained a station on the Yazoo & Mississippi Valley Railroad, and by the early 1900s it had "several good mercantile establishments, two hotels, a large sugar mill, a money order post office, express and telegraph offices, and a population of 600." But then the convent burned down, the college closed, and modern highways made Gramercy and Lutcher more convenient. Even with the courthouse, Convent has diminished to three-quarters its size from a century ago, its siting rationale having been gained from, and lost to, its own parish neighbors.[20]

As the highest feature on the deltaic plain, the Mississippi's banks (natural levees) are shedders of runoff, not collectors; they have distributaries, not tributaries, and they form forks, not confluences. Yet for humans, a distributary fork offers just as much advantage as a confluence, and creates its own web of traversable, inhabitable natural levees. What resulted on this otherwise sodden deltaic plain were navigable ingresses into productive regions, with sufficient high ground to host settlements. The two best examples of lower Mississippi fork sites are Plaquemine in Iberville Parish and Donaldsonville in Ascension Parish.

The city of Plaquemine owes its existence to a distributary flowing westward from a hairpin meander south of Baton Rouge. Known as Bayou Plaquemine, this discharge of sediment-laden water (as well as that of an intermittent parallel distributary known as Bayou Jacob) shored up the natural levee while enabling navigation back to Bayou Grosse Tete—which accessed Bayou Sorrel, Grand River, and all the riches of the Atchafalaya Swamp.[21] Pierre Le Moyne, Sieur d'Iberville, sensed the potential of this fork during his 1699 visit to a Bay-

Detail of 1820 *Map of Louisiana*, by John Melish, showing settlements along the lower Mississippi from Baton Rouge (*upper left*) down to the sea, and prominently featuring Bayou Lafourche at left, branching off at Donaldsonville. Library of Congress.

ougoula village (near a place still called Bayou Goula), when he noted "a creek [located] three leagues from their village, on the left going upstream . . . by way of which they go in canoe to the Outymascha and the Magenescito," two tribes living to the west.[22] Later in the 1700s, Acadian refugees used Bayou Plaquemine to reach the Attakapas region, and by the early 1800s Bayou Plaquemine became the premier gateway to south-central Louisiana.

To Thomas Ashe, writing in 1806, "the bayou or creek of Plaquemine [is] the principal and swiftest communication . . . to the two populous and rich settlements of Atacapas and Opelousas." To another observer, the site where Bayou Plaquemine forked off from the Mississippi was so beneficial that it was "hardly possible to secure a more desirable locality for a town."[23] That nodality became clear to a Tennessean named Thomas B. Pipkin, a veteran of the Battle of New Orleans who in 1817 purchased riverfront land abutting Bayou Plaquemine and opened a ferry and tavern. Two years later, he had the parcel subdivided as the town of Iberville, which he extolled as a "beautiful and important situation . . . scarcely equalled [*sic*] by any place in the union for its many advantages," namely "the Bayou Plaquemine, thro' which is the chief communication and passage . . . for all kinds of boats, nearly the whole of the year, [connecting] a large and rich portion of this state [with] the Attackapas [and] Opelousas" regions. Pipkin persuaded the state to clear out the bayou, and contracted the steamboat *Louisianais* to ply to the Attakapas region twice weekly.[24] Iberville grew, becoming the parish seat in 1835 and incorporating under the new name of Plaquemine in 1838, by which time the town was as much an administrative and service center as a port and portal. From the late 1820s into the 1850s, more people lived in Iberville Parish than East Baton Rouge Parish, and the plurality lived in Plaquemine.[25]

Today, that situation is reversed. East Baton Rouge Parish has over thirteen times more residents than Iberville Parish, and the city of Plaquemine is home to only one-fifth of Iberville Parish's population, some 5,800 people. While Baton Rouge's rise is chiefly traceable to its designation as the state capital in 1849, Plaquemine's regression came about as its siting advantages soured. Being on the cutbank of a particularly sharp meander, erosion gnawed away at the town's riverfront, and springtime freshets sometimes brought flooding through the bayou. Federal involvement in river control starting in 1879 engendered efforts to seal off distributaries in favor of higher and stronger levees—the so-called "levees only" policy—which resulted in the closure of Bayou Plaquemine in the 1890s. All the while, railroads had reconfigured western access, outcompeting the waterborne routes across the Atchafalaya.

Plaquemine rebounded with the 1909 completion of the Plaquemine Lock, which enabled shipping to complement adjacent timber and moss industries. "The town of Plaquemine," wrote the editors of a state history in 1892, "is the point where there centers an accumulation of logs from an interior pregnant with the largest and finest of cypress trees. [Its] saw-mills and planing-mills, as well as the shingle factories, are the largest and best equipped in the state."[26] Nearby White Castle, which shared access to the Atchafalaya's cypress forests, also got a mill, and the two communities prospered.

But when the cypress ran out, and when the circumventing Port Allen Lock opened in 1961, Plaquemine lost the last of its "scarcely equalled . . . advantages."[27] Yet it is still one of the largest urban riverfront populations outside of Baton Rouge and New Orleans, thanks to site advantages linking it to points west since the days of indigenous occupancy. In fact, a tiny community named Indian Village still endures where Bayou Plaquemine discharges into the Atchafalaya Basin.

While Bayou Plaquemine diverted only a fraction of the lower Mississippi, making the metaphor "fork" seem more like hyperbole, the next major distributary downriver carried off enough water to convince French mapmakers that it was *la fourche,* "the fork." Starting some 3,500 years ago, Bayou Lafourche constituted the main channel of the Mississippi, until around 1,100 years ago, when most water avulsed into the current channel.[28] Those two millennia of sediment deposition created a pair of eighty-mile-long interbasin ridges (natural levees) paralleling Bayou Lafourche—which had *its* own forks and distributaries with *their* own ridge systems, among them Bayou Terrebonne,

Bayou Little Black, and Bayou Blue. With the ecologically rich Barataria and Terrebonne basins on either side, and access to the Mississippi River and the Gulf of Mexico at either end, the main fork offered an attractive site for settlement—today's Donaldsonville.

Indigenous inhabitation led French colonials to describe this site as La Fourche des Chetimaches, and by one 1770 account the main village had a population of sixty warriors plus women, children, and elders. In the decades ahead, as Spanish administrators stepped up their granting of land to settlers, Natives were steadily displaced to the coastal fringe. One of those grantees was an Acadian named Pierre Landry, who in 1775 secured title to the main fork site, next to where a Capuchin priest had established La Ascensión de Nuestro Señor Jesucristo de La Fourche de los Chetimaches in 1772. Landry sold his parcel to William Donaldson in 1806, the same year that an observer declared the spot to be second only to Plaquemine for its access to the "populous and rich settlements of Atacapas and Opelousas." William Donaldson would do for Bayou Lafourche what Thomas Pipkin later did for Bayou Plaquemine: site a settlement here as a portal to the south and west.[29]

To design the town, Donaldson hired the French-born *ingénieur géographe* Barthélémy Lafon, who at the time was laying out today's Lower Garden District in New Orleans. Intimately familiar with regional geography, Lafon had a keen sense for land value and acquired a parcel right next to Donaldson's. Folks initially called Lafon's new layout a variety of names, including Donaldson, Donaldstown, Nouvelle Ville de Donaldson, and Lafourche (the name of the nearby post office), before officially settling on Donaldsonville. By then, the term La Fourche des Chetimaches had fallen out of use, while official documents began to refer consistently to the distributary as Bayou Lafourche.[30]

Donaldsonville gained momentum, becoming the seat of the newly chartered Ascension Parish in 1807, an entrepôt for cargo coming in and out of Bayou Lafourche and a ferry landing (1846) for present-day Darrow across the river, and the largest steamboat stop between New Orleans and Baton Rouge. Donaldsonville became so central to country planters that, in their tussle with city merchants in New Orleans, it succeeded in becoming the state capital in 1830. It didn't work out, and legislators returned to New Orleans in 1831, though the "country argument" eventually prevailed in making Baton Rouge the state capital in 1849. Donaldsonville instead capitalized on its original siting advantage, hosting dozens of stores, banks, warehouses, and wharves, and becoming home to Catholic, Protestant, and Jewish institutions as well as a number of educational academies.[31]

That natural advantage, however, got steadily undercut by manmade arteries—

Ascension Parish Courthouse in Donaldsonville. Photograph by Richard Campanella.

canals and railroads. The Attakapas Canal to Lake Verret (1830), the Barataria & Lafourche Company Canal (1830), and the New Orleans & Opelousas Railroad (1850s) each enabled cargo to move east and west rather than up and down the bayou, cutting Donaldsonville out of the action. In 1904, Donaldsonville suffered the same blow as Plaquemine when government engineers, following the levees-only policy, dammed Bayou Lafourche, blocking vessel passage and emitting only enough river water to keep the bayou fresh. The city with so much momentum in the early nineteenth century settled into intermediary status in the twentieth century, during which time its population changes (4,100 in 1900 to 7,600 in 2000 and 6,800 in 2022) reflected the regional petrochemical industry more so than a robust local economy. Yet, ahead of Plaquemine, Donaldsonville is the largest non-metropolitan population cluster along the lower Mississippi, and its impressive collection of historical architecture speaks volumes for its salient siting story.

Ridges formed wherever water escaped from the Mississippi and deposited sediment at offshoot angles. Terrestrial traffic could thence move perpendicularly away from the river. Such road-topped uplands abounded, particularly at sharp meanders, where they crossed the main River Road. Crossroads are, of course, attractive sites for settlement.

One intermittent distributary created just enough of a lateral ridge and crossroads to attract an antebellum enclave named New River—today's Geismar, in Ascension Parish, whose petrochemical plants now tower over the abandoned distributary still known as New River.[32] Another example occurs a hundred miles downriver, where a distributary ridge formed the first crossroads site for travelers coming upstream. Periodically reactivated into the 1920s, the now-abandoned Bayou Terre-aux-Boeufs distributary discharged from English Turn and flowed eastward through St. Bernard Parish before bifurcating at Reggio (itself a crossroads), with one ridge extending out to Yscloskey and Hopedale, and the other down to Delacroix. That meant terrestrial traffic along the natural levee of the Mississippi could turn onto a ridge-top road and proceed fully fifteen miles out into marshes abundant with game, fur, shellfish, and finfish.

That crossroads developed into a settlement in French colonial times, when it comprised a prominent plantation owned by colony *ordonnateur* (treasurer) Pierre Gaspard de Rochemore. In the Spanish era it pertained to Antoine Philippe de Marigny de Mandeville, who in 1779 bequeathed it to his son Pierre. By this time, Spanish administrators had embarked on their land-granting effort to bring in more Spanish subjects. Starting in 1777, they began recruiting families from Málaga and Granada in Spain to settle west of the Acadian Coast, giving rise to today's New Iberia. In subsequent years, Governor Bernardo de Gálvez settled Canary Islanders on the coastal fringes of New Orleans, in the interest of economic development as well as military defense against nearby British colonies.[33] It was for these purposes that Pierre Marigny "donated the gigantic parcel behind [his] river frontage," wrote St. Bernard Parish historian William de Marigny Hyland, himself a direct Marigny descendant, "to the King of Spain for the colonization of colonists from the Canary Islands in 1779."[34] That grant brought a few hundred Isleños to the Bayou Terre-aux-Boeufs region. Another 150 Isleños had been settled across the river in what is now Laffite, but after getting pummeled by hurricanes and floods, in 1782 they joined their brethren at Bayou Terre-aux-Boeufs.[35] Together these settlements became known as the Poblacion de San Bernardo, forming the heart of the original ecclesiastic and civil parish of St. Bernard. Their descendants live in "da parish" to this day.

The Marigny plantation soon came into the possession of statesman and philanthropist Julien de Lallande Poydras. Because Poydras's holding adjoined the busy river/distributary crossroads, that site became known as Poydras and attracted residences and stores. Attesting to its centrality, in 1848 the parish courthouse was located near Poydras, two miles east in St. Bernard Village, and would remain there for over ninety years.

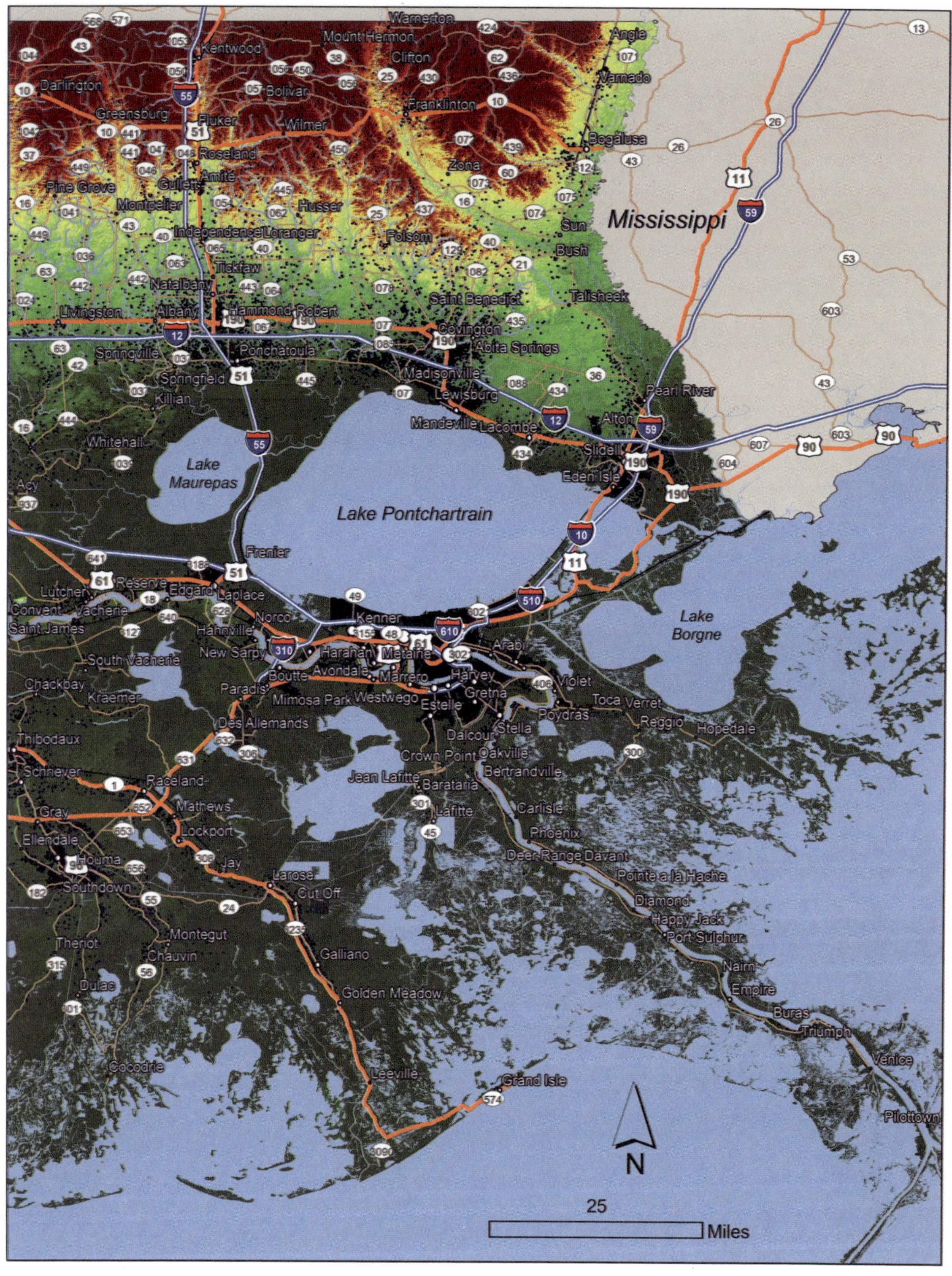

Warnerton
Mount Hermon
Clifton
Angie
Varnado
Kentwood
Darlington
Bolivar
Franklinton
Greensburg
Fluker
Wilmer
Bogalusa
Roseland
Amite
Zona
Gullett
Pine Grove
Montpelier
Husser
Mississippi
Independence
Loranger
Sun
Folsom
Bush
Tickfaw
Natalbany
Saint Benedict
Talisheek
Livingston
Albany
Hammond
Robert
Covington
Abita Springs
Springville
Ponchatoula
Springfield
Madisonville
Killian
Lewisburg
Pearl River
Mandeville
Lacombe
Alton
Whitehall
Slidell
Lake Maurepas
Eden Isle
Acy
Lake Pontchartrain
Frenier
Reserve
Lutcher
Edgard
Laplace
Convent
Vacherie
Norco
Kenner
Saint James
Hahnville
Lake Borgne
New Sarpy
Harahan
Metairie
Arabi
South Vacherie
Boutte
Avondale
Marrero
Harvey
Violet
Chackbay
Paradis
Gretna
Kraemer
Mimosa Park
Westwego
Estelle
Toca
Verret
Poydras
Des Allemands
Reggio
Hopedale
Thibodaux
Dalcour
Stella
Crown Point
Oakville
Schriever
Raceland
Jean Lafitte
Bertrandville
Barataria
Mathews
Gray
Lafitte
Carlisle
Lockport
Ellendale
Phoenix
Houma
Deer Range
Davant
Jay
Pointe a la Hache
Southdown
Larose
Cut Off
Diamond
Happy Jack
Port Sulphur
Theriot
Montegut
Chauvin
Galliano
Nairn
Empire
Dulac
Golden Meadow
Buras
Triumph
Venice
Cocodrie
Leeville
Grand Isle
Pilottown
N
25
Miles

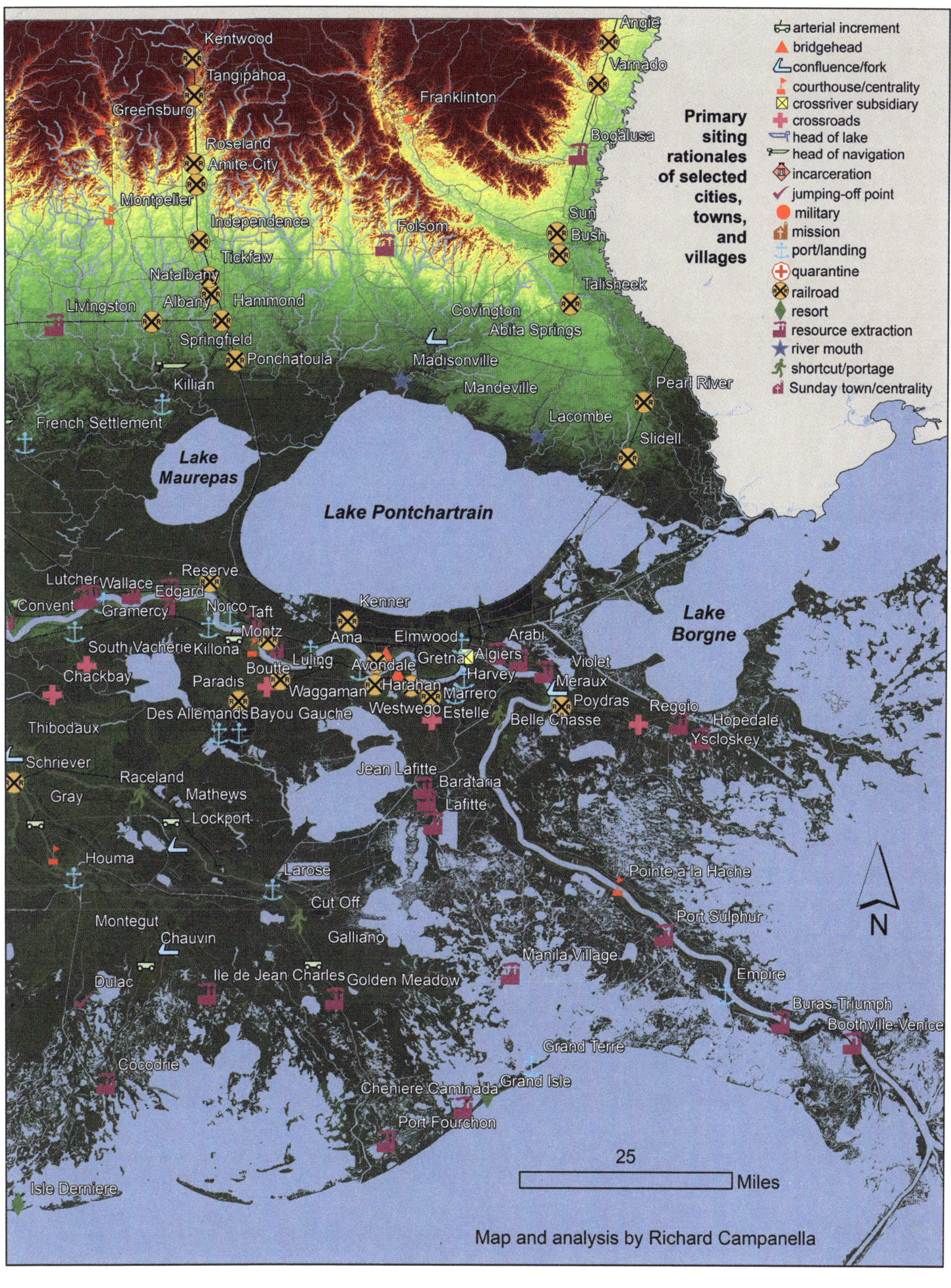
Primary siting rationales of selected cities, towns, and villages
arterial increment
bridgehead
confluence/fork
courthouse/centrality
crossriver subsidiary
crossroads
head of lake
head of navigation
incarceration
jumping-off point
military
mission
port/landing
quarantine
railroad
resort
resource extraction
river mouth
shortcut/portage
Sunday town/centrality
Kentwood
Tangipahoa
Greensburg
Franklinton
Angie
Varnado
Bogalusa
Roseland
Amite City
Montpelier
Independence
Folsom
Sun
Bush
Tickfaw
Natalbany
Albany
Hammond
Livingston
Springfield
Ponchatoula
Talisheek
Covington
Abita Springs
Madisonville
Mandeville
Killian
French Settlement
Pearl River
Lacombe
Slidell
Lake Maurepas
Lake Pontchartrain
Lake Borgne
Reserve
Lutcher
Wallace
Edgard
Convent
Gramercy
Norco
Taft
Kenner
Montz
Ama
Elmwood
Arabi
South Vacherie
Killona
Luling
Gretna
Algiers
Violet
Chackbay
Boutte
Avondale
Harvey
Meraux
Paradis
Waggaman
Harahan
Marrero
Poydras
Des Allemands
Bayou Gauche
Westwego
Estelle
Belle Chasse
Reggio
Hopedale
Yscloskey
Thibodaux
Schriever
Raceland
Gray
Mathews
Lockport
Jean Lafitte
Barataria
Lafitte
Houma
Larose
Pointe a la Hache
Cut Off
Montegut
Chauvin
Galliano
Port Sulphur
Manila Village
Dulac
Ile de Jean Charles
Golden Meadow
Empire
Buras-Triumph
Boothville-Venice
Grand Terre
Cocodrie
Cheniere Caminada
Grand Isle
Port Fourchon
25
Miles
N
Isle Derniere
Map and analysis by Richard Campanella

Railroads supplemented the value of the intersection. The Mexican Gulf Railroad, initially launched in 1837 from New Orleans, had by the late 1840s extended through "Poydras Junction" and out Bayou Terre-aux-Boeufs to the shores of Lake Borgne, creating a head-of-rail site known as Proctorsville (Proctor's Point, now Shell Beach).[36] By the 1890s, the New Orleans & Gulf Railroad forked out at Poydras and headed east along Bayou Terre-aux-Boeufs, with stations at Poydras, St. Bernard Village, Toca, Contreras, Reggio, Florissant, Yscloskey, and finally Shell Beach. Along with Hopedale and Delacroix, these enclaves became resource extraction sites—for fur, game, and fish in the early days, and for commercial and recreational fishing today, thanks to modern Highways 39 and 46. The *poblacion de San Bernardo* is now a fraction of its former size, demographically and geographically: its people and land base have been decimated by repeated storms and floods, while its ridges are sinking, its marshes eroding, its waters salinating, and its sea level rising. But the outlying fishing settlements remain economically viable as resource extraction sites at the continental fringe, and the only way to get there is through the crossroads at Poydras.

Luling occupies a very different part of the deltaic plain, but also arises from a crossroads. Its natural levee—comprising plantations since the 1720s, one of which came into the possession of the Luling family in the 1850s—was positioned at an erosive cutbank, the likes of which could spawn a distributary. That's what happened here, in the form of Grand Bayou, which created a slender ridge wending across the upper Barataria Basin. Insubstantial though it was, it formed a land bridge nearly reaching Bayou Lafourche, catalyzing present-day Raceland, rather like Vacherie did farther upriver by linking with present-day Thibodaux. Just as Vacherie's ridge became a road playing host to South Vacherie and Chackbay, Luling's ridge gave rise to the communities of Boutte, Paradis, and Des Allemands, the last of these arising at the crossing of Bayou Des Allemands. Previously known as St. Denis or Gassenville, Luling became a crossroads for traffic heading in four different directions: up or down the River Road, southward on the ridge, and northward via ferry. Houses and stores were built to tap into that spatial opportunity, and what resulted was the community of Luling.

Luling's siting story got a boost from railroads as they laid tracks down that rear ridge in their westward reach. By the 1890s, the Texas & Pacific Railroad passed through Luling, while the Southern Pacific forked down the ridge to Raceland. Luling by century's end had a post office, a river landing, a ferry to Destrehan, and a population of nearly 1,000. What worked for railroads in the

1800s did the same for automobile roads in the 1900s. With the construction of Highway 90 through Boutte in the late 1930s, followed by Interstate 310 across the Hale Boggs Bridge in 1983, the Luling/Boutte area became a modern crossroads accessible in four directions, home to 18,000 people.[37]

So too did LaPlace, with over 30,000 residents, two-thirds the population of St. John the Baptist Parish and one of the largest non-metro concentrations along the lower Mississippi. Yet LaPlace, like Luling, never had an early parish church or courthouse, nor does it have a nucleated historic downtown; it never even incorporated. Previously the area was known loosely as Bonnet Carré, a term inferring the entire square-bonnet-shaped river bend from here up to Reserve, and plantations occupied its entire natural levee. Some occupied a notorious cutbank where the river periodically tore open a crevasse, the worst of which inundated far-away New Orleans in 1871.[38] The feature that finally attracted settlement was the unusually broad natural levee just upriver from the crevasse (now the Bonnet Carré Spillway). Although hardly high, this upland extended far back enough to merge with the land bridge between lakes Maurepas and Pontchartrain, enabling riverfront traffic to veer northward toward the piney woods of what is now Tangipahoa Parish. In the 1880s, rail lines capitalized on that terrestrial connection, just as they would do for Luling across the river. One was originally known as the New Orleans & Baton Rouge Railroad, to which a French-born New Orleans druggist named Bazile LaPlace, who had recently bought land here, granted a right of way for tracks and a depot to be named after him. By the 1890s, the Louisville, New Orleans & Texas operated the line to the LaPlace depot, while the Chicago, St. Louis & New Orleans built its tracks up the land bridge and put a station at Frenier on the Lake Pontchartrain shore. The road built to connect the two stations became LaPlace's Main Street.[39]

In the early 1930s, the state built Airline Highway (Highway 61) inland from LaPlace to connect New Orleans and Baton Rouge, and Highway 51 to traverse up to another railroad town, Ponchatoula, and points north. Now automobiles could utilize that crossroads, drawing commerce and residences farther away from the old riverfront section of LaPlace. Next came I-10 and I-55 in the 1970s, further tugging development inland. Fueled by the exodus from New Orleans and the rise of River Road industry, LaPlace flourished as a sprawling interchange of four major arteries. Its siting story took a century to write and had a number of chapters, but ultimately it may be categorized as a crossroads site—just like Luling.

For need of labor, resource extraction and processing sites often spawn settlements. With its abundant natural resources and maritime access, the lower

Mississippi offers archetypes of such siting rationales, the earliest of which involve fisheries—and fishers from 5,000 miles away.

Immigrants from the Dalmatia region began arriving in coastal Louisiana in the 1820s and peaked during the 1880s through 1910s. Known variously as Slavs, Slavonians, Croatians, Dalmatians, Yugoslavs, or Austrians (for the Austro-Hungarian Empire), these seafaring people found opportunities akin to those in the Adriatic and Mediterranean. Plaquemines Parish particularly beckoned with its bounteous estuarine fisheries and briny oysters. Additionally, "some Yugoslavs began work as trappers and traders of muskrats, minks, and other peltries," wrote sociologist Frank M. Lovrich, and "from these revenues some invested in extensive orange acreage near Fort St. Philip," where they neighbored Creole families.

Settlements germinated in the 1830s as Slavic families constructed oyster "camps," isolated wooden houses built up on stilts, equipped with cisterns, and positioned on bayous where they docked their luggers and skiffs. "These camps were about a quarter of a mile apart, [and by] about 1840 several little hamlets or villages" arose among them. Some aggregated around preexisting enclaves, such as Quartiers des Burats, founded by an extended family whose surname later got anglicized to Buras. Most were too informal to garner proper names until the late 1800s, when the concurrent establishment of canneries, processing facilities, and wharves turned them into communities. One representative example was what Lovrich, in his 1963 dissertation, dubbed "Oysterville[,] a trade center [whose] influence projects out to . . . oyster camps nestled in the numerous bays and bayous around it."[40] Many other lower-river communities would form as resource extraction (fisheries) sites and trade centers. "Today they are referred to as Buras [formerly Burats], Empire, Ostrica, and Venice,"[41] the last previously known as Jump, for a former river crevasse, and renamed Venice in 1892 possibly by Dalmations familiar with the famed Italian city. Others such as Neptune, Sunrise, and Nicholls have since fallen off the map. With a combined population of 3,000 people, Buras, Empire, and Venice today retain the shellfish and finfish industries for which they were originally sited. They rank among the largest seafood ports in the nation, handling oysters, shrimp, menhaden, and other species—our last wild food, processed at what a sign in Venice describes as "the Southernmost Point in Louisiana, Gateway to the Gulf."[42]

A few miles upriver of Empire is a community with a very different siting story, but one also pegged to extraction and processing. The resource in this case was sulfur, a yellow, crystalline mineral used for fertilizer, insecticides, fungicides, and other applications. Solid deposits known as brimstone typically

Empire typifies what one researcher described generically as "Oysterville," those many lower-river settlements born as extraction sites for shellfish and finfish. Photographs by Jason Campanella and Richard Campanella.

coincided with oil and gas reserves, and Plaquemines Parish proliferated with both—along with the political will to extract them and the riverine access to ship them. Major sulfur deposits were found at Garden Island Bay, near the river's mouth, and at Grand Ecaille in Barataria Bay, the largest in the world at the time. In 1933, the Texas-based Freeport Sulphur Company dug a canal from Lake Grand Ecaille northeastwardly to a site it had secured on the west bank, where engineers established storage and processing facilities, a shipping port with conveying systems, and a company town. They named it Port Sulphur (spelled the traditional way), and both the facility and community prospered, the latter with homes, amenities, and a school.

All the while, sulfur industry technologies changed (as did the spelling), making the element obtainable from liquid crude. As brimstone lost its value, Port Sulphur lost its siting rationale. Grand Ecaille closed in 1978. Freeport merged with McMoRan in 1981, and in the early 2000s Freeport-McMoRan shuttered its operations at Port Sulphur. The facilities were battered by Hurricane Katrina in 2005, and two years later Freeport-McMoRan relocated its New Orleans headquarters to Phoenix, Arizona. Port Sulphur has since hollowed out, becoming a small service node (school, sheriff's office, firehouse, church, and cemetery) for about 2,000 people dispersed over twelve miles, its obsolete siting story written into its name. From a siting perspective, Port Sulphur may be considered a plant (processing) site, but since its location had been predetermined by proximity to the Grand Ecaille mine, its original siting rationale was resource extraction.[43]

Farther up the River Road, where brackish bays gave way to freshwater swamps, Louisiana bald cypress was the resource of value. While this gorgeous, durable wood had been selectively harvested since the 1720s, it was not until the 1880s that industrial-scale cutting began—the likes of which could spawn "huge industrial plants with sawmills at the center and scores of purpose-built company towns," as researcher Donna Fricker wrote. Behind the boom were a number of factors, among them the depleted supply of northeastern timber in the face of insatiable national demand, new southern railroads, northern investment capital, new steam-powered skidders, and "the availability of large tracts of timberland at low prices" prompted by an 1876 federal law that opened access to trees on public land. What ensued was not forestry, but more like wood mining, and it turned most of Louisiana's old-growth cypress, southern pine, and longleaf (yellow) pine into "stumpscapes." It also elevated Louisiana to the top of the national timber economy. "In 1880," wrote Fricker, "Louisiana ranked thirtieth in the United States for the dollar value of its timber product. By 1900, it ranked tenth . . . and by 1920, second. In some years in the 1910s the state led the country in timber production."[44] Lumber mills opened throughout Louisiana and Mississippi, from the piney hills down to the delta. While many facilities piggybacked on existing communities, such as Plaquemine and White Castle, others established their own company towns. Two prime examples are Lutcher and Garyville.

Lutcher formed when Pennsylvania timber tycoons Henry Jacob Lutcher and G. Bedell Moore, having moved down to Orange, Texas, in 1877 to cut and mill Sabine River cypress, aimed to duplicate their success along the lower Mississippi in 1889. The Lutcher-Moore Company bought the forty-arpent Chenet Plantation in St. James Parish for its proximity to the Maurepas Swamp, a site further enhanced by the 1892 establishment of a depot of the Mississippi Valley Railroad. Over the next few years, Lutcher and Moore erected what one journalist described as "the largest and most complete sawmill plant in the state . . . furnishing the beautiful crimson heart Pontchartrain cypress to every state in the union, up into Canada." The parcel adjacent to the planing and shingle mill "took on the air of a thriving village," named Lutcher, "laid out in wide, regular streets and shaded avenues lined with pretty and commodious houses." By 1896 they numbered over 100, home to over 700 people served with a purpose-built school. "A bare piece of cane field a few years ago," Lutcher began as a company town sited to support the company mill, which had been sited to extract company-owned timber. In 1895 the firm added "a big new sash, door, and blind factory[—]a blessing to the laboring classes, who will have opened a new door to employment," and an additional source of profit for the management class. "If we rich men of Louisiana did not show her wealth of products to the world," asked Henry Jacob Lutcher, "who would?" Old-growth cypress, however, is hardly a renewable resource, and after Lutcher-Moore felled the last trees on its holdings, the company shuttered the mill in 1931, leaving residents to resort to fur-trapping or return to agriculture.[45] Today, what remains of Lutcher's siting story are the former company houses, most of them still occupied, and the hatchet on the town logo.

As Lutcher grew, a competitor eyed the same resource and sited itself nearby. In 1903, the Lyon Lumber Company of Illinois purchased the Glencoe, Emilie, and Hope plantations just downriver in St. John the Baptist Parish, for their adjacency to the Maurepas Swamp—550 square miles of cypress and pine forests. Ambition does not begin to describe what Lyon accomplished in the next few years, by which time its slogan had become "We own the finest tract of cypress timber in the world and operate the most modern cypress sawmill ever built."[46] To house their workers, Lyon built Garyville, named to honor a company director. Featuring three train stations, blocks of houses for hundreds

Lutcher's siting story as a timber extraction site is remembered in its town logo, while nearby Garyville still retains the former office of the Lyon Cypress Lumber Company. Photographs by Richard Campanella.

of worker and executive families, and a commercial district with a bank, a hotel, a theater, stores, a meeting hall, and a church, Garyville is sometimes described as Louisiana's first planned community and company town. In fact, many mill or company towns were built statewide in this era, though Garyville ranks among the best examples. It hosted one of the largest non-metro populations below Baton Rouge, with over 1,000 people.

But as with Lutcher and other lumber towns, the boom did not last. Virgin cypress ran out by 1915, after which the mill switched to old-growth pine from St. Helena and Livingston parishes, where Lyon established another company town named Livingston. Then the pine ran out, while fires in the late 1920s destroyed stacks of stored lumber. The Lyon mill closed in 1931, the same year as Lutcher's plant, costing both communities their siting rationales. Starting in the 1940s, a new extraction and processing industry found advantages in the same geographies that had previously attracted plantations and sawmills. Lutcher and Garyville today, with a combined population of 5,000, now depend heavily on the River Road petrochemical industry. All that remains of Garyville's siting story is the old Lyon Lumber Company headquarters, recently a museum.[47]

Settlements may form where resources are extracted or where resources are processed—that is, transformed to market products, and leaving some of that "added value" in the local community in the form of employment, tax revenue, and development. Though their commodities differed, value-added processing sites explain the locations of Reserve, Gramercy, Waggaman, Avondale, Norco, and Arabi.

A stretch of natural levee on the east bank of St. John the Baptist Parish, known loosely as Bonnet Carré (square bonnet) for the shape of the river, had been used to raise sugarcane since late colonial times. Being across the river from the parish's courthouse and church, Bonnet Carré never developed into a service center, although it did have a secondary church named St. Peter. One particular plantation at Bonnet Carré/St. Peter came into the possession of the Boudousquié family in 1833 and, for reasons unclear, became known as Reserve by the 1850s. The holding spanned 19.5 frontage arpents, where stood the main house and milling facilities, and extended back to the 40-arpent line. The Boudousquié family house happened to be on the circuit of a French-born Jewish peddler named Leon Godchaux, who, after saving his earnings during his youth, moved to New Orleans and in 1845 opened a clothing store on Canal Street.

Godchaux did well, expanded in the 1850s, and managed to hold on to his money through the Civil War—unlike many planter families, like the Boudousquié at the moribund Reserve Plantation. With banks highly circumspect about lending, desperate planters instead turned to moneyed individuals for loans. It was under those circumstances that the widow Sophie Boudousquié reconnected with her old acquaintance—that young peddler of decades prior. "Leon spared Sophie Boudousquié the ignominy of foreclosure and bankruptcy," wrote Peter M. Wolf, Godchaux's great-great-grandson, by buying out her outstanding debts in 1866 and, three years later, fully purchasing the Reserve Plantation. "By bailing out Sophie Boudousquié, Leon entered the south Louisiana sugar business . . . without intending to do so."[48]

Now having nearly 800 arpents of fertile soil and processing equipment, the country peddler-turned-city clothier set himself on a path that would eventually make him the "Sugar King." He established the Godchaux Sugar Company in 1869, one year after Morris Edrington had acquired the neighboring Cornland Plantation and opened the Cornland Sugar Factory. Both companies built facilities, while Godchaux housed his workers and their families in company-built houses with community amenities. A post office opened in 1870, followed by a cemetery in 1871 and a railroad station in 1883, and the St. Peter Catholic Church expanded to accommodate the growing congregation. By 1893, the Godchaux Sugar Refinery had doubled in size and pioneered new processing technologies. Its tireless founder also became a major producer of the cane he refined, going on a "bold sugar lands buying spree," according to Wolf, scooping up the surrounding plantations of "Star, Diamond, LaPlace, LaBranche, Belle Pointe, New Era, Cornland, Elm Hall, Utopia, Upper Ten, Mary, Madewood, Foley, and Greater Raceland. He rejuvenated each place, raising their productivity. . . . Together they covered 72,000 acres, 10,000 of which were in sugarcane fields and the balance in marsh, pine woods, and valuable cypress timberland."[49]

Leon Godchaux died in 1899 at the age of seventy-five, but his sugar legacy continued into the 1950s, accounting directly or indirectly for most economic

The Godchaux-Boudousquie House was integral to the siting story of Reserve, a sugar production and processing settlement spearheaded by "Sugar King" Leon Godchaux. The late 1700s Creole plantation house has been restored since this scene was captured in 2012. Photograph by Richard Campanella.

activity in Reserve and beyond. "With Leon Godchaux's arrival," wrote local historian Gerald J. Keller, "the fortunes of [St. John the Baptist] Parish dramatically changed, from being a collection of small, rural settlements to an agricultural center of regional and national significance."[50] The operation subsequently changed hands a number of times, lastly as the Godchaux-Henderson Sugar Company, which closed in 1985, around the same time Godchaux's famed clothing stores finally folded.

The former Reserve Plantation is now the Globalplex Intermodal Terminal of the Port of South Louisiana, and the site that came to prominence over 150 years ago is still a major source of employment for Reserve's 8,500 residents.[51] Their siting story is congruent to those of other plant sites and company towns, but differs in one key way: Godchaux "selected" this site for purely incidental reasons—courtesy of a personal favor that begot a real estate deal, without any intention of getting into the sugar business, much less reinventing it. In that regard, Reserve could have happened anywhere, so to speak—anywhere along the lower Mississippi, where an immigrant youth born as Lion Godchot began his Louisiana life as a peddler, and ended it as the Sugar King.

Gramercy's siting story is comparable to that of Reserve, except that it remains physically active and visually salient in the town it spawned. The Louisiana Sugar Refining Company (Imperial Sugar) plant sits right on East Main Street, across from the Sacred Heart of Jesus Catholic Church, near fields cultivated with sugarcane for centuries, and a few blocks from the levee on which locals build elaborate bonfires to guide Papa Noël on Christmas Eve. Gramercy, in short, exudes French Louisiana culture, as does its neighbor Lutcher. But just as Lutcher spawned from a timber plant site created by Pennsylvanians by way of Texas—and got a German name in the process—Gramercy happened when railroad tycoons from New York City launched a sugar mill and named it for, of all things, their toney Manhattan neighborhood.

The firm, called Colonial Sugars, represented an ongoing effort of capitalists to consolidate plantation-based sugar mills from antebellum times into centralized industrial facilities with dedicated workforces. "Gramercy is a product of the Railroad Era of the last quarter of the 19th century," explained former manager George P. Meade, who ran Colonial Sugars from 1923 to 1956. "The Illinois Central wanted to locate a sugar house on the Yazoo & Mississippi Valley right-of-way from New Orleans to Baton Rouge." In late 1894, Illinois Central executives found the perfect spot, the former Golden Grove Plantation in St. James Parish, originally a Colapissa Indian village. It had rail access and a riverfront perch, and it neighbored Lutcher, whose labor and infrastructure could be tapped without competing with its timber trade. The site marked the heart of the nation's premier sugar region, halfway between Baton Rouge and New Orleans.

What to call the operation? It so happened that the president and vice president of the Illinois Central, both major stockholders in Colonial Sugars, "lived at the then-fashionable Gramercy Park area in New York. . . . The name of the town, and the sugar company, came directly from New York's Gramercy Park."[52] Initial plans called only for a mill to process Golden Grove cane, but in 1902 the company erected a full-scale refinery to granulate sugar for a national market, for which it built worker housing along with a school, church, and recreational facilities. As Gramercy grew, the refinery changed hands, becoming the Cuban-American Sugar Company, then Savannah Foods and Industry, and today Imperial Sugar. The St. James Parish plant is now second in size to the circa 1912 Domino refinery in St. Bernard Parish, and both played key roles in launching the respective communities of Gramercy (population 2,700) and Arabi/Chalmette (26,700).

Waggaman and Avondale, two unincorporated communities with a combined population of 15,400 on the west bank of Jefferson Parish, emerged cour-

Gramercy is one of the few Louisiana communities whose original siting story, a century-old sugar refinery, is still vital to the town's economy and prominent in its landscape. Photograph by Richard Campanella.

tesy of late 1800s rail access to the east bank. Trains in that era crossed the Mississippi on transfer ferries, ungainly tug-pushed barges onto which locomotives and cars rolled on and off at bankside terminals. The largest was known as the Mastodon, measuring 366 feet long and capable of carrying two locomotives plus tenders and up to twenty-four loaded freight cars. It crossed from the foot of today's Hickory Avenue—thus activating today's city of Harahan—to a part of the former Waggaman Plantation known as Avondale, where the Southern Pacific line came closest to the Illinois Central tracks on the east bank. The intermodal ferry terminal built at that crossing later influenced the siting of the Huey P. Long Bridge, whose 1935 opening made the Mastodon extinct.[53] "The Huey P" also brought residential and industrial attention to this now-accessible section of Jefferson's west bank riverfront. As early as 1926, when plans for the future bridge were solidifying, developers proposed to create a "Belt City . . . at the spot where the automobile approach of the new bridge will reach ground level." A modern bridgehead site, Belt City would form the buckle of an envisioned beltway looping around the metropolis. As the bridge was constructed, streets were laid out and houses erected. In the mid-1940s, residents renamed their community Bridge City, now home to 7,200 people—despite the fact that the envisioned beltway never quite came to fruition.[54]

Motivated by the same new span, marine entrepreneurs Harry Koch, Perry Ellis, and James Viavant in 1938 formed Avondale Marine Ways, Inc., and leased land from the railroad company to establish a shipyard just upriver from the bridge. By the early 1940s, Avondale Marine employed hundreds of workers building Merchant Marine convoy ships and repairing tugboats, tank barges, and other war-related vessels; it later became the largest private employer in Louisiana, with upward of 12,000 workers. Realizing the housing need, developers sited subdivisions adjacently, giving rise to today's Avondale and Waggaman communities, both of which exemplify how industries catalyze settlements. But, unless they economically diversify, such settlements are prone to the fate of said industries, and just like the mill towns of times past, Avondale, Waggaman, Bridge City, and Westwego all suffered a terrible blow in 2014 when Northrop Grumman closed Avondale Shipyards and consolidated its shipbuilding activity in Pascagoula, Mississippi, eliminating 5,000 skilled jobs.[55]

No industry has so profoundly transformed the lower Mississippi as petrochemical processing, to the point of seemingly forming "a second system of cities[,] connected by heavy rail, helicopter flyways, and mineral pipelines" extending from "derelict rigs and storage tank farms to the luminous industrial skylines."[56] As vast as they are intricate, these "factories without walls" have affected riverine settlements in ways ranging from their employment, land values, and public health to their shape, existence, and, in one case, its very name: Norco, Louisiana, originally the New Orleans Refining Company.

What brought NORCO to St. Charles Parish was a 1916 federal maritime law, but we have to go back to 1901 to understand the industry behind it. That year, prospectors struck oil in Jennings, the biggest gusher in Louisiana to date, rivaling concurrent strikes in Texas. In rapid sequence, the drilling, refining, and exporting of petroleum products became lucrative new Louisiana industries. The best transport option was by vessel, for which lower Louisiana's intricate waterways were ideal. Refining required unlimited freshwater, underground brine, riverfront land, and deep-draft shipping access, all of which could be found along the lower Mississippi. The largest old plantations made for the best industrial parcels, and their owners, many of whom traced their titles to colonial times, savored their sudden rise in value. So did the owners of marshlands and swamplands once thought to be worthless. Industry executives and their local benefactors found friends in state government, who bent over backward to accommodate the industry's physical needs and regulatory wants. Louisiana's most powerful people partnered with what would become the world's most powerful industry in making the lower Mississippi into "the Industrial Corridor"—or what critics today decry as "Cancer Alley."[57] Both sides showcase Norco—that is, the former company town and the surrounding Shell Norco Manufacturing Complex—as Exhibit A of their argument.

The law that brought NORCO to St. Charles Parish was the 1916 Shipping Act, which, with Europe at war, aimed to augment the nation's river fleet by prohibiting companies from shipping products in their own vessels, thus forcing new entities to build up maritime capacity. Shell Oil Company, already active in the region, invested in the New Orleans Refining Company to fulfill that need for a separate shipping arm, and NORCO directors set out to find an apt riverside site. They found 460 acres at what had been the Good Hope Plantation, including the enclaves of Sellers (previously Sarpy) and Good Hope. NORCO also proceeded to build a refinery on the parcel, which Shell acquired in 1922 and expanded with the purchase of the Trepagnier family's adjacent Myrtleland Plantation in 1929. Descendants of former slaves from the Myrtleland and Diamond plantations (now the Bonnet Carré Spillway) had lived in a place called Belltown, which Shell relocated to a new site it called Diamond. Across the road from Diamond, Shell built a company town to house white workers and their families, and in 1934 named it Norco.[58]

In the decades ahead, the company known previously as Royal Dutch Shell and now as Shell, expanded its facilities to the point of practically encircling the

Mural in Norco. Photographs by Richard Campanella.

dual communities, including a new chemical plant abutting Diamond. White workers holding better-paying specialized jobs lived in the larger subdivision of Norco, while African Americans holding a small number of mostly janitorial positions resided in four-street-wide Diamond. The two populations, divided by race, class, and generations of lived experience, came to hold diametrically opposed views of Shell and the petrochemical industry, the former proscribing to the "Industrial Corridor" narrative, the latter to "Cancer Alley." With the rise of the environmental justice movement, community members in Diamond teamed with lawyers and activists in suing for relocation and compensation. After years of litigation, Royal Dutch Shell in 2002 agreed to buy out Diamond; the corporation eventually spent $30 million in purchasing 190 properties and relocating 400 residents.[59]

Norco today has around 2,800 people, over 81 percent of whom are white, among the highest rates along the River Road. Diamond's street grid is still in place, but its houses and residents are now mostly gone, with only seventy-four people remaining, of whom only 16 percent are white. Now a century old, Norco's siting story—and Diamond's un-siting—are rooted in the historical geography of the delta, where modern petrochemical plants and old slave plantations turned out to have the same spatial requirements.[60]

Now among Louisiana's most industrialized parishes, St. Bernard remained rural until the Mexican Gulf Railroad extended down St. Claude Avenue in neighboring New Orleans, triggering urban development along its tracks. What brought the action across the parish line was an industrial plant with a novel siting story.

The story began when residents in New Orleans filed complaints about the fetid *abattoirs* scattered about their city. Butchers had long slaughtered livestock at their neighborhood shops, a right that allowed them to process fresh meat on demand and deliver it swiftly to customers. But that same convenience also led to conflict, as workers dumped disgusting offal and effluent in gutters and lots. Angry neighbors petitioned the state to close the dispersed butcheries in favor of a single consolidated slaughterhouse, to be located on the margins of the metropolis. In 1869, the Reconstruction-era state legislature passed "An Act to Protect the Health of the City of New Orleans, to Locate the Stock-Landings and Slaughter-Houses, and to Incorporate the Crescent City Live-stock Landing and Slaughter-house Company."[61] In exchange for the regulation, the state granted the company a monopoly, making it almost like a public utility.

Citizens cheered, but abattoirs protested. Their attorneys filed lawsuits arguing that federal law protected Americans' right to practice their trade, and that no state law could supersede it. In fact, the attorneys noted, the recently ratified Fourteenth Amendment, which bolstered the Thirteenth Amendment in its prohibition of slavery, stipulated that "No State shall make or enforce any law which shall abridge the privileges or immunities of citizens of the United States." The abattoirs then formed their own association, countering the state-backed monopoly, and purchased land along the St. Bernard Parish line to build their own slaughterhouse. Dubbed Stock Landing, this semi-rural site had good riverfront wharfage, plenty of freshwater, and an outflow channel to drain off blood. The site was just close enough to the metropolis to serve city dwellers, yet evaded a legal clash with the city of New Orleans by being on the St. Bernard side of the parish line.[62]

Meanwhile, the state-backed Crescent City Company had secured Slaughterhouse Point on the Algiers riverfront for *its* livestock landing and processing facility. Algiers also made sense because, at that time, it sat within Orleans Parish but outside the city of New Orleans, in accordance with a subsequent health ordinance stating that the new slaughterhouse could not be within city limits.

The abattoirs now found themselves competing with each other, with one company in Stock Landing and the other at Slaughterhouse Point. In the interest of preserving solidarity and getting back to work, they settled their differences and, in March 1871, merged to become the Crescent City Slaughterhouse Company. When workers "were given a choice between the company's fairly makeshift original abattoir (in Algiers) and a larger, better-equipped one located on the same side of the river as the city," wrote historians Ronald M. Labbé and Jonathan Lurie, "the vast majority quickly abandoned the west-bank facility" and got to work at Stock Landing.[63] The resolution brought scores of meatpackers and their families to rural St. Bernard Parish. Soon, 700 to 1,100

Former Ford Motor Company plant and Domino sugar refinery in St. Bernard Parish. Photograph by Richard Campanella.

animals per day arrived to slaughter, earning the operation $1 per head for cattle and 30 to 50 cents for calves, sheep, and hogs.

Workers initially lived in adjacent faubourgs in New Orleans and rode horses to work, for which the company provided stables. But "in the 1870s and 1880s," wrote historian William de Marigny Hyland, "a small village evolved around the slaughterhouse." Having gained a post office in 1882, the community held a contest to coin a more uplifting name than Stock Landing. "The 1882 revolt of Arabi Pasha in Egypt [had been] highly publicized" at that time, wrote Hyland, and "because of the anti-British sentiment still prevalent in St. Bernard, the winning name in the contest was Arabi."[64]

The company modernized the plant in the 1890s and connected it to railroad lines. In 1906, surveyors laid out a street grid in Arabi, making it the first urban subdivision in the parish. In 1912, the American Sugar Refining Company opened a gargantuan plant farther downriver, which did for settlement in adjacent Chalmette what the slaughterhouse had done for Arabi. Ten years later, the Ford Motor Company sited an assembly plant between the meat and sugar plants, benefitting both communities.

The Arabi slaughterhouse operated under various names until 1963, by which time St. Bernard Parish was heavily industrialized and steadily suburbanizing. Arabi is now home to 4,300 people, while adjacent Chalmette and Meraux together have 30,000 residents—three-quarters the entire parish population in a fraction of its land area.

And what of that lawsuit? In 1873, the U.S. Supreme Court ruled in favor of the monopoly, implying that state law could trump federally recognized freedoms. Controversial ever since, "The Slaughter-house Cases" had the effect of curtailing the Fourteenth Amendment—and siting the community of Arabi.

A hundred river miles upstream, Carville claims an even more unusual rationale. At first, this riverfront community materialized rather typically, as a service center sited along a meander shortcut, halfway between Geismar and St. Gabriel across the Point Clair promontory. It got its name from postmaster and storekeeper Jules Alex Carville, whose father—a former Union solider who became a schoolteacher in Iberville Parish—had established a mercantile store here in 1868. After the elder died in 1899, Jules rose in prominence, as neighbors held him in "high esteem" for his "interest in all matters pertaining to the public welfare"—a trait recognizable in his famous grandson James Carville, chief strategist for Bill Clinton's 1992 presidential campaign.[65]

The community, too, would achieve fame for its public welfare, and what it wrought is now so thoroughly associated with Carville that it effectively rewrote its siting story. That story began in pestilential New Orleans, which had long suffered some of the highest death rates in the nation. Among the most dreaded maladies was leprosy, a bacterial infection causing the sort of lesions and deformities that, since biblical times, got patients exiled to remote "colonies." So too were they treated in New Orleans, where in the late 1700s "a quantity of land in the rear of the city" had been "appropriated for . . . that loathsome malady."[66] Other leper colonies later formed down Bayou Lafourche and at other isolated spots. Desperate for a normal life, some patients escaped and "strayed off to New Orleans," and when they formed "a considerable number [which] mixed freely with healthy populations," state officials intervened to force their isolation.[67]

In 1892 the state legislature passed Act 85 to confine lepers in a quarantine station. Two years later, it created the Board of Control for the Louisiana Leper Home, assigning it the controversial task of siting a colony.[68] A proposal to use an old fort by Lake Pontchartrain was met with protests over fear of water contamination, and just about any other suggestion met similar resistance. Board members decided to work surreptitiously, seeking a site close to most state residents yet distant from major cities, and accessible by water to keep the afflicted off of public roads.

The board finally found a viable site at a former sugar plantation two miles upriver of Carville. Established by Robert Coleman Camp in 1825, the land and buildings, including a neoclassical mansion erected in 1859, occupied a narrow promontory rarely transited, thanks to that Carville–St. Gabriel cutoff. "The site finally selected, Indian Camp [Plantation] in Iberville, had to be chosen secretly, and the hospital there was fitted up for the lepers," wrote a reporter at the time. "People of the neighborhood . . . protested rigorously, [some] waging a fierce war . . . but it was too late."[69] The first patients arrived on a coal barge on December 1, 1894, and were housed in seven former slave cabins.

A siting story that began acrimoniously ended up triumphant. Care for the afflicted became compassionate, thanks to the Sisters of Charity, so much so that Louisiana won national recognition for its handling of this difficult problem. In 1917, the National Leprosy Act required patients across the country to be quarantined at Carville, and in 1921 administration of the newly renamed National Leprosarium shifted to the U.S. Public Health Service. Patients and caregivers arrived from all over the world, making Carville economically stable and uniquely cosmopolitan. Life for the 500 patients became as contented as could be expected in a quarantine community equipped with schools, churches, farms, workshops, and recreational facilities set among attractive landscaping and architecture.

Leprosy became known as Hansen's disease, for the Norwegian physician who determined that its causative bacteria were nowhere near as contagious as thought. In the 1940s, Dr. Guy Henry Faget and his team developed sulfone drugs to cure the ancient malady—the "Miracle at Carville," according to patient Betty Martin, a former New Orleans debutante whose autobiography became a bestseller. By the 1970s, admission to the Carville facility became voluntary, and as Hansen's got recategorized as an outpatient disease, the complex became the Gillis W. Long Hansen's Disease Center. In 1999, after 105 years of service, the center was closed and the research program was moved to Baton Rouge, though some elderly residents chose to live onsite for the remainder of their lives.

In 2001, the Louisiana National Guard took over the campus and currently runs social programs in the old leprosarium. Still fronted by the circa 1859 Indian Camp plantation house and now home to the National Hansen's Disease Museum, "Carville," as everyone calls the place, is a rare example of a community sited for the grim spatial exigencies of quarantine.

Of the forty-nine cities, towns, villages, and other communities in the Lower Mississippi River region (excluding greater New Orleans) analyzed in this study, 14 percent had riverine- or water-based primary siting stories (half the state average of 29 percent), while 29 percent were primarily resource extraction or processing sites (mostly petrochemical), 8 percent were railroad sites, and 8 percent were crossroads (compared to state averages of 13 percent, 33 percent, and 10 percent, respectively). Settlements began forming here in the 1770s, crested in the 1870s, and ended in the 1930s; 57 percent emerged organically, above the state average of 49 percent, the remainder having been ordained.

Last of the "landings," along the River Road in St. John the Baptist Parish. Photograph by Richard Campanella.

3

BAYOU LAFOURCHE, BAYOU TERREBONNE, AND THE BARATARIA-TERREBONNE BASINS

Bayou Lafourche lends itself to metaphor. Iberville in 1699 described that "fork" as "a great arm of water coursing toward the southwest." French geographer Elisée Reclus viewed it in 1855 as one of many "fingers . . . spreading [from] a gigantic arm projecting into the sea." American geographer John McPhee imagined such channels as jumping "here and there within an arc about two hundred miles wide, like a pianist playing with one hand—frequently and radically changing course . . . in utterly new directions."[1] That dynamic characterization alluded to the fact that Bayou Lafourche had once been the Mississippi's main "arm," primarily from 1500 to 700 years ago (Lafourche Delta Complex), its later shift into the current channel (Plaquemines Delta) being the last of seven avulsions in as many millennia. By the colonial era, Bayou Lafourche had diminished to a secondary fork, but not before depositing enough alluvium to create a terrestrial "arm" (natural levee) with "fingers" (Bayou Terrebonne, Little Bayou Black, and Bayous Blue, Du Large, Grand Caillou, and Petit Caillou), all of which interspersed the marshy Barataria and Terrebonne basins with inhabitable ridges.[2] "Like a silver sickle," wrote Catharine Cole (a.k.a. Martha R. Field) of the Lafourche landscape in 1892, "the beautiful and historic bayou cuts its way across the rich, green country, making long sweeping swatches [through] cane and corn, oak grove and paddock, factory and farm, church and marsh, village and lagoon, until its liquid tip touches with narrow point the salt, blue waters of the Gulf of Mexico."[3]

Which evokes another Bayou Lafourche metaphor: "the longest village street in the world," an observation that writer Harnett T. Kane credited to locals in the 1940s, adding, "I don't know of any place that has attempted to refute the claim." Along 120 wending miles, from the bayou's divergence from the Mississippi River to its discharge in the Gulf of Mexico, "a single line of homes hugs the waterway," such that it "cannot be determined when a town ends and mere residences on the bayou begin." Yet "here and there towns appear," and for compelling reasons, for the same characteristics that have made Bayou Lafourche metaphorical have also made it an oracle of siting stories.[4]

Take Donaldsonville, which we had previously categorized as a navigable fork site, akin to Plaquemine at Bayou Plaquemine and Geismar at New River. Originally called La Fourche des Chetimaches, Donaldsonville stemmed from a 1770s Spanish land grant to Pierre Landry that came into the hands of William Donaldson in 1806, who in turn commissioned Barthélémy Lafon to survey a street grid. Donaldsonville soon became the seat of Ascension Parish, making it an administrative center as well as a major steamboat stop, ferry landing, and entrepôt for Bayou Lafourche, exporting its agricultural output and importing whatever its residents needed from New Orleans.

Thibodaux tells an equally compelling siting story. It sits on a ridge of fertile soil amid abundant resources, with a reliable freshwater source, among multiple forks and two crossroads. Later-constructed canals and railroads made Thibodaux that much more of a nexus, close enough to neighboring cities to maximize benefits while far enough to minimize competition. Thibodaux also happens to be halfway between the Pleistocene Terrace and the Gulf of Mexico, and roughly at the center of the Mississippi River Deltaic Plain—an intermediary between the greater New Orleans/Barataria region to the east and the Bayou Teche region to the west.

For all its advantages, colonial settlement came late to Thibodaux. Expansion under the French regime prioritized the high-value natural levees of the Mississippi, an effort that tended to displace Natives down onto secondary forks and backswamp ridges. The Houma and Bayagoula (Bayougoula) tribes, for example, got pushed down the New River distributary and were eventually negotiated out of their remaining land in what became known as the Houmas Claim. In the case of Bayou Lafourche, resistance to French intrusions got the Chitimacha and Washa (Oucha) tribes forced down to the extreme coastal fringes, where descendants barely hang on today. The violence delayed colonial settlement in the region, such that "for more than a half century," wrote Harnett T. Kane, "the bayou country had to wait for an event that was to change many things about Louisiana—the arrival of the Acadians."[5] Those French Canadian refugees made their way down La Fourche des Chetimaches starting in 1765, and were joined in the 1780s by Spanish immigrants from Las Islas Canarias who formed Valenzuela, now Plattenville. By some accounts, a trading post had formed down from Valenzuela by the 1790s, most likely where Bayou Lafourche's channel forked off southeastwardly to form Bayou Terrebonne. At the time, siltation clogged the fork, though both waterways were otherwise navigable and connected by a wagon path known as the Terrebonne Road.[6]

In 1808, that unnamed fork site had been selected to host the seat of justice for the newly designated Parish of Lafourche Interior. Shortly thereafter, a New York-born man of French Acadian descent named Henry Schuyler Thibodaux (originally spelled Thibodeaux) acquired land by the fork. Having arrived in Louisiana in 1794, Thibodaux attained a Spanish land grant, became a planter, and resolved to improve the region. Toward that end, in 1818 he donated his fork-side parcel to the parish police jury and committed to fund the construction of a courthouse. A year later, an adjacent landholder named Jean Baptiste Hebert donated space to build St. Joseph Church, and in 1820 Thibodaux worked with surveyor James Boyd Grinage to lay out a street grid that would be named Thibodauxville. Following his death in 1827, Thibodaux's widow, Brigette Belanger Thibodaux, donated an additional 100-foot-wide strip to reconnect the two bayous via a 4,000-foot channel to be dug by the Lafourche & Terrebonne Navigation Company. The canal stimulated Thibodauxville's original rationale as a navigable fork site, and imparted economic life to points all up and down both Bayou Lafourche and Bayou Terrebonne.[7]

Thibodauxville incorporated in 1838 and secured permanent designation as the Lafourche Parish seat in an 1852 special election, by which time most people called the town Thibodaux. It became "a shipping point of considerable importance . . . because of its strategic position on Bayou Lafourche," wrote

Detail of the Tanner map (1851), showing Plaquemine at upper left, "Thibodeauxville" and Houma at left center, and the mouth of the Mississippi River at lower right. Library of Congress.

archivists in 1942. "Most of the sugar and molasses from Terrebonne Parish passed through the town on its way to market, and the return freight and supplies came by the same route. In 1846, 8,000 hogsheads of sugar and as many barrels of molasses were shipped from the wharves at Thibodaux, [as were] moss and cotton." The town itself had a full cadre of middlemen, along with merchants, skilled craftsmen, and dockworkers—a miniature New Orleans on the bayou, with an Acadian accent and a country flair. All evidence indicates that it was the reopened Lafourche/Terrebonne fork that spurred Thibodaux's growth; all other site advantages (crossroads, ferry landings, bridgeheads) and roles (administrative centers, institutional hubs, rail stops) were either secondary or subsequent.[8]

Visiting from New Orleans, travel writer Catharine Cole was smitten with the result. "The best managed, the cleanest and neatest town in the state is the unhesitating verdict of any visitor to Thibodaux," she wrote in 1892, raving of its well-maintained streets and "deep, clean gutters . . . well lighted by gasoline lamps," lined with brick sidewalks as fine as those "in London or Paris." Thibodaux also had "first-class shops and a large bank," as well as "several factory industries, boiler works, an ice factory, two good newspapers . . . two fire companies, a theater, churches, including the finest Catholic Church outside New Orleans, excellent schools and a refined and cultured social life."[9]

Over the twentieth century, Thibodaux's secondary siting rationales became primary, while its original *raison d'être* became *passé*. Shipping faded when Bayou Lafourche was closed off from the Mississippi in 1904. Its fork with Bayou Terrebonne soon sedimented and is now paved over by Canal Boulevard. Most cargo by then had shifted to canals, rails, or roads to get to market. Yet Thibodaux thrived, thanks to the oil and gas industry as well as Nicholls State University, and in recent decades the city has leveled off at 15,000 residents. Both the Lafourche Parish Courthouse and Thibodaux City Hall are still located a stone's throw from the city's original fork site—or perhaps we should say a ball's throw. "The Lafourchais describes his manner of elbow-to-elbow existence by saying that the boys can toss a baseball along the bayou from one front yard to the next," from Thibodaux all the way down to Golden Meadow.[10]

Perhaps the most unusual Louisiana settlements were sited not on hard land but on soft marsh, throughout what one ethnographer characterized as Louisiana's "Asian Coast," from the Barataria Bay to eastern St. Bernard Parish. Here, Asian immigrants built wooden platforms with dwellings and warehouses, all raised up on pilings, for the processing of shrimp and other fisheries. Chinese predominated at the Bassa Bassa shrimp-drying platform,

The Lafourche Parish Courthouse overlooks the former fork of Bayou Lafourche and Bayou Terrebonne that gave rise to Thibodaux. Photograph by Richard Campanella.

while Filipinos and Chinese together operated at least ten other sites, including Manila Village (1873) twenty miles south-southeast of Lafitte.[11] Shrimp-drying entailed boiling the crustaceans in saltwater, drying them under the sun, and stacking them thickly on the platform, whereupon community members would wrap their feet in burlap and dance to the rhythm of a chant to remove the spiky heads. The dried shrimp were then packed 220 pounds to the barrel and shipped to New Orleans at a cost much cheaper than canned shrimp, making them a popular delicacy and seasoning. The industry originated probably in the late 1700s with Filipinos at Saint Maló in eastern St. Bernard Parish, and grew substantially in the 1870s thanks to a San Francisco investor named Lee Yam and his son Lee Yat. The Lees eventually came to own over 700 acres of marsh plus platforms, dwellings, and warehouses, employing up to eighty people and operating some of the largest shrimp seines in the world.[12]

Fascinated outsiders exoticized the Asian shrimp-drying platforms. Lafcadio Hearn described the "Malay fishermen" of Saint Maló on the south shore of Lake Borgne as "strange, wild, picturesque . . . poised upon slender supports above the marsh, like cranes or bitterns watching for scaly prey."[13] The *Daily States* published this description of an unspecified community in 1899:

> Here on these low grass-covered islands . . . lives this queer colony of Chinese shrimpers in fragile huts curiously constructed of palmetto, bamboo and other light material. Huge platforms are built . . . about four feet above the water level. Around the outer edge of these structures are arranged the houses of the colonists forming what may be called "grand plazas" [behind which are] fine gardens, which might very appropriately be likened to the "Hanging Gardens

> of Babylon." These consist of huge boxes filled with earth [in which are grown] peculiar vegetables known only to the Celestials.[14]

A literal example of a resource extraction settlement site, these "stilt villages" could have been located wherever shrimp could be caught and processed for market. Explaining the locations of the circa 1900 Asian shrimp-drying platforms probably comes down to marsh ownership within adequate salinity regimes—for example, where Lee Yam and Lee Yat were able to gain title to those 700 acres. These fascinating sites have all since disappeared, the last of Manila Village having been destroyed by Hurricane Betsy in 1965. Louisiana's "Asian Coast," however, has only grown, with the arrival of Vietnamese and Laotians from the Mekong Delta starting in 1975, many of whom have become mainstays of the Gulf fishing industry.

A thousand years ago, when the Mississippi discharged through Lafourche, its turbid waters splayed out into a shallow bay with weak tides, yielding multiple braided distributaries with diminishing sinuosity. Together they formed a sort of "horsetail pattern" dangling into Terrebonne Bay.[15] Viewed around Houma, the feature looks more like an octopus, with the city proper being the head, and eight or so tentacles (distributary bayous) emanating in every direction. Unique on the deltaic plain, the splayed feature made a fine settlement site within the newly formed Terrebonne Parish ("good earth"), which had been carved out of the much larger Lafourche Interior Parish in 1822. A hamlet with the unlikely Anglo name of Williamsburg (now Bayou Cane) initially served as Terrebonne's seat of government but never gained momentum, perhaps because it had no particular geographical advantage.

Hubert M. Belanger and Richard H. Grinage identified a better site on Bayou Terrebonne. At the "head" of the "octopus," the Bayous Black, Du Large, La Carpe, Chauvin, Grand Caillou, and Little Caillou flowed out in all directions, making this spot a junction of both navigable waterways as well as passable roads on inhabitable ridges. From the old Haché land grant, Belanger and Grinage obtained a parcel measuring one arpent on the right bank of Bayou Terrebonne and ten arpents back to Bayou Black, and in 1834 donated it to the Terrebonne Parish police jury to build a new courthouse. Sited at multiple confluences and crossroads in a more centralized position to the new parish's growing population, "Houma," named for the Natives, made an ideal maritime, trade, and administrative center.[16]

For decades smaller than Thibodaux, Houma surpassed its upstream rival in the early 1900s thanks to two prospects for which Houma was well situated:

the growing coastal petroleum industry and plans by the U.S. Army Corps of Engineers to excavate a free public peri-coastal shipping channel from Texas to Florida. What became known as the Gulf Intracoastal Waterway, dug through Houma in the 1930s, reinstated the city's siting advantage from a century earlier—and just in time, because navigability on the natural bayous had been in decline since the 1904 closure of Bayou Lafourche. Houma's population surpassed 10,000 during World War II, and more than tripled during the subsequent oil boom. Since the 1980s it has stabilized in the low 30,000 range—double the population of Thibodaux, but more dependent on petroleum.[17]

Whereas the Gulf Intracoastal Waterway reinvigorated Houma's original siting story, other manmade canals created new siting opportunities along Bayou Lafourche. Their excavation represented attempts to reconcile the latitudinal forces of economic supply and demand, emanating mostly from New Orleans, with the longitudinal orientation of Bayou Lafourche. What resulted, thanks to ditchers and barge-mounted steam shovels, were new "lines of least resistance," as Richard Hurd described them, creating new "convenient point[s] of contact."[18] Among them were Lockport, Larose, and the aptly named Cut Off, for that is what all of them were: shortcuts to the outside world.

Lockport originated from the 1829 effort of the Barataria & Lafourche Canal Company to dig and dredge a channel from what is now Westwego across Lake Cataouatche and Lake Salvador marshlands to join Bayou Lafourche. The investors' goal was to connect the lucrative New Orleans market with points west, reducing 130 sinuous river and bayou miles to a breezy thirty-five-mile sail on tidal waters. Where precisely to connect with the bayou? That answer came from William Field, who in 1823 acquired bayou frontage that happened to be well-positioned for the company's planned canal. Upon learning of the project, Field in 1833 donated five arpents to the Barataria & Lafourche Company in exchange for its commitment to build the lock. "The canal would provide a continuous navigable stream from Bayou Lafourche to New Orleans," wrote local historian Jeffrey J. LeBlanc, "and as a consequence, would greatly enhance the value of Field's adjoining lands."[19]

Workers dug the eastern leg of the Company Canal in the early 1830s, whereupon surveyor Allou D'Hemecourt in 1835 laid out a street grid for what would be called *Longueville.* They completed the leg to Bayou Lafourche by 1841, installed a cypress timber lock by 1847, and replaced it with a masonry lock in 1853, the ruins of which still stand. By then, Longueville residents had changed their community name to reflect its reason for being, and it's been called Lockport ever since—despite the fact that railroads later supplanted the canal, bayou commerce diminished, and Lockport lost its advantage. It had not

Downtown Houma (*top*) developed at the junction of navigable bayous and ridge-following roads. Lockport formed where workers built a navigational lock (*left*) to join the Company Canal with Bayou Lafourche. Photographs by Richard Campanella.

been intended to serve as the terminus of the Barataria & Lafourche Canal; company officials had planned to continue digging westward to the Atchafalaya River port of Brashear City (today's Morgan City, originally named for Walter Brashear, cofounder of the Barataria & Lafourche Company.)[20] Lockport, formed as a head-of-canal and lock site, is today home to 2,400 people, a size it has maintained for the past sixty years.

In the years following the establishment of Thibodaux and Houma, settlers farther down the bayou took advantage of the long growing season to cultivate oranges, potatoes, and vegetables. Time was of the essence in delivering the produce to market, but long was the journey up the bayou and down the river to New Orleans. An alternative came to light once the Barataria & Lafourche Company cut its channel across Lake Salvador to connect with Lockport. Local landowners followed suit by dredging their own direct channel from Bayou Catahoula to Catahoula Bay at the southern end of Lake Salvador. By some accounts, a navigable passage had opened by the late 1840s, after Octave Harang acquired land in 1846 for a sugar plantation; other sources indicate a dredged shipping channel was not fully in place until 1877.[21] It became known as the

Canal Harang, for the family involved in the project on the adjacent Banana Grove Plantation. The settlement that formed at the head of the canal, known as Harang, soon got Our Lady of the Rosary Church, followed by a post office in 1890, each serving some fifty families. As often happened in rural hamlets, the post office inspired a formal renaming. Community leader Dr. Willie Harang had recruited a pharmacist named Joseph Felicien Larose to move to Harang, and it was Larose who was able to secure postal service and serve as postmaster: hence Larose, Louisiana.[22]

The Canal Harang, which had given Larose its head-of-canal siting advantage, resuscitated the community in 1925 when the U.S. Army Corps of Engineers incorporated the channel into its Gulf Intracoastal Waterway. In 1943, the Corps completed a widening project that cut the GIWW straight through town; roads were built parallel to its flanks, and Larose became the maritime and terrestrial crossroads it is today.[23]

From 1905 to 1971, Larose hosted an agricultural experiment that would permanently alter its topography. At a site abutting the Canal Harang, Cincinnati investors acquired 3,200 acres of marsh, erected levees, and drained the land for vegetable production. Known as Delta Farms, it had its own residential community built within the impoundment overlooking the croplands. Along with nearby Clovelly Farms and thirty similar reclamation/agriculture projects in the region, the Delta Farms settlement had a peculiar siting story, born of "Lifting Farms out of Water," as *The Country Gentleman* put it in 1919. By that year, fully 7,000 acres had been drained, of which 4,000 acres had been sold to "actual settlers . . . about 150 families living on the land."[24] Dewatering wetlands creates economic opportunities but comes at a cost. A topographic map from 1939 shows parts of Delta Farms to have subsided five feet below sea level, making it one of very few places outside greater New Orleans to have sunk so deeply. It did not bode well: the levees breached in 1961 and again in 1971, after which Delta Farms, once home to families and crops, became a rectangular lake popular with sport fishermen.

Cut Off has a similar siting story to Larose, on a bend of lower Bayou Lafourche abutting bays that accessed the underbelly of New Orleans. It also spawned its own agricultural reclamation experiment—Clovelly Farms, still functioning today, also below sea level. All the bend needed to become valuable was a shortcut to the bays, and that came in the form of the State Cut Off Canal, dug by the dredge boat *Harmanson* during 1856–1859 as a shipping and outfall channel, thirty-five feet in width and five feet deep. The channel triggered settlement at *La Coup*—The Cut, or Cut Off—enabling residents to sail straight east to Bayou des Amoureux through Lake Salvador to reach greater

New Orleans.[25] "The canal was to be used not only for navigation," wrote one correspondent, "but also for drainage of lands and in particular to help prevent crevasses by offering an outlet for the waters of Bayou Lafourche."[26] Cut Off's population swelled by 200 people following the Chênière Caminada Hurricane in 1893, which caused great destruction and displacement of communities to the south. Today, Cut Off is not a nucleated settlement, as when it originated as a head-of-canal site; rather, it is an elongated Census-Designated Place, with a population of over 5,500—comparable to its historical siting partner, Larose, which as a CDP has 6,700 residents.

If any two words characterize Bayou Lafourche, they are "long" and "leaky." We have already seen how sheer length can yield settlements—those five-mile and ten-mile communities, or arterial increment towns—and Bayou Lafourche would render plenty. Now consider the role of "leakiness"—that is, how historic crevasses (breaches) sprang distributaries of varying sizes, depositing sediment and building ridges branching off the main bayou road. Like forks and confluences, such crossroads are magnets for human settlement, and Bayou Lafourche has its share.

Napoleonville's siting story is illustrative. This quaint village may have germinated from its centralized position within Assumption Parish when it was created in 1807, earning it the parish seat, dubbed "Courthouse" on maps. But why this particular bend in the bayou? A clue comes from another informal name ascribed to this spot, "Canal," likely for what became the Attakapas Canal cut to access Lake Verret and points west. How to get there? By taking a slight ridge extending six miles southwest from Bayou Lafourche, the product of a long-ago distributary, now today's Canal Road (Road 401).[27] This made "Courthouse" a crossroads for westward travel, and it helped that it was centrally positioned within the new parish, bringing it to attention as an administrative center. In 1813, the hamlet got its first post office, named Assumption, and in 1818 a land parcel was donated for a new courthouse. In 1832, streets and parcels were laid out, with the central artery (today's Canal Street) leading out to the ridge-top Canal Road accessing that channel to Lake Verret. Land for the town had been donated by a merchant and shopkeeper named Ruellan Napoleon, for whom the town and post office were officially named in 1879, one year after the community gained incorporation. Travel writer Catharine Cole found Napoleonville in 1892 to be "a quiet, pretty, very French little village, strung out all in a row . . . along the bayou's banks, [with] several large stores and a good hotel; it is the parish seat and has good schools and churches." Cole noted the channel that gave rise to Napoleonville: "A canal runs across the country to the bayou and lake to the West, and along this are pleasant homes."[28] Today, Napoleonville is a village of 530 inhabitants, and while its crossroads with Highway 1 is still vital, no longer can it take you very far west. Instead, Paincourtville, to the north, has become the new crossroads for access into the Atchafalaya Basin.

The origin of Raceland's name is a mystery; a favored hypothesis—that it referred to race courses operating here in the late 1800s—fails to explain why the name was first documented in 1842. Raceland's siting rationale, however, is clear: it represented the perigee (shortest distance) between Bayou Lafourche and greater New Orleans. That is, Raceland started on a passable pathway connecting Bayou Lafourche with the Mississippi River, along the same interbasin ridge that had given rise to Luling and Boutte. At Luling, that pathway followed an abandoned distributary called Grand Bayou; at Raceland, it followed a similar distributary ridge created by Bayou Chactimahan. Between the two ridges flows Bayou Des Allemands, where the riverside community of Des Allemands now stands. That topographic connection hosted a road, which made Raceland into a crossroads, all the more when the tracks of the New Orleans, Opelousas & Great Western Railroad were laid upon berms and trestles paralleling the natural ridge. Later operated by Southern Pacific, that railway at first did no favors for Raceland, because it swooped behind the town, taking advantage of cheaper rights-of-way. In doing so, it spawned the station-stop enclaves of Raceland Junction and Bowie, the latter of which became home to the Bowie Lumber Company's Cypress King Mill. Its worker housing had a population of 1,000 until a fire in 1917 sent residents packing for Raceland proper.

Eventually the railroad did benefit Raceland, when in the late 1920s an automobile road (today's Highway 90) opened parallel to the track bed, reinvigorating the crossroads. That advantage strengthened when Road 182 was built to connect Raceland southward to Houma via a crossroads at Savoie.[29] Today, Raceland remains a gateway and portal between greater New Orleans and lower Bayou Lafourche. Whatever the origin of its name, Raceland has been a crossroads site for two centuries, and is now home to 11,300 people living within Census-Designated Place boundaries.[30]

The sheer length of Bayou Lafourche itself exerts a force for settlement. That is, even with sites at forks, canal heads, crossroads, and elsewhere, extensive stretches of "the longest village street in the world" still lacked basic services, such as general stores, supply depots, or doctor's offices. Tiny service hubs thus materialized: entrepreneurs opened stores and depots; religious institutions established churches; and government entities opened post offices or built bridges, which in turn attracted settlers and more services. In 1937, one 107-mile stretch of Bayou Lafourche had fully twenty-four bridge

Assumption Parish Courthouse and commercial buildings in Napoleonville, on Bayou Lafourche. Photographs by Richard Campanella.

crossings—one every 4.5 miles—and most of them had clusters of houses and businesses on either side. What resulted was a sequence of settlements with some mix of stores, services, post office, church, and/or bridge, spaced at consistent intervals.[31]

Note, for example, how Belle Rose (home to two churches, a grocery store, a bar, a post office, and a bridge crossing) is located halfway between Donaldsonville and Paincourtville, each four to five miles away. And how Labadieville—originating as a mission site in 1843 at what is now St. Philomena Catholic Church—is similarly positioned between Napoleonville and Thibodaux, each eight miles away. Gray is halfway between Thibodaux and Houma; Savoie, between Houma and Raceland; Mathews, between Raceland and Lockport; and

Jay, between Lockport and Larose. Likewise, the communities of Bourg and Galliano are evenly distributed between Houma and Golden Meadow (which itself was activated by a navigation channel cut to its east, named Canal Yankee), the fork sites of Montegut and Chauvin are halfway between Houma and Cocodrie, and Leeville is halfway between Golden Meadow and the "land's end" settlements we shall examine next.[32]

South of Bayous Lafourche and Terrebonne are historical coastal settlement sites whose fates range between "going" and "gone." Dulac, Isle de Jean Charles, Du Large, and Cocodrie occupy the last habitable ridges formed by those two bayous and their distributaries; their topography is down to a few feet, and their populations down to a few hundred. Grand Terre, Grand Isle, Chênière Caminada, and Isle Dernière (Last Island) occupy barrier islands, and only one retains a sizeable population. While their initial rationales vary, all these current and former settlements may be considered land's end sites, products of their perch along Louisiana's "great thalassic littoral" with the Gulf of Mexico.[33] And then there is Port Fourchon, at the mouth of Bayou Lafourche, whose siting story is Louisiana's most recent, and whose space is largely manmade.

What initially brought "settlers"—really survivors—to the coastal fringes of Bayou Terrebonne's horsetail-shaped delta was colonial displacement. Remote ridges, some so intermittent they were known as isles or islands, provided refuge of last resort to indigenous tribes and bands who had been forced out of higher interior lands. The ridges paralleled Bayou Du Large, Grand Caillou, and Little Caillou in the region south of Houma, while down the main channel of Bayou Terrebonne they followed the distributaries of Bayou du Chien and Bayou St. Jean Charles, whose fork later gave rise to Montegut. Details of tribal or band identities and territories are as convoluted as they are disputed, but the broader pattern of displacement is all too clear. Through pressure, deception, disease, discrimination, and violence, European settlers pushed Natives off their homelands southward to the ends of the Earth. Among them were the Houma, Biloxi, Chitimacha, and Choctaw, and over the centuries members intermarried with other ethnic groups, and their descendants assimilated to varying degrees. Yet a cultural memory endures of the journey from hard earth to soft marsh. Oral tradition holds that the Houma Nation had lived on the loess bluffs of what is now West Feliciana Parish into the 1700s, until they were relocated by French colonials to Bayou St. John in present-day New Orleans in 1706, moved upriver to the present-day Burnside area in Ascension Parish in the 1720s, and then forced down Bayou Lafourche and Bayou Terrebonne in the late 1700s. White settlement in Thibodaux and Houma in the early to mid-

1800s further dislodged the Natives down to Isle de Jean Charles, Pointe aux Chene, Grand Caillou, and Dulac.[34]

In the case of Isle de Jean Charles, colonial settlement began when two French brothers named Naquin arrived in the late 1700s. In testimony to the subsequent intermixing, the surname Naquin is now common among Biloxi-Chitimacha-Choctaw Indians, whose chief is Démé Naquin Jr. In the case of the Grand Caillou and Dulac communities, Natives arrived to what by then was considered federal lands following the Louisiana Purchase. Records from the late nineteenth century list a few dozen families identified as "Indians" living in places with names like Felix Canal, Deer Island, Bayou LaButte, Bayou Chene, and Bayou Mauvais Bois, with Cocodrie serving as a fishing and shrimping launch. What would become the Dulac Community Center began in 1882 when George C. Cragen donated an acre of land on behalf of the Methodist Episcopal Church, which "Houma Indians [used as] a place to tie their house boats during non-trapping seasons."[35]

Native coastal settlement survived for generations on farming, trapping, fishing, and shrimping. By the late 1900s, however, a labyrinth of oil and gas extraction or pipeline canals had been scoured throughout the Terrebonne Basin, triggering erosion and saltwater intrusion. Freshwater had been reduced by the damming of Bayou Lafourche, hardly any new sediment arrived, and rising seas swallowed sinking marshes. Hurricane after hurricane wrought travails, leaving an aging population facing mounting risk. Starting in 2016, a federal program offered Biloxi-Chitimacha-Choctaw tribal members the option to relocate to a subdivision called New Isle north of Houma, making them, according to media reports, "America's first climate refugees." Their ancestors had sought refuge at these land's end sites; now, as that land comes to its end, the government that once drove them there is granting them refuge from it. Among those reluctantly moving inland is Chief Naquin, whose biography reads as the siting story of the old isle. "I was raised on the island," he said in reference to Jean Charles, "the son of a commercial fisherman. He was an oyster fisherman and a shrimper, trapper. Whatever it took to get by, he did."[36]

When the Mississippi overflowed with extreme floods, it jettisoned heavy sand particles to the farthest perimeter of its deltaic lobe, where longshore currents swept them westward into the shape of barrier islands. What resulted was a rarity in the otherwise marshy delta: white, sandy beaches fronting clear Gulf waters. Settlement gravitated to the most substantial and accessible islands, the easternmost of which was Grande Terre, at the mouth of Barataria Bay. Grand Terre's siting advantage was its deep-draft harbor, the product of strong currents moving through narrow Barataria Pass, marked by a Spanish tower and pilot station around 1780. That channel made the western tip of Grand Terre attractive as a transshipment base for moving cargo between seafaring vessels and interior craft.

But Grand Terre did not become a standard seaside port; rather, its isolation made it attractive to smugglers seeking to evade official regulation and taxation in moving cargo in and out of lower Louisiana. And plenty of illicit cargo there was: "When it came to obeying the rules of mercantilism," wrote historian Lawrence Powell, "Louisiana ranked among the New World's worst scofflaw. The entire economy was steeped in smuggling[;] it thrived on contraband trade."[37] Contrabandists arriving from throughout the Caribbean and Gulf basins rendezvoused at Grand Terre with a loose coalition of buccaneers coordinated by the brothers Jean and Pierre Lafitte. From that island site, the so-called Baratarians ferried the contraband, including enslaved people, through backswamp bays and bayous to reach New Orleans. Up to 3,000 smugglers worked Grand Terre's not-so-clandestine entrepôt during its early 1800s heyday, making it the largest "settlement" along the Louisiana coast.[38]

Grande Terre's rogue days came to an end in 1814, when the U.S. Navy's Master Commandant Daniel Todd Patterson raided the racket to prevent the Baratarians from siding with the British in their pending attack on New Orleans. The Americans gave Grand Terre a new mission, as a defensive site, eventually leading to the construction of Fort Livingston. The masonry bastion is now in ruins, a relic of Grand Terre's contentious history.[39]

Across Barataria Pass from Grand Terre is the much larger Grand Isle. Despite sandy soils and limited freshwater, permanent occupancy of this barrier island began as an agricultural effort. During 1781–1787, Spanish governor Bernardo de Gálvez granted tracts to four Frenchmen, who proceeded to establish commodity plantations, food farms, orchards, and cattle pastures. Others arrived to partake of finfish and shellfish, and lived on the *chênière*—that is, oak groves on the island's topographic crest, which held together the soil and provided shade and lumber.

What precipitated settlement in this otherwise agrarian environment was the recreational appeal of Grand Isle's sandy beaches, complete with deep water and breaking waves—rarities in Louisiana. Motivated by pleasure-seeking as well as fear of late summer pestilence, New Orleanians began frequenting Grand Isle regularly in the 1840s, and grand hotels began opening in the 1850s. Following the Civil War and its aftermath, Grand Isle was poised to prosper as a resort site: investors renovated the Barataria Plantation into a

Some of the last historic structures remaining on Grand Isle (*top*); all that remains of historic Chênière Caminada (*left*). Photographs by Richard Campanella.

luxury inn, converting its former slave cabins into guest rooms, while others built seaside lodges sparing no expense. Patrons arrived via steamers coming down the Harvey or Company canals, or by an 1888 railroad line connecting Algiers with a transfer dock for boat service. Patrons bathed, fished, feasted on seafood, and sailed to see sights like old Fort Livingston and the curious Asian shrimp-drying platforms at Manila Village. Affluent Creoles in particular relished Grand Isle, where they "shed city clothing and some degree of inhibitions," according to three historians, in "an exotic, almost erotic atmosphere, markedly different from the rigid mores" of the day. Literary figures such as Lafcadio Hearn, George Washington Cable, and Kate Chopin wrote extensively of Grand Isle; it was "the Riviera of the South," and the pleasurable beach was its siting rationale.[40]

Twentieth-century Grand Isle continued as a tourism destination, and once Highway 622 (now Highway 1) opened in 1931, visitation became more of the middle-class weekend warrior variety. What separated the age of exotic resorts from that of fishing rodeos was a trauma that would severely damage Grand Isle and utterly destroy its neighbor to the west, Chênière Caminada.

Whereas a deep harbor activated Grand Terre and sandy beaches catalyzed Grand Isle, Chênière Caminada was ideal for extracting finfish and shellfish. The compact island offered decent docking, access to Bayou Lafourche, and rich fisheries on both the Gulf and bay side, including oyster reefs. Originally labeled as the Isle of the Chitimachas (the corollary of the Fork of the Chitimachas, or Bayou Lafourche), the island was first granted in 1763 to Monsieur Du Roullin and saw agricultural development in subsequent decades, including by a landholder named Caminada. It did not really form an agglomerated settlement until after the Civil War. Only thirty-three people lived on the island in 1850, according to census records; that figure swelled to 736 in 1880, 1,047 in 1890, and 1,471 in 1893, by which time most households were engaged in harvesting finfish, crabs, shrimp, and oysters and shipping them to "cannery row" in Westwego.[41] Also known as Caminadaville, the settlement at the eastern tip of the island comprised "a long row of little gray, pleasant homes, set close together, [each with] a grassy yard," wrote Catharine Cole in 1892. "In the corner of nearly every yard will be a shed, where luggers are lying bottom up, out of the sun, or where a new boat is being beautifully built. . . . In the bayous are luggers, schooners and pirogues pulling at their anchors[;] the fishermen are busy getting ready to sail off to the winter fishing grounds [and] will not come back again until next spring. When they get a load of fish they will sail with it to New Orleans and then return to their fishing ground. Everything whispers of the sea."[42]

On the evening of Sunday, October 1, 1893, the whispering sea heaved and surged as a tremendous hurricane landed directly upon Chênière Caminada. Monday's sunrise brought to light astonishing havoc: at least 822 dead or missing, 396 of 400 structures destroyed, the entire fishing fleet gone, and oyster reefs buried in sand. Sited to harvest the riches of the sea, Chênière Caminada instead became its victim. Grand Isle, perched upon a slightly higher ridge, lost about thirty of its 300 permanent residents, and would have lost hundreds of visitors had the hurricane struck during summer—as had happened on Isle Dernière (Last Island) in August 1856, when a storm cut the island into pieces. Isle Dernière never recovered as a resort site after 1856, nor did Chênière Caminada return as a fishing site after 1893, and Grand Isle would never quite be the same. Its 2020 population of 1,005 residents diminished greatly after Hurricane

Ida struck on August 29, 2021, causing even more structural damage than the 1893 storm. As for Chênière Caminada, it had nothing left to lose.[43]

Which brings us to Port Fourchon. One could argue that Port Fourchon is not a settlement with a siting story, but rather an industrial complex with no true residential population. Yet it is nonetheless a community of workers operating on a built environment, sited strategically and designed for permanence. The facility was born of a shift in oil production from onshore to nearshore and offshore, which forced the industry to devise more efficient ways of moving crude oil through Louisiana's processing plants for national and international distribution. Supertankers being too large to navigate up the Mississippi, the industry would have to meet them halfway—and that meant Highway 1 down Bayou Lafourche, the only direct arterial connection to the central Louisiana coast. Companies formed a consortium to build floating mooring stations twenty miles offshore for supertankers to discharge crude into pipelines leading to "a hollowed-out underground salt dome for storage prior to distribution to regional and national refineries."[44] Legislation enabled the creation of the Louisiana Offshore Oil Port (LOOP) in 1972, as construction ensued on a vast array of pipelines as well as on Port Fourchon itself, completed in 1981. Its operators describe the facility as "a multi-use coastal port that functions primarily as a land base for multiple offshore energy support service companies," each of which leases space on the elevated platform and runs its operations independently.[45]

Port Fourchon has an otherworldly appearance, like a spaceship landing on the littoral. Yet it is rooted by a similar set of spatial exigencies underlying most other siting stories. It had to be near its resource (offshore crude) and requisite geographical features (salt domes), and reachable by vessels, pipelines, and trucks, which in turn needed access to the processing plants. It required freshwater and enough of a land base to host a raised platform, all of which pointed to Highway 1 following Bayou Lafourche down to the sea. On a coast replete with river mouths, Port Fourchon is Louisiana's best example of a mouth site—of a bayou, that is—though it is also fittingly categorized as an end-of-artery entrepôt.

Of the twenty-eight cities, towns, villages, and other communities in the Bayou Lafourche and Terrebonne region analyzed in this study, 36 percent had riverine- or water-based primary siting stories, while 21 percent were primarily resource extraction or processing sites, both above the state average of 29 percent and 13 percent, respectively. Only 4 percent were railroad sites and none were crossroads, compared to 33 percent and 10 percent statewide. The rarity of these terrestrial siting stories speaks to the utter historical dependence of this region on water and waterways. Lasting settlements along these bayous began forming in the 1790s, crested in the 1850s, and ended with Port Fourchon in 1981. Fully 75 percent of Bayou Lafourche and Terrebonne-area settlements emerged organically, the other 25 percent having been ordained, compared to a statewide ratio of 49 percent/51 percent emergent/ordained.

4

GREATER BATON ROUGE AND POINTE COUPÉE

Baton Rouge is a cultural Venn diagram. Originally straddling Houma and Bayougoula tribal hunting grounds, the city became more Anglo than the adjacent French Creole and Acadian regions, yet more French than the former British and Spanish colonies to which it once belonged—while also more African than the piney woods to its east. It is more Protestant than south Louisiana, yet more Catholic than the north, and in recent decades it has adopted the foodways and traditions of the Acadian and Creole regions. Economically, Baton Rouge is an administrative and industrial center, yet also academic, agricultural, and "the nation's most inland seaport," 253 river miles from the Gulf of Mexico.[1] Politically, it is a sort of "forward-thrust" capital, positioned "as the forward post of a non-French power," wrote geographer Milton B. Newton, "set to watch the affairs to the south."[2] Geographically, Baton Rouge's northern half occupies the lowermost Mississippi Valley, sitting upon a terrace just high enough to send tributaries into the river, while its southern flank slopes down to the deltaic plain, yielding the river's first distributaries, Bayou Manchac and Bayou Plaquemine. Perhaps it is appropriate, then, that the eminently liminal Baton Rouge has multiple siting stories spanning over a century, with no consensus on a foundation date or *raison d'être.* But one early rationale stands salient: that of a militarized site of two rival powers.

Baton Rouge's name came from what the Natives called *Istrouma,* or *iti humma* in Choctaw—the red pole first documented by Iberville in 1699. Strewn with bear skulls and fish bones, the *bâton rouge* most likely stood on Scott's Bluff, now the campus of Southern University, and signified that the tributary at the base (Bayou Baton Rouge, now Baton Rouge Harbor) demarcated Houma and Bayougoula hunting grounds. What is less clear is when, where, and why a settlement germinated to become the Baton Rouge we know today. Some sources speculate that a French fort had been built in this vicinity in 1719, but evidence is lacking. Documents show that in 1722 the Company of the Indies had granted a concession here to the Dartaguette family, on which formed an enclave known as Dirombourg (Dironbourg). But the site had been abandoned by 1727, and for the rest of the French colonial era the words *Baton Rouge* remained on maps only as a navigational reference.[3]

After the French and Indian War, Britain took possession of West Florida as a hostile neighbor of Spanish Louisiana. Both powers erected forts at the Bayou Manchac distributary on the Mississippi River. The British named theirs Fort Bute, and the Spanish Fuerza San Gabriel. In 1770 the British laid out a community near their bastion under the name of New Town, which may have morphed into a similar project under the name of Harwich. That town had been fully laid out in 1772 about one mile north of Fort Bute. But its parcels had few takers, even after a 1777 attempt to revive the project, and Harwich soon faded as British attention shifted to fighting the American Revolution.[4]

Some may consider this militarized defensive/distributary fork site and its embryonic towns to mark the beginnings of Baton Rouge—except that they were located well south of today's downtown. A more convincing case can be made that the future capital germinated from a warehouse and a handful of houses built by the British later in the 1770s in today's downtown area.[5] Why here? This was the spot where the terrain rose along an unusually straight segment of the otherwise wending lower Mississippi, offering better harborage than the sharp bend at Bayou Manchac. Siting at this potential break-of-bulk point may also have been informed by the difficulty oceangoing sailing ships had in proceeding upriver, due to a steeper channel gradient, making this spot a head of navigation for larger vessels.[6]

By this time, as American patriots battled Red Coats elsewhere, military leaders in British West Florida erected a fort named New Richmond near their warehouse to defend it from the Spanish, who supported the Americans. In 1779, Spanish soldiers captured Fort Bute as well as Fort New Richmond and, after two subsequent victories in the Battle of Baton Rouge, took control of West Florida. The next year they erected Fort San Carlos and made Baton Rouge into a Spanish government post.[7]

Most inhabitants, however, were anglophone Protestants, and leery of Spanish Catholics. Those in adjacent Spanish Louisiana, meanwhile, were mostly Francophones, and equally unenthused about being Spanish subjects, much less British ones. The *dons* in Baton Rouge sought to ameliorate the tensions by issuing documents in all three languages—our Venn diagram, circa 1780s. But they were not about to make further concessions. In 1790, Baton

The 1796 plan of Fort Baton Rouge attests to the future Louisiana capital's origin as a militarized site. Library of Congress.

Rouge became an ecclesiastic parish, and two years later it got its first Catholic church.

A decade later, the Baton Rouge area had a population of over 1,500 people and appeared at the brink of a boom, as the pending American acquisition of Louisiana would make Baton Rouge a valuable Spanish port on the Mississippi. Landholder Elias Toutant Beauregard prepared by hiring Arsène Lacarrière Latour to subdivide his riverfront holding. Latour devised an elaborate Grand Manner (Baroque) plan, akin to what Pierre Charles L'Enfant had done for Washington, D.C., fifteen years earlier, featuring radial streets, plazas named Florida and Mexico, an *iglesia* and Palacio del Gobierno near a *prado* (lawn) and *coliseo,* and *mercados* by the Camino Real fronting the river. Over one long century, 1699 to 1805, Baton Rouge went from an indigenous landmark to a designed city.[8]

Though its envisaged grandeur never came to be, modern Baton Rouge retains elements of Latour's plat, including radial streets and toponyms such as Florida Avenue and Government Street. Its underlying siting rationales embodied everything from a land grant to a distributary fork, to a head of navigation for oceangoing vessels, to a riverside bluff with good harborage, and eventually a service, trade, and administrative center. But Baton Rouge's use as a militarized site predated all other rationales and persisted for years.[9] Relics of Baton Rouge's military origins may be found in the shadows of the state capitol, where an old powder magazine stands across from the four remaining Pentagon Buildings, built in 1822 to house the U.S. Barracks.

Baton Rouge grew following the 1821 ratification of the Adams-Onís Treaty, which officially transferred Spanish West Florida to the United States. Yet it remained a country town compared to cosmopolitan New Orleans—the largest city in the South, and the state's economic, cultural, and political epicenter.

Discontent over that imbalance prevailed among rural planters, and when time came to rewrite the state constitution in 1845, delegates' country-versus-city discord came to light. One way to rebalance power was to decrease New Orleans's number of seats in the Senate. Another way was to relocate the legislature and governor farther inland, a shift called "forward thrust" in geography. It was no coincidence that the interior of Louisiana tended to be more Anglo-American, while Francophone Catholics predominated in the coastal region, principally around New Orleans. After years of wrangling, legislators during 1846 to 1849 took the official steps to relocate state government to Baton Rouge, a city that, in 1840, was 2 percent the size of New Orleans.[10]

Today, the city of Baton Rouge is 60 percent the size of New Orleans, and its parish population exceeds that of Orleans Parish by 20 percent. That growth had many drivers, among them the establishment of the Standard Oil refinery in 1909 and the subsequent navigation improvements that enabled Baton Rouge's harbor to become a seaport. But the premier driver has been the stabilizing presence of state government—precisely the goal of forward-thrust siting, in which a state administrative center is relocated from the coast to the interior to counterbalance disproportions of power, people, and space. International examples include Australia's creation of Canberra in 1908 to shift power inland from coastal Sydney and Melbourne, Pakistan's 1957 relocation of the capital at Karachi to Islamabad, and most famously Brazil's bold 1960 launch of inland Brasilia to host the capital previously in coastal Rio de Janeiro. The 1849 shift to Baton Rouge parallels the inland thrusts of other southern capitals since colonial or early American times: Galveston to Austin in Texas, Biloxi to Jackson in Mississippi, Mobile to Montgomery in Alabama, Pensacola to Tallahassee in Florida, Savannah to Atlanta in Georgia, and Charleston to Columbia in South Carolina. Baton Rouge's siting story is ultimately that of a militarized site that grew into an administrative center through the political logic of the forward-thrust capital.[11]

Because Baton Rouge occupied an elevated terrace and not the deltaic plain, expansion was not confined to a slender river-fronting natural levee. What happened instead was inland expansion along transportation arteries. For example, Florida Avenue and Government Street, both in Latour's original plan, were extended eastward as country roads across a patchwork quilt of farms, pastures, and plantations. Along them arose, at regular intervals, settlements serving local needs with services such as stores, churches, and post offices. Similarly, with the advent of railroads, stations and depots were spaced regularly, not too close together, not too far apart. Such roads and railroads formed the spatial framework within which modern Baton Rouge would be fitted, and early arterial-interval settlements became nodes of commerce still evident today.

A major example of arterial expansion occurred along Highland (originally High Lands) Road, which follows the brow of the Pleistocene Terrace as it slopes steeply down to the coastal plain. Traffic on this scenic route flowed from Baton Rouge southeastwardly for a dozen miles, and residences were built all along, some for plantations, others for farms, still others as country villas. Each was nigh within sight of the next, amid greenery and gardens, but rarely more than one deep. The linear community extended for such a distance that outlying residents tended to gravitate not to Baton Rouge for their needs, but to country service centers along Highland—places with names like Magnolia Church, Morning Star Church, and Staring's Store, each one to two miles apart. None grew into true towns, as they were too close to Baton Rouge to garner that sort of economic magnetism. Instead, the reverse happened: each remained locally salient while Baton Rouge expanded and eventually subsumed them. Magnolia Church, for example, no longer has its house of worship, but its salience continues in the form of the busy Parker Boulevard intersection with Highland Road, at the South Gate of Louisiana State University. Morning Star Church, meanwhile, is now the commercialized Kenilworth Parkway intersection, and Staring's Store is the Staring Lane intersection. Highland Road today retains its bucolic feel, with well-appointed residences and the occasional antebellum manse, and remains interspersed with commercial clusters, just as it was historically.[12]

Another artery wended southeasterly and parallel to Highland, earning it the descriptors "Middle Highland Road" or "the Road from Baton Rouge to Amite River." It got renamed for the Perkins family of Kentucky, who in the early nineteenth century operated the 2,800-acre Hundred Oaks sugarcane plantation here, said to be among the largest east of the Mississippi. By century's end, the holding had been broken into farmsteads along Perkins Road, which, like Highland Road, developed its own roadside centers. One formed around New Gideon Church, which is now the congested College Drive intersection. Another formed around Kleinpeter's Store, the Kleinpeter family having received a Spanish land grant in this vicinity in 1786; it is now Perkins's busy Siegen Lane intersection.[13] Siegen Lane itself intersected Clay Cut Road, originally an extension of the Marietta Road (1863) and now Jefferson Highway. That crossroads spawned an enclave called Nesser, which today is a commercial cluster along Highway 61.

If in the early 1900s you headed west from Nesser along Clay Cut Road, you'd pass Priestly Chapel (now Esson Lane at Jefferson) and proceed on to a fork with

Louisiana State Capitol grounds, circa 1935 (*top*), just east of the colonial-era militarized site overlooking the Mississippi. At right, an ancient Indian mound underlies the fort site that eventually grew into Louisiana's capital. At bottom, the Pentagon complex is the last major landmark of Baton Rouge's original militarized siting story. Photographs by A. L. Barnett/ Library of Congress and Richard Campanella.

Benton's Ferry Road (now the Old Hammond Highway). That fork with North Harrell's Ferry Road gave rise to the crossroads community of Harrell's Store as well as a ferry landing at Jones Creek. As for Benton's Ferry, that operation had been founded by planter and lawyer Robert Benton to cross the Amite River just below its confluence with the Comite River. Benton's Ferry later became Marietta's Ferry—hence Marietta Road. That ferry/confluence site became known as Marietta, which today marks the Old Hammond Highway intersection with Highway 190—the easternmost point of the greater Baton Rouge conurbation.

The ferry landing proved too flood-prone for permanent residency, so Robert Benton instead established a small community on higher ground to the east, where a post office named Benton's Ferry opened in 1856. That settlement gained the name Amite Springs, and was later renamed for Robert Benton's brother-in-law, William Denham—today's Denham Springs.[14]

The Yazoo & Mississippi Valley Railroad became one of Louisiana's most prolific place-makers, having starred in the siting stories of Harahan, Convent, and Gramercy, among others. Incorporated in 1882 as part of the Illinois Central system, the Y&MV line eventually linked New Orleans to Memphis, generating new station-stop settlements and reconfiguring older riverine settlements. The tracks came into Baton Rouge from the southeast, roughly paralleling Highland and Perkins roads (the latter of which had its own Louisiana Railway & Navigation Company line, laid in 1905–1906). The Y&MV's station at Bayou Paul spawned a settlement whose post office was named Iberville; today this is the crossroads community of the same name in Iberville Parish. Next came the stations of Rhodes, Burtville, Gardere, and Arlington, all still on the map as neighborhoods, after which the tracks ran along the Baton Rouge riverfront and proceeded northward. The Y&MV's right-of-way was later paralleled by today's Nicholson Road (Highway 30), along which are now the college neighborhoods flanking Louisiana State University. On and among these and other historic arteries we see various siting rationales—stores, service centers, Sunday towns, forks, crossroads, ferry landings, train stations, flag stops, depots—and while few became municipalities, most remain nodal spaces amid residential and commercial suburbs, home to tens of thousands of people.[15]

"Leaving Baton Rouge and going eastward along the Greenwell's Springs road," wrote surveyor Samuel Lockett of another such artery in 1869, "the country is, in general, level, but somewhat cut up by ravines, and even inclining to be undulating. . . . The soil is a dark orange yellow silt[,] quite fertile, the natural growth being beeches, magnolia[,] oak and the occasional gums."[16] Now known as Greenwell Springs Road, this route was both the cause and effect of settlements that would later comprise the eastern part of greater Baton

Rouge. Through arterial increment siting, the road birthed periodic clusters of houses, such as those at Mount Olivet Church and Poor Hill Church, both now commercial intersections in the Park Forest and Monticello subdivisions of North Sherwood Forest. Continuing eastward, the road connected with two communities on the Amite River, Burlington and Greenwell's Springs.

The siting rationale for Burlington was a ferry landing, and the settlement grew to the point that an 1840s map shows a rather impressive urban grid for the little riverside community. But once other bridges were built over the Amite, traffic found paths of least resistance elsewhere; the ferry closed, and Burlington disappeared.

Greenwell Springs is a different story, with an epilogue its founder never would have imagined. According to one account, "three young hunters accidentally chanced upon the springs, in the autumn of 1850."[17] Supposedly medicinal, the clear, cool waters bubbled up from ten wells throughout lovely woodlands—enough to convince entrepreneur Robert W. Greenwell to turn it into a health resort named Greenwell's Springs. He hoped to do for Baton Rougeans what Christy Springs (today's Abita Springs) did for New Orleanians: offer a wholesome retreat convenient to the congested city, and yet apart from it, during an era of frightful yellow fever epidemics. But when the Civil War erupted, patronage all but ceased, and the hotel became a Confederate encampment; afterward, the facilities were dismantled for the lumber needed in rebuilding. The community revived in the early 1900s when the state opened a tuberculosis sanitorium here, but when subsequent medical advances called into question the alleged benefits of such sites, Greenwell Springs and other Louisiana health resorts lost their siting rationales and risked economic irrelevance.[18]

Against all expectations, however, Greenwell Springs has become a "neighborhood" in a large and prosperous "city" whose bland name, Central, belies its unusual "siting" story. It came from a phenomenon described as a breakaway city, in which citizens, resolved to secure or deter something, legally secede from existing jurisdictions to create their own government with the power to enact the desired change. One example was today's Old Metairie, whose ridgetop road leading out of New Orleans made it a popular getaway in the 1920s. Cabarets and illicit casinos opened to serve the day-trippers, vexing locals with noise and nuisance. Aiming to expel the gambling halls, residents convinced legislators in 1927 to break away from Jefferson Parish governance and incorporate as a municipality named Metairie Ridge. But the breakaway proved legally tenuous, and in 1928 the Louisiana Supreme Court withdrew Metairie Ridge's municipal status. Like the rest of Metairie, the area has been an unincorporated part of Jefferson Parish ever since.[19]

Denham Springs has two *raisons d'être*, one involving a ferry landing at the confluence of the Comite and Amite rivers, and the other a spring, marked by this sign at Spring Park, where an entrepreneur in 1855 built a health resort. Photograph by Richard Campanella.

Whereas the city of Metairie Ridge floundered in 1928, the city of Central succeeded in 2005. It now touts 30,000 residents distributed over sixty-three square miles, but has no urban core or historic downtown. Central comprises an assemblage of modern subdivisions nestled among fields and forests, sprinkled with older enclaves having their own siting stories. Why is Central now officially a city, with a mayor and city hall? Businessman Russell Starns, who spearheaded the breakaway, explained it succinctly. "We didn't start out wanting to be a city. We wanted to get our own school district."[20]

Central had previously been an unincorporated part of East Baton Rouge Parish, through which it elected representatives, paid taxes, and received services. But residents felt their grievances went unaddressed amid the much larger populations in Baton Rouge proper, and topping the list were public schools—a volatile issue intertwined with race and class, as the city proper is far more African American and lower in income than outlying areas. The tension is a common one: majority-white Zachary (to the north of Baton Rouge) and the St. George area (to the southeast) both became what two sociologists called "white breakaway districts," in which better-educated, predominantly white areas used political geography to remap educational jurisdictions. To hear advocates tell it, it's not about race or class but local control in the face of an unresponsive bureaucracy. Along those lines, Zachary created its own community school district in 2011, while St. George has battled for years to become its own municipality—each to strident accusations of racism and classism.

In 2005, Central's breakaway advocates got the state to incorporate their sub-rural populations and empower the new municipality to create its own school district. Almost overnight, Central became Louisiana's fourteenth-largest city, and among the whitest (nearly 90 percent), best-educated (55 percent with college degrees), and most prosperous (median household income $64,484). Along with Zachary, Central also has a top-ranked public-school system.[21] Its siting story started in the 1800s with arterial increments, crossroads, resources, and resorts; it restarted in the 2000s as a political breakaway, motivated by reasons on which supporters and critics will never agree.[22]

Denham Springs has dual siting stories, both involving water. The first was the Comite and Amite rivers' confluence, where cotton planter Robert Benton had established Benton's Ferry (Marietta's Ferry) for traffic to and from Baton Rouge. Opposite the ferry terminal was land previously owned by a Scotsman named Alexander Hogue, who had migrated from Georgia in 1828 and settled here with his family. Hogue's daughter married a Mississippian named William Denham, and their daughter, Sarah Denham, eventually married Robert Benton, who would open the ferry. With the land now accessible to regional traffic, the two extended families learned they had a valuable resource underfoot, one that would become the second siting story: spring water, arising from the same subsurface hydrology beneath Greenwell's Springs. In 1855, a new owner named Stamaty Covas from New Orleans opened a hotel resort here and named it Amite Springs; the next year, Benton replaced his ferry with a floating bridge, which "of course, will render communication with [Amite] Springs more facile and agreeable," reported the *Baton Rouge Daily Comet.*[23] An ad in the *Daily Picayune* later that year extolled Amite Springs's accessibility and attractions, among them the Watering Place Hotel and "the woods surrounding the Springs, [which] abound with every species of game and afford visitors the most agreeable pastime with the gun. The Amite River is celebrated for the abundance of its fish, and angling here is not surpassed by any place in the South."[24] A fire in 1860, followed by Civil War skirmishes, set back Amite Springs, but it recovered with a modest resort economy and, thanks to that bridge, an economic lifeline to Baton Rouge. In 1898, Amite Springs was renamed Denham Springs to honor William Denham; in 1903 the community incorporated as a village; and in 1929 it became a town. The road to the old ferry landing and floating bridge became today's Highway 190. Today, Denham Springs is home to 9,300 people, and while the springs have dried and the resorts are gone, the city is now a thriving bedroom community of Baton Rouge, still linked to the capital via Highway 190 as well as Interstate 12.[25]

The area north of Baton Rouge is undergirded by a framework of track beds and paralleling roads, with communities at their intersections. Understanding how they materialized entails going back to 1824, when the state legislature split Feliciana Parish into West and East divisions. That reconfiguration made the former seat of justice at Jackson, centrally sited in the original Feliciana Parish, now inconvenient to both new parishes. Authorities thus designated St. Francisville to be the seat of West Feliciana Parish and conducted a survey to identify the geographical center of East Feliciana Parish, resulting in the creation of Clinton. As cotton plantations and small farms developed, Clinton became a quintessential southern courthouse town, complete with majestic Greek Revival architecture. What it and other interior areas did *not* have was a navigable river, forcing planters to transport their bales overland to distant landings on the Mississippi.

In fact, there was a waterway for floating cargo to the Mississippi, but it was inconsistently navigable. Thompson's Creek provided enough interior access to warrant a rudimentary circa 1730 French stockade, and later a small port at its mouth, home in the early 1800s to the Cochran & Rhea Store. Operated by a shipping firm of the same name in New Orleans, the store had a landing where small barges and keelboats struggled up shallow Thompson's Creek to reach the present-day town of Jackson in East Feliciana Parish. For this reason, the landing at Cochran & Rhea gained the name of Port Jackson, home to abodes, a church, a cemetery, and the ruins of the fort.[26]

The unreliability of Thompson's Creek led cotton-growers to seek an alternative. In 1833, investors incorporated the Clinton & Port Hudson Railroad and began work on a twenty-seven-mile track linking East Feliciana Parish to a landing on the Mississippi River, specifically a bluff/batture site superior to Port Jackson to be called Port Hudson. The new railroad turned both Clinton and Port Hudson into shipping terminals, and led to a station stop midway between—named Midway. From there, a spur line was later built to Jackson, which revitalized that former Louisiana courthouse town. Midway would get renamed Ethel, which remains a railroad community today.[27] As for that new river landing, in 1838 the state legislature authorized its incorporation and officially named the settlement "Port Hudson" for its railroad terminal. The new town burgeoned as swiftly as Port Jackson waned, and in time all that remained of the latter were "vestiges of a decayed Fort, Mission House, Cemetery and Store House." Port Hudson, on the other hand, became a "rough and rowdy" river town, in the right place and time to become a regional intermodal transshipment node.[28] Port Hudson, and not Baton Rouge, became the most economically vital settlement in East Baton Rouge Parish. It had a lofty bluff to protect from high water, a sandy batture suitable for a vessel landing, and

Detail of J. H. Colton map of 1855, with Port Hudson and Clinton appearing in the upper left corner. Library of Congress.

a virtual monopoly on flat, fertile cotton country to its rear. Most of all, "Port Hudson's strategic value," wrote historian Milledge L. Bonham Jr., came from "being the terminus of the Clinton and Port Hudson Railroad" and a network of inland roads.[29]

All that changed with southern secession, when Port Hudson's many advantages turned it into a military target. The town's siege and capture by Union forces in July 1863 ended Confederate control of the Mississippi River, and with its tribute plantations in ruins, rail lines torn up, and houses and facilities bombarded, Port Hudson never recovered. It met its fate when the river channel shifted away from the landing, while new railroads bypassed Port Hudson altogether. The siting rationales of the 1830s had lost all their value, and the settlement they rendered has so thoroughly disappeared that most Louisianians today understand "Port Hudson" to be not a town but a battlefield.[30]

The legacy of Port Hudson lives on through the arteries built to access the lost town, which came to form the settlement framework of the plains north of Baton Rouge. One such artery had been planned to connect Clinton and East Feliciana Parish with the capital region, but when it fell through, investors in 1852 instead created the Baton Rouge & Clinton Plank Road Company, aiming to charge tolls for use of its road "paved" with wooden boards. Plank Road (now Highway 67) spawned two arterial increment/crossroads communities,

Some of the last vestiges of the lost town of Port Hudson, outside of the preserved Civil War battlefield. Photograph by Richard Campanella.

known as Fred and Olive Branch, which are now on the outskirts of Zachary and Slaughter. Plank Road's corridor into the state capital, meanwhile, became the axis for the north Baton Rouge communities of Istrouma, Brookstown, North Highlands, and Garden City.

Additional arteries in the settlement framework included the Bayou Sara & Port Hudson Railroad, which in 1842 linked those two river termini with Baton Rouge as well as Woodville and Jackson in Mississippi. Its pathway is now partly Highway 61, the main axis for a number of north Baton Rouge communities near Southern University. Another artery was the Yazoo & Mississippi Valley line, linking New Orleans to Yazoo City in Mississippi starting in 1882. Later part of the Illinois Central system, the line was extended to Memphis and renamed the Louisville, New Orleans & Texas Railway in 1892. The tracks would become a major settlement-maker across the South, including here on the "Plainsland" north of Baton Rouge, where Zachary, Baker (including Leland College), and Scotlandville (including Southern University) would form.

Not a true prairie, these slightly elevated flatlands gained their descriptor Plainsland from a memory that it had once been "completely cleared of trees and undergrowth by the Indians." Early settlements included St. John's (Buhler's) Plains, White Plains, Brown Plains, The Plains Store, and others, some of which live on as crossroads on old routes to Port Hudson.[31] Later settlements on the Plainsland formed largely along railroads. During 1883–1884, workers laid 456 miles of track between Memphis and New Orleans along a pathway selected in part because landowner Darel Zachary enthusiastically sold a 650-foot-long by 50-foot-wide strip to the railroad company for "the great sum of one dollar." There the company built a station and created a definitive southern railroad town—Zachary, Louisiana, "the hub of the Plainsland."[32]

Baker has a similar siting story, born of a train station established in 1884 and a post office in 1888, both on the former plantation of Josephus Baker. For four decades, Baker also became an academy town, home to Leland College. Founded by Baptists and originally named Leland University, this institution of higher learning had since 1873 educated emancipated people and their descendants at a St. Charles Avenue campus in New Orleans. By the early 1900s, Leland found itself in need of funding and surrounded by pricey Uptown real estate. Damage inflicted by a hurricane in 1915 spurred a decision to stabilize finances by selling the valuable urban campus and relocating to rural Louisiana. But the institution encountered racist resistance at prospective sites statewide. After years of limbo, officials finally settled on a former plantation in Baker, only four miles from Southern University in Scotlandville—which also served African Americans. Too far from alumni's children and too close to a competing university, the new site never quite worked out, and Leland College closed in 1960. Its former campus is now the Leland Community subdivision in Baker, and together with nearby Zachary, the two railroad-sited cities are home to 30,000 people.[33]

Southern University has fared better in Scotlandville, but it too arrived there after a siting struggle of its own. The community of Scotland had formed at the junction of the aforementioned railroads, just east of Scott's Bluff, where in 1699 Iberville had first spotted the famous *bâton rouge.* Two factors in the early 1900s turned that enclave into the Scotlandville neighborhood of today. One was the establishment of the Standard Oil Company refinery in 1909, which brought in workers, some of whom settled in Scotland. The other was

Oil refineries dominate most of four miles between the Capitol Building and Southern University in north Baton Rouge. Photograph by Richard Campanella.

Southern University, whose relocation here would influence the racial makeup of north Baton Rouge.

That institution grew out of efforts by the biracial state legislature to educate emancipated people after the Civil War. In 1879–1880, lawmakers created Southern University with the stipulation that it be sited in New Orleans. After six years in provisional buildings, Southern built a beautiful campus on Magazine Street for an enrollment mostly drawn from greater New Orleans. Persistent financial problems were partly alleviated with the passage of the Morrill Act in 1890, which made Southern an agricultural and mechanical college and gave it new revenue streams. But the designation also required that Southern shift its curricula to agronomy, which meant finding a new site where it could build experimental farms and labs. After years of legal battles and racial acrimony, authorities finally identified a viable site at an isolated old plantation north of Baton Rouge. "No valid complaint can be made against the location of the Southern University on the Scotland Plantation," reported the *Daily Picayune* in February 1914, alluding to the prejudice encountered at other sites. Prime real estate it was not, being "bounded on the west by the river, on the north by a swamp, on the south practically by the Standard Oil, and [having] no public road running in front of it." No wonder leaders in Baton Rouge saw the move to Scotland as good economic development.[34]

Southern achieved that and more, becoming a major educator and employer of African Americans, and making Scotland a magnet for their settlement north of downtown. Now a Baton Rouge neighborhood, Scotlandville is synonymous with Southern University and Agricultural & Mechanical College, and while its siting story can be traced to historical railroads and racial politics, it feels like a modern American college town—except for the vast petrochemical plant still to its south.

* * *

"I, Michel Mahier, do send this to his Majesty's government, this prayer: To build a city on the West Bank of the Mississippi, above the King's Fort in the district of Baton Rouge, Louisiana territory. The name of this city to be San Miguel." So wrote a French-born physician in a 1798 letter to Governor Esteban Rodríguez Miró, after six years working at the Spanish Royal Hospital at Manchac and Baton Rouge. Mahier proceeded to lay out San Miguel (Ville de St. Michel) on his plantation across the river, a project that took the final ten years of his life, and was continued by his widow until her death in 1822. During that time, the site's dominion switched from the Spanish to the French to the Americans, who in 1807 created West Baton Rouge Parish. San Miguel eventually got swept away by the river in the 1820s, but by then the parish courthouse had been operating adjacently, along with some stores, depots, houses, and a ferry landing. What became known as the town of West Baton Rouge might qualify as an administrative center or a river landing in its original siting rationale, but it is better classified as a cross-river subsidiary. Mahier said as much in his entreaty, as there was no other reason for a city here—no bluff, fork, portage, resource—except for being across from the King's Fort.[35]

What gave West Baton Rouge new life, and eventually a new name, was its selection as a terminal for the Baton Rouge, Grosse Tete & Opelousas Railroad, chartered in 1853. As they did for Algiers and Westwego on the west bank of greater New Orleans, railroads made the west bank of greater Baton Rouge a jumping-off point to western cattle, rice, and timber regions, while also reinvigorating its riverine relevancy. Combined with the ferry landing, the new railroad spurred demand for housing, and West Baton Rouge expanded along the tracks. Local planter Henry Watkins Allen, owner of the nearby Allendale Plantation, became a prominent investor in regional railroads, and after he served as a Confederate brigadier general and state governor, neighbors honored him by renaming their community Port Allen in 1878.

In 1905, a former slave named Alexander Banes, who in 1874 purchased riverfront land north of West Baton Rouge, sold his holding to the Sunrise Realty Company. Subdivided for houses, "Sunrise" grew in 1906 when the Missouri-Pacific Railroad opened a transfer ferry named Anchorage adjacently, and together they pulled Port Allen's urban and industrial development northward. Sunrise faded when the Huey P. Long-O. K. Allen Bridge, serving both rail and automobile traffic, opened in 1940, killing the Anchorage transfer ferry. Traces of Sunrise's street grid are still visible in the layout of the ExxonMobil Port Allen Lube Plant, and while people no longer live on Banes's land, the Sunrise community played a key role in shaping Port Allen.[36]

Port Allen incorporated as a village in 1916 and as a city in 1923, and grew commensurately with the opening of the Port of Greater Baton Rouge in 1954 and the Horace Wilkinson Bridge in 1968. The span obviated the old ferry service, which dated to the days of Ville St. Michel, but it reinvigorated Port Allen's original siting rationale as a cross-river subsidiary. Today the city of Port Allen is home to 4,900 people, and most of them can get to downtown Baton Rouge faster than most Baton Rougeans.[37]

West Baton Rouge Parish and Pointe Coupée Parish occupy a transitional zone between the Mississippi River's valley and delta. Precisely where one feature becomes the other is debatable, but their distinction is not. Northward, upraised bluffs and terraces confine the river to a meander belt—a valley by any definition, one that extends a thousand miles upstream. But southward, those topographies dissipate, allowing the channel to avulse broadly and deposit sediment liberally, as it did for 7,200 years in forming its deltaic plain.

Within this Pointe Coupée Parish transition zone is a fluvial feature favored for settlement sites. Known as cutoff meanders or oxbow lakes, they result when a river curves so circularly that the narrow neck separating the C-shaped channel gives way to filtration, to the point that the current scours across the loop. Finding a steeper gradient, the river then lunges through and "cuts off" the old meander, which thence clogs with sediment and becomes a lake shaped like an oxbow or horseshoe.

Meander cutoffs of both natural and manmade origin are common throughout the lower Mississippi, but the specimen in Pointe Coupée Parish stands salient. One geomorphologist described it as "the lower-most cutoff[,] the oldest to be completed within historic times, and one of the longest meander loops ever formed by the Mississippi." It began breaking off in the late 1600s, in time for early historical documentation. La Salle alluded to it during his 1682 expedition downriver, and in 1699 Iberville's crew, having been advised by Natives of this convenient shortcut, cleared debris along a 350-foot-long, six-foot-wide flow to get their longboats upriver, putting the term *Pointe Coupée* (cut point) on the map. More and more river water coursed through the cutoff, widening it, while lesser quantities flowed through the meander loop, gradually sedimenting it.[38]

Some accounts hold that as early as 1708 Pointe Coupée became an encampment for French Canadian *coureurs de bois*—"forest runners" who traded furs with the Tunica village to the east and Red River tribes to the west. Other sources contend that in 1717 Iberville's younger brother Bienville established

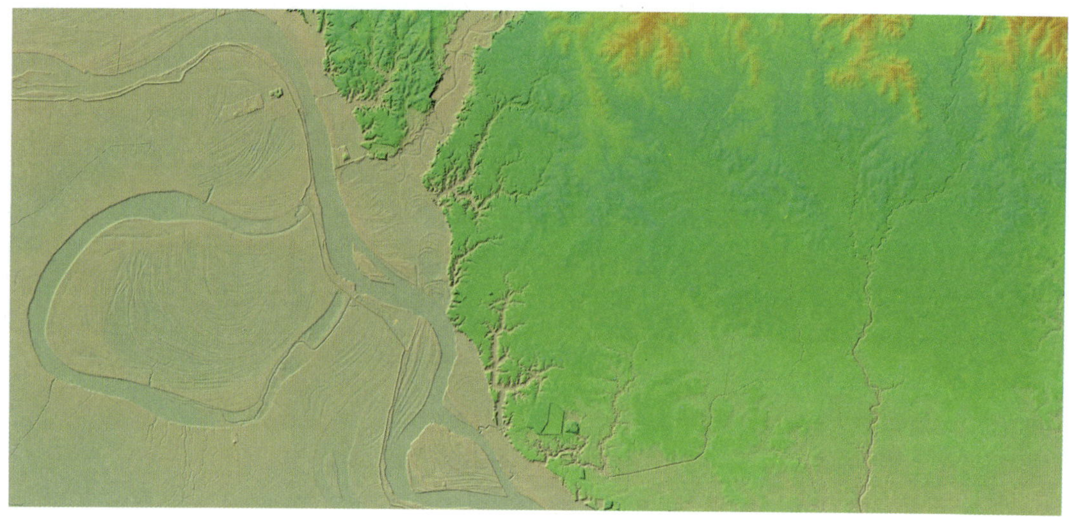

This LIDAR elevation map shows the deltaic False River region at left, starkly contrasting with the loess bluffs across the Mississippi. New Roads appears at left center, at the northern end of the False River meander cutoff. State Lands Office.

a Poste de la Pointe Coupée here. "Though it is possible that Europeans could have temporarily occupied what is now Pointe Coupée Parish at those dates," wrote historian Brian Costello, "no evidence of such has been found [until] 1722, when Pointe Coupée is included in a census of the Louisiana colony."[39] Over the next four years, French authorities established a fort and barracks at Le Poste de la Pointe Coupée, where in 1726 the visiting Father Raphael recommended building a church for a resident missionary.[40] By then, the main channel of the Mississippi had largely scoured through the cut, leaving behind what early settlers called the *fausse rivière*—"false river." A map by Sainte d'Anville from 1732 shows the *ancien cours du Flueve* with striking clarity, depicting its motionless water with a slender squiggly loop. That map also shows the Fort de la Pointe Coupée at the cut point, roughly where the communities of Waterloo and Anchor are today. That redoubt and garrison constituted the first nucleated settlement in colonial Pointe Coupée, sited for defensive reasons as a response to the Natchez Indian uprising of 1729, and aimed at protecting the fifty-five French settlers, fifty-three African slaves, and three indigenous slaves in the vicinity.

In 1736, a Capuchin priest from Luxembourg named Anselm de Langres visited Pointe Coupée to found a church honoring the order's patron saint (for whom St. Francisville was later named). The first Church of St. Francis of Pointe Coupée, built in 1738, played the nucleating role of a Sunday town, drawing the faithful from afar and helping actuate a site. In 1760, St. Francis Church was replaced by a larger edifice built adjacently to the fort, which itself had been moved to the modern-day enclave known as Pointe Coupée (located where the St. Francisville/Bayou Sara ferry landed until 2011). By that time, thirty-eight soldiers manned the garrison, and by 1766 some 500 French settlers and 700 slaves inhabited 117 plantations spanning the natural levees (*côtes* or coasts) in and around False River.[41]

Over the course of the 1760s, two belligerent political regimes found themselves on either side of la Côte de la Pointe Coupée. The west side came under Spanish rule, and their fort at Pointe Coupée by this time consisted of a stockade quadrangle with four bastions and an officer's house, barracks, storehouses, and a prison, with a nearby church served by a Capuchin priest. On the opposite side of the Mississippi were the British, who took possession of West Florida following their victory in the French and Indian War. The two enemy powers endeavored to fortify their respective frontiers and populate their interiors, for a colony without compatriots is neither defendable nor productive.[42]

As General Alejandro O'Reilly took command of Louisiana for the Spanish in 1769, he worked speedily to reinforce interior posts, such as Rapides, Natchitoches, Opelousas, Attakapas, and Pointe Coupée, where he had settlers take oaths to their new king. What was now officially called Punta Cortada became a priority to populate as a *barrera* against the nearby British; accordingly, Spanish officials granted land parcels to white colonists and imported hundreds of Africans from the Bight of Benin region to cultivate fields of indigo, tobacco, corn, and cotton. False River became particularly useful in this regard, in that its natural levees provided extensive high ground and access to the interior regions of the Atchafalaya and Red River. Nearby meanders were so sinuous that their natural levees fused at points of tangency, allowing for shortcuts to be blazed across promontories. By 1774, according to a British map, a settlement called Raccourci (French for "shortcut") formed upriver, across from Tunica. In the late 1770s, a similar shortcut was blazed southward from the garrison to False River, which locals described as the *chemin neuf* or *camino nuevo* (new road) of the main Royal Road, the Camino Real.[43]

Over the next generation, as Spanish, French, and British colonials left the stage, defensive priorities gave way to the needs of American civil governance. In 1804, U.S. authorities used the ecclesiastic parish of St. Francis Church to delineate Pointe Coupée Parish, and in 1806, as military troops departed, the former fort and garrison became the parish courthouse. All the while, the Chemin Neuf running south from the courthouse had brought traffic to the property of a free woman of color named Catherine Depau (also known also as La Fille Gougis, or Gougis's Daughter). In 1822, Depau "created a six-block, 20-lot subdivision of the front part of her False River plantation, bordered on the east by the New Road [and now] bounded by False River, Second Street, New Roads Street, and St. Mary Street."[44] Thus was born New Roads, Louisiana, courtesy of a shortcut to the natural levee of an oxbow lake. In 1847 New Roads became

New Roads was sited where a *chemin neuf* connected a fort and courthouse to the False River property of a free woman of color named Catherine Depau. In 1822 Depau laid out the subdivision seen here, whose main artery is still named New Roads Street. Above is the sign fronting St. Francis of Pointe Coupée, located near the old fort site and ferry landing. Photographs by Richard Campanella.

an administrative center, after the old courthouse burned down and the parish seat was moved three miles south to its current location.

The siting story of New Roads echoes that of the upriver communities of Batchelor, Spokane, Lake Bruin, Newellton, and Lake Providence, in that all formed on the natural levees of oxbow lakes. New Roads also has commonalities with Carville and Belle Chasse farther downriver, as well as New Iberia and Franklin on Bayou Teche, in that they emerged at shortcuts across promontories. It is one of the few municipalities in Louisiana to have been founded by a person of color or by a woman, let alone a free woman of color. As a seat of justice, it is also unusual for being at the periphery of its parish—testimony to New Roads's demographic dominance, with 4,300 people, nearly a quarter of the parish population. Regarding the old fort and church site, still called Pointe Coupée, it remained a key river landing into 2011, when its 200-year-old ferry service to Bayou Sara was supplanted by the John James Audubon Bridge. Yet even today, most traffic in and out of New Roads arrives via that *camino nuevo* shortcut from the late 1770s, still called New Roads Street. Another lasting consequence of New Roads's siting story is that it imparted better access to the convex (outer) bank of False River, as opposed to the inner concave side, which locals call "the island" because that's exactly what it was when it first broke off from the Mississippi three centuries ago. To this day, populations and property values are lower on False River's island side, home to only two named places, Ventress and Jarreau.[45]

So dominant was False River that maps from the early 1800s named hardly any other places nearby. This began to change as roads were blazed along ridges emanating southward and westward from the oxbow lake. One headed south along Bayou Sere and Bayou Poydras, giving rise to Lakeland, whose lakeside perch mirrored that of New Roads. Another road heading west to Opelousas catalyzed the formation of Parlange, also on the natural levee of False River. The largest settlement along that road to Opelousas had attracted human occupancy as far back as AD 1200, when Natives built ceremonial mounds at present-day Livonia, three of which still stand. Livonia formed in 1846 where the road to Opelousas crossed Bayou Grosse Tete, just below the confluence of its two feeder bayous, and just above the head of navigation. Those arteries spawned their own settlements, among which are Frisco heading up to Parlange; Fordoche heading north to Melville and Morganza (the two linked by the narrow "waist" between the Mississippi and Atchafalaya rivers, now State Road 10); and Maringouin, Rosedale, and Grosse Tete heading south into Iberville Parish.[46]

Postbellum conditions beleaguered Pointe Coupée Parish's plantation-based economy, and bankside erosion and crevasse floods damaged its landscape—to the point that the historic landings at Pointe Coupée and Waterloo have all but disappeared. What partly revived the region was the construction of the New Orleans & Pacific Railroad along the Bayou Fordoche natural levee during 1878–1882. This artery launched or revitalized settlements in the southwestern corner of the parish, among them Red Cross, Aban, McKneely Spur, Fordoche, Quick, Valverda, Kenmore, and Sparks at the Iberville Parish boundary. After the Texas & Pacific took over the line, it laid separate tracks starting in 1899 from Port Allen through New Roads on to Ferriday and points north. Itself a vector for flag stop or station settlements, the T&P's main impact on Pointe Coupée Parish was the right-of-way it created for the 1920s construction of Louisiana's longest state highway, today's Highway 1. The twin arteries spawned a sequence of toponyms, though most have negligible populations: Majors, Ploup, Beaud, George Spur, Frederick Spur, Morrison, LaBarre, Schwab, Morganza, Lacour Spur, Batchelor, Lettsworth, Keller, and finally Legonir, across the Atchafalaya from Simmesport.

The railroad and highway also imparted a recreational economy to False River for its placid beauty, rich history, and popular water sports. The weekend getaway economy benefits from the fact that New Roads happens to mark the state's population centroid, meaning Louisianians are evenly distributed around this locale (a bronze "Louisiana Center of Population Monument" marks the theoretical spot in False River Park). Visitors now tour the historic plantations where enslaved field hands once toiled, stroll New Roads Street in downtown New Roads, and water-ski on the oxbow lake where once churned the avulsing waters of the Mississippi River.[47]

Of the fifteen cities, towns, villages, and other communities in the Greater Baton Rouge/Pointe Coupée region analyzed in this study, 47 percent had riverine- or water-based primary siting stories (above the state average of 29 percent), while 33 percent were primarily railroad sites, the same percentage found statewide. However, there were zero resource extraction/processing sites or crossroads sites, compared to the statewide figures of 13 percent and 10 percent. Settlements began forming in the Greater Baton Rouge/Pointe Coupée region in the 1770s, peaked in the 1850s, and ended by the 1900s. Roughly 54 percent of settlements in this region emerged, while the other 46 percent were ordained—close to the statewide split of 49 percent/51 percent emergent/ordained.

Louisiana population centroid monument in New Roads. Photograph by Richard Campanella.

5

THE WESTERN FLORIDA PARISHES

Most of Louisiana is both flat and fertile (alluvial valleys, deltaic plains, prairies, swamps, marshes), or neither flat nor particularly fertile (terraces, hills, wolds, cuestas).[1] The Feliciana parishes, however, are both undulating and bountiful—the only part of the state where antebellum plantations traversed rolling hills. What set this area apart geologically was loess (from the German *löss,* "loose"), silt particles that had been left exposed on postglacial outwash plains, mobilized by prevailing winds, and dropped across the Mississippi Valley. The particles that fell within the river's meander belt were swept away by fluvial forces, while those falling on terraces, such as in the Felicianas, accumulated in a dusty reddish mantle. Runoff eroded the silty deposits into hillocks and steep ravines known as loess bluffs.

Along the western base of the bluffs flowed the Mississippi, which deposited its alluvium along beach-like banks and islands. While the uplands made for good town sites, it was the riverine lowlands that had the most commercial value as vessel landings. Thus, throughout the loess region, from Port Hudson and St. Francisville up through Natchez and Vicksburg, as well as Columbia and Harrisonburg on the Ouachita, river towns had hilltop *and* landing sections. The dual sites operated in unison, but were separated by architecture and land use (residential versus commercial); by class, race, and prestige; and by highly divergent reputations. "Natchez is situated on a bluff," wrote a boatman in 1822, with its "streets wide and straight, and the houses well built[;] the upper town being so elevated, is very pleasant." But down at Natchez Under the Hill, all hell broke loose. "At the foot of the bluff," he continued, "is a small river bottom . . . where the Prince of Darkness is, I believe, the only acknowledged superior—It is without exception, the most infamous place I ever saw—where villainy, hardened by long impunity, triumphs in open day."[2] Similar reputes colored other bluff/landing sites, including St. Francisville and Bayou Sara in West Feliciana Parish.

What set the loess region apart politically was its interstitial position amid four rival powers—"a fierce and fractious frontier" over which ten flags would fly.[3] Victory over France secured the region for England and launched the colony of British West Florida in the 1760s; subsequent conflict with American revolutionaries and Spanish troops shifted dominion from British to Spanish rule in the 1780s. All the while, Anglo settlers trickled into the region, attracted first by the British presence and later by Spanish land grants. As the English-speaking contingent grew, so too did their discontent with Spanish governance, especially after Spain retroceded its adjacent colony of Louisiana to France, which in 1803 sold it to the United States. Seven years later, rebellious factions defied Spanish authorities and declared themselves the independent Republic of West Florida in what is now West and East Feliciana, East Baton Rouge, St. Helena, Livingston, Tangipahoa, Washington, and St. Tammany parishes—to this day, Louisiana's "Florida parishes."

Launching a new nation proved more than the rebels had bargained for, and within months the nascent republic acquiesced to American occupation. But because Spain vehemently rebuked the insolence, it refused to transfer any land titles, calling into question all prior settlement. Diplomats on both sides recognized the rift and negotiated a series of compromises culminating in the Adams-Onís Treaty of 1819. Ratified in 1821, the so-called Florida Purchase clarified a number of issues "of Amity, Settlement, and Limits Between the United States of America and His Catholic Majesty," among them the transfer of all of Florida as well as the Sabine Neutral Ground to the United States. The western tip of Florida and the entire Sabine strip thus officially became part of Louisiana, giving the boot-shaped state its toe and heel. Settlement ensued in the fertile loess bluffs north of Baton Rouge, the only part of either acquisition that had access to the Mississippi. That river was now completely under American control, flowing through a valley with growing populations, plied by increasing numbers of new steamboats. Things were looking good for Louisiana.[4]

The key settlement to emerge from the geopolitical resolution was the dual river landing/dry-point site that would become Bayou Sara and St. Francisville in West Feliciana Parish. This was the best of a handful of sites where one could (1) sail on the Mississippi, (2) enter a navigable tributary, (3) pull within a couple thousand feet of uplands, and (4) establish a vessel landing at the foot of a flood-safe bluff suitable for a town. The tributary was the waterway described in the 1730s as Riviere a la Chaude Pissie ("River of Hot Urine"), perhaps due to its silty reddish coloration. The Brits gleefully translated that toponym to Clap

Creek (slang for gonorrhea), and the Spanish called it Bayou Sara, reportedly for a woman who lived alongside.[5] The landing, a batture-like deposition of sand and swamp, became the commercial town of Bayou Sara, and the bluff behind it came to host the residential district called St. Francisville. The latter community did not occupy just any faint rise; rather, "it was built on the crest of a mile-long ridge overlooking a creek and river part of its length, and sloping on either side to valleys heavily wooded and traversed by vari-pebbled streams"—a truly beautiful site.[6]

One may reckon St. Francisville to have originated as a fort site, for some early French maps show a redoubt in this vicinity labeled as Ste. Reine (Ste. Reyne). Nearby on Rivière des Tunicas (Bayou Sara) had been a Tunica village, suggesting Ste. Reine may also have been a trading post for a concession made in 1720, located downriver at the mouth of Thompson's Creek. But unlike other Louisiana fort site settlements, there is no clear progression from this military use to modern St. Francisville. Whatever primitive stockade may have existed here in the 1720s had been abandoned before 1765 and did not spin off a lasting settlement.[7]

A stronger case can be made that St. Francisville originated as a missionary site. Catholic missions had spawned towns throughout the Spanish colonial world, including in Texas and Florida, but less so in Louisiana; among the few are Los Adaes, Zwolle, Labadieville, and Abbeville. Here on the loess bluffs, Capuchin monks in 1775 established a mission known as La Villa de San Francisco under the authority of the Bishop of Santiago de Cuba. The site comprised a hillslope granted by the King of Spain, where Capuchins built a monastery and named it after their patron saint, St. Francis of Assisi. It was likely here where, "in a novel episode in Spanish colonial history," wrote historian Gilbert C. Din, authorities brought in English-speaking Irish priests in an attempt to convert Anglo Protestant settlers in Spanish West Florida to Catholicism. The area where they circulated came to be known as Feliciana, literally the land of happiness, but likely named for the wife of Spanish governor Bernardo de Gálvez, Marie Felicité.[8]

The monastery burned down around 1789, the religious conversions did not go swimmingly, and the Capuchin monks eventually departed. But the effort apparently left behind the name La Villa de San Francisco; alternately, the name came from Father Francis Lennan, one of those Irish priests whose name happened to be the same as the Capuchins' patron saint. In either case, the Spanish name got anglicized to St. Francisville.

Starting in 1787, Spanish officials granted land along Bayou Sara to settlers, among them John Mills and his family. In 1799, two settlers from Ohio

Cemetery in St. Francisville thought to be the site of the La Villa de San Francisco mission and monastery. Photograph by Richard Campanella.

attained bayou-side property, opened a store, and by some accounts laid out a place called New Valencia, which would soon evolve into the town of Bayou Sara. By 1802, a Catholic parish church was in operation at Bayou Sara, and by 1810 enough people had agglomerated in adjacent St. Francisville (which today claims a foundation date of 1807) to earn it designation as the capital of the West Florida Republic. After the American acquisition, the Feliciana region became Feliciana Parish, and in 1824, when that jurisdiction was split into west and east sections, St. Francisville became the seat of justice of West Feliciana Parish. Soon it became an administrative center and a genteel bedroom community with upward of 150 houses, many of which still stand—Louisiana's premier British-American inheritance. St. Francisville and the surrounding countryside became a place where English-speaking Protestants outnumbered Francophone Catholics, where Federal and Neoclassical architecture prevailed over Creole, and where British metes-and-bounds surveying demarcated fields through which mounted gentry hunted foxes, "as in Maryland and Virginia."[9] The surrounding region was as beautiful as it was productive. "The district of Feliciana is considered by many as the garden of Louisiana," wrote a national observer in 1817. Planters here "are very rich—some of them have as many as 600 acres of land in a state of cultivation[;] they all have slaves, and some as many as 300. . . . A New-England farmer can hardly form an adequate idea of the wealth of these planters."[10]

Bayou Sara played a key role in their enrichment. Flourishing cotton plantations and steamboat traffic made it the busiest river port between New Orleans and Natchez—and like Natchez Under the Hill and later Port Hudson, it had a

This weathered sign identifies the railroad depot in the distance as the last vestige of Bayou Sara, the river landing settlement "under the hill" from St. Francisville, abandoned in the late 1920s after repeated flooding. At right are the few remaining houses in Bayou Sara inundated by the high springtime waters of the Mississippi River in 2011. Photographs by Richard Campanella.

reputation to match. "Monday October 21 . . . Came to about 10 oclock at night, at Bayou Sara," wrote a weary boatman in 1816; "Very much disturbed by a company of riotous young men who came aboard this evening, and deprived us of our rest."[11] Commerce nevertheless burgeoned, though much of the bounty seemed to pass *through* the community. "Between three and four thousand teams traverse our streets annually," wrote a St. Francisville editorialist in 1825, "bringing to our landing the produce of the finest cotton growing country upon earth, and carrying therefrom the products of the states of Virginia, Pennsylvania, Ohio, Kentucky, Tennessee, Indiana, Illinois, and Missouri." But most cargo transferred from wagon to vessel without any value getting added by local industry. "We ourselves are lost in wonder that the growth of our village does not keep pace with our commerce."[12]

Bayou Sara got a boost from a bold idea that initially circulated in 1828: to build a railroad from the inland cotton region of Wilkinson County, Mississippi, to the river landing at Bayou Sara, so bales could be shipped from Woodville to New Orleans. State charters for America's first interstate railroad were attained in 1831, and after eight costly years of construction, the West Feliciana Railroad fully opened in 1842. Because it used a gauge (4 feet, 8½ inches between rails) that became standard in 1886, engineers were able to incorporate the line into larger systems, such as the Louisville, New Orleans & Texas (in 1888), the Yazoo & Mississippi Valley (in 1892), and finally the Illinois Central. Each line would become a major siting vector through both Louisiana and Mississippi, and all may be traced in part to Bayou Sara. The original circa 1834 office and banking house of the West Feliciana Railroad still stands in Woodville, facing the courthouse square.[13]

At left, Ferdinand Street slopes down "under the hill" to the former river landing site of Bayou Sara, while its fork rises up to Our Lady of Mount Carmel Catholic Church, "on the hill" in St. Francisville, a few blocks from the West Feliciana Parish Courthouse (*below*). Photographs by Richard Campanella.

Bayou Sara's siting rationale served well for as long as the benefits of river commerce exceeded the costs of periodic inundation. Among the worst floods were in 1844, 1846, and 1849. Referring to the latter, one traveler declared that "the town of Bayou Sara is a complete Venice."[14] And yet its greatest boom followed, during the 1850s, when, aided by a new ring levee, Bayou Sara's population exceeded 500 people and its "river front was crowded with wharves, warehouses, and offices of commission merchants, [while] large steamboats were constantly loading and unloading both freight and passengers."[15] But after the Civil War disrupted cotton production and railroads subsequently shifted commerce inland, repeated river floods as well as fires tilted the equation toward decline, particularly after a terrible deluge in 1912. "Of Bayou Sara's 630 residents in 1910, only 234 remained in 1920," wrote a team of archaeologists. "The town was unincorporated in 1926, [and] the flood of 1927 effectively destroyed what remained."[16] Most former inhabitants moved up the hill into St. Francisville, whose population nearly tripled between 1920 and 1960, aided in part by automobile roadways that put it within commuting distance of Baton Rouge.

Now a serene bedroom community of the state capital, historic St. Francisville remains the administrative center of West Feliciana Parish and enjoys a modest level of weekend getaway tourism. One of the most beautiful places in town is the Grace Episcopal Cemetery and adjacent Old Catholic Cemetery, which is said to be the site of the original Spanish Villa de San Francisco Mission. Bayou Sara is beautiful too these days, but for different reasons: the waterway's lush bottomlands teem with life, including the occasional alligator. The last remaining historic structure is the Bayou Sara Depot, built in 1888 for the West Feliciana Railroad, which continued to roll as the Illinois Central up until 1978. Bayou Sara's river landing, bustling for two centuries, finally came to rest in 2011, when ferry traffic to New Roads shifted to the new Audubon Bridge.

Around 1802, a few Anglo settlers secured land parcels on a loess bluff where two streams merged with Thompson's Creek, the area's second-largest tributary of the Mississippi after Bayou Sara. The creek flows today like a placid brook, with clear water wending through a sandy-bottomed meander belt. But prior to modern river management, it was voluminous enough to be navigable by small barges and longboats part of the year, and prone to dangerous torrents following heavy rains. Because of this confluence as well as a nearby crossing (Murdoch's Ford, said to be used by black bears), a settlement formed here under the name Bear Corners. One settler, John Horton from North Carolina, made Bear Corners into a larger hamlet he called Buncombe, for the Appalachian county from which he hailed.

Buncombe turned out to be in an opportune location. In 1811, Louisiana officials created Feliciana Parish in what had briefly been considered the independent West Florida Republic—and what Spain still held to be Spanish West Florida. Undaunted, the state legislature in January 1815 called for a survey to find a centralized site for a parish courthouse. By then, a military route known as General Wilkinson's Road had been blazed across the Florida region, from the Mobile River to St. Francisville, opening up the middle of Feliciana Parish. The surveyor determined the center to be on parcels owned by John Horton and James H. Ficklin, which were near Buncombe and its landing on

Bear Corners (*top*), marking the center of Jackson since 1832, sits one block from the original Feliciana Parish Courthouse (*left*). Photographs by Richard Campanella.

the creek. Horton and Ficklin donated land to host the courthouse, and Buncombe was on its way to becoming an administrative center. Around the same time, news circulated of Major General Andrew Jackson's rousing victory over the British at the Battle of New Orleans. Residents renamed Buncombe in his honor, and Jackson, Louisiana, became the new seat of Feliciana Parish.[17]

Jackson's centrality lasted only four years. In 1824, legislators divided Feliciana Parish into West and East sections, using Thompson's Creek as the boundary. Jackson's courthouse became inconvenient, and new seats of justice were designated at St. Francisville to the west and Clinton to the east.

Such reconfigurations could kill a courthouse town. But Jackson managed to stay relevant by returning to its innate advantages. It developed its access to Thompson's Creek into a flatboat and keelboat landing, which worked in unison with Port Jackson, located fifteen miles downriver at the confluence with the Mississippi.[18] Jackson also developed a professional community. In 1825, the state legislature located the College of Louisiana here, which later grew into Centenary College and, according to boosters, made Jackson "the Athens of the South." In 1847, Jackson landed the East Louisiana State Hospital, a mental institution with a large workforce that is still in operation today. All along, Jackson developed into a regional crossroads for overland traffic and early railroads, enabling it to become a trade and banking center for cotton planters and a bale depot for shipments to Port Hudson. Unlike river towns, Jackson benefitted from the late 1800s shift to rail transit, by which time its population exceeded 2,000 people. In 1890, a parish advocate tallied Jackson's siting benefits: "Within *six* miles of three railroad stations and within *twelve* miles, by good wagon roads, of three receiving and forwarding points on the Mississippi river; with one railroad penetrating its borders from east to west, and another railroad running its whole breath from north to south[.] Jackson's cheap, easy and free intercourse with the outside world and her exceptionally good educational advantages have attracted from abroad numerous accessions of capital and labor. . . . to a point bigger than they reached in *ante bellum* times."[19]

Jackson tripled in population over the next half century, but all the while each of its siting logics lost sway. Cotton cultivation moved west, large-scale agriculture never really came back, no new industry filled the void, no major highway or interstate passed through, and Thompson's Creek was, in the end, little more than a placid brook. Now down to 3,900 inhabitants, scenic Jackson, replete with historic structures, has nevertheless ranked as the largest municipality in East Feliciana Parish for well over a century, and is currently triple the size of the parish seat of Clinton. Its siting story is unusual in that Jackson emerged naturally and then became ordained as an administrative center—only to lose that status and yet endure, by making the most of those natural advantages. Through it all, the building at the center of town is still called Bear Corners ("no matter what the restaurant is," a waitress once explained to me as she served Mexican food), and it sits one block away from the original Feliciana Courthouse, standing since 1816.[20]

Clinton, a dozen miles to the east, has long been a sister to Jackson—part partner, part rival, equally beautiful, and with rhyming siting stories. Following the splitting of Feliciana Parish in 1824, officials in East Feliciana had their new parish surveyed to determine the center. It fell in "an old worn out field . . . entirely destitute of forest or fountain," not worthy of their envisaged seat of justice. So they scouted nearby and found, 2.5 miles to the east, a dome-like rise "well watered by perennial springs and by Pretty Creek, and wooded by dense forests of pine and hardwoods."[21] Better yet, General Wilkinson's Road

East Feliciana Parish Courthouse (*left*) and Lawyers Row (*right*) in Clinton, exhibiting the Greek Revival style in vogue in the 1840s, at which time Clinton was known as a center for jurisprudence. Photographs by Richard Campanella.

ran nearby, providing east-west access. As had happened in Jackson, the lucky owners, chief among them John Bostwick, sealed the deal by donating land for the courthouse and street grid. Bostwick named the town Clinton in honor of New York governor De Witt Clinton, who at the time oversaw the excavation of the Erie Canal. "By 1830 the community was booming," wrote the town historian; "Clinton became known as the legal center of the area, and when the Clinton & Port Hudson railroad was established in the mid 1830s, the town found prosperity as the cotton trading center for a large area." It was also the premier crossroads in East Feliciana Parish, with five wagon roads plus the railroad all intersecting here by 1850.[22] Like Jackson, to which it was linked by road and rail, Clinton took pride in its academies, including Silliman Female College and later Silliman Collegiate Institute, founded in 1852 and reopened in 1965 in the same antebellum edifices. Clinton also attracted "intellectual recruits from the law schools all over the Union" to settle intricate land title questions, many arising from the area's irregular British metes-and-bounds surveying system and multiple political regimes. Locals called the town's many esquires "the East Feliciana Bar," and their striking Greek Revival-style offices, known as Lawyers Row, still face the majestic East Feliciana Parish Courthouse. Ordained in the standard fashion of a seat of justice, Clinton added to its rationales by also becoming an arterial hub, a trade and services center, and a home to "a brilliant Society of Intellectual Athletes."[23]

With Bayou Sara and Port Hudson serving as the main river landings, and Jackson and Clinton as interior hubs, most other Feliciana settlements developed along arteries interconnecting the four nodes. They were few in number and small in size, for two reasons. First, throughout the 1800s, extensive plantations dominated this landscape, though they were significantly outnumbered by small farms. As we saw in the sugar region, large plantations formed de facto communities—communities of forced residency and policed movements, with their own living quarters, food production, and services. Their presence tended to stymie town formation because they effectively *were* towns. Second, this was loess terrain, and unlike the compacted flat clays of the prairies and terraces, the silty topsoil eroded into hillocks and ravines sloping down to unnavigable streams—a fragmented landscape unfavorable to town formation. Nor was this timber country, nor oil, nor industrial; it even ceased to be plantation country after the Civil War, with the emancipation of the enslaved workforce and the erosion of the topsoil. (All around East Feliciana Parish, wrote a local observer in 1890, "are many large bodies of abandoned lands, which were once highly esteemed for their great productive capacity, but which have had a rest of twenty-five years, since the old system of labor was abolished."[24]) Thus, postbellum populations tended to be strewn lightly along back roads and rails crisscrossing patchy pastures and woods. An inspection of the 1906 Bayou Sara quadrangle of the U.S. Geological Survey, the first mapping effort to depict detailed loess topography, shows far more rural houses scattered hither and yon than clustered in named communities. To this day, 90 percent of West Feliciana Parish's population of 15,500 resides in unincorporated areas, and its sole municipality, the town of St. Francisville, falls well short of qualifying as a city.

Four of these back roads emanated from Bayou Sara/St. Francisville along Little Bayou Sara, chief of which was the Old Tunica Road. Their destination was a remote landing named Tunica serving steamboats on the Mississippi and plantations along Tunica Bayou. By the early 1900s, the roads were supplemented by two tracks laid through Bayou Sara, that of the Louisiana Railway & Navigation Company, which hugged the base of the Tunica Hills, and that of Woodville & Bayou Sara Railroad, which became a branch of the Yazoo & Mississippi Valley line. Together with the roads, these arteries gave rise to the rural population clusters of "Laurel Hill, Ratcliff, Riddle, Rogillioville, Row Landing, Star Hill, Wakefield, and Weyanoke," as well as Solitude, Bains, Catalpa, Converse, Brothers, McGehee, Wilcox, Flower Hill, Rosebank, Turnbull, and Retreat. Some formed as arterial increments, post offices, or station stops; others germinated around old plantation houses. None had a population of more than a few score, and only a third endure today.[25]

From the standpoint of modern human geography, the most influential outcome of West Feliciana's historic arteries, starting with the Old Tunica Road and ending with today's Highway 66, was the access they provided to a remote plantation at the base of the loess bluffs. That river-fronting bottomland is now home to 6,300 "residents" and 1,800 workers, by far the highest concentration of humanity in the region. Officially the Louisiana State Penitentiary, it is universally known by its historical plantation name—Angola. How the nation's largest maximum-security prison got sited in "the land of happiness" is the story of a highly controversial policy and one determined man.

The policy was convict leasing, devised in 1844, in which the state contracted a firm to hire out prisoners for gang labor, such as picking cotton, building levees, or laying tracks. From the state's perspective, convict leasing turned an expense into a revenue stream; from the perspective of retributive justice, it made prisoners into slaves; and from the perspective of Samuel L. James, it represented a lucrative opportunity when in 1869 he became the leaseholder of all the state's convicts imprisoned at Baton Rouge. A civil engineer and former Confederate major, James needed labor to build levees, and so he effectively became the manager of the entire state prison system.

In 1880, James and his associates purchased, in the northwestern corner of West Feliciana Parish, a plantation known since the 1840s as Angola, Angora, or Woodyard. The land in that era had come into the possession of interstate slave trader Isaac Franklin of Tennessee, who had a penchant for exotic-sounding names; "Angora" inferred Ankara in Turkey, and a similar allusion probably explains "Angola" (it was not a reference to the slaves' African origins).[26] Now in the hands of Samuel James and his company, the Angola Plantation became the destination of a subset of James's leased prisoners, where they were put to work raising crops or hired out to external projects—all for James's profit. According to a later government report, "James reportedly maintained the most cynical, profit-oriented, and brutal prison regime in Louisiana history. Approximately 3,000 prisoners died under the James lease between 1870 and 1901."[27]

After the abuses of the "James Prison Camp" came to light, reformers succeeded in banning convict leasing in Louisiana in 1898. Three years later, the state ended the James lease, purchased his camp, resumed direct oversight of the prisoners, and renamed the place Angola State Farms. Following a bad river flood in 1922, neighboring landholders opted to sell six adjacent plantations to the state, and Angola grew to its current size of 18,000 acres, most of it croplands. In the century since, Angola has been a place of notoriety, reform, life, and death. Nearly everything associated with the penitentiary is controversial, from its name and history to its old electric chair ("Gruesome Gertie") and its annual prison rodeo, which detractors have compared to Roman gladiators. Angola is also the major employer in the region, and even has its own ferry to Pointe Coupée Parish, called Angola Landing.

To the question of why 8,000 people now occupy this remote bottomland, it's probably true that Samuel James could have secured a comparable field elsewhere, and the availability of this particular plantation ultimately explains Angola's siting. But this parcel was well-positioned for James's brand of convict labor, and for what the State of Louisiana later needed for its penitentiary. It was located near Baton Rouge, home to the prior prison, and accessible via road, rail, and river, close to most of the state's people (in fact, Angola is just a few miles from Louisiana's population centroid, at New Roads).[28] Being fertile bottomland abutting the Mississippi River, Angola needed levees and could yield bumper crops, both of which would enrich James, a levee builder who fancied himself a planter. Angola was also isolated, and when the state purchased it to become the state penitentiary in 1901, officials valued its out-of-sight, out-of-mind location all the more because it was also accessible and convenient. Angola's siting thus has a spatial rationale, and it strikes a common theme in the geography of incarceration.[29]

Like its western neighbor, East Feliciana Parish had its own web of antebellum roads, but to look at its population distribution today, it is plain to see that the primary settlement vector was the Yazoo & Mississippi Valley Railroad (later the Louisiana, New Orleans & Texas and now the Illinois Central). We have already seen how the men behind this influential artery, commenced in 1882 to link New Orleans to Yazoo City and beyond, ordained today's Scotlandville, Baker, and Zachary in East Baton Rouge Parish. Originally station stops, these settlements were later paralleled by Highway 19 and are now collectively home to over 40,000 people. As the tracks proceeded northward, the economic magnetism of greater Baton Rouge diminished and the rurality of East Feliciana Parish prevailed, yielding smaller communities at longer intervals.

First across the parish line was Slaughter, which germinated as a train station and rail junction, where Y&MV officials had taken over the old Woodville & Bayou Sara Railroad and made it a westward branch of their main line. While the site selection of Slaughter was completely deferential to the needs of the railroad company—the name salutes property owner William S. Slaughter, on whose parcel the station was built—Slaughter ended up with decent geography, according to parish advocate Henry Skipwith writing eight years after its 1884 founding. Slaughter was indeed a railroad junction, Skipwith affirmed, and one that made it the possessor of "natural tribute without a competitor, all the country west of it, between it and the Mississippi, and [over to] the Amite river." More so, this "thriving, fast growing, incorporated town of two hundred houses" benefitted from being "situated on a well-chosen rolling site[;] its natural drainage is so perfect that the heaviest downpours of rain, pass out of

The siting stories of Slaughter and Zachary are evident in their railroad-based town centers. Photographs by Richard Campanella.

sight as if by magic, leaving its streets and sidewalks clean and dry." Skipwith predicted that Slaughter, home to 400 people by 1892, would soon "increase ten-fold." But like his other statements, that prediction proved overly enthused. Slaughter flatlined through 1960, and only in the 2000s did it surpass 1,000 residents. Most of that growth came not from rural tribute from points north, but suburban sprawl from Baton Rouge.[30]

The next stop north on the Y&MV was a site that had as much potential as Slaughter. Once called Midway for its centrality, Ethel formed at the junction with the old Clinton & Port Hudson line, which had been built in 1840 to activate Port Hudson. When the Y&MV took over those tracks, it closed the line to Port Hudson and made the stretch to Clinton into a spur of its larger system, the eastern counterpart to the Bayou Sara spur. The junction alone justified a station, but it benefitted additionally by being located at the standard arterial increment of five miles from Slaughter, which itself measured five miles from Zachary. Named for the daughters (both named Ethel) of two local advocates who secured space for the station, Ethel was well-positioned to benefit from the expected commercial tribute of East Feliciana Parish. By 1892, it had fifty houses and a hundred inhabitants, and boasted a decent perch on Redwood Creek, "fed by perpetual springs, and which reward the fisherman with fine strings of perch, trout, and blue catfish."[31] But in the twentieth century railroad travel declined, automobile traffic bypassed Ethel, the rural parish diminished economically and demographically, and Ethel sat too far from Baton Rouge to grow like Baker or Zachary. Today, Slaughter is one-twentieth the size of Zachary, and Ethel is one-twentieth the size of Slaughter.[32]

The march of the arterial settlements proceeded up the Y&MV as tracks were laid in the 1880s. Starting from New Orleans and continuing beyond Baton Rouge with an average increment of 4.7 miles, those station stops were Scotlandville, Baker, Zachary, Slaughter, Ethel, McManus, Gayden (Gurley), Wilson, and Norwood. By 1890, Wilson resembled Ethel: a hundred houses, 300 people, on a slight rise above the same Redwood Creek, its station named for the company president. Wilson is now a village of about 500 people, as is Norwood, the last community before the Mississippi state line. Most of those Louisiana settlements caused by the Y&MV 140 years ago remain in place today, where freight trains still rumble by on the "Main Line of Mid-America," the Illinois Central.[33]

Of the twelve cities, towns, villages, and other communities in the western Florida parishes region analyzed in this study, 17 percent had riverine- or water-based primary siting stories (below the state average of 29 percent), while 25 percent were primarily railroad sites, 8 percent were resource extraction or processing sites, and none were crossroads (compared to state averages of 33 percent, 10 percent, and 13 percent, respectively). Settlements began forming in this region in the 1770s, crested in the 1840s, and ended in the 1900s. Only 33 percent of western Florida parishes-area settlements emerged organically, the other 67 percent having been ordained by a founder—compared to a statewide ratio of 49 percent/51 percent emergent/ordained.

The caboose on display at Bayou Sara commemorates the role of the West Feliciana Railroad—chartered in 1831, completed in 1842, and last served by the Illinois Central line—as a primary settlement and development artery in the western Florida parishes. Photograph by Richard Campanella.

6

BAYOU MANCHAC AND THE MAUREPAS BASIN

The area southeast of Baton Rouge is a geomorphological potpourri—part older terrace, part younger delta, flat but with differing land covers (piney woods, savannah, prairie, cypress swamp), and all sloping from higher elevations down to lowlands tidally influenced by Lake Maurepas. It was the last-settled and least-populated area between Louisiana's two largest cities, and saw more than its share of subverted siting schemes. Two reasons explain why: a persnickety distributary known as Bayou Manchac, and a flummoxing legal case that took a century to resolve.

Bayou Manchac flowed out of a hairpin meander south of the Pleistocene Terrace upon which Baton Rouge sits, making it the Mississippi's first distributary on its deltaic plain. Water flowing in the bayou and its tributaries—Manchac is a rare example of a distributary with tributaries—had a down-cutting effect on the terrace clays, after which the sluggish current meandered through swamplands and discharged into two tidal lagoons (Lakes Maurepas and Pontchartrain) connected with the Gulf of Mexico. That access made Bayou Manchac more valuable to humans than its twisting channel might have merited, because it formed an *imashaka*—"rear entrance"—into the interior, circumventing some 200 miles of countercurrent navigation on the Mississippi. For this reason, a Tchefuncte and Coles Creek Culture site existed at the confluence of Bayou Manchac with Bayou Fountain into the 1500s.[1] Similarly, in 1718, Bayou Manchac came close to becoming the site for New Orleans. While Bienville's men cleared vegetation from what is now the French Quarter, officials in Paris perused maps of Louisiana to select a site for the headquarters of the Company of the West. They saw cartographic squiggles depicting a back door to the Mississippi—a bigger, better shortcut than the Bayou St. John/Bayou Road portage marked farther downriver on maps. "These different considerations," wrote

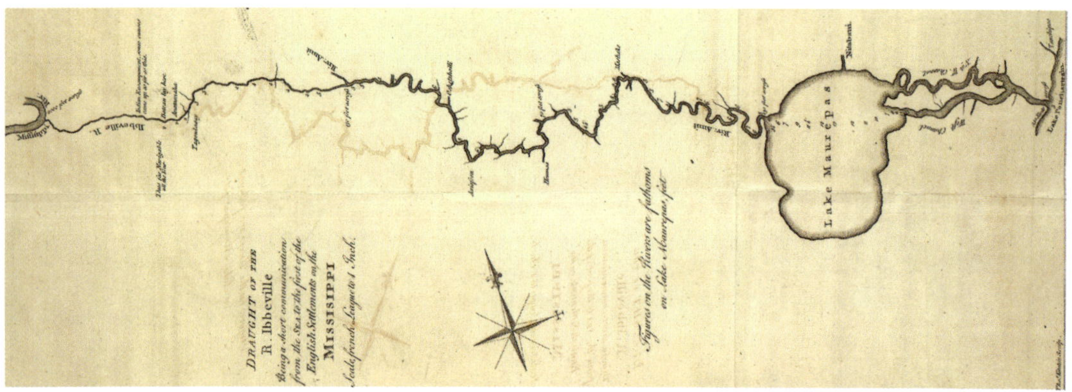

1770 map by English captain Philip Pittman of what he called the "R. Ibbeville" (Bayou Manchac), flowing as a distributary from the Mississippi River (*left*) near Baton Rouge, joined by the Amite River draining uplands to the north (*left center*), and discharging into Lake Maurepas and Lake Pontchartrain (*right*). Library of Congress.

an official on April 14, 1718, "make us think . . . that the most suitable place is on the Manchac stream." The company dispatched chief engineer Paul du Perrier to transmit the recommendation; had he inveigled Bienville, the French Quarter site might have been countermanded and the effort relocated up to Bayou Manchac. But Perrier perished en route, and with him died the notion, seemingly absurd today, that New Orleans would be sited near Baton Rouge.[2]

By the 1770s, colonial geography had changed radically. With the French departed, the Bayou Manchac fork at the Mississippi River now had two enemy bastions on either side, British to the north and Spanish to the south, while the bayou itself became an international boundary between British West Florida and Spanish Louisiana. In an effort to populate their side, the British planned the communities of New Town and Harwich to be built near their fort, and envisaged a third town, Dartmouth, for where Bayou Manchac merged with another river to form the Iberville (now the Amite) River. All three British site selections had ascribed navigational importance to Bayou Manchac, but none ever came to fruition, because British attention turned to hostilities with American colonists and their Spanish allies. Yet the proposed Dartmouth area did manage to attract some British settlers, for reasons all their own. Starting in 1776, some British noncombatant families, seeking refuge from violent skirmishes, furtively crossed Bayou Manchac and settled on the Spanish side, at its confluence with the Amite.[3]

All the while, Spain had been recruiting its own people to populate Louisiana, aiming to boost productivity and defend against British interests. Upon receiving immigrants from Málaga, Granada, and the Canary Islands, Spanish leaders debated whether they should be dispersed to the north and west, as Lieutenant Governor Francisco Bouligny recommended, or kept closer to New Orleans, as argued his superior, Governor Bernardo de Gálvez. In something of a compromise, Bouligny led some immigrants, mostly the *peninsulares* (main-

The 1778 plan for La Villa de Gálvez reveals an ambitious vision for a Spanish city on the Amite River. But in the decades ahead, Galveztown gradually lost its siting rationales, and the settlement eventually disappeared. Library of Congress.

landers) from Málaga and Granada, west to the Attakapas region, where he eventually established New Iberia, while Gálvez led others, mostly the Isleños, to a site "he glowingly described," according to historian Gilbert C. Din, at "the confluence of Bayou Manchac and the Amite River, where he proposed to establish Villa de Gálvez and a fort." Because Bayou Manchac marked the border with British West Florida, this site would be the perfect place to fortify and populate with Spanish loyalists.[4]

A little too perfect, it turned out. When Gálvez arrived at the confluence in 1778 with a group of Isleños, they happened upon those apprehensive British noncombatants huddling in refuge. Realizing they were harmless, Gálvez granted asylum to the erstwhile enemies so long as they accepted the Isleños. As Spanish troops erected a small fort and garrison, surveyors laid out a plaza and street grid for what they called Villa de Gálvez, or Galveztown. By 1785, the confluence site had 242 residents of various nationalities, while Manchac at the main distributary fork had seventy-seven inhabitants. Galveztown peaked in 1793 with 262 people in eighty-four households.[5]

The growth would not last. Tribulations ranging from disease and hunger to hurricanes and floods beset the remote outpost. Galveztown also lost its military importance, as Spanish troops defeated local British forces and American patriots prevailed in the Revolution, bringing an end to British West Florida. The Bayou Manchac distributary lost its strategic value, and its navigability hardly made it an economic prize, being intermittent and sinuous. Surviving Isleños departed Villa de Galvez for land grants in San Bernardo (today's eastern St. Bernard Parish), while others relocated to what is now Spanish Town in Baton Rouge, or downriver on the Amite River, or to the slightly higher ground five miles to the south, forming a community still known as Galvez today. By 1804, Galveztown was down to only twenty-eight families, and most of them had departed by 1810.

In late 1814, Major General Andrew Jackson sealed off Bayou Manchac in preparation for the British assault that was ultimately repelled at the Battle of New Orleans. The distributary has never flowed freely since, and aside from a smattering of houses at Claybank, no true Bayou Manchac town would form again, either at its former fork by the Mississippi or its confluence with the Amite. History had bypassed Galveztown, and its "beautiful and advantageous situation" became obsolete.[6] "Not a vestige of the ancient town remains," wrote an Ascension Parish resident in 1888. "The spot is to-day the sole property of a lineal descendant of the brave explorers who founded the town. Mr. Miguel Gonzales, who has attained more than fourscore years, is the lone inhabitant and owner of the site of this ancient city."[7]

The demise of Galveztown and the closure of Bayou Manchac steered subsequent settlement farther downstream, to where two tributaries from the north, known today as Gray's Creek and Colyell Creek, joined the main channel of the Amite (formerly Iberville) River. That infusion made the Amite navigable for schooners and luggers sailing up from Lake Maurepas. Some former residents of Galveztown had resettled at this head-of-navigation site, taking advantage of slightly elevated terrain nearby. That ridge allowed for roads to be cleared into

Spanish West Florida, connecting to what are now Denham Springs and Walker in Livingston Parish. By 1833, American settlers numbered enough to warrant the establishment of a post office, called Beech Hill and later Coelk. Among them was an Italian-born merchant and schooner captain named Vincent Scivicque, who regularly plied the Amite and brought cargo into the region. Scivicque donated land for a cemetery in 1824 and a church in 1839, and opened Scivicque's Ferry for travelers en route between Livingston and Ascension parishes. Renamed Port Vincent in his honor, the settlement served as Livingston Parish's seat from 1872 to 1881, at which time it also became a Sunday town and regional service center. "Port Vincent was a thriving community in the days when the Amite River was the primary means of transportation," wrote a local historian, in reference to its head of navigation and ferry landing site advantages. Port Vincent was also a crossroads, administrative center, and a resource extraction and processing site, featuring "the Port Vincent Brick and Stave Mill, sawmills, a cotton gin, a warehouse, boat docks, schools, churches, boarding houses, and many business establishments." When railroads were built regionally, both the Amite River and Port Vincent lost their economic rigor, subverting yet another siting story of the Maurepas Basin. Yet unlike its upstream predecessors, Port Vincent managed to endure, gaining incorporation in 1952 and becoming by 1970 "a resort for many fishermen, boaters, skiers, and persons retreating for a weekend from the crowded cities." Port Vincent is now home to about 400 people, many of them retirees enjoying the placid beauty of this once-vital site.[8]

Downstream and east of Port Vincent, the banks of the Amite and its tributaries become too low and marshy to host settlements. Roads thus became the main vectors, particularly where they crossed terrain high enough to allow for intersecting pathways. French Creoles who settled along the Amite River, earning it the name La Côte Française, constructed roads extending to what are now Port Vincent and Springfield, gaining access to Livingston and St. Tammany parishes. As river traffic declined in favor of the roads, La Côte Française shifted to what is now the crossroads of Highways 16 and 444, becoming today's village of French Settlement, population 1,100.

Take 444 toward Springfield and you'll get to the crossroads site of Verdun, where Highway 63 takes you up to Frost and the former lumber company town of Livingston, now the Livingston Parish seat of justice. Head down on Highway 16 from French Settlement, and you'll get to the crossroads site of Head of Island, which gets you down to Sorrento, or up to another crossroads at Killian, born as a landing site on the Tickfaw River. Exactly in between on Highway 22 is the community of Maurepas (historically Amite), whose landing on the Amite River made it a jumping-off point to extract Maurepas Swamp cypress timber.[9]

The Amite River near its confluence with Bayou Manchac—once the "rear entrance" (*imashaka*) into the region, later a boundary between hostile empires, now a placid paradise. Photograph by Richard Campanella.

The southernmost expression of the Pleistocene Terrace east of Baton Rouge is a grassy neck of land protruding into the Maurepas Basin, "mantled with 10 to 30 feet" of consolidated clay, "composed of many coalescing Pleistocene coastal rivers and streams that have left behind remnants of former channels forming low ridges."[10] Two distributaries of the Mississippi have incised their channels through this oval-shaped protrusion. One is Bayou Manchac, which joins the Amite and discharges into Lake Maurepas, and the other is New River, which forks off at today's Geismar as the Blind (Petite Amite) River, and discharges into the same lake. Motorists on Highway 61 today traverse this topographic feature driving from Old Jefferson in Baton Rouge through Prairieville and Gonzales (passing right over New River) and down to Sorrento, after which they drop into the Maurepas Swamp. Spanning some fifty square miles, the landscape here is something of an anomaly: a flat, grassy terrace, scored by just enough downcutting streams to create the occasional ravine—and yet surrounded on three sides by deltaic deposits that somehow manage to be even lower and flatter.

The protruding terrace also had an unusual settlement history, having paused for nearly a century and restarted with a U.S. Supreme Court ruling. The problem originated with French and Spanish colonial policies that, in a dubious display of munificence, "allowed" indigenous tribes to continue to reside on their homelands. The Houma and Bayagoula (Bayougoula) tribes occupied this territory up to 1774, whereupon three colonists led by Maurice Conway claimed to have bought out their right of occupancy and sought permission to secure the title. The Spanish governor concurred, and in 1776 he dispatched Louis Andry to survey lines for Conway's acquisition, which Andry did by starting at the fertile frontage along the Mississippi and continuing back to the forty-arpent line. The next year, a Spanish administrator doubled the depth to eighty arpents, which had the effect of negating some of Andry's surveying. Making matters worse, Andry had only qualitatively described the rear of the acquisition, reckoning it to be worthless wetlands. In fact, being a prairie terrace made the land dry, arable, and useful. Conway and later "holders of this grant subsequently claimed that it extended back to Bayou Manchac, Amite river and Lake Maurepas, covering the enormous area of 211,478.61 acres."[11] Their purported titles became known as the Houmas Claim.

The problem came into relief when Louisiana became American, its economy developed, and the Houmas Claim became valuable. A parade of American investors came to buy or petition adjacent tracts, among them prominent names like Daniel Clark, William Donaldson, Wade Hampson, John Slidell, and John McDonogh. Each tract depended on the exactitude and legitimacy of that colonial-era claim, especially its nebulous rear flank. Starting in 1806, American courts found the Houmas Claim to be neither exact nor legitimate, the result of "poor documentation under a foreign government," according to one historian.[12] Lawyers argued, judges opined, appeals were filed, missives were published, and the Houmas Claim remained largely vacant—for fear of trespassing charges, lawsuits, and more court cases.

Finally, in 1884, the U.S. Supreme Court ruled against the colonial documents and cleared the way for titling. Not wanting to evoke the controversy, people started calling the area by a new name—the New River Territory. When it was fully opened for settlement in 1888, the New River Territory became an Oklahoma-like bonanza of homesteading opportunities, situated between Louisiana's largest city and its capital, a situation unique in regional history.[13]

From a settlement perspective, the century-long legal freeze had a number of lasting spatial effects. First, it nullified colonial-era surveying throughout the terrace except along the Mississippi riverfront, where Andry had surveyed fixed boundaries. The area was thus resurveyed afresh, using the township-range-section lines of the American Public Lands Survey (PLS). Homestead claims were made in American-style units of 40 to 160 acres, rather than in arpents, and each parcel was delineated within straight lines and right angles, rather than flailing French long lots. Look at any map or satellite image of the Gonzales area in Ascension Parish, and you will see a checkerboard of orthogonal streets following section lines, something as rare in southeastern Louisiana as it is common on midwestern prairies.[14]

Accordingly, clusters of houses formed at the grid intersections—places today named Hobart, Little Prairie, Galvez, Brignac, Duckrose, and Cornerview. The pattern follows geographer Walter Christaller's Central Place Theory, where, given an isometric surface, settlements are predicted to emerge at regular spatial intervals. Being a flat prairie terrace wiped clean of prior placemaking, this is the centralized settlement array we would expect to see.

At right, an 1859 letter from John Claiborne and John Slidell explains the Houmas Claim controversy to a state official; below, an 1864 map by Helmuth Holtz labels "The Houmas Grant" at the lower center left of this Maurepas Basin detail. Library of Congress.

THE HOUMAS CLAIM.

A Letter to the Hon. Cyrus T. Bemis, Member of the General Assembly of Louisiana.

New Orleans, April 12, 1859.

Dear Sir,—In accordance with your request, made several weeks ago, that I would furnish you with authentic information as to the nature and history of the Houmas Land Claim, and its present condition, I have examined into the official archives at the Land Office in this city, as also into other official documents, and shall proceed, as briefly as may be compatible with a full and fair view of the subject, to state the result of my labors.

The French and Spanish laws for the government of the Colony of Louisiana, as those Powers successively held it, permitted to the Indian tribes the occupation of the lands upon which their villages and fields were situated, but the Crown reserved to itself the title to the soil. Previous to the year 1774 the Houmas and Bayagoulas, together occupied a considerable tract fronting on the Mississippi, in what is now the parish of Ascension. About that date three gentlemen, Messrs. Maurice Conway, Latil and McNamara, with the consent of the Colonial authorities, bought of the Indians their rights to a tract occupied by them, about twenty-two leagues above this city, on the left bank of the river, with the customary depth of forty arpents, by a river front of ninety-six arpents. Subsequently, Maurice Conway purchased the rights of his associates, and became thus the sole proprietor of the land. In the month of September, 1776, Conway presented to the Governor of the Colony his petition, in which he alleged his ownership of the tract above described, and stated that, owing to the absence of timber on it, the Cypress Swamp being then, as he said, more

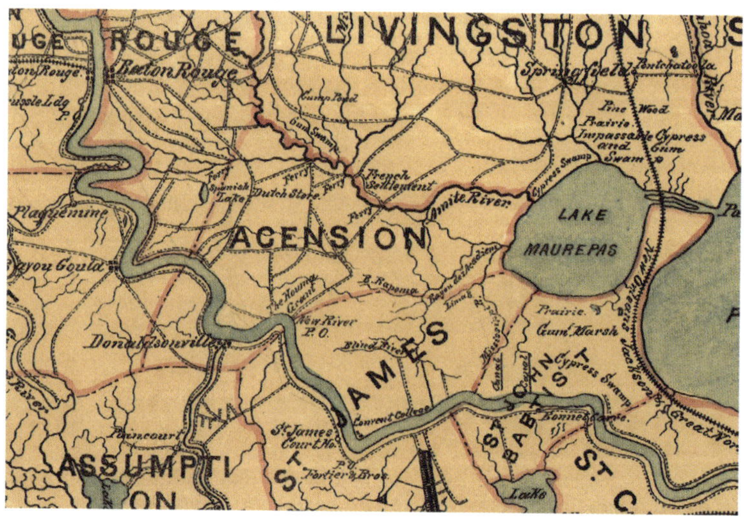

The legal freeze of 1806 to 1884 also had the effect of vacating three generations of land users and land uses, be they for enslaved commodity agriculture, truck farming, grazing, industry, or town formation. To be sure, there were some squatters on the prairie who managed to scratch out a living. But most land remained vacant and unutilized for most of that time, and the few settlement sites were tenuous and tiny until century's end.

Prairieville is an example. People initially settled in this vicinity in the Spanish era, as evidenced by the circa 1785 land donation by Joseph Dupuy to create Prairieville Cemetery. Why here? As one of the higher elevations on this neck of the upraised terrace, this spot marked the halfway point along a road blazed in 1805 to connect the St. Gabriel/New River (now Geismar) area on the Mississippi with Galveztown on Bayou Manchac.[15] After Galveztown was abandoned in 1810, the Old Galveztown Road endured in its southward reach to the Mississippi, but gradually fell out of use in its northern reach—which probably explains why today's Highway 73 follows the old road more closely from Geismar to Prairieville than Highway 42 does up to the ghost town of Galveztown. Settlement in the region then abated as courts grappled with the Houmas Claim, and did not resume until after the U.S. Supreme Court resolved the case in 1884. Soon, Prairieville came upon the map, as a post office and store run by Hercule Landry to serve small farmers now tilling the fertile grasslands. "Two and a half miles farther south," wrote parish advocate H. Thompson Brown in 1888, "is Dutchtown, formerly known as Dutch Stores," which like Prairieville also originated as a stop along the Old Galveztown Road. Now at that enclave "there are to be found a large store, two-story cotton gin, saw and grist mill, an extensive sugar plantation, and the largest and best equipped sugar-house in the New River section."[16] Its operator was Leon Picard, who was also the postmaster at the Dutchtown Post Office. Now along the I-10 corridor, Dutchtown is a neighborhood outside Geismar and a bedroom community of Baton Rouge.

Post offices, stores, depots, processing facilities: enough settlements emerged on the savannah to motivate the Louisiana Railway & Navigation Company to lay tracks in 1905–1906 as the last leg of its venture to connect Shreveport, Alexandria, Baton Rouge, and New Orleans.[17] Later named the Louisiana & Arkansas, the railroad produced new towns by establishing stations, or nudged preexisting towns toward its tracks.

Such was the case in Prairieville, where the new train station acted like a magnet for growth. Thirty years later, the routing of Airline Highway (Highway 61) parallel to the railroad's right-of-way had an even stronger magnetism. Today, Prairieville is fundamentally shaped by Airline Highway, to the point that one might surmise that this Main Street-like artery explains the community's existence. In fact, the highway followed the railroad, whose station iterated a preexisting settlement, which originated as a halfway point on an old road to a furtive colonial community dating to the Revolutionary War. Prairieville today, considered a Census-Designated Place, has over 33,000 residents, and wending among its subdivisions are relics of the centuries-old claim dispute: an abandoned distributary called New River, a bayou named Conway, an enclave called Galvez, and a plantation house named Houmas.

Like Prairieville, Gonzales began tentatively during the era of the Houmas Claim, when by 1851 some Acadian settlers had either acquired or squatted upon a parcel abutting the New River distributary near its head of navigation up from Lake Maurepas. (Comparable sites downstream birthed the settlements of St. Amant and Acy, and all three were linked by New River Lane, parts of which are today's West New River Street, Weber City Road, and Highway 429.) By the 1860s, inhabitants at what they called Lower New River operated a small cotton gin at the site, followed in 1880 by a sugar house. In 1887, Joseph Gonzales, a descendant of Galveztown Isleños and the son of a well-known sheriff, opened a store and became postmaster at a new post office named Gonzales.

Gonzales was nearly renamed Edenborn by the Louisiana Railway & Navigation Company to honor its president, William Edenborn, as it constructed tracks through the area in 1905. The company had sited its station 2,000 feet north of Gonzales's perch on New River—enough, it was thought, to warrant a different name. Aggravated residents felt otherwise and took the matter to legislators, who passed a state law in 1910 compelling railroad companies to name their stations after adjacent post offices—and it has been "Gonzales" ever since.[18] The community got a surveyed street grid in 1906, incorporated as a village in 1922, and gained a vital perch on Airline Highway a decade later. That artery made Gonzales into a crossroads town at Burnside Avenue, the "main street" of the old Houmas Claim, transecting it perfectly north-to-south along a section line.[19]

Gonzales is now officially a city, and in the last thirty years its urban footprint has gravitated toward Interstate 10 in the style of an "edge city"—so much so that I-10 commuters might perceive modern Gonzales to be mostly the sprawling outlet malls surrounding Exit 177. But a century ago, that very spot was anything but Anywhere, USA, as Ascension Parish historian Sidney Albert Marchand described in 1931: "COLORED SETTLEMENT is situated two or three miles in a southwesterly direction from Gonzales, and consists almost entirely of ex-slaves and their descendants. When the vast New River territory was opened up for homestead entry (about 1888), nearly all of the settlers in the area made homestead claims, and were granted tracts of land ranging from forty to one hundred sixty acres. The homes of many of these old darkies, however, have passed into other hands. There are comparatively few white settlers in this section at present."[20] Colored Settlement is now gone from map and memory, having been subsumed by Gonzales (population 12,000), which itself has transformed into a bedroom community of Baton Rouge. The same is true for the next major settlement of the old Houmas Claim, Sorrento.

The siting story of Sorrento has more in common with far-away Gramercy, Garyville, and Livingston than with nearby Prairieville and Gonzales. That commonality was resource access, Sorrento being at the very brink of the grassy terrace—and thus a good jumping-off point into the 250-square-mile Maurepas Basin. What brought an Acadian family here in the 1860s was Bayou Conway (named for the same Maurice Conway behind the Houmas Claim), to which they gained access via a slight upland that became a road—today's Highway 22. "Conway" remained a small hamlet until the Louisiana Railway & Navigation Company built its track bed in 1905, at which time the settlement got a post office named for postmaster Edmund Landry. Two years later, the name of the post office was changed to that of the new station, Sorrento, said to have been selected by railroad president and German immigrant William Edenborn because he had taken his bride to Sorrento, Italy, for their honeymoon.

The railroad drew attention from lumbermen, who viewed Sorrento as a perfect milling location for cypress and tupelo trees cut from the Maurepas Basin. By 1910, the Opdenweyer-Fisher Cypress Company and the Ascension Red Cypress Company established mills here or in nearby Elroy, and workers and their families settled in the new timber/railroad community of Sorrento. But soon the old-growth timber began to disappear, and the Opdenweyer mill closed in 1921, though a veneer mill opened in 1925. Sorrento became an extraction site for other Maurepas resources, including Spanish moss, bullfrogs, and, in 1929, petroleum, whose subsequent bust was mitigated by the circa 1933 opening of Airline Highway. Sorrento incorporated as a village in 1956 and as a town in 1962. Now home to over 1,500 people, Sorrento still has a small lumber and oil sector (Shell Sorrento), but mostly relies on Airline Highway and Interstate 10 for its economy.[21]

Together, the communities of the old Houmas Claim—Prairieville, Gonzales, Sorrento, among others—evidence a number of "laws" geographers have observed in the hierarchy of urban functions: that proximate cities (in this case, Baton Rouge and New Orleans) grow *toward* each other, that cities tend to subsume outlying communities, and that with greater mobility (in this case, Interstate 10) larger cities relinquish some dominance to the very outlying communities they subsume.[22] Compare any historical map to a modern satellite image, and it is remarkable how Louisiana's two largest metropolises have drawn closer together in their sprawls—particularly on the old Houmas Claim, through which still wends Bayou Manchac.

Nine cities, towns, villages, and other communities were analyzed in the Bayou Manchac/Maurepas region for this study. Roughly 78 percent had riverine- or water-based primary siting stories (close to triple the state average of 29 percent), while 11 percent were primarily railroad sites, 11 percent were resource extraction or processing sites, and none were crossroads (compared to state averages of 33 percent, 10 percent, and 13 percent, respectively). Settlements began forming in this region in the 1760s, climaxed in the 1850s, and ended by the 1910s. Fully 78 percent of Bayou Manchac/Maurepas-area settlements emerged organically, the remaining 22 percent having been ordained by a founder—well off from the statewide split of 49 percent/51 percent emergent/ordained.[23]

7

THE EASTERN FLORIDA PARISHES

You can get there from here. Second only to ecological productivity, waterborne accessibility drew humans to lower Louisiana. Few places offered better ingress and egress to abundant resources than the Maurepas, Pontchartrain, and Borgne basins, with their rivers, creeks, bayous, lakes, passes, and bays spanning from terrace to delta. By pirogue, portage, and pluck, one could venture from timbered hills to tide-washed islands, traversing all the eco-zones from as high as 370 feet in elevation down to the level of the sea—all within twenty miles. Previously, we explored settlement in the western Florida parishes; now we move eastward to St. Helena, Livingston, Tangipahoa, Washington, and St. Tammany parishes.

Waterborne access led Natives to call this region Balbancha, for the many dialects heard along crisscrossing trade routes. Principal tribes north of *Okwa-ta*—"Big Water," Lake Pontchartrain—were the Tangipahoa, Acolapissa (Colapissa), and Choctaw, each of which favored riverside perches as settlement sites. One Acolapissa village was located four leagues up the river named Talcatcha (Taleatcha, later Hatcha), meaning "rock" or "stone." It was here where Bienville visited in 1699 and found the water good to drink, suggesting this site was above the head of tides, a plausible rationale for the village. Later, an English mapmaker translated *talcatcha* as "pearl," for the calcium accretions Natives collected from the shells they used to scrape out their dugout canoes. "Pearl" got applied to the larger river to the east, which is where a branch of the Choctaw tribe lived into the twentieth century—likely on Indian Village Road in eastern Slidell, overlooking a secondary channel of the Pearl River.[1]

Shortly after Bienville's visit, the Acolapissa moved to Castembayouque—Bayou Castine, in today's Mandeville—near another creek the Choctaw called Chinchuba, "alligator," now a bayou and neighborhood name. It flowed west of the larger Bayou Lacombe, where the Choctaw had an encampment known as Butchu'wa. Still farther to the west were the Bogu Falaya (Long River, now the Bogue Falaya) and its tributary, the Kefonctei (River of Oaks, now the Tchefuncte), and the Tanzipao, Choctaw for corncob or white corn, possibly indicating maize cultivation along today's Tangipahoa River.

All told, by the time of the French arrival, some 700 Acolapissas lived in six villages on the west bank of the Pearl River system near present-day Slidell. A few hundred Tangipahoas lived along their namesake river and a series of trails near present-day Madisonville, and another 500 Quinipissas-Mugulashas inhabited the Amite River area. Combined with those farther west, roughly 3,000 Natives occupied the 5,000 square miles between the Pearl and Mississippi rivers. Those numbers proved inadequate to marshal any sort of unified defense against European intrusion—and the tribes were hardly unified, what with shifting alliances, conflicts, mergers, and transpositions.[2] Incredibly, after two centuries of demise and displacement, some Choctaw persevered in remote corners of St. Tammany Parish long enough for ethnologist David I. Bushnell Jr. to record their folkways for the Smithsonian Institution. But then, "by an act of Congress on July 1, 1902," wrote Bushnell dispassionately in his 1909 bulletin, "they were persuaded to remove to the Indian Territory and receive an allotment of land."[3]

Under the new colonial regime, a few French settlers in what is now St. Tammany Parish made their livelihoods from the pine derivatives of charcoal, tar, pitch, and resin, used as sealant for roofs and ship hulls. "It is usually towards the mouths of the river, and along the sea-coasts, that they make tar," La Page du Pratz pointed out, "because it is in those places that the pines chiefly grow," and where the tar could be shipped across Lake Pontchartrain. As early as 1722, a Frenchman named Rousseau et La Combe established an operation presumably at the mouth of Bayou Lacombe where he and his slaves sent wood, charcoal, and bricks by schooner to help build New Orleans. By 1727, a census recorded sixteen colonists and thirteen slaves living north of the lake.[4] Three or four tar works operated elsewhere along the lakeshore by the 1730s, including up Bayou Liberty and the Tchefuncte River, where Antoine Aufere had up to forty slaves laboring on the largest tar works. But these rustic industries never really spurred settlement agglomeration, probably on account of their arboreal nature, as well as the entrepreneurs' lack of title to the land. They extracted resources and moved on, with little need for permanency. The same may be said of two other early industries in the eastern Florida parishes, pelt harvesting and cattle ranching.[5]

The slow pace of land-granting reflected the limited fecundity of the region's hard clay soils. French authorities prioritized instead on the rich alluvial

Detail of the John Melish map shows the eastern Florida parishes as they stood in 1820, from the Amite River (*left*) to the Pearl (*right*). Library of Congress.

soils along the Mississippi River and its distributaries, where arpenteurs laid out elongated lots for concessionaries to create plantations. Before the French could turn their attention to less fertile areas, their devastating 1763 defeat in the French and Indian War incurred the surrender of the lands across the lake to the British.

In 1766, English authorities inventoried their new colony for opportunities, and in what is now St. Tammany Parish they found "a Town on Lake Pontchartrain call'ed Tangipahou . . . inhabited by frenchmen & Choctaws," probably the first of its size in this era. A smuggler's paradise, Tangipahou saw deer pelts harvested by Indians come in on packhorses led by English traders. Instead of getting exported through Mobile to Great Britain, the pelts went south illegally to enemy New Orleans, "where they sell for as much as they do in London." Also shipped southward were pitch, tar, lumber, charcoal, lime, and cattle, all "contrary to Act of Parliamt." Imported from New Orleans, also illegally, were "Liquor &c," to which the French added "Rum, Powder, Ball & Blankets" to pay off their Choctaw trading allies. Worse yet, from the British perspective, "the French give them bad talks and poison their Minds against the English," a reminder of the lingering animus from the recent war.[6]

It is unclear where the rambunctious trafficking outpost of Tangipahou was located. Local historian Frederick S. Ellis put it on Bayou Bonfouca, Bayou Liberty, or Bayou Lacombe, making it an antecedent of Slidell or Lacombe; it also may have been at the mouth of the Tchefuncte or Tangipahoa, making it a forerunner of Madisonville. What all these sites had in common was their head-of-lake setting: each was at or near the mouths of navigable rivers emptying into a lake or bay, enabling trade with communities rimming the basin. Other examples of head-of-bay/head-of-lake sites in Louisiana include Pierre Part, Lake Arthur, Lake Charles, and Grand Lake.

In recognition of this siting advantage, British land grants in this region were all made "at the head of Lake Pontchartrain." They started with the "Tanchipaho Plantation" grant made for Francis DuPlanly (a.k.a. François Hery), continued with a grant "on a creek named Chefuncte" for John Jones, and proceeded as far east as the Rigolets into the 1770s. French travelers had given the lower Tchefuncte River area the name Coquille ("little shell") for its many rangia clams and oysters, which Anglophones shortened to "Cokie." Yet the British land grants never amounted to much; indeed, only seven in this area would be later recognized by American authorities, and none developed directly into modern towns. British authorities focused instead on the fertile loess bluffs by the Mississippi River to the west, or the seaports of Mobile and Pensacola to the east. Concerning the lands in between, the British, like the French prior, got distracted by a distant war, this one with American revolutionaries. After Spain declared war on Britain in 1779, the conflict came home to West Florida, resulting in the expulsion of the British. Now Spain would control West Florida, plus New Orleans and all of Louisiana, not to mention most of the hemisphere to the west and south.[7]

From 1779 to 1810, Spanish authorities increased the number of land grants elevenfold within the Distrito de Chifoncte, today's Washington and St. Tammany parishes. There was good reason: with New Orleans constantly rebuilding after six hurricanes and two fires between 1776 and 1794, resources across the lake took on new value. "The wild lands are finely timbered with pine, live oak, cypress, magnolia, plum, gum, bay, cottonwood, ash, [and] willow," wrote an observer two decades later. "The pine timber is remarkably tall and strait, with trunks from 70 to 80 feet high before coming to the limbs, [and] will furnish an inexhaustible supply" of lumber, tar, and pitch "for a century to come."[8] The underlying Pleistocene Terrace also provided fine clay that was superior for brick-making compared to the clay particles deposited by the Mississippi River.

One grant went to Jean Baptiste Baham in 1783 for 1,000 arpents along the Tchefuncte River. Another went in 1785 to district commandant Charles Parent, where he would amass a herd of 1,500 cattle along the lower Tchefuncte. Being at the head of a lake by the mouth of a navigable river above its head of tides, this site, formerly Coquille or Cokie and now Chifoncte, was ideal for boat building, with its harbor-like setting and timber and tar nearby. Enough people had settled near the mouths of the Tchefuncte, Bayou Bonfouca, and

Bayou Lacombe between 1797 and 1805 to enable the construction of a number of schooners. Around that same time, two Spanish officials with the titles of "Alcalde [Mayor] of the Tchefuncta" and the "Syndic of Bayou Lacombe and its dependencies" were living in the area, further indicating community formation.[9]

Ten river miles up the Tchefuncte, a French Creole named Jacques Dreux (Drieux) attained a Spanish land grant on the west bank of the Bogue Falaya, at its head of navigation above the two rivers' confluence. It made an ideal site for an interior landing, dubbed the Barrio de Buck Falia, working in tandem with the lake port of Chifoncte. Around 1805, Dreux laid out four squares along the Bogue Falaya River, intending to build a town he would call St. Jacques. Although Dreux never followed through on the project, his intent signaled the promise many saw in this pleasant and resource-rich region.

Geopolitical changes helped agglomerate early rural dispersions into lasting settlements. First came the secret retrocession of Louisiana by Spain to France in 1800, followed by the subsequent sale of Louisiana by France to the United States in 1803. Seven years later, unhappy Anglo colonists in West Florida rebelled against the Spanish, launched the Republic of West Florida, and ended up under the dominion of the United States. Spain and the United States eventually signed the Adams-Onís Treaty of 1819, which, after ratification in 1821, officially gave Louisiana its boot shape. It was during those interregnum years that colonial-era settlers dispersed along the Lake Pontchartrain shore began to cluster into bona fide towns—namely Barrio de Buck Falia at a river confluence and head-of-navigation site (today's Covington), and Chifoncte at a head-of-lake site (today's Madisonville).

The creation of Covington involved an Anglo-American family originally from Philadelphia, starting with Captain William Wharton Collins, who shipped mail from New Orleans up the Tchefuncte River into Spanish territory. Recognizing the region's opportunities, William urged his brother, John Wharton Collins, to come to Louisiana and open a mercantile firm in New Orleans. Their two sisters came as well, and as the newcomers sailed across the lake on William's schooner, they apparently liked what they saw—in more ways than one. Both sisters eventually married members of the Badon family, who owned land on the Bogue Falaya just down from Jacques Dreux's stalled St. Jacques town project at Barrio de Buck Falia. John Wharton Collins, meanwhile, set his eyes on land adjacent to the Dreux tract, for which he obtained a Spanish grant. A few years later, under American governance, he purchased 1,600 acres from Dreux and designated a section as the town of Wharton. Collins then hired New Orleans surveyor-engineer Joseph Pilié to lay out a street plan. Pilié's grid

Columbia Landing on the Bogue Falaya River (*left*) represents Covington's origin as a head-of-navigation site among multiple confluences, in a region rich in resources and resort opportunities. At right is the 1819 former courthouse in the Claiborne Hill section of Covington, now among the oldest surviving structures in the vicinity. Photographs by Richard Campanella.

contained unusual features: each square had at its center "a plot of 120-by-120 feet that was set aside for public use [and] accessed by alleys to adjacent streets." The interior spaces "became known as 'ox lots,' because farmers and draymen who brought produce or products . . . such as bricks, lumber, tar, pitch and charcoal, sheltered their ox teams and wagons or carts there."[10] In 1816, the state legislature incorporated the town but changed its name to honor Leonard Covington, the late brigadier general who had helped get the short-lived West Florida Republic annexed into the United States.[11] Following a century of ad hoc settlement, the town of Covington finally blossomed, and with compelling rationales: a landing among multiple confluences at the head of navigation in a region ripe for resource extraction as well as resort opportunities.[12]

Covington would later become an administrative center, but not before getting some cross-river competition. In 1819 the Claiborne Company planned an adjacent town for the express purpose of hosting the St. Tammany Parish courthouse. Two decades on, Claiborne failed to garner momentum, probably for its lack of natural advantages, and in 1837 the parish seat was relocated back across the Bogue Falaya. Covington has been the St. Tammany Parish seat of justice ever since, and is now a prosperous city of nearly 12,000 people, a bedroom community to New Orleans, and, increasingly, an economic hub in and of itself. Its well-maintained downtown features access to scenic river landings, a historic hotel dating to Covington's resort days, and those old ox lots still set within Pilié's squares. In regard to the erstwhile cross-river subsidiary, old Claiborne is now the neighborhood of Claiborne Hill, and still has the majestic circa 1819 Creole structure that for eighteen years served as the parish courthouse.

If Covington were to succeed on the Bogue Falaya, it needed to work in tandem with Chifoncte at the head-of-lake site, where Jean Baptiste Baham had his land grant and where cattle ranching and boat building had been ongoing. Sometime between 1810 and 1813, Baham identified a dry point near the mouth of the Tchefuncte, named it Madisonville for the U.S. president who oversaw the annexation of West Florida, and had it surveyed into lots. Three subsequent developments reinforced Baham's site selection: the 1815 construction of a military road linking Madisonville with the Natchez Trace, the 1819 advent of steamboats plying Lake Pontchartrain, and the 1820 construction of a larger military road heading north-northwest to Nashville. Within a few years, Madisonville became the "best harbor for vessels in lake Pontchartrain" and a waypoint for those "travelling from New-Orleans to Natchez by the route of the latter lake." It incorporated as a town in 1817, serving as a terrestrial crossroads and maritime hub, home to a U.S. Navy shipyard.[13]

In 1817, immigration advocate Samuel R. Brown published a glowing account of the "handsomely situated" new town of Madisonville, "unquestionably destined to become a great commercial city. It is favorably situated for the coasting and West India trades," implying that its perch by brackish Lake Pontchartrain effectively made Madisonville a coastal city. It was also a resource extraction site and shipbuilding harbor, "convenient for the necessary supplies and materials for repairing and building vessels, [such] that government have fixed on the site of a navy yard near the mouth of the Chefuncti." Enjoying lake breezes and far from the urban multitudes, Madisonville "is believed to be a more healthful situation, and less infected with musquetoes, than New Orleans." Madisonville became a chief supplier of forest products and beef on the hoof, the latter to an extraordinary degree. "The country above Madisonville," wrote Brown, "is peculiarly adapted to the rearing of hogs and cattle; for they neither require salt, nor attention in winter; and nowhere in the United States are they raised in greater numbers than [here]. The reed cane, and the grass of the prairies constitute their principal food."[14] Madisonville was the perfect place to ship the fattened beasts to city abattoirs across the lake.

In the century ahead, Madisonville's marine economy did well enough to grow the population to over 1,000, not far behind Covington. Boat building became the principal economic sector, involving some fifteen family-owned outfits. The largest was the Jahncke Shipyard, which during its 1910s heyday employed hundreds of men to construct deep-draft vessels in five enormous shipways. But contracts greatly diminished after World War I and World War II. Unable to compete with Avondale, the shipbuilding industry petered out by the 1960s. Isolated from modern interstates, Madisonville has since diminished to a fraction of the size of Covington. Few locals seem to mind, as their community has happily transformed "from a sometimes rough-and-tumble shipyard," as one journalist put it, "to a quaint and quiet corner of St. Tammany Parish that managed to maintain its small-town charm while coping with explosive growth." Today Madisonville is a bedroom community and watersports destination, still very much tied to the Tchefuncte River and Lake Pontchartrain.[15]

History buffs point out that ten flags have flown over Louisiana since La Salle first planted the Fleur de Lis in 1682. "In reality," wrote historian Samuel C. Hyde Jr., those ten banners "enjoy association exclusively with the Florida parishes; only eight flew over the remainder of the state."[16] Hyde took that disparity to draw attention to the "more curious, colorful, and perhaps contentious" history of this "fierce and fractious frontier," one that involved four rival nations, disputed borders, ethnic hostilities, duplicitous treaties, and a bold rebellion whose resolution brought the American flag to the region. The first priority for the United States was to blaze military roads to secure the rogue territory. Spain, after all, had rebuked the 1810 West Florida Rebellion and did not recognize the subsequent American annexation; while the two nations had long enjoyed amity, conflict now seemed possible.

The new military roads, parts of which had followed old Indian and game trails, were difficult to blaze and rough to ride. One, constructed during 1811–1812 to connect northern Alabama with the Mobile area and extended westward to St. Francisville, came to be known as General Wilkinson's Road. Another, blazed in 1815, ran from Madisonville northward to Jackson, Mississippi, and was known as General Carroll's Road. The third, General Jackson's Road, proposed by Old Hickory himself and completed in 1820, ran from Nashville through Florence in Alabama and Columbus in Mississippi, to Covington and Madisonville in Louisiana.[17] Together with spurs and connectors, the eastern Florida parishes' network of military roads became the premier settlement-makers of the 1810s through the 1850s.

General Wilkinson's Road, for example, helped pinpoint a site for St. Tammany Parish's original seat of justice. That jurisdiction had been created in 1810 as part of Louisiana governor William C. C. Claiborne's effort to annex West Florida; its name honored Chief Tamanend, the Delaware Indian peacemaker who was later lionized as the "Patron Saint of America" and became a popular namesake. Like most of Louisiana's original parishes, St. Tammany was laid out expansively, incorporating all of present-day Washington and much of Tangipahoa, which meant that a centralized parish seat would be inconvenient to most inhabitants who lived near the Lake Pontchartrain shore. That's where General Wilkinson's Road came in, as it crossed the Bogue Chitto River near the center of the parish, making the interior more accessible and thus viable as a seat of justice. Marked on maps simply as St. Tammany Court House, the parish seat became a ferry crossing and country crossroads. But when Washington Parish was carved out of St. Tammany in 1819, the tiny administrative center relinquished its role southward to Claiborne in 1819, followed by Covington in 1837, while the new Washington Parish seat went northward to Franklinton during 1823–1826. Now in the proverbial middle of nowhere, the site of old St. Tammany Court House is marked only by a historical plaque four miles west of Enon.[18]

Continuing east along General Wilkinson's Road was a crossroads on the Bogue Luca River near its confluence with the Pearl, a decent landing site except that navigation on the Pearl was often impeded by logjams. What instead brought settlement to this spot was a forerunner of a future industry based on the parish's upwellings of refreshing artesian water. Marked as Mineral Springs on two 1820s maps, this crossroads with General Jackson's Road may be categorized as a resource extraction site near today's Sheridan, between Franklinton and Bogalusa.[19]

Proceeding west of Madisonville, three settlements could be found along a spur of General Wilkinson's Road. The oldest and largest was Springfield, whose siting story began in 1763 under the British regime as Bookter's Landing, head of navigation on the Natalbany River. For that same reason the site later became a Spanish defensive position, and was surveyed for parcels in 1801, making it one of the earliest towns in the vicinity. The new military road put Bookter's Landing on a pathway linking Madisonville with the Natchez Trace, making it an alternative route between the two most important cities on the lower Mississippi River, New Orleans and Natchez. The town became a seat of justice and administrative center after Livingston Parish was carved out of St. Helena in 1832, and incorporated in 1838 under the name of Springfield to herald its natural wells. The circa 1835 courthouse still stands, despite the fact that Springfield has lost all its formative siting rationales—including as parish seat, relinquished to Port Vincent in 1872, to Centerville (a.k.a. Springville) in 1881, and to Livingston in 1941. Historic Springfield has nevertheless managed to retain a stable population of around 400 residents.[20]

The next community from Madisonville out to General Wilkinson's Road is marked as St. Helen Courthouse on the 1820 Melish map. This site became a parish seat starting in 1812, when the military roads were being blazed, and later gained the name Montpelier. Adjacent to its courthouse was the Land Office, an important federal clearinghouse for the titling and distribution of public lands between the Pearl and Mississippi Rivers. It was also home to an early post office (1814) and the Montpelier Academy (1833). But around that time, St. Helena Parish was split to create Livingston Parish to its south, thus

At left is the old Livingston Parish Courthouse (1835) in Springfield, a head-of-navigation site that became a defensive position and later an administrative site, but has since lost all its historical rationales. At right, the Greek Revival–style former Federal Land Office stands adjacent to the Art Deco–style St. Helena Parish Courthouse in Greensburg. Photographs by Richard Campanella.

killing Montpelier's centrality. In 1832, the new seat of justice went to better-positioned Greensburg, sited on a bluff above the Joseph Branch near General Wilkinson's Road, and where, in 1837, land was donated by William Kendrick for a new courthouse. Montpelier has since settled into village status, no longer an administrative center or a stopover to Natchez, but still managing to retain 200 residents for the past century. Greensburg, home to 630 people, remains the seat of justice, and its Greek Revival–style Land Office still stands in Kendrick Square, in the shadow of the Art Deco–style St. Helena Parish Courthouse.[21]

At the crossing of the Madisonville spur of General Wilkinson's Road arose a settlement marked prominently enough in 1820 for one to expect that it might endure today. But the vagaries of human geography gave "Spillers" no such destiny, for it does not appear to have any siting rationale beyond those two old military roads. All that remains today is a creek named Spillers just west of Amite City. The military roads had a similar fate: despite remaining in use well into the twentieth century, most eventually returned to field or forest. Only one short segment running northeast of Covington, designated as Highway 1082, is still officially known as the Old Military Road.

The 1830s brought invigoration to cross-lake relations. The Pontchartrain Railroad and New Basin Canal had just opened, giving New Orleanians direct access to Lake Pontchartrain. Combined with the Old Basin Canal and Bayou St. John, these three arteries motivated the formation of Milneburg, West End, and Spanish Fort as jumping-off points to the entire basin. A fleet of steam packets began regular lake service, busying Madisonville and other landings with raw materials, cargo, passengers, and new opportunities.

One opportunity came in 1831 via the Pontchartrain Railroad, whose terminal served the New Orleans faubourg (suburb) developed by Bernard Xavier Philippe de Marigny de Mandeville immediately below the French Quarter. A maverick and *bon vivant,* Marigny was a major real estate developer, and among his properties across the lake was Green Point, a shoreline promontory he had purchased in 1829 and made into the Fontainebleau Plantation. Marigny subsequently acquired lakeshore land to the west of Fontainebleau, between Bayou Chinchuba and Bayou Castine, where he created a resort for New Orleanians now able to travel comfortably across the lake. There was good reason to do so during the late summer "sickly season," when people of means sought to escape the fetid metropolis and its frightful epidemics. Physicians viewed the city's backswamp as the source of miasmas causing maladies such as yellow fever and malaria (literally "bad air"), while the fresh air and pine forests across the lake struck them as both a respite and remedy. In 1834, Marigny had his land subdivided as a resort town named Mandeville, and stipulated that its lakefront would remain without "any edifice whatsoever[,] forever free and for common usage," so that patrons could bathe and bask in unobstructed breezes.[22] Aided by ferry service that Marigny provided from Milneburg, Mandeville became popular for its hotels, eateries, and recreational facilities, and it would grow to become the largest community directly fronting Lake Pontchartrain.

Mandeville's rationale was that of a resort, sited for access to appealing environs. The happenstance of Marigny's land acquisition also played a role, though the site did have natural advantages, being slightly higher than the lake's otherwise marshy shore.[23] It was also adjacent to Bayou Castine, Little Castine, and Bayou Chinchuba, the last of which gave rise to a sister community known as Lewisburg. A savvy real estate developer, Marigny knew what he was doing in connecting his namesake resort with his namesake New Orleans neighborhood. "For Mandeville and Madisonville," read a typical ad in *Daily Picayune* in the hot August of 1841. "We take this opportunity to announce . . . that the steamboats *Mazeppa* and *Walker* will leave this afternoon for the above pleasant places of resort. Now, any of you who wish to put out, must be at the Pontchartrain Railroad by 4 o'clock, P.M., or you'll miss out."[24]

Mandeville demonstrated that the eastern Florida parishes could turn their aseptic environs into moneymakers. With lake breezes, pine forests, and clean springs and rivers, the undulating countryside seemed the antithesis of pestilential New Orleans. City dwellers of means who previously fled in droves every August through October for distant Grand Isle or Biloxi now arrived at nearby Mandeville, Madisonville, or Covington.

Artesian springs became a particularly attractive siting rationale, providing

Lakefront recreational opportunities (*left*) near Bayou Castine (*right*) explain the siting of Mandeville in St. Tammany Parish. Photographs by Richard Campanella.

a refreshing alternative to the gritty river water and stagnant cisterns of New Orleans. Among the first was Mineral Springs in Washington Parish, though this remote roadside stopover probably never garnered permanent settlers. In the early 1850s, investors Joseph Bossier and William Christy acquired land by an upwelling in the scenic woodlands east of Covington. They named it Christy Springs, built cottages, and established an omnibus line to connect it with steamer service to New Orleans. A journalist who visited in 1855 raved of "the sparkling liquid that gushes from the springs" and "the bracing air, impregnated with the odor of the pine," recommending Christy Springs for "the healthy as well as the invalid."[25] By 1856, the community changed its name to that of a nearby river, the Abita, reputedly of Indian origins, and its tourism trade fared well into the twentieth century. Now a bedroom community and still a weekend getaway, scenic Abita Springs continues to benefit from its artesian groundwater, brewing popular Abita Beer and exporting bottled springwater region-wide. The steadily growing town of 2,700 people is a paragon of a resort site predicated on the best type of resource extraction: the renewable type.

Mandeville and Abita Springs demonstrated the economic viability of health tourism, just as Madisonville and Covington had previously done for natural resources and shipping. All three sectors made clear that developing the Florida parishes depended on transportation access. Impressed by the success of the Pontchartrain Railroad, investors in the mid-1830s conceived a second line from New Orleans, this one going westward around the lake and up to Jackson, Mississippi. They got so far as to identify one Peter Hammond as the owner of a key Livingston Parish property through which the tracks would have to pass. But the Panic of 1837 derailed their plan, and it would take another decade, plus out-of-state financial support, to get it back on track. In 1851,

The spring that gave rise to Abita Springs is memorialized with a statue of a Native American, while the health resort economy that helped Abita Springs grow is remembered in the town's logo, "Where Nature Performs Miracles." Photographs by Richard Campanella.

investors from Illinois teamed with locals to form the New Orleans, Jackson & Great Northern Railroad Company and attain everything they needed to lay the tracks, including permission from landholders like Peter Hammond. Work began in 1853, and by the next year New Orleans's first interstate railroad became a whole new settlement vector in what was then Livingston and St. Helena parishes.[26]

In September 1855, a group of excited journalists joined the president of the NOJ&GN on a junket up the so-called Grand Trunk Railroad. Waxing poetic on the "verdure, delicate flowers of every hue" amid the "innumerable other denizens of the vegetable kingdom that flourish on our fertile soil," the journalists recorded the embryonic communities forming around the railroad's flag stops and depots. There were "clearings and fields, cottages and gardens, log-huts and small-stock, villages and hotels, stores and work-shops, mills and wells" all around "crowded stations, filled with produce and freight lately received or awaiting transport." Among the new communities were "Kennersville . . . on the plantation of Mr. Kenner," followed by "the next stopping place, Frenier," in St. John the Baptist Parish, which was about to get a post office. Next came the isthmus between lakes Maurepas and Pontchartrain and across Pass Manchac to "Ponchatoula station, forty-seven miles from the city," gateway to the "far famed 'Piney Woods.'" Then on to "Tickfaw, [which] has the river Tangipaho flowing past it . . . and the Natalbony, a branch of the Tickfaw." Next were "the pretty and flourishing village of Amite" with "its inviting hotel [and] fine steam saw mill," and "Tangipaho station," its depot full of "waiting passengers, and of freight of all kinds: oxen and wagons, laden with cotton," and finally Osyka, across the Mississippi state line. "A more pleasant day is rarely spent on such an excursion," the reporter concluded. "Success, we say, to the Grand Trunk Railroad."[27]

Ponchatoula is a quintessential railroad town, founded in 1855 along the New Orleans, Jackson & Great Northern as one of a number of stations from Kenner to Kentwood. Another site activated by the railroad was Hammond (note the locomotive in the mural at right), established in 1861 as a rail-side shoe manufacturing facility. Hammond today is the only railroad siting story in Louisiana that grew large enough to qualify as a U.S. Census Bureau Metropolitan Statistical Area. Photographs by Richard Campanella.

Maps of the late 1850s show these station-site settlements already sprouting crossroads. Each was separated by approximately ten miles, enough to create opportunities for sites to arise in between. Five miles from Ponchatoula, for example, became a perfect spot for a station, not just because it was halfway to Tickfaw but because two investors in 1861 had acquired land by Peter Hammond's holding to establish the C. E. Cate & Company, which manufactured shoes and milled lumber. "Hammond's Crossing" was ideally sited, being convenient to urban demand yet isolated enough to host a malodorous tannery, near cattle pastures for cowhides, and by woodlands for timber. It benefitted additionally when Confederate commanders established Camp Moore by "Tangipaho station," to train soldiers to fight Federal troops. In 1862, Cate & Company won a contract to supply footwear for the Confederacy, and soon Hammond Crossing bustled with more work than it could handle. That ended decisively in 1863, when Union troops destroyed the shoe factory, sawmill, and railroad, putting Cate & Company out of business—and Hammond out of the Civil War.

Hammond recovered with the rebuilding of the railroad, which in 1874 became the New Orleans, St. Louis & Chicago, and in 1878 the Illinois Central (IC). By then the state had carved out Tangipahoa Parish (1869) from parts of St. Helena, Livingston, Washington, and St. Tammany. In testimony to their importance, the railroad and its station-stop settlements determined the elongated shape of the new jurisdiction, a peculiarity among Louisiana's sixty-four parishes.

In 1885, the IC initiated a marketing strategy that would have lasting impact on the eastern Florida parishes. Looking to invigorate business in the South, the Chicago-based corporation designated Tangipahoa Parish "a land point, to be advertised throughout the Northwest [today's Midwest] as having some special attractions in the way of good climate, cheap lands, nearness to New Orleans, etc., and to which point Home Seekers' tickets would be sold monthly from all Illinois Central points north of the Ohio River."[28] The effort emulated what the Southern Pacific Railroad had been doing since 1883 in southwestern Louisiana, recruiting Anglo-Saxon farmers from Iowa to settle on the prairie so that they would pay tribute to its line (thus the town of Iowa near Lake Charles.) Extolling warm climes and fertile soils, agents advertised for midwestern farm families to pack up, climb aboard, and resettle down in Kentucky, Tennessee, Mississippi, and Louisiana.

Here in Tangipahoa, IC officials persuaded the Cate family to sell some of their land, which had formerly pertained to Peter Hammond. In 1887, the affiliated Iowa and Louisiana Land and Lot Company began laying out parts of modern-day Hammond. Well into the twentieth century, the IC Passenger Department employed a General Immigration Agent based in Iowa who worked specifically with Tangipahoa Parish, using Hammond as its "land point" in arranging ticket sales and land deals. Combined with local and regional settlement, the IC strategy helped triple the parish population, from 9,600 people in 1885 to roughly 30,000 by 1910. Hammond became the main trade center, attaining incorporation in 1889 and surpassing 1,500 in population in 1900. After gaining highway access and landing a state university, Hammond has grown nearly every decade since, surpassing 21,000 people in 2022 and remaining the largest city in Tangipahoa Parish, triple the size of second-place Ponchatoula.[29]

At first glance, Hammond's siting story is that of a classic railroad town, with its vibrant downtown organized around a still-active Amtrak passenger station. The story has served Hammond well: of all Louisiana's railroad towns, Hammond is among the most robust, with a diversified economy, a four-year university, and double interstate access to two nearby metropolises. But that story has some interesting twists. While Hammond postdated the railroad tracks, it predated the train station, having arisen initially as a trackside manufacturing center. Yet its urban grid postdated the station, thanks to the Iowa and Louisiana Land and Lot Company. And to this day, downtown Hammond has a midwestern ambience, just as the company's name insinuated.

As for the IC land-point strategy, it did for the eastern Florida parishes what the Southern Pacific had done for the southwestern prairie: impart a Protestant Anglo-Saxon demographic and midwestern farming heritage to Louisiana's piney woods. The policy helped create greater New Orleans's dairy belt—that peripheral region where intensive agriculture, including dairy cows and strawberry and vegetable farms, found fertile soils and inexpensive land linked to urban demand. Wrote one contented IC-line transplant from Peoria, Illinois, in 1903, "Nine years ago this fall we moved to Hammond, Louisiana, where I have been engaged in gardening, fruit culture and dairying, receiving reasonable compensation for my efforts. Our climate is second to none. An artesian well is easily secured at a very nominal figure, producing the purest of water. . . . We like it here; the North has lost its attractions."[30]

The IC sprouted additional settlements at five-mile intervals up and down Tangipahoa Parish. Midway between Hammond and Tickfaw, for example, arose the trackside community of Natalbany, halfway between Tickfaw and Amite sprouted Independence, evenly distributed between Amite and Tangipahoa were Roseland and Fluker, and midway between Tangipahoa and Osyka was Kentwood. Independence went from merely "a siding in the pine woods" in 1885 to a town of 1,200 residents in 1910, amid 4,000 acres producing 282 carloads of strawberries annually, thanks to midwestern transplants as well as Sicilian immigrants—to the point that the town became known as Little Italy and now celebrates a Sicilian Heritage Festival. Kentwood, "not on the map in 1885, now [in 1910] claims a population of 4,000," with budding potential for "dairying, strawberry growing and truck farming." The same was said of Roseland, "another northern settlement" of families from places like Michigan and Pennsylvania, which had been "a field covered with pine stumps twenty years ago [and is now] an interesting city of 600 people."[31]

Many of the IC towns also got sawmills, and all benefited from artesian springs. One well in Roseland, owned by S. E. Hostetter, looked like a Texas-style oil derrick; another in Kentwood produced highly desirable water that is bottled and exported to this day. Amite did doubly well in this era, as the 1869 creation of Tangipahoa Parish earned it a courthouse and made it an administrative center as well as station-stop site. Taken together, the ten communities traceable to that circa 1855 railroad are home to one-third of the population of Tangipahoa Parish. Every station became a highway crossroads, and some got railroad spur lines. Those emanating arteries sprouted their own settlements, among them Robert, Loranger, Wilmer, and Bolivar to the east, and Baptist, Pumpkin Center, Albany, Holden, and Livingston to the west.

The Livingston Parish community of Albany has a particularly interesting settlement history. Initially a standard Louisiana railroad town, Albany's timber attracted the Brackenridge Lumber Company, which in 1896 advertised in northern cities for dollar-a-day workers to come down to its milling operation. Some immigrants in Cleveland, Ohio, saw the ads in the Hungarian newspaper *Szabadság* and moved their families down to Albany to work at the lumber mill. By 1906, however, sawyers had denuded the forests, and Brackenridge "cut and ran" to the Pacific Northwest. Before departing, the company surveyed its "stumplands" into twenty-acre plots and offered them to the highest bidder. The Hungarians sent letters back to Ohio to persuade kin and kith to come down to Louisiana to buy the parcels. Being farmers by tradition, dozens more families rode the IC south to Hammond. By 1910, there were nearly 200 Hungarian immigrants in Albany, forming the community of Árpádhon; by the 1930s they numbered well over 1,000 living at what folks called Hungarian Settlement. Albany's siting story may well be that of a train station and sawmill, but what sustained it was a recruitment effort that produced the largest rural Hungarian-American community in the nation.[32]

Over the course of the nineteenth century, the eastern Florida parishes transformed from a politically contested landscape of pine savannahs, with the occasional cattle ranch and tar works, to a patchwork quilt of productive farms, industries, villages, and health resorts nestled among networks of roads and rails. The area's claim to fame was its wholesome environment, dubbed "the ozone belt" for the widespread belief that pine trees charged the atmosphere with balsam, a fragrant resin used as a salve (balm). Balsam, it was thought, yielded an electrical property understood to be ozone, which people perceived to cleanse the air of the malignant organisms causing miasmas. Adding to their argument were the cool artesian springs, clear sandy-bottom streams, and refreshing breezes rolling off the brackish lake, all of which exhilarated urbanites seeking respite from the congested metropolis.[33] Aiming to serve that city market, Mandeville-based investor George Ingram established in 1870 the New Orleans & Northeastern Railroad Company. Coordinating with steamboat and barge services, the company sought to run trains linking New Orleans with Mandeville, Lewisburg, and Sulphur Springs in Covington—not by going west through Manchac as the Grand Trunk Railroad had done in 1855, but by going east across the Rigolets and through St. Tammany Parish.

After seven years of work, a change in leadership, and the construction of a seven-mile trestle over water and marsh, the NO&NE Railroad in 1883 began service from a terminal named Halloo, later known as Pearl, Pearlville, and now Pearl River. Halloo became a hub for other tracks laid westward. In 1887, the East Louisiana Railroad opened from Pearl River to Abita Springs, followed in 1888 by trains to Covington, and in 1892 to Mandeville.[34]

Wherever rails went, stations sprouted, though not all would bloom into towns. Guzman, for example, was too flood prone, being a mere flag stop where the NO&NE first rolled off the trestle. Guthrie, meanwhile, was too far from lake resources, and only became an outpost called Alton. The station between Guzman and Guthrie, however, had various advantages, being on the higher Pleistocene Terrace, at the head of navigation of Bayou Bonfouca, aligned with the lakeshore communities of Lacombe and Mandeville to the west, and convenient to the densely forested Pearl River Basin to the east and north. One may also consider this site to be the dry point nearest to a head-of-lake location, akin to Lacombe and Madisonville. For these reasons, a sawmill, creosote works, and grocery store opened at what folks called the "Robert brick house," which itself became a lodge. Officials with the NO&NE used the Robert area as an encampment for their track layers and erected a station here in 1882. The following year, they surveyed the adjacent land for a town to be called Slidell Station. The name honored the late Louisiana politician and Confederate ambassador John Slidell, whose daughter married the French baron Frédéric d'Erlanger, an investor in the NO&NE.

By 1890, Slidell had 364 residents; by 1910 it had nearly 2,200, at which time historian Alcée Fortier described it as "one of the largest towns in the southeastern part of the state since the railroad was built," a "shipping and banking town for the large lumber district [at] the junction of two lines, [with] sawmills, brickyards, several factories [and] mercantile establishments."[35] Slidell became the new gateway to the eastern Florida parishes. Boarding in New Orleans at 6 a.m., one could arrive at Slidell by 7 a.m. and at Abita Springs by 8:40 a.m., enjoy a full day at a resort, and return by nightfall. Railroads made St. Tammany Parish into what promoters called "The Healthiest Place in America, in the Center of the World's Greatest Ozone Belt, the Most Famous Winter and Summer Tourists' Resort in the South."[36] Junctions at Slidell connected all of Orleans and St. Tammany parishes with Hammond and Kentwood in Tangipahoa Parish, with Bogalusa and Franklinton to Washington Parish, and with points beyond in every direction.

Two generations later, Slidell became home to a new type of junction, a rare triple merger of federal interstates and the busiest traffic interchange in the state. Opened in stages, I-10, I-12, and I-55 enabled a major exodus from New Orleans, making Slidell one of the fastest-growing cities in the nation in the 1970s. Today, Slidell is by far St. Tammany Parish's largest city, with 28,700 people living in subdivisions sprawling among the three vehicular "rivers." Slidell's siting story is that of a station-stop settlement with preexisting geographical advantages; today it is a bedroom community and travel center for motorists heading every direction of the compass.[37]

The lower Pearl River, like the Sabine at the opposite side of the state, was about as inviting to settlers as a gator's nest. Born of a compact watershed and named for the accretions in oysters, the Pearl River diverges into intricately braided channels meandering within a broad forested basin and discharging out multiple mouths. Native people made provisional use of this lush delta, but Europeans bent on settlement steered clear of what they saw as a murky

At left, a mural across from the train station on Front Street commemorates the siting story of Slidell in St. Tammany Parish. The postcard below shows the railroad-accessed lumber mill that birthed Bogalusa as an industrialized resource extraction and processing site. Photograph by Richard Campanella; postcard from Wikipedia Commons.

gateway to a mediocre interior. Samuel R. Brown advised as much in his *Emigrant's Directory.* "The swamps skirting this river for eight or ten miles from its mouths," he wrote in 1817, "are too subject to inundation to admit of extensive settlements," while its bottomlands are "covered with a heavy growth of cypress trees [and] rendered almost impassable by the reed cane." In terms of navigation, "rafts of driftwood" blocked sloops around seventy-five miles inland, where "during dry summers, is little more than ancle deep." The few minuscule settlements on the Louisiana side of the basin—Lima, Gordon Town, Violin, and Lee's Creek—materialized despite the Pearl, not because of it, and all have since disappeared. Their siting rationales were as jumping-off points to ferry across to the more solid Mississippi side of the Pearl, which had two better-suited landings, Gainesville and Pearlington. In this regard, what happened on the lower Pearl mirrored the lower Sabine 250 miles to the west, where the Texas side got all the action and the Louisiana side remained wild.[38]

What brought Louisianians closer to the Pearl River was the dovetailing of railroad construction and resource extraction—not to mention an enormous injection of New York capital. Starting in 1904, the Buffalo-based Goodyear lumber barons bought up vast acreages "in the very heart of the heavily wooded yellow pine belt," while affiliated investors launched the Great Southern Lumber Company and built the New Orleans & Northeastern Railroad (1906–1907) up from Slidell. Later called the New Orleans Great Northern and nicknamed "the Ozone Route," this line engendered a sequence of station-stop communities, including Florenville, Talisheek, Bush, and Sun in St. Tammany Parish and Varnado and Angie in Washington Parish. Once remote backwoods, the western Pearl River Valley was now ready for industry and settlement.[39]

So ready, in fact, that the Goodyears had a tent encampment set up for workers to build the kingpin of their bold enterprise: a sawmill unequaled in size and capacity, with a company town to match. It would be named Bogalusa, for the Pearl River tributary known as Bogue Lusa—"black water" in Choctaw.[40] An ordained settlement if ever there was one, Bogalusa had a carefully devised siting story, with criteria laid out point by point. "The transportation problem having been solved" by the construction of the company railroad, wrote Alcée Fortier in 1913, and with "water facilities provided by the Pearl river, the mill and town site was selected midway in the company's holdings, giving access to all sides of their timber." New Orleans architect Rathbone DeBuys laid out the town by zoning the north side of the Bogue Lusa River for commerce, the south side for the railroad terminal and massive mill, and the west and east sides for "homes of mill operatives"—whites to the west, and "colored and foreign" to the east, literally on the other side of the tracks.[41]

Built so swiftly that it was dubbed the Magic City, Bogalusa incorporated in 1914 and counted over 8,200 residents by 1920, most of them employed in what was said to be the largest mill in the world. Others worked at the magnificent Great Southern Hotel, built by the same timber/railroad interests as an "ideally situated home for Winter Tourists . . . in the heart of the Ozone Belt, the healthiest spot in the whole world"—despite the fumes of the nearby mill.[42]

During the 1920s, as old-growth yellow pine grew scarce and the Ozone Belt lost its credibility, Bogalusa shifted to paper and chemical manufacturing and avoided the fate of so many other timber towns. Its population surpassed 14,000 in 1930 and peaked in 1960 at over 21,000, placing Bogalusa second to Baton Rouge as the largest city in Louisiana's Florida parishes. Bogalusa also had outsized labor and racial discord over mill jobs and working conditions, circumstances more associated with the industrialized North or interior South than lower Louisiana. Problems of economic geography came to light as well, as Bogalusa's siting rationales—railroad transportation, old-growth timberlands, a water source, and spatial centrality—lost value by the late 1900s. In the decades since, Bogalusa's mill employment has plummeted, its population has halved, crime has soared, its environment has become polluted, and its isolation has become a liability. A plaque mounted at the entrance to one of Bogalusa's subdivisions, intended "as a memorial to Charles W. Goodyear, one of the founders of the city," reads like an epitaph: "On this tract of land there was a forest of virgin pine trees from which was cut the first log that was manufactured into lumber, at the sawmill of the Great Southern Lumber Company in 1908, and also the last log at the end of the lumber operations in 1938."[43]

If Bogalusa is the epitome of a company town sited for resource extraction, Franklinton is an exemplar of a parish seat sited for centrality. Selecting a viable spot near the center of 670 forested square miles, however, is a subjective task, especially in 1819, when the state legislature created Washington Parish. Clearly the courthouse ought to be by the Bogue Chitto River, being a semi-navigable waterway transecting the parish. The initial site, selected in 1819, may have been a preexisting settlement at a ford or ferry landing, and was named Franklin to match the parish name of Washington in honoring a Founding Father. Here, starting in March 1820, Colonel Thomas C. Warner presided as judge in a provisional courthouse.

But as often happened, a landholder elsewhere offered to donate space to build a proper courthouse, knowing that doing so would enhance real estate values. The donation came from John Bickham, who had settled along the Bogue Chitto River in 1799 at age twenty-two, participated in the West Florida Rebellion and the War of 1812, and had been sufficiently involved in politics to foresee the creation of Washington Parish in 1819. He offered thirty acres to host the new parish's courthouse and jail, as well as space to build a public school and for home sites to be sold for the benefit of the parish. There were geographical advantages as well: Bickham's land abutted the Bogue Chitto River at the crossing of the well-traveled Old Choctaw Trail, marking a spot area more centrally positioned within the parish. Too good to pass up, parish officials in 1823 departed the provisional courthouse for Bickham's land, which voters officially approved as the parish seat in 1826. By then, the town's name had been changed to Franklinton to avoid confusion with Franklin in St. Mary Parish. Both the town of Franklinton and the Washington Parish Courthouse have been on Bickham's land ever since.[44]

Maps for the rest of the century show Franklinton as the only substantial community in Washington Parish, all other settlements being little more than rural stopovers or crossroads. It had enough momentum to survive the loss of a third of its parish land to Tangipahoa Parish in 1869, a move that offset the town's spatial centrality and could have killed it. Franklinton instead regained traction with the 1907 opening of the Bogue Chitto Branch of the New Orleans Great Northern Railroad from Bogalusa, which made timber available to regional mills and birthed a sequence of new flag stops and stations to the east (Rio, Isabel, Zona, Pinecliff, and Jenkins) and northwest (Clifton and Warnerton). All these toponyms remain on the map, but hardly any have more than a handful of houses following the removal of the tracks. Modern highways have since supplanted railroads as settlement-makers in the eastern Florida parishes, yielding hamlets such as Mt. Hermon, Pine, Sheridan, and Enon. At the midway point southward between Franklinton and Covington is the St. Tammany village of Folsom, initially a sawmill site.[45]

Recent decades have been tough on rural Louisiana, and Washington Parish is no exception. Its population has flatlined since 1960, while Franklinton has declined by 12 percent since peaking in 1980. Located twenty miles from the nearest interstate and seventy miles from the closest metropolis, the town of 3,600 people relies heavily on its original role of administrative center, thanks to John Bickham's land donation of 1819—the same year the Florida Purchase officially gave Louisiana its eastern tier.

Despite being in southern Louisiana, the Florida parishes have a settlement-siting legacy more like that of northwestern Louisiana, limned mostly along overland roads, railroads, and highways. The region's main rivers—Bayou Sara, Thompson's Creek, the Comite, Amite, Tickfaw, Tangipahoa, Bogue Chitto, and the Pearl—have played only a secondary role in inferring where people live today, due to their limited navigability and untillable banks. With a political history as varied as its physical geography, the Florida parishes represent a counterpoint to the settlement patterns of the next southern Louisiana region to which we will turn our attention.

Of the twenty-six cities, towns, villages, and other communities in the eastern Florida parishes analyzed in this study, only 12 percent had riverine- or water-based primary siting stories (less than half the state average of 29 percent), while 62 per-

cent were primarily railroad sites, 8 percent were resource extraction or processing sites, and none were crossroads (compared to state averages of 33 percent, 10 percent, and 13 percent, respectively). Settlements began forming in this region in the 1810s, peaked in the late 1850s, and ended by the 1900s. This was railroad country, and communities mostly formed around train stations. Only 12 percent of eastern Florida parishes settlements emerged organically, the other 88 percent having been ordained, mostly by railroad executives or timber barons, far off from the statewide ratio of 49 percent/51 percent emergent/ordained.

8

THE ATCHAFALAYA BASIN

From the 1700s into the 1860s, settlers endeavored to get across or around the Atchafalaya Basin, not into it. Outposts formed primarily as cross-basin transit nodes between population centers to the east and prairies to the west. Not until the late 1800s did this vast bottomland offer advantageous settlement sites therein, the reason being the Atchafalaya River itself—a hydrological system whose natural complexity is exceeded only by what humans have done to it.

A millennium ago, the present-day Atchafalaya was the lowermost channel of the Red River, draining runoff as far away as New Mexico and discharging it broadly through what are now St. Mary and Terrebonne parishes. This began to change in the 1400s, when a crevasse opened on the Mississippi at the point where it came the closest to the Red, allowing water to lunge westward at Turnbull's Bend. The two rivers joined forces, and depending on their relative volumes, either's waters would veer down the other's channel. But because blockages formed on the lowermost Red, most waters within the converged systems made their way down the Mississippi, effectively making the upper Red an influx (tributary) of its larger neighbor. The little water that continued down the lowermost Red became an efflux (distributary) of the Mississippi, which the Choctaw described as "long river" and pronounced in a way than got written as "Chafalaya, Chiffalie, Chaffalia, Tchafalaya, Atchafa-Laya [or] Atchafalaya."[1]

What had been blocking the Atchafalaya was a colossal tangle of trunks, branches, and roots just below Turnbull's Bend, much like the logjams ("rafts") that clogged the Red River's upper valley. What also affected Atchafalaya hydrology was its many braided channels, which tended to disperse sediment broadly across the floodplain, like the Pearl River, instead of building up natural levees, like Bayou Lafourche or the Mississippi River. Lacking such ridges, most early Atchafalaya communities emerged as jumping-off sites along the basin's perimeter, intended to get people and cargo around or across the morass. The basin itself was one big settlement lacuna—"impassable by man," declared Amos Stoddard in 1812, "except along the water communications." Indeed, some travelers circumvented the Atchafalaya Basin altogether, sailing the "sea route" from points east and up Bayou Teche to the west. Others went northward on overland roads through Pointe Coupée, Avoyelles, and St. Landry parishes and dropped down into the Opelousas region on the other side.[2] Those who ventured across the basin needed points from which to make the jump, and that's why settlements formed along the perimeter.

On the eastern flank, the premier example was Plaquemine, that Mississippi River town sited at the distributary fork of Bayou Plaquemine. During springtime high water, that distributary became navigable back to Bayou Grosse Tete, and thence to Bayou Sorrel, Grand River, and interconnecting lakes and waterways, including the Atchafalaya River itself. Navigators could thus float their way to the western flank of the basin, where awaited what Thomas Ashe described in 1806 as "the two populous and rich settlements of Atacapas and Opelousas," today's St. Landry and Lafayette parishes. Here lived eager trading partners as well as fine cattle pastures, rice plantations, and all of Texas and the western frontier.[3] In 1817, Thomas Pipkin, who had established Plaquemine under its original name of Iberville, got state officials to clear out the bayou for steamers to provide regular service to the Attakapas region.[4] The journey across the Atchafalaya swamp was long, circuitous, and potentially dangerous. "We ran down the bayou [Plaquemine]," reported one navigator during the spring 1852 freshet; "the waters of which rush . . . with fearful violence, forming a continuous series of foaming rapids [with a] vast amount of drift timber."[5] Nevertheless, if the cargo and passengers came from the Mississippi River region, the Bayou Plaquemine route was the best option to cross the Atchafalaya Basin.

If the transit involved the Bayou Lafourche region, then the circa 1820 Attakapas Canal could be used to jump across the basin, from Napoleonville to Lake Verret and westward. This route activated the tiny Acadian community of Pierre Part, sited at the head-of-lake point of Lake Verret, as well as Belle River on the western shore and Stephenville to the south. Accessible only by boat well into the twentieth century, these communities were overwhelmingly Acadian, and until two generations ago mostly spoke French.

On the western side of the basin, a jumping-off site materialized where a slight ridge adjoined the navigable fork of Bayou La Rose and the Atchafalaya River, not far from where the Whiskey and Grand River channels connected with Bayou Plaquemine. Named Butte La Rose, this remote entrepôt became so strategic to cross-basin traffic that Confederate officials defended it with Fort

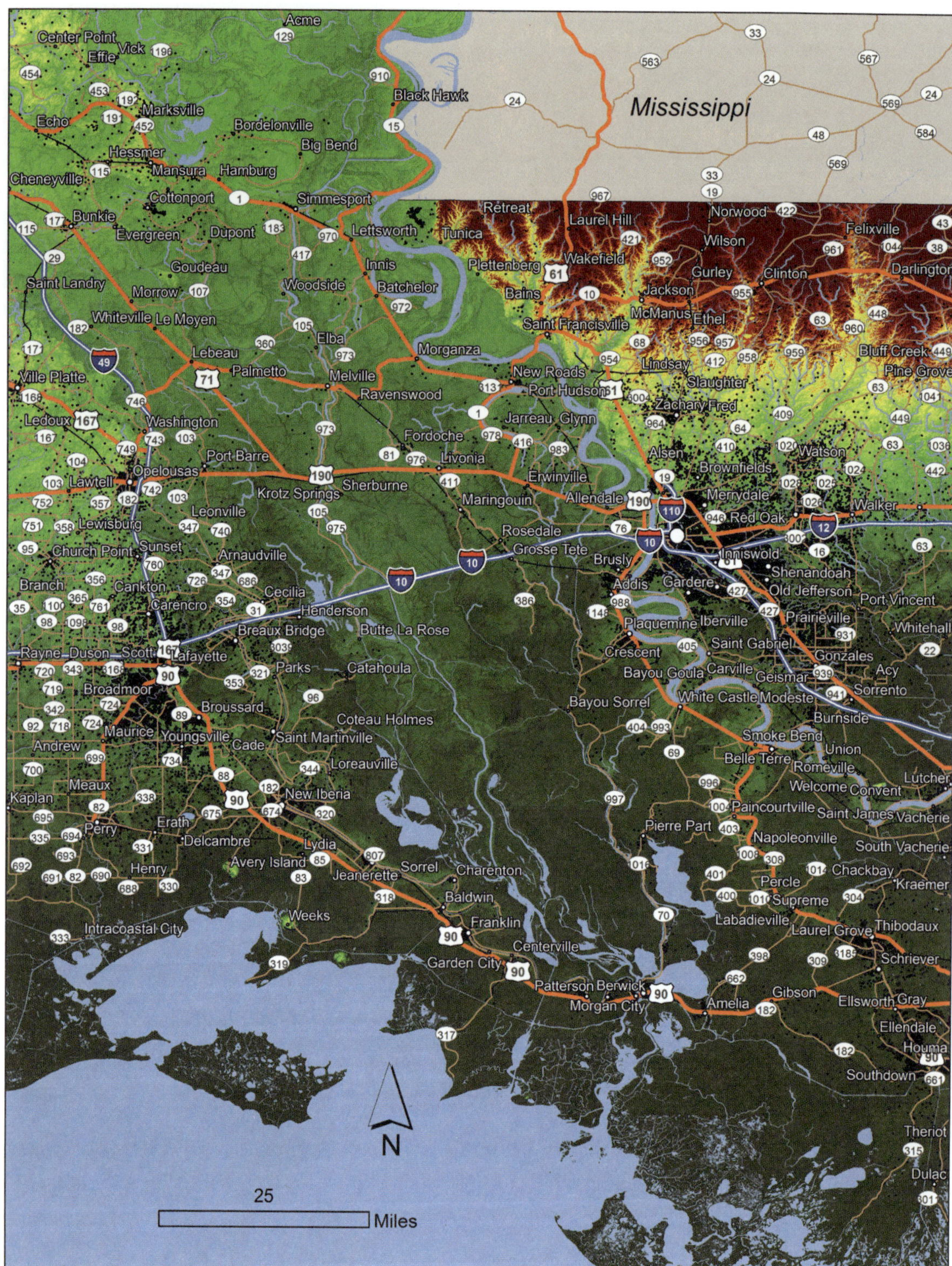
Mississippi
Acme
Center Point
Vick
Effie
Black Hawk
Marksville
Echo
Bordelonville
Big Bend
Hessmer
Mansura
Hamburg
Cheneyville
Cottonport
Simmesport
Bunkie
Evergreen
Dupont
Lettsworth
Tunica
Retreat
Laurel Hill
Norwood
Felixville
Wilson
Innis
Plettenberg
Wakefield
Gurley
Clinton
Darlington
Goudeau
Saint Landry
Woodside
Batchelor
Morrow
Bains
Jackson
Whiteville
Le Moyen
McManus
Ethel
Saint Francisville
Elba
Morganza
Bluff Creek
Lebeau
Palmetto
Melville
Lindsay
Pine Grove
Ville Platte
New Roads
Slaughter
Ravenswood
Port Hudson
Zachary
Fred
Ledoux
Washington
Jarreau
Glynn
Fordoche
Alsen
Watson
Port Barre
Livonia
Brownfields
Opelousas
Lawtell
Sherburne
Erwinville
Krotz Springs
Maringouin
Allendale
Merrydale
Walker
Leonville
Red Oak
Lewisburg
Rosedale
Sunset
Grosse Tete
Inniswold
Church Point
Arnaudville
Brusly
Shenandoah
Branch
Cankton
Addis
Gardere
Old Jefferson
Cecilia
Carencro
Port Vincent
Henderson
Plaquemine
Iberville
Prairieville
Whitehall
Breaux Bridge
Butte La Rose
Rayne
Duson
Scott
Lafayette
Saint Gabriel
Crescent
Gonzales
Parks
Catahoula
Carville
Acy
Bayou Goula
Geismar
Sorrento
Broadmoor
White Castle
Modeste
Broussard
Bayou Sorrel
Burnside
Coteau Holmes
Maurice
Youngsville
Saint Martinville
Smoke Bend
Union
Andrew
Cade
Belle Terre
Romeville
Loreauville
Lutcher
Meaux
Welcome
Convent
Kaplan
New Iberia
Paincourtville
Saint James
Vacherie
Erath
Pierre Part
Perry
Lydia
Napoleonville
Delcambre
South Vacherie
Avery Island
Sorrel
Chackbay
Henry
Charenton
Jeanerette
Percle
Kraemer
Baldwin
Supreme
Labadieville
Thibodaux
Franklin
Laurel Grove
Intracoastal City
Weeks
Centerville
Schriever
Garden City
Patterson
Berwick
Gibson
Gray
Morgan City
Amelia
Ellsworth
Ellendale
Houma
Southdown
N
Theriot
Dulac
25
Miles

Primary siting rationales of selected cities, towns, and villages
arterial increment
bridgehead
confluence/fork
courthouse/centrality
crossriver subsidiary
crossroads
head of lake
head of navigation
incarceration
jumping-off point
military
mission
port/landing
quarantine
railroad
resort
resource extraction
river mouth
shortcut/portage
Sunday town/centrality
25
Miles
N
Map and analysis by Richard Campanella

Butte La Rose in 1861, and Union forces targeted it for capture in 1863. A primitive road, and later a canal and railroad, linked Butte La Rose with St. Martinville on Bayou Teche, giving rise to the enclave of Catahoula as a secondary jumping-off site. Now fishing camp communities, Butte La Rose and Catahoula remain among the more populated spots in the lower Atchafalaya Basin, each with about 1,000 people.[6]

Another jumping-off point along the western basin was Port Barre, at the juncture of Bayou Teche and Bayou Courtableau, the latter of which flowed into the Atchafalaya River and offered access to Butte La Rose and Plaquemine. Originally a trading post where French *couriers* and Opelousas Indians bartered whisky and furs, the fork site came into the possession of Sieur Jacques Guillaume Courtableau, who in 1820 sold it to Alexander Charles Barré, who founded Barré's Landing. Later renamed Port Barre and serving as a steamboat dock for Opelousas-area cotton, the fork site was incorporated as a village in 1898 after gaining new life as a railroad junction and timber extraction site. Now a town along Highway 190, Port Barre, population 1,750, proudly calls itself the "Birth Place of Bayou Teche" on its town logo. Other jumping-off sites in the vicinity include the Bayou Teche communities of Charenton ("Indian Village"), Centerville, and Arnaudville, which, under the right conditions, connected by road and water with Livonia on Bayou Gross Tete—whose peninsula-like natural levee protruded into the Atchafalaya Basin and hosted the communities of Maringouin and Grosse Tete.[7]

Most other Atchafalaya residents lived not in towns or villages but in isolated camps or houseboats hither and yon, catching turtles, bullfrogs, alligators, and finfish or trapping furbearers for wholesaling. "Development of a fishing economy resulted in a dispersal of population, with remaining nodal points being Pierre Part, Butte la Rose, and Bayou Chene," wrote geographer Malcolm Louis Comeaux. "The reason[:] these people were now largely hunters and gatherers, with the only income being from the sale of fish. Since transportation was slow, fishermen had to live near their work, and population was thus dispersed and oriented toward streams."[8]

New settlement opportunities began to emerge in the 1840s, as contractors steadily dislodged the logjam obstructing the Atchafalaya River. Like the concurrent removal of the Red River rafts in northwestern Louisiana, this work aimed to open up regional navigational access, and in the process transform the Atchafalaya Basin from obstacle to asset. After most debris had been removed by the 1860s and 1870s, the navigable river enabled human movement and settlement to reconfigure basin-wide.

But the uncorking had unintended consequences. Water volume and alluvium augmented in the Atchafalaya River, and both flooding and sedimentation increased throughout the basin. That excess water came from the Red/Mississippi confluence, because, since the logjam was removed, it found a steeper and therefore shorter path to the Gulf via the Atchafalaya—140 river miles straight south, versus 315 miles to the southeast. If left unchecked, the Atchafalaya would eventually capture most or all of the lower Mississippi, upending every siting rationale in Louisiana's most important region. Such an avulsion had happened before, roughly once per millennium going back 7,000 years, and Native populations adapted by relocating. European colonizers, however, were not about to make such concessions; their settlements were designed to extract and accrue value, and the societies behind them intended to defend them from nature, just as they defended them from imperial rivals. Now, centuries later, the alterative was unthinkable: if the Mississippi River jumped into the Atchafalaya River channel, utter catastrophe would ensue for southeastern Louisiana, particularly for New Orleans, which would be left on one long estuary with neither a port nor potable water. In theory, such an avulsion would do the opposite for south-central Louisiana, making it the main portal in and out of the Mississippi Valley, and bolstering the value of the first high ground near the mouth of the Atchafalaya. That site is today's Morgan City, and its siting story is one of the most confounding in all of Louisiana.

What complicates Morgan City's siting story is the fact that its land base may be described as a variety of geographical features: a natural levee along a small bayou, a bank along a large river, an island, a peninsula (or two), and even a strait. Likewise, its adjacent water features may be labeled as lakes, bays, marshes, swamps, bayous, rivers (with multiple channels), passes, cutoffs, canals, and waterways, not to mention a delta and a spillway—each tidal to varying degrees, with salinity regimes ranging from fresh to brackish.

The area came upon the colonial docket in the 1780s, when Pennsylvania-born Thomas Berwick, who worked as a surveyor for the Spanish government in the Opelousas district, settled in the lower Atchafalaya region with his family. In 1797, Berwick's widow, Eleanor Wallace Berwick, and their son, Joseph, received a grant from Spanish governor Héctor de Carondelet for "seventy arpents of Tiger Island facing the east bank of the river Teche."[9] Other settlers attained nearby grants or purchased tracts, and some established sugarcane plantations, the largest of which was also on Tiger Island (named for its bobcats). That holding came into the possession of Walter Brashear (Brassier), a Maryland-born doctor of French origin. By that time, cattle raised in the Opelousas and Attakapas country found conduit to market by coming down Bayou Teche through Tiger Island—an area also known loosely as Berwick's

Bay—and proceeding eastward to New Orleans. Seeking to streamline the passage, Brashear invested in the Barataria & Lafourche Canal Company, and that corporate effort commenced in 1829 to dig a navigation channel from today's Westwego to Lockport on Bayou Lafourche (reached in 1841) and westward to Brashear's island on Berwick's Bay.[10]

Enough people settled in and around Tiger Island to warrant the establishment of a Catholic chapel in 1843, and the community that aggregated around it came to be known as St. Mary by 1849. Vessels by this time could enter the Atchafalaya River and make their way up Bayou Teche into St. Mary Parish, making St. Mary into a fork site. Economic vectors from every direction were now converging on Berwick's Bay, that strait-like feature straddling the lower Atchafalaya River.[11]

What finally motivated formal settlement was not the belated extension of the Barataria & Lafourche Canal, but a new competing conveyance. In 1853, investors obtained a state charter to build the New Orleans, Opelousas & Great Western Railroad "to a point on the Sabine River most favorable for the purpose of constructing said Road through the State of Texas to El Paso [and] thence to the Pacific Ocean."[12] That ambitious project had to first get around the Atchafalaya Basin, and to do that tracks had to be laid along that strait by Berwick's Bay.

The Great Western Railroad would start in Algiers across from New Orleans, connect with Thibodaux on Bayou Lafourche, proceed on trestles to Berwick's Bay, and follow a series of topographic ridges (today's Highway 90) to Opelousas, with eventual plans to reach Natchitoches and Texas. Work began in October 1852. By fall 1854, the line had made it to Bayou Lafourche, and in spring 1857 it reached Berwick's Bay.[13]

The coming conveyance motivated Walter Brashear, owner of a Tiger Island sugar plantation, to start subdividing urban lots where the tracks approached a trestle. In 1855, the town of Brashear was established on the east bank of the Atchafalaya, with Robert Brashear as postmaster. The early settlement of St. Mary, meanwhile, morphed into a cross-river counterpart known as Berwick. The Great Western began regular rail service just as the Atchafalaya River was being cleared of debris, promising a rosy future for both Brashear City and Berwick City, as dual railroad station sites—as well as seaports, river ports, and bayou ports.[14]

The Civil War and its aftermath brought deprivations to this key portal, including wrecked infrastructure, renascent logjams, basin-wide floods, yellow fever epidemics, and the bankruptcy of the Great Western Railroad. What got the twin cities back on track was the purchase of the line by Connecticut magnate Charles Morgan, a proponent of intermodal transportation—which was essentially the siting rationale of both Brashear and Berwick. Morgan expanded the rail yards in Algiers, added a steam-driven cotton press, extended the tracks westward into Texas cotton and cattle country, and built steamships of varying capacities. Morgan's Louisiana & Texas Railroad and Steamship Company offered "Steamers and Rail Connections to Points in Texas, New Mexico and California, Havana, Vera Cruz, Cedar Keys and New York" with a major terminal at Algiers and a key cog at Brashear, where wharves, pens, turntables, and other improvements were built. Cattle, cotton, sugar, timber, Spanish moss, furs, and seafood moved through Brashear heading to points east, while migrants bound for Texas and the frontier headed west.[15] "In a few years," predicted an 1869 company petition to city fathers, "Brashear will be placed in competition with the largest cities in the state, if not in the union and the world."[16] In 1873, Congress designated Brashear an official Port of Entry, home to a federal tax collector and inspector of revenue, a valued status held previously by Franklin and originally by New Iberia. Three years later, the community renamed itself Morgan City in honor of the magnate who rejuvenated its intermodal siting rationales—as a river landing, mouth site, bayou fork, railroad stop, basin bypass, jumping-off point, and crossroads.

The twentieth century saw the rise of the shrimp and petroleum industry, making Morgan City also a resource extraction site. Its population rose from around 2,000 in 1880 to over 5,000 in 1910 and peaked at nearly 16,600 people in 1970, at the height of the oil boom. Today, 11,000 people call Morgan City home, while another 4,500 live in the town of Berwick across the Atchafalaya River. Both communities are encircled by manmade levees or floodwalls, the largest population center outside of greater New Orleans to be so treated. Together, the twin cities on this strait-like feature tell a convoluted siting story, testimony to the fickle nature of the Atchafalaya River and the complex basin through which it flows.

And flow it did, more and more of it, through the cleared logjam—gaining perhaps 5 percent of the Mississippi's volume, then 10, 15, and 20 percent, increasing gradually enough to elude alarm. What changed that illusion came in the spring of 1927, when heavy rains in the Midwest swelled the tributaries of the Ohio, Missouri, and upper Mississippi rivers. The lower Mississippi rose to stages never seen before, breaching levees throughout the valley and inundating 26,000 square miles from Cairo to the sea, including most of the Atchafalaya Basin. At its apex, the Great Mississippi River Flood of 1927 practically fused the lower Mississippi and Atchafalaya river systems into one vast debris-strewn lake, with countless houses and settlements under water.

The catastrophe taught the U.S. Army Corps of Engineers a stinging lesson. Convinced that constraining the Mississippi exclusively with high, strong levees would deepen the river's trench and thus create extra space for high water volume, the federal government in the 1880s had committed to a "levees only" policy, eschewing spillways or diversions and even sealing off natural distributaries such as Bayou Plaquemine and Bayou Lafourche. It seemed to work, at least superficially. But in fact, the scouring of the bedload did not happen fast or deep enough, not even to store the additional water retained by way of the leveeing and sealing of the channel. So the river rose higher, which called for the levees to be raised—which further raised the river. The entire lower Mississippi gradually rose above its floodplain, and as it did, the growing water volume exerted ever more pressure on the levees—and on the prudence of the levees-only policy. The epic deluge of 1927 showed that policy to be arrogant folly, and Americans by the hundreds of thousands paid the price in a catastrophe of epic proportions.

Congress responded with the Flood Control Act of 1928, which cemented the federal government's commitment to controlling the Mississippi, even as it absolved itself of liability should it fail. As before, levees would be realigned, raised, broadened, strengthened, and extended. But now, "safety valves" would also be incorporated into the strategy, such that levees would be the first but no longer the only line of defense. Spillways, floodways, and reservoirs would be positioned to divert excess water laterally, as rivers are wont to do, on lands officially conceded to nature's will, as humans are loath to do.

The first "valve" was the Bonnet Carré Spillway, a weir built in 1931 at a low spot on the east bank between Norco and LaPlace, capable of releasing up to 250,000 cubic feet per second through a five-mile-long floodway into Lake Pontchartrain. Next was the Morganza Spillway west of New Roads, started in the late 1930s and completed in the 1960s, where an additional 600,000 cubic feet per second could be diverted into a series of floodways, chief of which was the Atchafalaya Basin itself.

Building the Atchafalaya Floodway entailed a wholesale replumbing of the basin, for the safety of over a million people in external cities and towns, but at the expense of hundreds of families in internal enclaves, camps, and houseboats. The floodway would be bordered by two "guide levees some twenty miles apart," wrote environmental lawyer Oliver Houck, as well as "interior levees walling off the [Atchafalaya] river itself, and a 60,000-square-foot dredged canal down the middle to speed it south," past Berwick and Morgan City, plus an additional outlet cut across Bayou Teche at Wax Lake. Flowage easements were imposed on landholdings within the floodway, giving the federal govern-

Morgan City has one of Louisiana's most complex siting stories, traceable to a river landing, a bayou fork, a train station, a rail junction, a crossroads, a basin bypass, and a jumping-off point. These scenes were taken along its Atchafalaya River floodwall. Photographs by Richard Campanella.

ment the legal right to store water on those spaces in the event of a Morganza Spillway opening.[17]

The changes made life tenuous for "swampers" dwelling in the Atchafalaya Basin, and coincided with an era when outside towns and cities beckoned with modern conveniences and lifestyles. An outmigration ensued, as predominantly Francophone Acadian families moved westward to larger settlements, such as Butte La Rose and Henderson, eastward to Pigeon and Pierre Part, or southward to Berwick and Morgan City. English-speaking swamp families tended to migrate to Bayou Sorrel as well as Berwick and Morgan City.[18]

By the 1950s, human inhabitance of the Atchafalaya Basin had become centrifugal, emptying out in the core and gravitating to the periphery. Paved roads now crossed the basin, with Highway 190 to the north and Highway 90 to the south, while smaller roads linked once-isolated Pierre Part and Belle River, and plans were afoot for a federal interstate to be raised up on concrete pilings. All the while, the guide levees and dredged channel of the Atchafalaya Floodway had the effect of lowering water levels and drying out former wetlands in the northern portion of the basin, thus enticing private development into the very areas that could be legally inundated if the Mississippi ran high. The new conditions forced adaptations in three upper-basin communities: Simmesport, Melville, and Krotz Springs.

At first glance, Simmesport has a striking location, near the state's geographical center, where the Red River converges with the Mississippi and from which emerges the Atchafalaya. Theoretically accessible in four directions, one might expect a nodal settlement to form here. One British map from 1748 suggested as much, showing a place called Guachoia at the confluence, from which a "Road to New Mexico" extended off to the west.[19] But hydrologically, the area was more of a vortex than a node, liable to logjams, perilous to navigate, prone to deluge, and with limited terrestrial access—in sum, a great situation, but a sketchy site. As travelers circumnavigated the mess, they found that the nearby confluence of Bayou des Glaises with the Atchafalaya River made for a slightly more viable ingress and egress into Avoyelles Parish. One source described the locale as "an island of about ten thousand acres, formed by [the Atchafalaya] on one side, Bayou des Glaises on another, and Yellow Bayou on the third."[20] It was here in 1836 that Virginia-born settler Bennett Barton Simmes purchased seventy-nine acres from Thomas Stouts and Francis Breaux "situated in the Parish of Avoyell[e]s on the waters of the Bayou des Glaze."[21] Simmes built a warehouse and dock at the confluence, acquired more land, and later purchased the nearby White Hall Plantation. By 1840, "Simmes Port" had a post office. In 1854 the Masonic Lodge had formed, and in 1857 Grace Catholic Church opened, making the community into a Sunday town for surrounding areas. Simmesport became a rendezvous for troops involved in the Union's unsuccessful Red River Campaign in 1864, and appears prominently on wartime maps as "Semmesport."[22] After the Civil War, federal officials continued their decades-long effort of clearing debris from the lower Atchafalaya, which buoyed river trade at Simmesport and later led to the building of two railroad lines.

But the debris removal had the effect of releasing increasing quantities of Mississippi River water into the Atchafalaya system, of which Simmesport was the head. Predicting the Mississippi could jump channels within a generation, the U.S. Army Corps of Engineers between 1954 and 1962 built the Old River Control Structure near Simmesport, designed to regulate 70 percent of incoming water to flow down the Mississippi and 30 percent down the Atchafalaya. Nearly every community from Simmesport down to Morgan City and out to Venice—roughly half the state's population, including Baton Rouge and New Orleans—directly depends on the engineering marvel at Old River. Its Promethean nature stands in stark contrast to modest Simmesport, which incorporated as a village in 1925, became a town in 1949, and retained a population of around 2,000 people in 2000, only to lose nearly a third during the 2010s. Simmesport's lifeline today is no longer the bayou confluence or the railroad, but Highway 1—which brings us to the next Atchafalaya town downriver, Melville.[23]

Melville's siting story is encapsulated by the settlement's original name of Centerport.[24] Sited initially as a ferry landing and loading wharf on the west bank of the Atchafalaya River, Centerport was centralized within the upper Atchafalaya Basin, halfway along the road from Point Barre to Williamsport, and midway between the Mississippi River region to the east and the Opelousas Prairie to the west. A 1904 article described the town, incorporated in 1889 and renamed Melville for the son of a steamboat captain, as located "in the center of large lumber tracts and fertile cotton lands, and its fame as a fish market is widespread," particularly for catfish and buffalo fish. Bayous with ridges emanated in a spider-like fashion, giving Melville good terrestrial access, while steamboats from Natchez and New Orleans stopped regularly at its landing. By the 1890s it became the junction of the Texas & Pacific and Opelousas, Gulf & Northeastern railroads, and it specialized in wholesaling basin-caught fish to train-based buyers. "Few places in the State are as advantageously located from either a geographical or topographical point of view," gushed a journalist; "Melville is destined for a brilliant future." With a population of over 1,000 and home to the only bank, post office, church, telegraph, and telephone for miles around, Melville by 1914 became "the shipping and trading point for . . . the eastern part of the parish."[25] It was also briefly on the main automobile route between New Orleans and Shreveport, where motorists would line up to take the toll ferry across the Atchafalaya River.

But then Highway 71 was paved and Highway 190 was laid through Krotz Springs, leaving Melville off a main thoroughfare. It lost its ferry to a bridge, and lost its original town site to a new federal levee—which altered the river ecology, and thus Melville's fishing economy. The centrality that once looked so promising now had the effect of isolation. Melville has managed to hang on, capitalizing on catfishing, and adapting to the federal floodway by building a ring levee around itself. Today the freight trains roll by with little economic impact, the port and ferry are long gone, the timber has been felled, and the cotton and cane ship out elsewhere. Melville's population is down by 60 percent from its 1970 peak of nearly 2,000 residents, and it shows no signs of reversing.[26]

Krotz Springs has a more secure lifeline than Simmesport and Melville, being on the Highway 190 thoroughfare between Opelousas and Baton Rouge. It also has a more multifarious backstory, with siting rationales varying depending on what one views as the taproot of the modern community. Antebellum maps show no named community here, but two charts from the 1860s indicate the old road from Arnaudville to Livonia here crossed the Atchafalaya River, which had its own paralleling pathway, evidencing that future Krotz Spring began as a ferry landing and crossroads. Perhaps that's how Charles William Krotz got here in 1899, when immense acreages of woodlands went up for sale and investors came from afar to bid. A son of German immigrants from Ohio, the maverick Krotz bought thousands of acres in the Melville and Latanier area, clearing some, flipping others for a quick profit, and looking for opportunities all around. He acquired the Soniat-Lyon timber tract in St. Landry Parish, and partnered with the Soniat lumber enterprise to establish a bankside mill. By this account, future Krotz Springs arose as a resource extraction site, perhaps with a future as a company town.

In 1900, Krotz, hearing rumors of petroleum reserves, partnered with an early wildcatter to drill "the first oil well in the Parish (possibly the first in the state)." At 2,400 feet deep, they struck not petroleum but "an artesian well of terrific pressure," sending up a gusher of water.[27] Undaunted, Krotz turned disappointment into opportunity by using the well to supply water for the community aggregating around the sawmill. Why stop there? Krotz began bottling the water, pedaling it as an antidote to ailments and "the finest bathing water in the world." He announced his next project as "The Coming Health Resort of the South" and began subdividing and selling lots to build houses around his new hotel. By this account, the community gained momentum as a resort site.

By 1909, twenty families lived in what some called Krotz's Mineral Springs and others called Latanier (not to be confused with another Latanier to the north). It had a school built by Krotz, as well as a train station negotiated by Krotz to be served by the Frisco Railroad line, rolling over the first train bridge over the Atchafalaya River. Krotz even arranged for a syndicate of parish investors to put up $100,000 to build the hotel resort, including a sanitarium and a carbonation plant for exporting the bottled spring water.[28] The community was officially incorporated as a village under the name Krotz Springs in 1917 and later became a town.

While Krotz's vision to create an elaborate resort never came to be, his eponymous community won a consolation prize in 1932 when it was selected for a bridge on Route 7, a.k.a. the East-West Highway, what is now the Huey Long–O. K. Allen Bridge on Highway 190. To motorists, Krotz Springs now serves as an arterial increment site—a place for a pit stop—though its true siting story includes a ferry landing, crossroads, resource extraction site, timber town, and health resort. Locals view their town as the "Gateway to the Atchafalaya," even as they live behind a levee separating them from the same. Indeed, Simmesport, Melville, and Krotz Springs all depend on ring levees for protection from their own siting stories, three little bowls within America's largest swamp basin.[29]

Of the seventeen cities, towns, villages, and other communities in the Atchafalaya Basin analyzed in this study, 82 percent had riverine- or water-based primary siting stories (close to triple the state average of 29 percent), while 12 percent were primarily railroad sites, 6 percent were resource extraction or processing sites, and none were crossroads (compared to state averages of 33 percent, 10 percent, and 13 percent, respectively). Settlements began forming in this region in the 1810s, crested in the 1860s–1870s, and ended in the 1930s. Fully 88 percent of Atchafalaya Basin settlements emerged organically, the other 12 percent having been ordained by a founder—one of the highest regional percentages statewide, where the ratio is 49 percent/51 percent emergent/ordained.

9

BAYOU TECHE, THE VERMILION RIVER, AND THE OPELOUSAS AND ATTAKAPAS DISTRICTS

According to legend, a giant fire-spewing snake once attacked the villages of the Chitimachan Indians. After tribesmen vanquished the writhing serpent, its carcass left a wending imprint in the mud that, upon filling with water, became Qukx Caqaad—Snake Bayou. How *Qukx* got transcribed as "Teche" is unclear; one researcher suggested it came from the Chitimachan word for worm, which is pronounced "cheesh," not far off from the *Teches* seen in early sources. Alternately, *Teche* inferred the Caddo word *techas* or *thechas,* meaning "friends"—which the Spanish used for the lands extending into Mexico, possibly the origin of "Texas." The etymologies point to three key aspects of Bayou Teche: its indigenous occupation, its meandering morphology, and its westward position within colonial Louisiana.[1]

Hydrologically, Bayou Teche is many things: a former channel of the Mississippi River, and partly of the Red; a tributary of the Atchafalaya, and a western edge of its basin; and the drain of a watershed extending into the Kisatchie Hills, which itself has multiple headwaters, tributaries, abandoned distributaries, and outlets. Nominally beginning at Port Barre as a fork of Bayou Courtableau, Bayou Teche has been a lifeline through lands used to raise cotton, rice, sugar, and cattle, with older Pleistocene prairies to the west, freshwater swamps to the east, and brackish bays to the south. Bayou Teche's waters have been diverted, pumped, and supplemented in and out of a twisting channel that has been severed, reconnected, and redirected. Even at its mouth one finds liminality: folks in Paterson view their town as the terminus of Bayou Teche,

Bayou Teche begins as a fork (*top left*) of Bayou Courtableau in Port Barre, a feature noted proudly in the town's logo (*top right*). It then wends downriver like a serpent, according to a Chitimachan legend depicted in this Breaux Bridge monument (*left*). Photographs by Richard Campanella and Town of Port Barre.

calling everything downriver "the Lower Atchafalaya River," whereas historical sources depict Bayou Teche as discharging into the Atchafalaya River at Berwick. From a geomorphological perspective, the impact of Bayou Teche's past land-building may been seen extending eastward to Morgan City, Amelia, and even Gibson, while the future looks bright southward at the Wax Lake Delta, a rare spot of land accretion along Louisiana's otherwise eroding coast.[2]

Home to the Opelousas, Attakapas, and Chitimachan peoples, Bayou Teche saw European settlement commence courtesy of the late 1770s Spanish policy of populating the Louisiana colony for military defense and economic development. The gateway to that western region had become known as the Poste de Attakapas, or simply the Attakapas ("man eater"), named for the most feared of its three resident tribes.[3] It was the Chitimachans, however, who numerically predominated in the Bayou Teche region—until displacement relegated them to isolation or assimilation with incoming Europeans, among them Spaniards recruited from Málaga, Granada, and the Canary Islands.

Coordinating this settlement effort was Lieutenant Governor Francisco Bouligny, a determined officer who had helped establish Spanish rule in Louisiana and now oversaw Indian affairs as well as immigration policies. Bouligny's superior, Governor Bernardo de Gálvez, thought it best to settle the newcomers close to New Orleans, a strategy that eventually spawned Galveztown, San Bernardo, and Gonzales. Bouligny favored a more dispersed strategy, eyeing the Ouachita region to the north and the Attakapas region to the west. Ouachita was deemed too risky, so Bouligny instead planned on leading twenty settlers from Málaga plus employees and slaves into the Attakapas region, namely Bayou Teche.

"Probably no group of immigrants received as much assistance in settlement as the Malagueños," wrote historian Gilbert C. Din in describing Bouligny's January 1779 expedition. But they were strangers in a strange land, new to all they saw. Heavy rain made matters worse—"fifteen days of Purgatory," one soldier put it—as they slogged across the Atchafalaya. Upon reaching Bayou Teche in late February, Bouligny and his advisers scouted optimal sites for what he would call Nueva Iberia, the name indicating these new colonists were *peninsulares,* from the Spanish mainland, like Bouligny himself, as opposed to the *isleños* (islanders) Gálvez had been settling closer to New Orleans.

In mid-March, Bouligny selected a bend on Bayou Teche twelve leagues (thirty-six miles) up from its mouth, because it struck him as particularly beautiful and accessible, something he may have deduced from the presence of a nearby Chitimachan village. Despite persistent rains, workers made progress clearing banks and building huts—until the bayou overflowed and inundated the town site. All the while, Bouligny had come to understand that most land along Bayou Teche had already been titled, such that he would have to purchase it from colonists. The expedition had to pull up stakes and head upriver to find an alternative site, putting Bouligny in the position of explorer as well as a buyer on the real estate market.[4]

In April he found a site that satisfied all requirements. It was located twenty-three miles above the first location, on the west bank of a promontory known as Petite Fausse Pointe. This hairpin meander, along an oxbow-like sequence of bayou bends, would force vessels to slow down while effectively doubling the length of the settlement's waterfront. Importantly, it had a portage cutting across the subsequent meander loop that replaced fifteen miles of navigation with a mere two-mile walk.[5] Nearby were freshwater lakes "filled with fish and game," Bouligny noted, as well as prairie to the west for crops and cattle, and ample timber in the Atchafalaya swamp to the east. Better yet, the site had access to the marshes of the Vermilion Bay via Bayou Petite Anse (Little Cove), which could be developed into a sea harbor, and where a potentially useful salt dome (now Avery Island) was located. This spot was also just above Bayou Teche's head of saline tides, a paramount attribute in regard to potable water and irrigation. What sealed the deal was that the real estate had a willing seller, in the person of Joseph Prevost *dit* Colette, who sold thirty arpents of frontage to Bouligny for 400 pesos.[6] Because the move had been carried out during springtime high water, it showed that the new site for Nueva Iberia would be relatively safe from inundation—unlike the former site by the Indian village,

"Queen City of Bayou Teche," New Iberia is Louisiana's purest example of a Spanish town—in its siting, founding, naming, layout, and in the ethnicity of its first European settlers. Its populace today, however, is as much of Acadian, Anglo, African, and indigenous descent. This mural (*top*) adorns an old warehouse wall (*bottom*) overlooking Bayou Teche. Photographs by Richard Campanella.

now Charenton, which remains the home of the federally recognized Chitimachan tribe today.

More Malagueños arrived and settled, as did some Germans, Irish, and others, but they did not ensure the success of Nueva Iberia. One of the guiles of settlement siting is that geographical advantages are all theoretical unless and until broader economic dynamics enliven them. A portage is worthless if nobody treks it; a harbor is just a riverbank if no vessels come to dock. For a while, that's what happened at Nueva Iberia—or rather, what didn't happen. There was not enough of a regional economy to impart value to this site, and local efforts to develop industries proved disappointing. Some Spaniards had been recruited to cultivate and process flax and hemp, but neither grew well along Bayou Teche, nor did corn and tobacco. Many Malagueños moved away from bayou life to tend to cattle on the prairie, and by the 1790s Nueva Iberia nearly failed again.

What saved the project was a subsequent influx of French Creole, Acadian, and Anglo settlers, who, with enslaved Africans, rendered the region productive. People and cargo in transit activated those site advantages Bouligny had discerned back in 1779, and the town he founded spurted to life. To the Francophones it was Nouvelle Ibérie, to Anglophones it was New Town, and to Hispanophones it remained Nueva Iberia. As the various ethnicities syncretized into Louisianians, they called their town New Iberia, which became the official name in 1847.[7]

By the early American era, New Iberia became the main Port of Entry and trade center for Bayou Teche plantations and the Attakapas cattle regions. The community incorporated as a town in 1839, during a period when New Iberia "became the radiating point for the trade of a large territory, extending some 60 miles in all directions," and when roughly one-third of the steamboats docking at New Orleans plied Bayou Teche.[8] New Iberia became the seat of the newly formed Iberia Parish in 1868, after which its population reached the low thousands, being now an administrative center and later a railroad depot.

A century later, over 30,000 people called New Iberia home, many with French or Spanish surnames. A city of graceful beauty and a bedroom community of Lafayette, New Iberia is at once an oxbow bend site, a point-bar or promontory site, a shortcut portage, and a head-of-tides site. It is also the paragon of a Spanish settlement in Louisiana, starting with its Malagueño founders and enduring with its Castilian name.

Once New Iberia is on the map, the spatial rationales of other Bayou Teche communities come into focus. Note that the waterway's four largest population centers—New Iberia, Breaux Bridge, Patterson, and Franklin, with a combined population of over 45,000—are all sited by sharp meanders, where vessels slowed, where waterfronts lengthened, and where portages cut across bends. Instead of following the long and winding waterway, one can take shortcuts from New Iberia to Daspit, from Breaux Bridge to Lafayette, from Patterson to Calumet or Berwick, and from Franklin to Katy or Baldwin. Note also that Franklin is roughly halfway between New Iberia and Patterson/Berwick/Morgan City, that Jeanerette is halfway between Franklin and New Iberia, and that New Iberia is approximately midway from Jeanerette to St. Martinsville. Indeed, along the entire length of Bayou Teche, communities have the same arterial increment siting characteristic as those along Bayou Lafourche, occurring every five to ten miles. Each settlement developed as a trade and service center, offering post offices, banks, supply stores, infirmaries, churches, and other needs. Three Bayou Teche communities—St. Martinville, New Iberia, and Franklin—gained further traction by becoming administrative centers, as the seats of St. Martin, Iberia, and St. Mary parishes.

Tradition holds that St. Martinville originated as the French Poste des Attakapas in 1756 and attracted Acadian settlers with the establishment of L'Eglise

Among Louisiana's best examples of a Sunday town, scenic St. Martinville initially formed around the church that would later become Saint Martin de Tours (*left*), known as the Mother Church of the Acadians. A statue commemorating an Attakapan warrior stands over the park fronting the church (*right*). Photographs by Richard Campanella.

de la Nouvelle Acadie aux Attakapas in 1765. But Bayou Teche historian Shane K. Bernard points out that Poste des Attakapas in that era was a broad regional reference, not a specific place, and puts the founding of the church at 1773, two years after a retired French military officer named Antoine Bernard Dauterive (Dautrive) donated land for Jean Berard to build a church. "On Dauterive's death," wrote Bernard, "his widow sold most of the remaining land to a handful of settlers, [and] around 1800, two settlers sold off land in lots to establish a town." By now known as Poste des Attakapas, the settlement was renamed St. Martinville upon being designated the seat of St. Martin Parish in 1811, at which time the church became Saint Martin de Tours.[9] What further developed the community was an "unusual semi-feudal arrangement" made in 1818, in which buyers of church-owned lots paid a stipulated sum for twelve years followed by an "annual and perpetual rent," effectively making the church the landlord of the town. According to the congregation, "this unique arrangement resulted in the firm establishment of the business district of St. Martinville around the church square"—a Sunday town in a nearly literal sense.[10] Also a port landing and bridge site, St. Martinville claimed 1,000 residents in 1870, peaked at nearly 8,000 in 1980, and now has 5,400 people, with majestic Saint Martin de Tours Catholic Church still dominating its center.

Accounts of Franklin's origins vary as well. Being on a bayou meander at a shortcut portage likely drew attention to this particular site, which some sources say became known as Carlin's Settlement in 1808. According to Clare D'Artois Leeper, conveyance records indicate that James Sanders bought land from Hugh Latiolais and laid out lots along what are now Jackson to Wilson streets—which point directly to Bayou Portage, which flows into West Cote

Blanche Bay and the Gulf of Mexico. (This connection positions Franklin, as well as Baldwin, closest of all Bayou Teche settlements to open coastal waters—only seven miles—and explains why the Charenton Canal and Franklin Canal were dug here around 1940.) Another account holds that, upon earning designation as the St. Mary Parish seat in 1811, Franklin took form when a Tennessean named Alexander Lewis in 1814 bought up bayou-fronting land, donated space for the courthouse, and laid out lots adjacently. Most accounts hold that the town was named for Benjamin Franklin, though one credible source contends that the name hails Franklin, Tennessee, the origin of some early settlers. Anglo planters came to dominate the economy, and soon Franklin rivaled New Iberia, becoming in 1830 the official Port of Entry on Bayou Teche, home to the collector of customs and inspector of revenue for trade with seaports as far away as Philadelphia and New York. Known for its stately neoclassical architecture (and Brutalist courthouse), this city of 6,500 people exemplifies a settlement that likely emerged from natural advantages, as a shortcut portage to a bayou landing, and gained traction by being ordained an administrative site.[11]

Then there's Arnaudville, a town of 1,000 people whose limits straddle the St. Landry/St. Martin parish line, and whose welcome sign reads "Deux Bayous." While located midway between Leoville and Cecelia (six miles from one, six miles from the other), Arnaudville's original impetus was as a confluence site, being at the juncture of Bayou Fusilier and Bayou Teche—thus its earlier name, La Jonction. The *deux bayous* had natural levees, along which roads were built, thus becoming a crossroads site. One of those roads followed a portage to Bayou Portage, where a hamlet aptly named Portage operated as a jumping-off site into the Atchafalaya Basin—all the more reason to settle at La Jonction. Renamed for two brothers who donated land for a church, Arnaudville may also be considered a head-of-navigation site, until the 1913 opening of a lock near St. Martinville, which enabled vessels to navigate up to Leonville. In addition to becoming Bayou Teche's new head of navigation, Leonville is also a crossroads site, initially settled by free people of color on yet another meander-crossing shortcut—connecting right back to Arnaudville.[12]

Similar siting stories explain Port Barre, founded at the fork of Bayou Teche and Bayou Courtableau, and offering a shortcut portage up to Melville on the banks of the Atchafalaya River. Sorrel and Centerville, meanwhile, formed at crossroads following abandoned distributaries: Sorrel's relict ridge afforded access down to Glencoe, Cypremont Point, and the Vermilion Bay, while Centerville's ridge did the same to South Bend and Burns Point on East Cote Blanche Bay. In sum, a web of interconnecting arteries, both hydrological and terrestrial, enmeshed the Bayou Teche region, and human movements on that system begot enduring communities at the nodes. Their siting stories are interlocking, interleaved, and interdependent.

And then there is Breaux Bridge, whose siting story is eponymous. In the 1770s, an Acadian named Firmin Breaux and his son Agricole had acquired land between the Vermilion River to the west (future Lafayette) and the Atchafalaya Basin to the east (future Henderson). A slight upland provided terrestrial access westward (now Highway 94), while a wending waterway (Bayou Portage) provided vessel access to the east. Connecting those two arteries pointed to the ideal spot where the Breaux men should install a footbridge over Bayou Teche, named Pont des Breaux. Like ferry landings, bridges funnel human movement and stimulate bridging point sites to form where waterbodies are sufficiently narrow, shallow, or otherwise crossable. That's what happened at Breaux's Bridge. In 1817, Agricole replaced the footbridge with a floating bridge for wagons. In 1829, Agricole died, leaving his thirty-three-year-old widow, Scholastique Picou Breaux, and their five children to fend for themselves. Scholastique understood the value the bridge had brought to their land, and drew up a Plan de la Ville Du Pont des Breaux with streets, parcels, a school, and a church. Parcels sold, houses went up, and Breaux Bridge was born. Scholastique remained active in bettering the town until her death in 1846, by which time the floating bridge had been replaced with a drawbridge. That span was replaced by a turntable bridge in 1852 and again in 1891; a steel vertical lift bridge was installed in 1950 and remains in service today, connecting the Lafayette and Henderson areas—as had the original footbridge starting in 1799. With a siting story of unusual clarity and endurance, Breaux Bridge is today the largest city in St. Martin Parish, home to over 7,500 people—and a bronze statue of Scholastique Picou Breaux, one of the few women founders of Louisiana cities or towns. The reputed Crawfish Capital of the World, Breaux Bridge can also call itself the City of Bridges, home to four spans over Bayou Teche, including that of Interstate 10, which has since become the community's economic lifeline.[13]

For two adjacent waterways originating from the same source and discharging out the same delta, Bayou Teche and the Vermilion River differ in fundamental ways. Bayou Teche was a land-builder, spewing sediment into a brackish bay and shoring up its banks higher than surrounding swamps. The Vermilion River, on the other hand, formed as an inlet from a brackish bay, where tidal regimes intruded inland according to the perturbations of a higher, firmer terrace—"an immense moist plain," wrote a traveler in the late 1850s, "being alternate tracts of grass and pine" known as the Attakapas Prairie.[14] Unlike the Holocene alluvial lowlands to the east and south, formed 5,000 to 7,000 years ago, this plateau dates to the late Pleistocene Epoch, 10,000 to 20,000 years

Breaux Bridge originated when Firmin Breaux acquired bankside land and erected a footbridge over Bayou Teche, drawing traffic to the bridge site pictured at the upper left. In 1829, Firmin's widowed daughter-in-law, Scholastique Picou Breaux, realizing the value the bridge imparted to the land, drew up a Plan de la Ville Du Pont des Breaux, creating today's downtown Breaux Bridge (*bottom*). Note the scrolled map in Scholastique's hand in her statue at upper right. Photographs by Richard Campanella.

ago, when melting ice sheets delivered alluvium in greater quantities to what are now south-central and southwestern Louisiana. The resulting terraces are thus higher and older than the coastal plain, but far younger and lower than the rocky hills of western and northwestern Louisiana, which are 10 to 55 million years old. Parts of the late Pleistocene Terrace tended to preclude the growth of trees, because their roots could not penetrate the hardened claypan horizon in the otherwise fertile soil profile; prairie grasses predominated instead. In Louisiana, the term "prairie" (e.g., the Attakapas Prairie, Mamou Prairie, Avoyelles Prairie) infers slightly elevated treeless plateaus from the late Pleistocene Epoch, environments altogether distinct from the forested natural levees and backswamps of Bayou Teche, Bayou Lafourche, and the lower Mississippi River.[15]

Augmented by tributaries, the waters of the Vermilion River carved the clay terraces downwardly toward the river's banks—unlike the Teche, whose natural levees slope upwardly to the bayou, and whose runoff flows away toward the backswamp. The clay particles gave the Vermilion a reddish color—thus its name, from the French *vermeil,* referring to a red dye. While both the Vermilion and the Teche may be described as deltaic waterways, and share enough water (through both natural and anthropogenic means) to be considered an integrated hydrological system, the Vermilion has the properties of a "consequence stream," in that its channel was determined by the slope and shape of its plateau-like watershed.[16] The Mermentau and Calcasieu rivers to the west have similar properties.

Landscape patterns further divulge the Teche/Vermilion distinction. Whereas flailing French long lots comprised the cadasters along Bayou Teche, the rectangular American township-range-section system undergirds those of the Attakapas Prairie. Topography differs too: the "Queen City of the Teche," New Iberia, sits sixteen feet above sea level, whereas Lafayette on the Vermilion River is nearly fifty feet in elevation, and Opelousas in the upper Vermilion Basin is seventy feet high.

From a settlement perspective, that topographical difference meant that people did not gravitate to the Vermilion River for lack of terrestrial alternatives, as was the case along Bayou Teche, Bayou Lafourche, and the lower Mississippi River. Quite the contrary: the Attakapas Prairie offered plenty of solid ground all around, regardless of proximity to the Vermilion. If people settled *on* the Vermilion, it was *because of* the Vermilion. Its surrounding grasslands made for fine cattle pasture, its flatness invited rice cultivation, its terrace topography kept floodwaters at bay, and its centrality made it a strategic military position.

One spot stood salient. It was a hillock that shed runoff down escarpments in every direction: northward into Bayou Courtableau, from which Bayou Teche forked, eastward into Bayou Little Teche, westward through Bayou Plaquemine Brûlé, and southward through tributaries feeding into the Vermilion River. Here on this high point, "far above sea level and very fertile," a tribe called the Opélousas ("man with black leg," according to one translation) could hunt, cultivate, and take refuge from deluges in the eastern lowlands.[17] Being a crest among hydrological basins also meant that trails crisscrossing here could get you anywhere. "East of Opelousas the streams flow to the Atchafalaya River," observed William Henry Perrin in 1891, "and west of the town they flow to the Vermilion River, thus forming a portage upon which Opelousas stands."[18] These advantages attracted colonists, including French and later Spanish soldiers, who in 1765 established a military post and garrison at Los Opeluzás. Land grants followed—fully 800 title transfers, from 1765 to 1805—as did the establishment of stores, houses, and a Catholic church. "Later when the fort was dismantled," wrote historian William J. Sandoz in 1925, "many of the soldiers preferred remaining and took up their permanent residence here, so that the nucleus of what is now the City of Opelousas was formed."[19]

They were joined by refugees from Acadie (Nova Scotia) in French Canada, who had been exiled into a diaspora by the British starting in 1755. They sought refuge in the American colonies, in French Saint-Domingue, and in France itself before finally opting to come to French Louisiana—only to learn upon their arrival in 1764 that the colony had been transferred to Spain. Incoming Spanish administrators tended to be magnanimous in granting land to *les Acadiens,* in the interest of increasing economic productivity and providing defense against their mutual enemy, the British. Because most parcels along the lower Mississippi were already titled, the granting tended to steer the Acadians well west of New Orleans, a cultural geography retained by their descendants today.

Westward the Acadians trekked, on Bayou Plaquemine and across the Atchafalaya, past Bayou Teche, and into the Opelousas and Attakapas districts—families with names such as "Broussard, Trahan, Braud, Bernard, Boudrot, Poirier, Bourgeois, Roy, LeBlanc, Thibaudeau, Arceneau, Guilbeau, Cormier and Doucet."[20] They were later joined by other Francophones named Guidry, Martin, Mouton, Landry, and Richard, and subsequently by Spaniards, Creoles, Anglo-Americans, and African Americans. Most settled in rural environs; others gravitated to the only sizeable settlement, Opelousas. In 1805, Opelousas became the seat of newly formed St. Landry Parish, making the portage and military garrison an administrative center.

Unlike Bayou Teche settlements, which were sited on a natural levee primarily for navigational reasons, nearby Opelousas occupies an elevated prairie terrace and traces its origins to a strategically positioned military garrison—but without the economic benefit of a waterfront. Photographs by Richard Campanella.

One drawback to terrace-based sites such as Opelousas was their limited river access. That economic need helped spawn small ports on whichever waterway was nearest. In the case of Opelousas, it was Washington, where many steamboat captains lived (*townhouse at left*), and where one circa 1830s cotton warehouse still stands on Bayou Courtableau (*right*). Photographs by Richard Campanella.

Yet inhabitants numbered only in the hundreds throughout the antebellum era because, unlike most south Louisiana settlements, Opelousas was a dry-point site—a slightly elevated dome *near* water but not *on* water, much less a navigable river. "As Opelousas was an inland town some miles from the nearest waterway," wrote historian Donald J. Millet, "it had to depend upon neighboring Washington, and to a lesser extent upon Port Barre, as its shipping center. It appeared for a time that these port towns would develop at the expense of Opelousas." Washington in particular had a compelling rationale, having the same topographical benefit of Opelousas's terrace plus a head-of-navigation port on Bayou Courtableau near three confluences. "All the cotton, corn and other produce for many miles south and west shipped through this port," wrote St. Landry Parish historian William J. Sandoz. "Washington became the chief shipping point" between a hinterland served by stagecoach lines and a foreland reaching all the way to New Orleans. Steamboat captains made Washington their home, large warehouses lined the town's waterfront, and for a while the bustling inland port edged out dry-point Opelousas in wealth and size.[21] A historic plaque summarized Washington's siting story succinctly:

> Prosperous ante-bellum inland port and Western frontier gateway.
> Texas stage and river packets interchanged passengers and mail.
> Passengers, freight were transferred to northbound craft.[22]

What resuscitated Opelousas was the same conveyance that spurred settlement all across the Attakapas Prairie: the railroad. "Things have brightened up wonderfully," exalted a local newsman in 1880 as trains began to roll in from Vermilionville. "The landing place . . . is crowded every evening[;] no one ever thinks of taking a walk in any other direction from that leading to the railroad tracks. . . . A very great change is taking place with our people. They are rapidly casting aside their old rustic country ways, and are becoming metropolitan-like in appearance and deportment. Old Opelousas is fast fading away. New Opelousas is now 'the boom.'" Trains gave Opelousas the accessibility it never had from waterways; conversely, they undercut Washington's port advantage on Bayou Courtableau. Being on a feeder line rather than a trunk, Opelousas still found itself at a relative disadvantage, and Washington continued to ship on the bayou. But railroads eventually prevailed fully, leaving the last steamboat to paddle out of Washington in 1900.[23]

Highways reenergized Opelousas in subsequent decades, as the city became the crossroads of Highway 190 and what is now designated as Interstate 49. With a population of 15,000, nearly twenty times the size of the historic village of Washington, the city of Opelousas remains the seat of St. Landry Parish and prides itself as a cultural hearth of south Louisiana, known for its zydeco music. High and dry, its site probably would have remained pasture were it not for a key eighteenth-century spatial advantage, as a crested portage between hydrological basins at the gateway to the Opelousas and Attakapas districts.

For every westward-trekking Acadian family that settled in Opelousas, another veered southward toward the Vermilion River. To them and their peers, Spanish officials "granted land freely along the bayous Carencro and Vermilion," wrote historian Harry Lewis Griffin, "and soon Acadians . . . began to settle along these streams and their tributaries."[24] They cut timber and built cottages; hunted, trapped, and fished; traded with Indians; raised cattle and planted crops; and opened stores and churches. The activity stoked traffic on prairie trails and twisting waterways, principally the Vermilion.

As debris and shallow draft made the Vermilion difficult to navigate, boatmen disembarked at the east-west route known colloquially as the Old Spanish Trail. Here, at what came to be called Petit Manchac ("little rear entrance"), Acadian settlers built a bridge at "Pin Hook," possibly derived from the Choctaw *pinashuk,* referring to basswood or linden trees. "The Pinhook Bridge area became a place where traders unloaded their boats and waited local transportation by horse and travois, and later wagons"—a paradigm of a break-of-bulk point at a head of navigation.[25] Entrepreneurs turned the Pin Hook bridgehead into a community by catering to transients, opening an inn for shelter, a canteen for food, a store for supplies, and a depot for storage, and by building houses for those who ran these enterprises.

In 1821, Jean Mouton, whose family owned land just to the north, assisted the settlement process by donating space to build L'Eglise St. Jean du Vermilion, now the Cathedral of St. John the Evangelist. Two years later, the state legislature designated the surrounding region to become Lafayette Parish, naming it for Revolutionary War hero Marquis de Lafayette, and made the Pin Hook area its seat of justice. Enthused by the momentum, Mouton in 1824 sketched out "a new development adjacent to the church and designed around a Court

Upon reaching the head of navigation of the Vermilion River, boatmen disembarked and interacted with overland travelers on what is now Pinhook Road (*top*), and together they needed victuals and accommodations. Out of these movements arose Lafayette, originally Vermilionville. Incredibly, a circa 1835 former inn (*bottom*) still stands near the city's initial site. Photographs by Richard Campanella.

House Square, [consisting] of 156 lots, each measuring 96 × 140 feet, with dirt roads aligned in a north-south grid and named for US Presidents."[26] Mouton's town would be called Vermilionville, and he hoped his Court House Square would host the Lafayette Parish seat of justice, which had been slated for Pin Hook a mile to the south. After some controversy, officials agreed to relocate the courthouse to Mouton's new city plan, though the spatial rationale of both sites clearly traces back to that break-of-bulk point where the Pinhook Bridge spanned over the Vermilion's head of navigation.[27]

Vermilionville was incorporated in 1836 and became the premier administrative and trade center of Lafayette Parish, so much so that folks tended to refer to the city and parish interchangeably. Railroads came through starting in

1880, and in 1884 Vermilionville was officially renamed Lafayette. Population surpassed 2,000 residents in 1890 and 3,300 in 1900, and proceeded to double every twenty years for eight decades, thanks largely to the oil and gas industry and the opening of Interstate 10.[28]

The midcentury petrol boom rendered modern Lafayette a crazy quilt of ranch house subdivisions and commercial arteries, rather mundane at first glance. But appearances can be deceptive: Lafayette is also the unofficial capital of Acadiana, a treasure trove of folk culture, and a good steward of its 200-year-old siting story. On the banks of the Vermilion River, preservationists have established a heritage village of restored vernacular structures capturing the ambience of old Vermilionville. Nearby, a road still named Pinhook passes over a bridge of the same name, at the Vermilion River's former head of navigation. And a short distance away from that original break-of-bulk point stands the circa 1835 Acadian-style Vermilionville Inn, recalling those early stopovers catering to travelers on the Attakapas Prairie. From that original site emerged Louisiana's fourth-largest city, home to 122,000 people.[29] "It is a well known law that wherever occurs a break in transportation, there will grow a city," wrote parish historian Harry Lewis Griffin. "The fact that Lafayette stands where it is today is due to the working of that law."[30]

As we saw with New Iberia on Bayou Teche, the rise of Opelousas and Lafayette elucidates the siting stories of their neighbors. The picturesque Acadian town of Grand Coteau, for example, sits roughly between Opelousas and Lafayette, as well as between Arnaudville and Church Point. Perched on a crest of the Pleistocene Terrace—thus its name, which translates to "large hillock"—Grand Coteau became a stopover, then a Sunday town (St. Charles Borromeo Catholic Church, 1819), and later an academy town (Academy of the Sacred Heart, 1821).[31] Carencro, in turn, is halfway between Grand Coteau and Lafayette, and also occupies a terrace crest. In the span from Washington to Lafayette, the intervening cities occur at that same five- to ten-mile interval detected on Bayous Teche and Lafourche.

Now let us look south of Lafayette, to Abbeville, whose history might at first make its geography seem incidental. The town was established in 1843 by a determined Capuchin missionary, Père Antoine Désiré Mégret, who collaborated with parishioners in getting the Vermilion Parish seat of justice co-located with their parish church by purchasing and donating a tract of land. One might suppose this acquisition, for which Father Mégret paid Joseph LeBlanc $900, might explain Abbeville's siting. But why had a church been located here in the first place? And why did enough people settle here to warrant an ecclesiastic parish? Abbeville, in fact, had good *terroir* for settlement. It is roughly halfway

Grand Coteau formed as a stopover, a Sunday town, and an academy town, with its most prominent landmark being St. Charles Borromeo Catholic Church, seen here. The scenic town is perched on a crest of the Pleistocene Terrace—thus its name, meaning "large hillock." Photograph by Richard Campanella.

between Vermilionville (Lafayette) and Vermilion Bay, and such midpoints—be they along roads, railroads, or in this case Bayou Vermilion—tend to offer opportunities and invite settlement. Additionally, Abbeville, like Lafayette and Opelousas, sits on the brink of the Pleistocene Terrace, where terrain rises to sixteen feet above sea level, compared to only five feet to the east or south. Finally, Abbeville is located by two tributaries of Bayou Vermilion, Valcourt Coulee and Coulee Kenny, making it also a confluence site.[32] Father Mégret, we may conclude, did not make his decision capriciously. He went on to sketch a town plan, enduring to this day, and named it for his birthplace, Abbeville dans la Somme in the Normandy region of France. Abbeville's siting story, then, had its genesis as a Sunday town (known originally as La Chapelle—The Chapel) at a confluence site, halfway between the region's largest city and the sea. The twenty-mile stretch separating the two communities gave rise to Maurice, which began as a store (le Magasin à Maurice, established by Jean-Maurice Villien), church, and service center situated precisely between Lafayette and Abbeville—in other words, a ten-mile town.[33]

Of the thousands of Acadians and other migrants who arrived at the Opelousas and Attakapas districts, most settled along the brow of the Pleistocene escarpment, or else in rural dispersions following bayous and rivers. "The

Picturesque Abbeville, like Lafayette, Grand Coteau, and Opelousas, sits on the brow of a terrace; it also abuts two tributaries of Bayou Vermilion, making it a confluence site. Photograph by Richard Campanella.

'Cajiens' love the streams," wrote a visiting newsman, "leaving the open prairie to the cattle and the newcomer." Another observer called the prairie "*terra incognita* to the outside world," for its crude roads, lack of navigable waterways, and paucity of nucleated settlements.[34] That began to change in 1880, when the Louisiana Western Railroad opened to link Morgan's Louisiana & Texas Railroad from the east with the Texas & New Orleans Railroad from the west. "These people build no towns," wrote the newsman of the earlier settlements strewn out along bayous; now, after 1880, he added, "the *railroad* is the town-builder."[35] Settlement geography had effectively shifted from emergent to ordained forces. But as historian Donald J. Millet pointed out, "the railroad alone could not have brought in settlers." What brought in settlers was the union of national wherewithal (capital, tools, expertise) with local resources (land, local know-how, workforces). Railroads brought in manufactured means of production and new people to work them, particularly midwesterners of Anglo-Saxon heritage; they also exported local commodities out to the rest of the nation. "Cotton compresses and oil mills, rice-processing mills, central sugar refineries, sawmills and other enterprises" were coeval with railroads in this region, and their ensuing geographies "were all town-centered."[36] Bearing in mind the prairie's flat topography and rectilinear surveying system, what resulted was an orthogonal landscape of railroads and roads tracing a grid of straight section lines, with each additional segment (a new feeder track, spur line, or road) yielding additional squares in the grid. Settlements of varying sizes materialized at the vertices of the grid, be they crossroads, flag stops for trains, stations for passengers, or cargo depots. Within two decades, 1880–1900, the Attakapas region's population doubled from 76,000 to 154,000 people. "While most of the towns in the early period were built on or near navigable streams," noted Millet, "those which came after 1880 were generally along the railroad."[37]

As per Christaller's Central Place Theory, the new towns were typically distanced by intervals of five to ten miles; indeed, the prairie between Lafayette and Lake Charles is the closest we have to the isotropic surface Christaller theorized—Louisiana's "Midwest," where arteries iterate section lines, and where communities occur at their 90-degree junctures. We see this Kansas-like regularity by extending lines straight westward from the three earlier cities of the Pleistocene escarpment—Opelousas, Lafayette, and Abbeville. For example, straight west of Opelousas is Eunice, straight west of Lafayette is Crowley, and straight west of Abbeville is Kaplan. Eunice's siting was predicated on Crowley's, just as Crowley's depended on Rayne's and Kaplan's—and as all depended on the railroad.

Crowley's siting story is illustrative. In 1886, two sibling real estate developers, C. C. and W. W. Duson, acquired a 174-acre tract in newly formed Acadia Parish, with the aim of hosting its seat of justice. Duson family members had been politically involved in detaching a part of St. Landry Parish to create Acadia Parish, thus calling into need a new administrative center.[38] It was not coincidental that the Dusons' tract was located roughly halfway between two existing communities already connected by the Louisiana Western Railroad. One was named Rayne, created in 1884 as a train stop and soon augmented by Pouppeville, a circa 1850s stagecoach stop settlement that was moved by ox cart to the new station a mile to the north. The other was Mermentau, which had initially formed at a Mermentau River crossing but was also moved to the railroad.[39] Wanting the same advantage for their real estate venture, the Dusons persuaded the railroad company's "roadmaster," Patrick C. Crowley, to relocate a spur line switch to their property, which would boost its value as a crossroads and station stop. To sweeten the deal, the Dusons promised to name the embryonic town to honor the compliant roadmaster. On January 4, 1887, Crowley was founded, and in February hundreds of lots were auctioned off.

Crowley resulted from a coordinated effort to create a parish seat and secure a railroad station. Today it is the "Rice Capital of America." Photograph by Richard Campanella.

Despite initial difficulties, the siting strategy worked. "By 1890," wrote historian Alcée Fortier in 1914, "the railroad's books showed that Crowley was the second-largest shipping point between Lafayette and Houston, Tex."[40] Over 400 residents lived in scores of houses set among a courthouse, schoolhouse, church, college, two hotels, butcher shops, drugstores, warehouses, and lumberyards. Industry followed, namely rice mills: six by 1900, more than any other town in the region and capable of producing 6,000 sacks per day. Prairie soils supported the rice cultivation, and modern engineering brought about the processing mills. The railroad enabled Crowley to become "the Rice Capital of America," and the spatial attribute of centrality helped turn this once-vacant grassland into an economic hub.[41] "The situation of Crowley on the Southern Pacific Railroad gives it advantageous communication with the outside world," wrote William Henry Perrin in 1891, using the new name for the Louisiana Western Railroad, "and the distance it is from Lafayette (about twenty-five miles) and Lake Charles (about fifty miles) must necessarily make it a heavy shipping point. It being also about the centre of the parish greatly adds to its business interests."[42] The historian Fortier similarly noted in 1914 that Crowley has "an ideal location, being half way between New Orleans and Houston, Tex."[43] And what about the fifteen-mile stretch between Lafayette and Rayne? There arose two additional circa 1880 station-stop towns, spaced precisely five miles apart: one is Scott, and the other is—what else?—Duson.

To the west, the Duson brothers became track-laying, town-ordaining tycoons. "While [W. W.] Duson's principal efforts were directed toward building up Crowley," wrote Fortier, "every possible aid and assistance was given his brother, C. C. Duson, in promoting and having built the New Iberia, Gueydan & Eunice branch of the Southern Pacific R. R., and the laying out and building of the towns of Gueydan, Morse, Midland, Egan, Iota, Eunice and Mammou."[44] Those seven communities, now with a combined population of 17,000, are all railroad stops along a south-to-north trajectory, befitting a flat prairie, and are each separated by four to twelve miles, or seven miles on average.

Eunice and Mamou demonstrate how the Dusons created these prairie communities. C. C. Duson conceived Eunice in 1894, named it for his second wife, Eunice Pharr, sketched its plat, auctioned off its lots, and led the effort to get it incorporated as a town in 1895. He did not, however, become its first mayor; that honor went to his son Walter Duson. The elder Duson instead busied himself founding *another* town, twenty miles west of Opelousas and exactly ten miles north of Eunice, by encouraging the Southern Pacific to extend its tracks to create a terminal there—which the company did in 1909. It would be called Mamou, the area's traditional name, of unclear origins. A 1907 *Opelousas*

Courier ad made clear the direction of C. C. Duson's marketing campaign: "Go west, young man, go west," read the copy. "Go west, and go to Mamou."[45]

Located north of the Attakapas region, Mamou occupied the Mamou Prairie, a grassland on which roads were blazed to connect points west toward Mexico with head-of-navigation sites to the east, such as Washington and Port Barre. One of those arteries has been identified as the old Spanish Royal Road or Spanish Trail, which is said to have given rise to Ville Platte ("flat town," on the Little Mamou Prairie), likely as a crossroads and stopover site.[46] Credit is attributed to a former adjutant major in Napoleon's army, Marcelin Garad, who, despite having lost his eyesight in battle, found his way to Louisiana and opened a tavern, where "travelers to Mexico and on the Rapides trail often stopped to hear the old soldier relate his experiences under the 'Little Corporal.'"[47] Garad's saloon became Ville Platte's post office, marking the halfway point between Washington and Chicotville (Bayou Chico). The community later became a Sunday town, trade center (incorporated 1858), and in 1911 an administrative center, as the seat of Evangeline Parish. Today the city of Ville Platte is home to 6,200 people. The community of Chatagnier, with a population of 360, also likely aggregated around a crossroads, halfway between Ville Platte and Eunice.[48]

On the southern flank of the Attakapas Prairie are Abbeville and Gueydan, two communities separated by twenty-two terrestrial miles with nary a waterway in sight. That distance generated need for the two towns to be linked—by the Southern Pacific Railroad, in 1902. The man making the arrangements was a Polish-born Jewish storekeeper named Abrom Kaplan, who, Duson-style, had pre-purchased a former plantation at the halfway point. By year's end, he created a town there and named it for himself. Kaplan, like its neighbors, became yet another example of an ordained five- to ten-mile town sited as a railroad station.[49]

Only one community in the heart of the Attakapas Prairie does *not* have that ordained railroad-based siting story. It can be discerned merely by looking at a map, because it abuts a wiggling waterway and its roads run diagonally rather than orthogonally. It is Church Point, on the banks of Bayou Plaquemine Brûlé, where in the early 1800s Pierre Louis Guidry—remembered as "M'sieu Guid"—established a *magasin* (store) to serve local Acadian settlers. Why here? Maps from 1814 and 1820 show two overland roads crossing here, one emanating from New Roads and the other from Opelousas—both at the same diagonal angle, and now traced by modern roadways. There was probably a crossing at this particular bayou bend (Plaquemine Point), making it a good spot for a country store.[50] Guidry's enterprise drew traffic, as did his offer to Catholic missionaries to use his home to celebrate Mass on Sunday, thus saving

Pointe de l'Eglise emerged from a crossroads near Bayou Plaquemine Brûlé, where a store and later a church opened to serve Acadian settlers. The community became a town in 1843 and anglicized its name to Church Point. Long known for its horse-drawn carriages, it celebrates a Buggy Festival every summer. Photograph by Richard Campanella.

rural neighbors the ten-mile trek to Grand Coteau. In late 1816, a bridge was built at Plaquemine Brûlé, further funneling people here.[51] The faithful built La Chapelle à la Pointe Plaquemine Brûlé at the spot, which got shortened to Pointe de l'Eglise and anglicized to Church Point, the name for the town established in 1843. Into the mid-twentieth century, well after it gained rail service in 1907, this charming Acadian community continued to draw Sunday faithful via a favored means of transportation on the Louisiana prairie: horse-drawn buggies. Harnett T. Kane reported in 1943 that "almost every family has its buggy, sometimes two, [and] thousands of the small vehicles jog along the innumerable back roads," where "the clop-clop of hoofs [is heard] among the heavy-powered delivery trucks and occasional passenger cars." Every town had a "buggy-and-blacksmith shop" for repairs, and everything from dance halls to doctor's offices had "hitching racks."[52]

Much would change in Cajun country after World War II, including the buggy scene. But the equestrian heritage lives on at Church Point in its summertime Buggy Festival, and in the traditional horseback Courier de Mardi Gras during Carnival season. Now an incorporated town of 4,100 people, Church Point has a siting story antithetical to most others on the Attakapas Prairie, being antebellum in its vintage, bayou-side in its geography, emergent in its formation, and a Sunday town in its rationale.[53] Church Point's main house of worship is now Our Lady of the Sacred Heart Catholic Church, and the town's welcome sign, which reads "Bienvenue à Pointe de l'Eglise," features a full-scale sculpture of a horse and buggy.

Of the thirty-seven cities, towns, villages, and other communities in the Bayou Teche, Vermilion River, Opelousas and Attakapas districts analyzed in this study, 35 percent had riverine- or water-based primary siting stories (above the state average of 29 percent), while 38 percent were primarily railroad sites, 5 percent were crossroads, and none were resource extraction or processing sites (compared to state averages of 33 percent, 10 percent, and 13 percent, respectively). The many river and rail sites, compared to the absence of resource sites, reflects the nature of Louisiana prairies, being transected by bayous and rivers, but also flat, relatively upraised, and treeless—good for small vessels and railroad trains, but not timber milling or petrochemical processing. Settlements began forming in this region in the 1760s, peaked in the 1870s, and ended in the 1900s. Some 59 percent of settlements in this region emerged organically, the other 41 percent having been ordained by a founder—compared to a statewide ratio of 49 percent/51 percent emergent/ordained.

10

SOUTHWESTERN LOUISIANA AND THE CHENIER PLAIN

Seven thousand years ago, when the Mississippi River discharged through the Maringouin and Teche deltas (today's Atchafalaya River and Bayou Teche), longshore currents swept alluvium westward along the flanks of the Pleistocene Terrace. Tidal marshes and sandy beaches formed, each intercepting more sediment and expanding the coastal plain. In doing so, beaches grew into narrow ridges, extending westerly five to twenty miles in length, up to twenty-five feet high, and only a few hundred feet wide.[1] Oak trees—*chênes* in French—took root on their well-drained soils, which Creoles called *chéniers*. In the 1930s, geographers coined the term Chenier Plain to describe this wave-dominated derivative of the river-dominated Mississippi Deltaic Plain. All the while, rivers and bayous drained the grasslands and piney woods of the inland Pleistocene Terrace, the largest of which were the Sabine River, Calcasieu River, Bayou Lacassine, and Mermentau River. Each formed estuarine lagoons (a.k.a. bays or lakes) as they neared the coast, respectively Sabine Lake, Calcasieu Lake, Grand Lake, and Lake Arthur.[2]

Coast, plain, beach, chenier, lake, river, terrace: what all this meant to settlers was a paucity of inhabitable sites set within a lattice of access vectors. The longitudinal vectors were the rivers flowing north to south into the Gulf. The latitudinal vectors were roads on chenier ridges extending westward from points east. Most of humanity in southwestern Louisiana, from the nineteenth century to today, sited themselves at the nodes on this lattice, and most other spaces remain marsh or water.

We'll start with the region's easternmost river, the Mermentau (sometimes spelled Mermenton). Tracing the western edge of the Attakapas Prairie, this

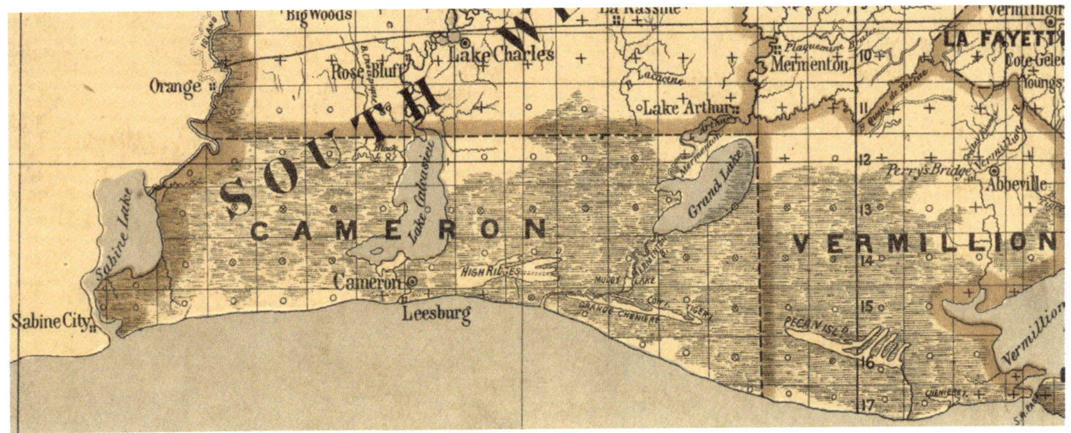

This detail of an 1876 General Lands Office map distinguishes between the prairie terrace and the coastal Chenier Plain (marshy hachures at bottom) of southwestern Louisiana. Library of Congress.

placid waterway is the product of three small bayous merging in a swampy basin. Their confluence allowed for navigability, as the resulting river gained enough volume to deepen its draft and push back tidal influences. It also had sufficiently stable banks for travelers to cross on an overland road, one of two pathways in the vicinity known collectively as the Old Spanish Trail.[3] The crossing may have been where a band of Attakapas Indians, on the move following a series of land sales to the Spanish, settled in 1799. Their chief, named Nementou, is probably the origin of "Mermentau."[4] The road appears on the 1820 John Melish map, connecting this spot with Opelousas, and the words "Head of Tides" are written here in the 1851 H. S. Tanner map. A settlement appears to have formed at Mermentau during the 1820s and 1830s. By the late 1840s, it became large enough to warrant a voting district and tally 100 votes in an 1855 election, and in 1857 Mermentau attained a post office.[5] Steamboats now were able to ply the Mermentau River, making the village a good site for cattle stockades in the shipment of beeves eastward to New Orleans; later, it became a useful processing point for lumber shipped southward to international markets. "The Mermentau River is a navigable stream," explained William Henry Perrin in 1891, "formed by the junction of the Canes, Plaquemine Brule and Nez Pique. Vessels ascend it for more than seventy miles and load with lumber for outside markets, much of it going to Havana and to Mexican ports." Mermentau also became an agricultural hub. "When the timber is cleared," Perrin continued, "the land, which is extremely rich, grows immense quantities of sugar, rice, cotton, corn, sweet and Irish potatoes, peas, melons, pumpkins, fruits, gardens, etc. No richer lands are to be found anywhere."[6]

Multiple siting stories—river crossing, head of navigation, head of tides, transshipment point, resource extraction site—thus explain Mermentau, whose potential was limited only by its river's modest catchment area. Then

Scenic Lake Arthur originated as a head-of-lake site, while riverine and lacustrine resources explain its two enduring economies, as a commodities shipment port and a recreational resort—"Louisiana's Best Kept Secret," according to town advocates. Photographs by Richard Campanella.

came the railroad in 1880, which led the community to relocate to its present position and reinvent itself as a train stop. Mermentau incorporated as a village in 1899 and is now home to 600 people. They reside among the lasting expressions of their siting stories: along Old Spanish Trail Road, where it parallels Railroad Avenue near the village rice mill, and where both the tracks and Highway 90 cross bridges over to the shipyards on the Mermentau River.[7]

As the Mermentau flows southward, it is joined by Bayou Queue de Tortue where the Pleistocene Terrace slopes down to the Chenier Plain. "The lowest part of the Mermentau," wrote geographer Jedidiah Morse in 1819, thence "opens into a spacious lake, and . . . empties into the sea."[8] That waterbody, once called Little Lake and now Lake Arthur, is really a broadened channel of the river as it dilates into Grand Lake, previously Mermentau Lake.[9] According to a local history, settler Atanas Hebert came to the area in 1811, after which two settlements eventually developed on the shores of Lake Arthur. The one at the southern tip was named Lakeside, and the other on the eastern shore was called Shell Beach; both were reachable by schooners sailing in from the Gulf, where sea breezes and balmy winters made for good citrus growing. Timber also beckoned: a sawmill opened at Shell Beach as early as 1840, and a lumber industry grew around the lake. By the 1850s, Lakeside also became something of a resort town, with stores, a post office, orange orchards, and a few comfortable homes favored by French Creoles on holiday from New Orleans.

But two hard freezes killed the orchards, and as the interior prairie developed, economic activity shifted to the firmer soils of the lake's northern shore. One of the first settlers in the new spot was Arthur LeBlanc, and people began referring to both the waterbody and the emerging settlement as Lac d'Arthur, or Lake Arthur—the name of the post office in the 1850s.[10] In testimony to its viability, officials with the Texas & New Orleans Railroad, aiming to link up with Morgan's Louisiana & Texas Railroad being built westward from Algiers, planned for their tracks to go through Lake Arthur as the halfway point between New Iberia and Lake Charles.[11]

The Civil War delayed the rail project, but in the meantime rice, timber, and cattle industries developed in the vicinity, making Lake Arthur a transshipment point between prairie and sea. In the 1880s, the Lake Arthur Town Lot and Land Company managed vessel traffic at the port, laid down a street grid adjacently, and built the "Hotel Arthur . . . finest hotel west of New Orleans" for wintertime tourists who swapped "northern blizzards" for "the fragrance of the rose and the luxury of the vegetable every day of the year[—]the most pleasant winter resort in the south."[12] Surmised William Henry Perrin in 1891, "Lake Arthur begins to consider itself a town, and started a newspaper last year . . . the *Lake Arthur Herald.*"[13]

Now in Jefferson Davis Parish (created in 1912), Lake Arthur is a congenial community of 2,600 people with a weekend getaway air, and its scenic perch on its eponymous waterbody, by Lake Street at the foot of Arthur Avenue, is still the heart of town. Lake Arthur's rationale may be classified as a head-of-lake site, while riverine and lacustrine resources explain its two enduring economies, as a commodities shipment port and a recreational resort—"Louisiana's Best Kept Secret," according to town advocates.

Consider now the next longitudinal vector in our lattice of southwestern settlement sites, the Calcasieu River, which has a similar river-lake-sea transition as the Mermentau and Vermilion, and transects the same hill-terrace-plain profile. But there was a biogeographical distinction here: the Calcasieu Basin was more wooded compared to the grassy prairie interiors to the east. An observer in the late 1850s called its landscape a "hummock," that is, forested land rising above a marsh, and described it as a "tract of more fertile, oak-bearing land, known as the Big Woods."[14] What this implied for future settlement was timber cutting and mill towns.

Another distinction involved political geography. During the eighteenth century, Spanish authorities had viewed the strip of land between the Sabine River and the Arroyo Hondo/Calcasieu River as the easternmost territory of New Spain, while their French counterparts understood it to be the westernmost flank of Louisiana. To everyone else—indigenous tribes, African maroons (escaped slaves), *mestizos,* trappers, stragglers, rogues—it was an ungoverned sanctuary, dangerous but free. In these forests and swamps, Natives displaced from as far away as eastern Tennessee and western Texas, among them members of the Koasati (Coushatta), Choctaw, Caddo, Adai, and Apache tribes, found refuge.[15] The territorial dispute persisted after the Louisiana Purchase in 1803, at which point the Americans inherited France's position in contesting Spanish Mexico over the so-called Sabine Strip. Neither side wanted war, but nor did either wish to lose ground to the other. In 1806, both parties agreed to treat the no-man's land as a demilitarized neutral ground. As historian J. Villasana Haggard put it, "the Neutral Ground was recognized as a well-known area lying between two sovereign nations but under the authority of neither."[16] Others called it the Sabine Free State, Louisiana's "wild west," where ruffians outnumbered settlers, where settlers were squatters, and where neither law nor order prevailed. By one account, some 250 parties had "settled in the western region under what were termed Rio Honda claims," the Spanish name for the region, home to a "race of people of mixed ancestry, known as Red Bones."[17]

Nature does not like a vacuum, and neither does politics. The border dispute was peacefully resolved in 1819 when Spain and the United States signed the "Treaty of Amity, Settlement, and Limits Between the United States of America and His Catholic Majesty." Known also as the Florida Purchase, the agreement stipulated the "boundary-line between the two countries . . . shall begin on the Gulph of Mexico, at the mouth of the river Sabine, in the sea, continuing north, along the western bank of that river, to the 32d degree of latitude."[18] After ratification in 1821, state officials arrived in the region and stewarded land sales under the auspices of St. Landry Parish and subsequently as Calcasieu Parish. The latter, created in 1840, initially had been so large it was nicknamed "Imperial Calcasieu," until its coastal flank became Cameron Parish in 1870.[19]

What steered settlers toward the Calcasieu River was an overland road extending westward from Opelousas across the "Great Carcasui [Calcasieu] Prairie," likely named for Attakapas Indian chief Quelque Shoue.[20] Where that road met a lake, fed by the Calcasieu River as it flowed from hummock to plain, represented a site with many advantages. It was astride a navigable river at a head-of-lake site; it had timber, croplands, and fine pasture to the north, as well as fisheries and other coastal resources to the south; and it was accessible to foreign ports through the Gulf of Mexico. The settlement that formed here gained the name of Italian-born lakeside homebuilder Charles Sallier—today's Lake Charles.

As for that overland route, "the road was now distinctly marked enough," wrote Frederick Law Olmsted when he trekked it in the late 1850s, "but had frequent and embarrassing forks, which occasioned us almost as much annoyance as the clouds of musquitoes."[21] One of those forks had given rise to Lisbon, today's Westlake, founded as a timber mill and shipping site on the Calcasieu River. Other forks activated settlements such as Comasaque Bluff, Marsh Bayou Bluff, Centre, Faulk's Bluff, and the ferry site of Buchanan's Crossing. Calcasieu Parish's police jury had initially selected Comasaque Bluff as the parish seat, but in 1852 the jurors changed it to Lake Charles, thanks to the advocacy of local lumberman Jacob Ryan. Another lumberman, Daniel Goos, who arrived in 1855, established a wood mill and built a wharf (now Goosport) for schooners to trade with Texas and Mexico.

Lake Charles gained incorporation in 1861 under the name of Charleston, though most people still called it Lake Charles. "We were not prepared to find the Calcasieu a superb and solemn river, two hundred and thirty yards across and forty-five feet deep," Olmsted wrote of the waterway. In allusion to its potential as a port site, he noted "it is navigable for forty miles, but at its mouth has a bar, on which is sometimes only eighteen inches of water, ordinarily thirty inches. Schooners of light draft ascend it, bringing supplies, and taking out the cotton raised within its reach. Lake Charles is an insignificant village, upon the bank of a pleasant, clear lakelet, several miles in extent."[22]

In 1867, the unpopular "Charlestown" was officially changed back to "Lake Charles," home to about 400 people, and by now an administrative center, port, and resource extraction site. Thirty years later, Lake Charles had grown more than fifteenfold and boasted two railroads, three major banks, nine churches, telephony, electrification, municipal water, multiple schools from elementary to college, a shipping industry, five wood mills, and a foundry. By 1877, the

Detail of Lake Charles panorama in 1923. Photograph by A. L. Barnett/Library of Congress.

timber industry became the principal economic sector in Calcasieu Parish, as scores of sawmills sent lumber onto sixty schooners to be shipped to ports in Texas, Mexico, and the West Indies. "It is estimated that, at least, four-fifths of the people of Calcasieu Parish depend . . . upon this timber business."[23] In the century to come, Calcasieu Parish would develop an oil and gas industry that would eventually dominate its economy, over which time Lake Charles has consistently ranked as the premier city in southwestern Louisiana, and among the ten largest in the state.[24]

Lake Charles's siting story rhymes with that of Lake Arthur. Both sites were activated by roads meeting navigable rivers where they broadened into "lakelets," both straddled the terrace-to-plain transition zone, and both eventually hosted communities sharing a name with their adjacent waterbodies. Historian A. Michal McMahon described Lake Charles's site as being on "the upper rim of an estuary on the eastern shore of a small lake, the northernmost of several estuarial lakes along the lower Calcasieu River." That waterway forms the second longitudinal vector in our settlement lattice of southwestern Louisiana.[25]

The third vector, the Sabine River, hosts only a single bankside town on the Louisiana side of its 300-mile border with Texas. The question: why, or rather, why not more? Caddo and Attakapas inhabitants lived provisionally along this temperamental river, moving when better conditions beckoned elsewhere—and often, they did. Europeans came with different imperatives, but also found few advantages along the Sabine. The aforesaid Spanish/French/American border dispute further deterred settlers, and the rogues who came in their stead further stigmatized this *terra incognita*—although they and others did give rise to a number of ferry crossings. Some later became steamboat landings, such as Ballieu's, Donoho's, and Hickman's Ferry, the last a forerunner of today's Burr Ferry. But none developed into villages or towns, much less cities.[26]

The main reason for the lack of Sabine siting stories was its bankside morphology, which, starting from its headwaters near Dallas, was either too swampy (*sabine* means "cypress" in Spanish), too steep, or altogether too inaccessible. The channel itself was sinuous, occasionally narrow, prone to shoals, and at one point liable to develop "rapids at low stage of water," while its hinterland was a small watershed of hard clay soils.[27] Worse, Louisiana's side of Sabine Lake and Sabine Pass was all but uninhabitable—"soft sea marsh" and "deep sea marsh," according to an 1840s state land map—just like the Pearl to the east.[28] The Texas side, on the other hand, was sufficiently elevated to host two riverside settlements, today's Orange and Port Arthur, and together they sucked the hope out of a settlement gaining traction on the bedraggled Louisiana side.

Those that tried failed. One rare settlement formed on a high bank at Niblett's Bluff, which was once an Old Spanish Trail crossing point and became a Civil War post and lumber camp. But it faded fast once the Louisiana Western Railroad bypassed it in favor of connecting Vinton directly with Orange. The railroad did install a station on the Sabine, at "a very pretty and pleasant location, with timber and prairie interspersed," according to an observer in 1891, but it too petered out. "Why it has not a good school and church facilities, with all other necessary business houses, seems to be an unanswerable question."[29] Such was the fate of a number of other landings and crossings along Louisiana's western border.

The problem was largely the river itself. Archaeologist Ryan M. Seidemann characterized the Sabine as "both a blessing and a bane" to its neighbors, "prone to massive, devastating floods [and] too treacherous to support substantial steam travel, thus limiting the economic development of the region." Well into the twentieth century, it "remained largely untamed and forgotten in the timberlands of East Texas and West Louisiana," and came to public attention only when plans were made to dam it into the Toledo Bend Reservoir, opened in 1969.[30] Today, the only community-scale features on Louisiana's bank of the Sabine are the town of Logansport at the northern end (examined later), and a massive Sabine Pass Liquefied Natural Gas terminal at the southern end, built entirely on reclaimed land. For the purposes of understanding the peopling of southwestern Louisiana, this third longitudinal vector in our settlement lattice is a study in absence.

"Calcasieu, Cameron and Jefferson Davis Parish are intersected with good highways and three railroad systems," raved the North American Land and Timber Company in a 1916 campaign to sell farmlands. Intersected they indeed were, by east/west arteries crossing north/south rivers, the arteries being roads along the coast and rails through the interior.[31]

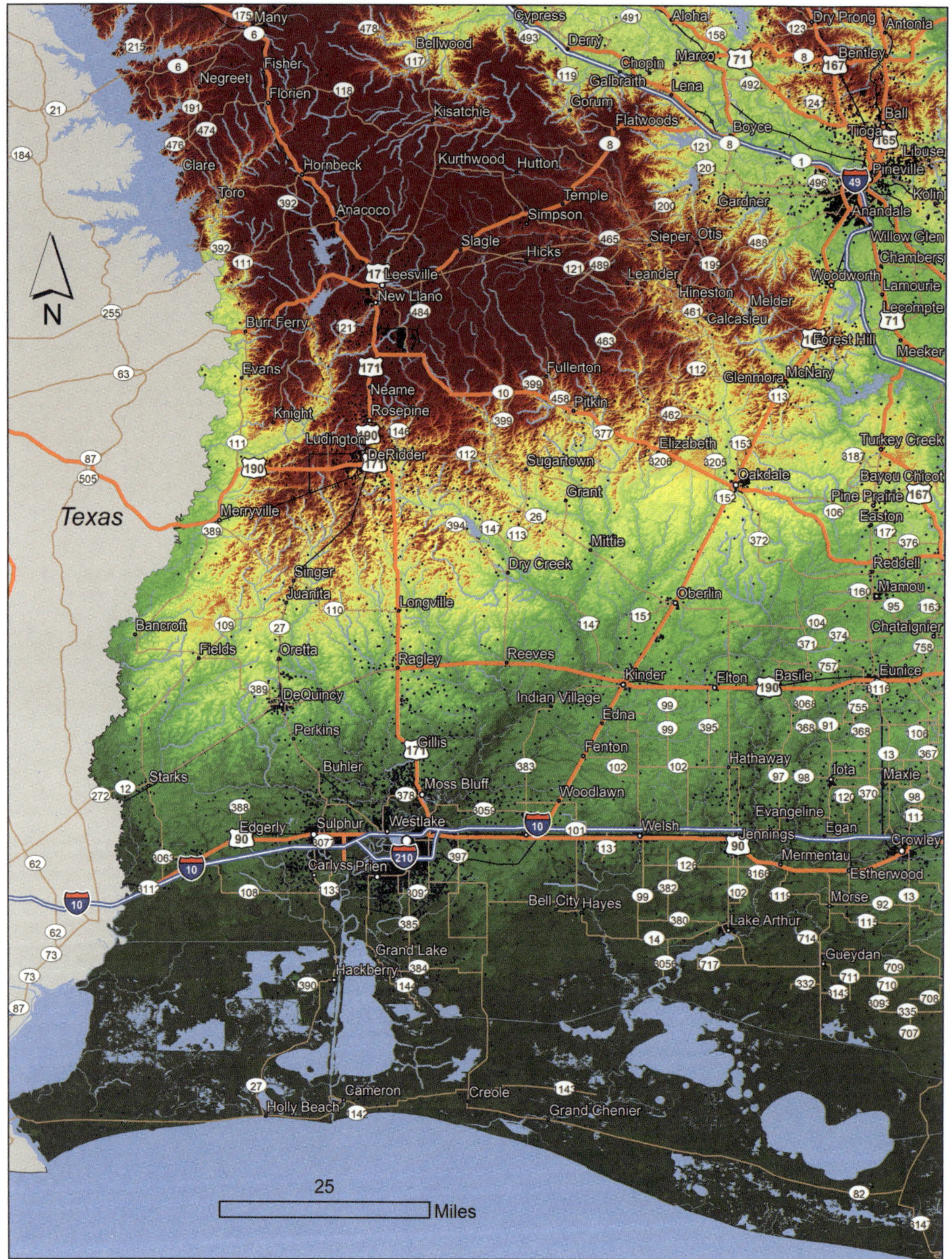
Texas
N
25
Miles
Many
Fisher
Negreet
Florien
Clare
Toro
Hornbeck
Anacoco
Bellwood
Kisatchie
Kurthwood
Hutton
Temple
Simpson
Slagle
Hicks
Leesville
New Llano
Burr Ferry
Evans
Neame
Rosepine
Knight
Ludington
DeRidder
Merryville
Cypress
Derry
Chopin
Galbraith
Gorum
Flatwoods
Aloha
Marco
Lena
Boyce
Dry Prong
Antonia
Bentley
Ball
Tioga
Libuse
Pineville
Kolin
Anandale
Willow Glen
Chambers
Woodworth
Lamourie
Lecompte
Forest Hill
Meeker
Gardner
Sieper
Otis
Leander
Hineston
Melder
Calcasieu
Glenmora
McNary
Fullerton
Pitkin
Elizabeth
Sugartown
Grant
Oakdale
Turkey Creek
Bayou Chicot
Pine Prairie
Easton
Reddell
Mamou
Chataignier
Eunice
Mittie
Dry Creek
Oberlin
Singer
Juanita
Longville
Bancroft
Fields
Oretta
Ragley
Reeves
Kinder
Elton
Basile
DeQuincy
Indian Village
Edna
Perkins
Gillis
Fenton
Buhler
Moss Bluff
Woodlawn
Hathaway
Iota
Maxie
Starks
Evangeline
Edgerly
Sulphur
Westlake
Welsh
Jennings
Egan
Crowley
Mermentau
Estherwood
Carlyss
Prien
Bell City
Hayes
Morse
Lake Arthur
Gueydan
Grand Lake
Hackberry
Cameron
Holly Beach
Creole
Grand Chenier

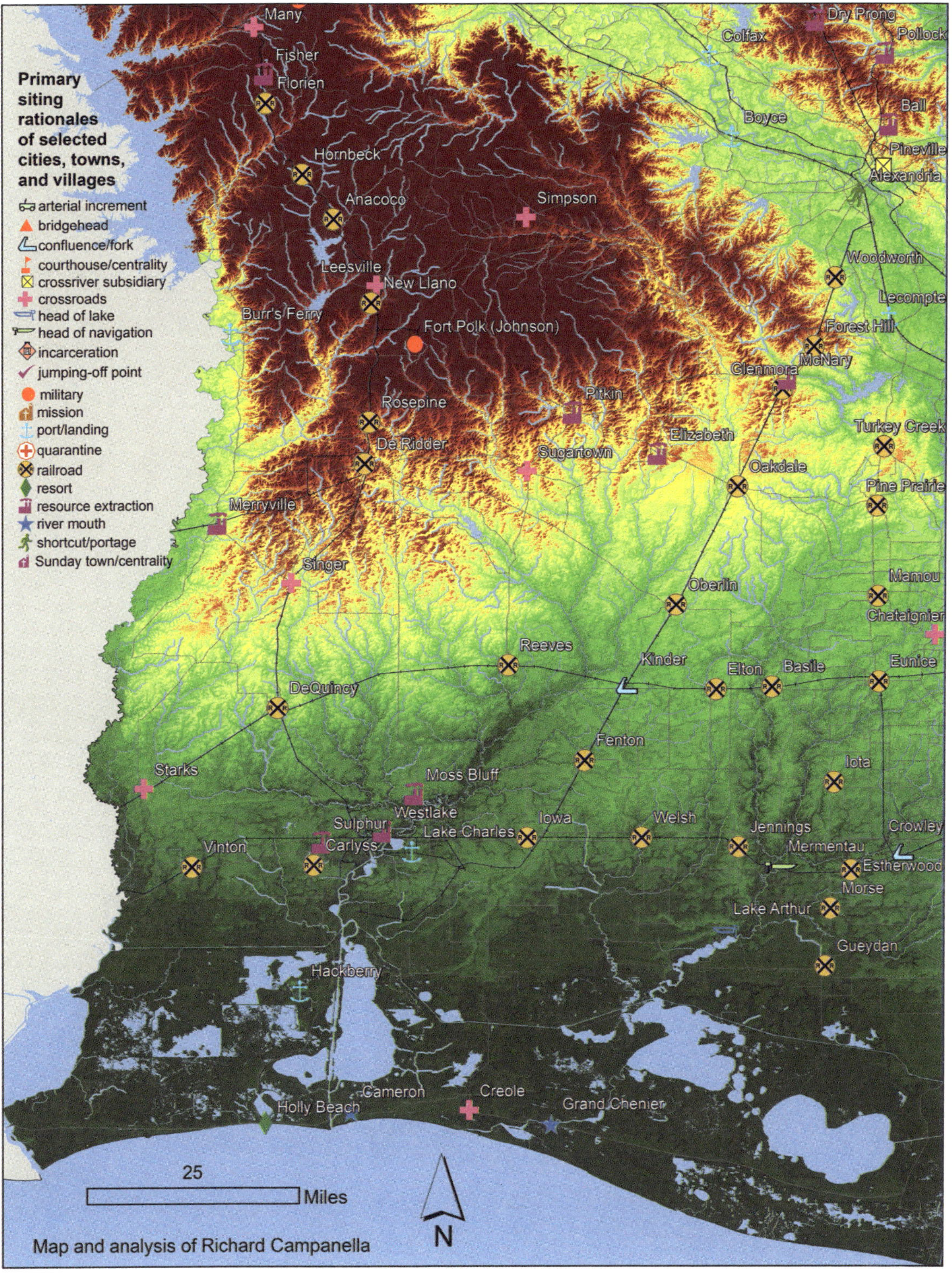

Primary siting rationales of selected cities, towns, and villages
arterial increment
bridgehead
confluence/fork
courthouse/centrality
crossriver subsidiary
crossroads
head of lake
head of navigation
incarceration
jumping-off point
military
mission
port/landing
quarantine
railroad
resort
resource extraction
river mouth
shortcut/portage
Sunday town/centrality
Many
Fisher
Florien
Hornbeck
Anacoco
Leesville
New Llano
Burr's Ferry
Fort Polk (Johnson)
Simpson
Rosepine
De Ridder
Pitkin
Sugartown
Elizabeth
Merryville
Singer
Dry Prong
Pollock
Colfax
Boyce
Ball
Pineville
Alexandria
Woodworth
Lecompte
Forest Hill
McNary
Glenmora
Turkey Creek
Oakdale
Pine Prairie
Oberlin
Mamou
Chataignier
Reeves
Kinder
Elton
Basile
Eunice
DeQuincy
Fenton
Starks
Moss Bluff
Iota
Westlake
Sulphur
Carlyss
Lake Charles
Iowa
Welsh
Jennings
Crowley
Vinton
Mermentau
Estherwood
Morse
Lake Arthur
Gueydan
Hackberry
Cameron
Creole
Grand Chenier
Holly Beach
25
Miles
N
Map and analysis of Richard Campanella

The roads closest to the coast followed cheniers, those long, narrow ridges of wave-swept sediments comprising the only inhabitable land, so much so that locals called them islands. From Vermilion Bay westward to the Sabine River, they included Pecan Island, Tiger Island, Indian Point Island, Grand Chenier, Oak Grove, Creole, Cameron, and Johnson's Bayou, while nearby were the Gulf-side hamlets of Holly Beach, Constance Beach, and Ocean View Beach.[32] Today, only about half of these communities endure, none with more than 400 residents, some without street grids, and not a single one incorporated as a municipality. Yet chenier settlements tell informative siting stories, because, along with Grand Isle, they represent Louisiana's purest—and most vulnerable—examples of coastal communities. Their rationales are straightforward. "Islands" such as Pecan, Tiger, and Indian Point, as well as Johnson's Bayou, may be characterized as dry-point jumping-off sites for the extraction of fur, game, fish, and other natural resources. Oak Grove and Creole are crossroad sites, being on chenier roads where they intersect an artery (now Highway 27) connecting with Lake Charles. Another coastal road proceeding up to Sulphur gave rise to Holly Beach, while the halfway point between Holly Beach and Sulphur helped spur the Calcasieu Lake-side community of Hackberry.

As dry-point sites at river mouths, Grand Chenier and Cameron have long been Louisiana's largest chenier settlements. Both originated in the 1840s as a consequence of the Preemption Act, which, in the interest of westward expansion, gave first option to purchase federal land to squatters, and second option to incoming homesteaders. In the case of the cheniers, once the government decided it did not need their oak trees for naval ship wood, it opened up the region for preemption. Another program granted lands to military veterans, many of whom subsequently sold their titles to speculators, who in turn sold them to homesteaders. "In the 1830's and '40's, a wave of migration from Virginia, the Carolinas, Georgia, Alabama, and Mississippi swept into the cheniers," stated a Cameron Parish history; "they were for the most part of Celtic or Anglo-Saxon lineage," followed later by Acadians or Creoles.[33] The Smith and McCall families were the first to settle at the mouth of the Mermentau River, while the Wakefield and Doxey families settled by the Calcasieu's mouth, and those that followed had surnames like Hall, Griffin, Root, and Miller.

Settlement on Grand Chenier was emphatically linear, a coastal corollary to the adage about throwing a baseball from house to house all the way down Bayou Lafourche. The only nucleated section was a place called Riverside on the Mermentau, where by the 1890s there were four churches, "excellent" schools, "three stores and several residences, post-office and shipping post" where transacted "at least two hundred thousand dollars' worth of shipments," plus the Stafford Ferry accessing Creole and Cameron. Along the rest of the chenier, some 200 families cultivated what seemed like "one continuous, unbroken farm," yielding sugar, corn, oranges, melons, and poultry, as well as cotton for shipment to Galveston, while the surrounding marshes abounded in "ducks, brant, geese, etc." Grand Chenier was also a key point for cattle raised on the Louisiana prairie to be shipped down the Mermentau River en route to New Orleans.[34]

Twenty chenier-miles to the west is Cameron, a dry-point site near the mouth of the Calcasieu River, where the ridge runs through a marshy strait between Lake Calcasieu and the Gulf of Mexico. Settlement here also began in the 1840s and stayed small until the designation of Cameron Parish in 1870, at which point the riverside houses gained the name Leesburg and became the parish seat. That status made the outpost into an administrative and trade center as well as a shipping point, particularly for cattle. Leesburg by the 1890s consisted of "a court house, one small store, and, perhaps, half a dozen other buildings."[35] But to visionaries it had great potential—if only the mouth of the Calcasieu River could be deepened. This was, after all, the largest river between Texas and the Atchafalaya, and its hinterland resources had markets all along the Gulf Coast. "Cameron has not yet had her day," predicted a state agent around 1890. "Her parish seat, Leesburg, is right on the Gulf of Mexico, at the mouth of the Calcasieu River, [ideal for] canning fish, oysters and shrimp" as well as transshipping cotton and cattle. "If deep water ever comes to the mouth of the river, Leesburg will be a great place by reason of that alone, [where] the largest ocean steamers can ascend the Calcasieu River, which is a deep stream, to the town of Lake Charles, some fifty-five miles from the gulf."[36]

Others saw the potential too. Arthur Stilwell, founder of the Kansas City, Pittsburg & Gulf Railroad, aimed to connect Kansas City slaughterhouses with Louisiana cattle country by extending his trade network to an intermodal port on the Gulf Coast. He built his rails through western Louisiana and laid out the train-stop town of DeQuincy in 1897, at which point he had to finalize the decision of where to reach the sea. "Stilwell visited Cameron, seeing it as a possible site for a port on the Gulf," wrote historian Donald J. Millet. "But being unable to come to terms with the large property owners in that parish, he turned his attention to Texas." The rails from DeQuincy instead veered westward through Beaumont, and the port that Cameron could have become for the Calcasieu River mouth instead went to a site on the other side of the Sabine River mouth. So proud was Arthur Stilwell of his new city that he named it after himself: Port Arthur, Texas.[37]

Leesburg also got a new name. Because Louisiana already had a Leeville and a Leesville, Leesburg's post office was named Cameron, while the community remained Leesburg. The confusion led to both the post office and community getting named Cameron, something requiring no great paperwork because the community had never incorporated. As for that channel-deepening project, it did come to fruition, but not to Cameron's advantage. The Calcasieu Ship Channel, dug in the 1920s, did indeed bring economic action—but to Lake Charles. Vessels could now beeline for the larger port inland, which would only grow larger, developing extensive petrochemical and natural gas facilities. Once again, Cameron got bypassed.

One of the state's few unincorporated seats of justice, Cameron, home to only 220 people, serves a storm-battered parish that is Louisiana's largest in area but second-lowest in population, home to only 5,000 residents. Port Arthur, incidentally, has 55,000, while Lake Charles has 81,000.

What cheniers were to the southwest Louisiana coast, railroads were to its interior, forming latitudinal settlement vectors in our lattice. Recall the Louisiana Western Railroad, the station-siting town-maker that opened in 1880 to link New Orleans with Texas, and how it ordained the prairie towns of Scott, Duson, Rayne, and Crowley, each at five-mile increments. Continuing westward, at a 4.7-mile average increment, gets us to Esterwood, Midland, and Mermentau, the first two of which were also ordained by the railroad, and the third having shifted *to* the railroad. Beyond the Mermentau River basin, the landscape rises back up to a prairie terrace, where we find the same flatland settlement geography we saw by Lafayette and Abbeville, with a township-range-section cadastral system, rectilinear roads, and Christaller's centralized places. This was Louisiana's "Midwest"—and in more ways than one: the same companies that laced southwestern Louisiana with rails now set about to people it with midwesterners.

The man behind the effort was Iowa-born Sylvester L. Cary, who, as agent for the Southern Pacific Railroad in 1883, advertised the region's attributes to populations back home. "So successful was he in this endeavor," wrote historian Donald J. Millet, "that the railroad company promoted him in 1887 to the position of Northern Immigration Agent with headquarters in Manchester, Iowa."[38] Anglo-Saxon farming families by the hundreds came to French Acadian country, lured by fliers declaring "Go South, Young Man—PROSPERITY, I Hear You Calling Me."[39] They brought their culture with them, including vernacular architecture such as the "I-house" (so named for their Indiana-Illinois-Iowa origins), distinctive for what geographer Fred Kniffen described as its "sideward-facing gables and one-room depth, in addition to its two storeys," some shaped "square with a pyramidal roof." In the 1930s, Kniffen mapped vernacular house types statewide and found the I-house "strikingly and sharply confined to the heart of the prairie region of southwestern Louisiana, where it was imported from the Corn Belt about forty years ago." He estimated that I-houses made up as much as 60 percent of the Jennings area, nicknamed the Iowa Colony.[40] Why here? That's where agent Sylvester Cary had his Louisiana office, and the circa 1880 train depot where he was based became Jennings—named for Jennings McComb, president of the Louisiana Western Railroad Company, and located roughly halfway between Lafayette and Lake Charles. Within ten years of its 1881 founding, Jennings boasted 400 platted acres around its centralized train station, along with twelve stores, five hotels, a school for 250 students, three churches, facilities for the all-important rice industry—and lots of I-houses.[41]

The development of that regional crop occurred thanks to a concurrent Midwest connection. Enter Seaman A. Knapp, president of Iowa State College of Agriculture, who the North American Land and Timber Company had contracted in 1885 to conduct agronomic research on southwestern Louisiana. Recognized today as a pioneer of agricultural extension, Knapp demonstrated the region's viability for rice cultivation. Collaborating with Sylvester Cary, he "attracted a group of Iowans to come down en masse and settle in Louisiana." What resulted, in part, was the Louisiana town of Iowa (pronounced "eye-uh-way"), sited at the fourth station stop (after Roanoke, Welsh, and Lacasinne) west of Jennings. Each was distanced by approximately five miles, along a railroad, through rice fields. And each was sprinkled with I-houses.[42]

At around this time, a new industry burst from beneath the Gulf Coast, and it would soon transform the world. Locals had long happened upon petroleum leaks, but either the quantity or the means of extracting and utilizing the sludgy substance fell short of economic feasibility. As technology progressed, "wildcatters" prowled the coastal region in search of accessible reserves. They found some in Calcasieu Parish as early as 1859, but it was not until the new century that all the requisite variables fell into place. January 1901 saw the famous Spindletop gushers in the Texas town of Beaumont, September brought strikes in Evangeline outside the Louisiana town of Jennings, and by year's end both states had a corporate oil industry. Soon, settlements were sited in its service, some as company towns (for example, Norco), some as end-of-artery entrepôts (like Port Fourchon), and others as resource extraction sites, such as Port Sulphur in southeastern Louisiana. The extreme opposite corner of the state also produced sulphur (sulfur), that yellow brimstone extracted from crude and used for fertilizer, and here too it became a siting story.

Make no mistake, it was the Louisiana Western Railroad that nourished Sulphur into a city, and its train station marked the center of town, ten miles west of Lake Charles. But Sulphur germinated as a resource extraction site, starting in 1865, when prospectors detected surface oil by a salt dome and found pure sulphur and gypsum below layers of quicksand. Using a dangerous extraction process, they launched a mining enterprise, and although it yielded only sporadic profits, they hired men and housed them in an adjacent community. One prospector, Eli Perkins, started a sawmill at nearby Rose Bluff, and in 1876 he opened a general store "to serve the workers in the oil and sulfur industry that were taking up residence near the sulfur dome northwest of modern-day Sulphur."[43] As the Louisiana Western Railroad tracks were under construction, plans were made by Thomas Kleinpeter in 1878 to lay out Sulphur City, which soon got a train depot named Brimstone (or Sulphur Mine Station, according to one map) and in 1884 its first post office.[44]

In 1890, the noted German chemist Herman Frasch came to Sulphur City and, in the employ of the Union Sulphur Company, developed the technique of superheating water to melt and push molten brimstone up to the surface with compressed air. The Frasch Process, safer and more profitable than earlier methods, transformed the industry and put Sulphur on the map. ("City" was dropped from its name in 1895.) Sulphur's population surpassed 1,500 people in the early 1900s, and in 1914 the community incorporated as a town. Local boosters claimed its *raison d'être* was "the largest Sulphur Mine in the world[;] the product is 98% pure and several hundred skilled and unskilled workmen are employed on this property," while "Calcasieu Parish has the largest Oil producing fields in the State."[45] In the decades ahead, oil and gas would replace brimstone as the area's main economic driver. Today, Sulphur, population 20,000 and now part of greater Lake Charles, remains rooted in its original siting story of resource extraction and processing—a site where, from the 1890s through the 1920s, workers "were producing more [sulphur] in one little city than . . . the rest of the world combined. It was massive."[46]

Vinton, at first glance, might appear to be a standard station-stop town along the Louisiana Western (Southern Pacific) Railroad, roughly halfway between Sulphur and Orange. At second glance, it might seem like a resource extraction site, as evidenced by the forest of derricks that once covered the Vinton oil fields, as well as the literal forest of yellow pine to the north.[47] Trains, oil, and trees all certainly boosted Vinton, but they did not birth it. Vinton is situated along the narrowest neck of land between the Sabine and Calcasieu rivers—a perigee of sorts—and aligns with Niblett's Bluff, the only high point along Louisiana's bank of the Sabine, and a crossing point of the Old Spanish Trail.[48] Vinton is also riverine, being along Hampton Coulee just above its confluence with Coon Gully. Topographically, it sits upon the edge of the prairie

Sulphur's siting story is told in a museum recounting the brimstone mine where new extraction technologies were developed. Photograph by Richard Campanella.

terrace, elevated above the coastal plain. Relatedly, according to an 1840s state lands map, it marks an intersection of the Old Spanish Trail. "It has a position of commanding commercial importance," noticed an observer in 1891, "only six miles to the Sabine, navigable for three hundred miles, and with the bar at the mouth improved for the passage of ocean steamers, and nine miles southeasterly to tide water on Bayou Choupique, which flows into the Calcasieu river. North is a vast forest of yellow pine, which can best be penetrated by a railroad from Vinton."[49]

The founding of Vinton involved the same visionaries behind Jennings: Iowa agronomist Seaman Knapp, who ascertained the rice-growing potential of Calcasieu Parish, and his railroad partner Sylvester Cary, with whom Knapp devised the successful midwestern recruitment plan. Also critical was Jabez B. Watkins, a Kansas-born farm mortgage entrepreneur who in 1883 purchased 1.5 million acres of government land in the Calcasieu region and worked with agricultural interests in selling farmland to incoming midwesterners. In 1887, Knapp himself bought 2,700 acres of federal land through which ran the Southern Pacific tracks, and selected a 160-acre section with particularly auspicious geography—the aforementioned waterways, topography, intersection, etc. In May 1888, Knapp had a grid of streets laid out around the train station, after which came a store, a post office, and houses. Another account credits Robert F. Evans, Frank H. Banker, and William Kirkman with involvement in key land purchases, and dates Knapp's purchase and platting to 1890. Most accounts credit Knapp for naming the community Vinton, in honor of his prior residence of Vinton, Iowa, but here too there is debate. One researcher suggests the name came from a group of Buckeyes from yet another Vinton, in Ohio, who formed a Vinton Colony in Lake Charles, one of whom later bought land in the new Louisiana town and brought the name with him.[50]

Today, Vinton, Louisiana, is an incorporated town of 3,100 people, and its cofounder Seaman Knapp is recognized by the U.S. Department of Agriculture as the father of the Cooperative Extension Service.[51] As for Vinton's siting stories, they fall in two categories: those emergent from history and geography, and those ordained by visionaries with means. The latter gave rise to Vinton proper, but the community would not have happened at this locale were it not for the former.

Of the eighteen cities, towns, villages, and other communities in southwestern Louisiana and the Chenier Plain analyzed in this study, 39 percent had riverine- or water-based primary siting stories (above the state average of 29 percent), while 28 percent were primarily railroad sites, 17 percent were resource extraction or processing sites, and 11 percent were crossroads (compared to state averages of 33 percent, 13 percent, and 10 percent, respectively). Settlements began forming in this region fairly late, due to political uncertainties. They got underway in the 1840s, peaked in the 1870s, and ended in the 1920s. Settlements in this region were precisely split between those of emergent versus ordained origins, as they were statewide.

11

THE RED RIVER REGION

After establishing footholds on the Gulf Coast and lower Mississippi River, French colonization moved inland to secure indigenous alliances and trade routes before imperial rivals did. One of the few men to have participated in nearly every settlement effort since 1699 was the French Canadian soldier and explorer Louis Antoine Juchereau de St. Denis, and it was he who Governor Antoine de la Mothe Cadillac selected in 1713 to secure the western frontier. Seeking to preempt threats from Spanish Mexico and to ally with tribes to trade for furs and horses, St. Denis spearheaded settlement along an idiosyncratic river channel in which water seemed uniquely prone to jamming, damming, and avulsing. The French called it the Rivière Rouge, born in today's New Mexico and tinted cimarron by sediment. St. Denis aimed to build a fort and trading post as far up that reddish-colored river as he could sail, row, pole, or tow.

It was no easy task navigating Louisiana rivers in this era. Currents ran strong during spring freshets, and sandbars lurked during dry autumns. In deeper waters, timbers with rock-entangled roots bobbed beneath the surface and threatened to smash hulls, while dense thicket limited docking opportunities along the banks. As the flow gradient steepened, crew members used whatever combination of oars, poles, sails, and cordelles (towlines) could beat the current. All too often, a thin line of trees out on a shoal obscured the distinction between the main channel and cutoff meanders or side lakes, causing confusion. Particularly perplexing was the confluence of the Red and Mississippi rivers, where an enormous logjam created a hydrological maze that would bedevil Louisianians for generations to come. Conditions hardly improved farther up the Rivière Rouge, as a colleague of St. Denis experienced in 1716. "I shall say only that this river floods during high water and one cannot find any

This detail of *Le Missis-sipi ou la Louisiane dans l'Amérique septentrio-nale* depicts a portage site at upper left, in which Natives carry their canoe on a pathway connecting two water-bodies. Portages were a frequent siting rationale for many early Louisiana settlements. Library of Congress.

ground to camp on, [and] when it is down, navigation is impossible because of the lack of water."[1]

As St. Denis ventured upriver, floodplains gave way to discernible topography on the east bank, including the Pleistocene Terrace at future Baton Rouge and Scotlandville, and the loess bluffs at Port Hudson, St. Francisville, and Tunica. Once he veered up the Red, however, bottomlands prevailed up to the point where the river incised siltstone and sandstone facies of the undulating Kisatchie Wold. Here in the Red River Valley, a series of logjams known as rafts had long impeded flow and impounded natural reservoirs (raft lakes), from which water discharged sporadically. At one point, it cut through sandstone outcroppings to form two cataracts over a span of two miles, including a 640-foot-long rocky stretch with a vertical drop of seventeen feet. A rarity in Louisiana, "the Red River rapids" impeded navigation, particularly during the low water months of July through January. Boatmen could either wait for a freshet or lighten their load and gingerly float over them, or they could land and carry (*porter* in French) their longboats and cargo on a path (*portage*) circumventing the obstacle.[2]

Portages invited overnight stays that sometimes grew into lingering encampments. Some sources claim a settlement materialized near the cataracts as early as 1723, though it was probably little more than reutilized shelters.[3] As Red River traffic increased and more people circumvented the falls, some settled to form the Poste du Rapides in the late 1700s, which in 1818 became Alexandria, Louisiana. "Alexandria is just below the 'Falls,'" wrote an observer in 1860, and "by this location, it secures uninterrupted water communication with the outside world much more continuously than do its neighbors, Natchitoches, Shreveport, and other towns far up the stream," because "when the river is low, the falls. . . . are impassable, the shallow water boiling furiously over the rocky bed."[4] Abetted by that pause in navigation, and subsequently by overland roads, timber milling, and railroads, Alexandria grew to the point of spawning a cross-river subsidiary named Pineville—all ultimately traceable to the rapids and their effect on human passage. Now home to over 164,000 Louisianians, the Alexandria/Pineville metro area shares the siting story of Niagara Falls in New York, Willamette Falls in Oregon, and Louisville on the Ohio River, in that all emerged from circumvention portages. Alexandria's parish is still named after the colonial-era Poste du Rapides, even though the cataracts of Rapides Parish have long disappeared underwater, thanks to modern river management.[5]

St. Denis managed to get past those falls, but the Red's shallow drafts did not bode well, nor did rumors about logjams farther upriver—the main Red River Raft and the lakes behind it. Sensing his explorations had reached their apogee, St. Denis surveilled for a fort site, for which indigenous allies served as critical informants.

A fortified post somewhere along the Red meant a lot to the colonization of Louisiana. It would secure the French side of the vague Spanish borderlands, tap into the region's furs and fertile lands, and open trading opportunities with Spanish communities to the west as well as the Caddo nation to the north, including the Kadohadacho, Nacogdoches, Adai, and Natchitoches tribes. The Caddo were key trading partners, offering salt, pottery, and bow wood to tribes of the Plains, and receiving horses and textiles from Spanish settlers in Tejas—Texas, likely from the Caddo word *techas,* meaning "friends."[6]

As for an optimal site, none came to attention along the Red's flood-prone

The Red River rapids, labeled as "Lower Falls" in this detail of a Civil War–era map, created the need for a portage that eventually gave rise to the city of Alexandria. The waterfalls also explain the name of Rapides Parish. *Sketch of the Two Breakwaters Above Alexandria in the Red River* (1864), by F. H. Gerdes and Lewis G. De Russy, Library of Congress.

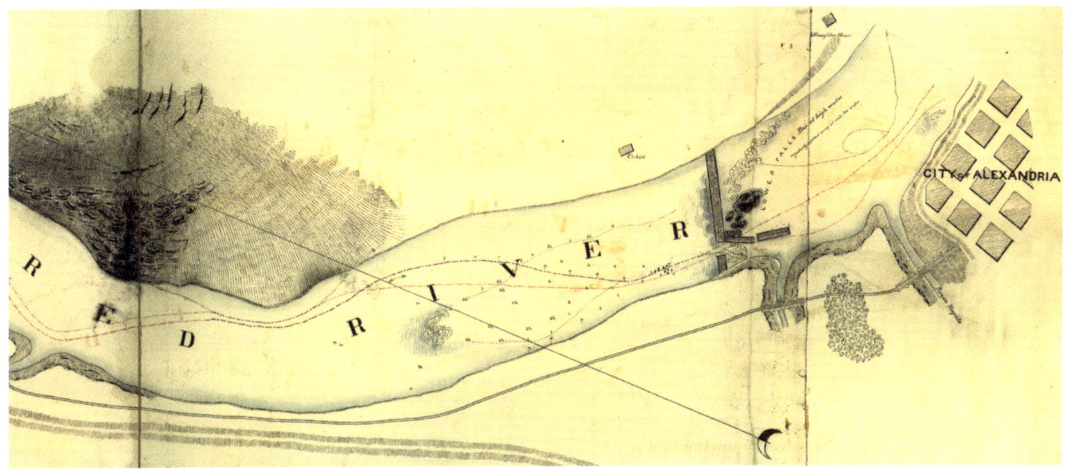

banks. But up a subsidiary channel known as the Rivière aux Cannes, the water had cut through outcroppings of the Nacogdoches Wold, giving it firmer banks. An indigenous village already sat on this upraised edge of the Red River Valley, which caught St. Denis's attention—evidence of geographer Milton Newton's observation that colonials often selected sites based on the actions of Indians, in this case a Tunica chief known as Bride de Boeufs.[7] In 1714, St. Denis chose a bankside spot on the Cane River for Fort St. Jean Baptiste des Natchitoches, on which construction commenced in 1716. The fort covered a 150-by-125-foot area and comprised a timber stockade with four corner blockhouses, inside of which were barracks, warehouses, a commissary, and a church.[8]

Over the next two decades, bankside erosion and occasional high water made the original fort site untenable, so in 1735 St. Denis's colleague Ignace François Broutin began building a new fort 1,000 feet inland, on a bluff known as Musler's Hill.[9] Decades later, after the departure of the French, Spanish administrators moved the fort and its accompanying settlement to another bluff a half-mile north, directly overlooking the Cane River—today's Front Street in Natchitoches. The three sites of eighteenth-century Natchitoches together constitute the first permanent European settlement in present-day Louisiana, and the oldest permanent European settlement within the expanse of the Louisiana Purchase, traceable to 1714—four years before New Orleans, as locals are quick to point out.

Why here? Natchitoches marked the Red River's head of navigation, by virtue of an *embaràs d'arbre* ("tree trap," or logjam) in the Cane River, as well

This reconstruction of Fort St. Jean Baptiste des Natchitoches (*right*) marks the site selected by St. Denis in 1714 for a French military outpost at the head of navigation on a branch of the log-jammed Red River. The settlement was later moved to a high bluff overlooking the Cane River, today's Natchitoches (*below*). Photographs by Richard Campanella.

The Spanish response to French Natchitoches was to build their own fort and mission nearby at Los Adaes (*left*). The easternmost point of Spanish Mexico, Los Adaes was linked to San Antonio and Mexico City by a network of trails known loosely as the Camino Real (Royal Road, a.k.a. Old Spanish Trail), whose ceremonial Zero Milestone (*right*) is marked today in San Antonio, Texas. Photographs by Richard Campanella.

as the much larger Red River Raft farther upstream, one so massive it would effectively barricade navigation well into the 1800s. The two subsequent relocations put the present-day city of Natchitoches on a dry-point site, the first high ground nearest to advantageous but flood-prone waterways.[10]

After the French planted their flag at Natchitoches, the Spanish felt compelled to respond in kind on their side of the borderlands. It would have to be somewhere accessible to their Camino Real de los Tejas—the Royal Road, or King's Highway, a network of backcountry trails emanating from Mexico City through present-day Texas and into Louisiana. As this pathway neared its easternmost terminus, it passed two wooded hills with a spring and stream—a wet-point site, with road access and a topographic perch, sufficient for the Spanish to take a stand against the French a dozen miles to the east. On one hill, Spanish officials in 1717 erected La Misión de San Miguel de Cuellar de los Adaes, named for the Adai Indians they hoped to convert, while on the other hill, in 1721, Gil Ybarbo and a group of Mestizos from Nuevo León built El Presidio de Nuestra Señora del Pilar de los Adaes, a wooden stockade roughly matching Fort St. Jean Baptiste in design and materials.[11] For the next half-century, remote Los Adaes served as the capital of the Province of Texas, and became a node for missionary and military operations—as well as for illicit trade with the French at Natchitoches. Borderlands tend to brew shifty alliances.

By the 1770s, after the departure of the French, the Spanish now controlled Natchitoches and all of *Luisiana,* thus obviating the siting rationale for Los Adaes. Authorities closed the fort and mission in 1773 and sent the soldiers back to San Antonio. But many remained, having married into various indigenous and mixed-race groups, and some obtained land grants as part of Spain's policy of populating Louisiana.[12]

One such Spanish grant for lands near Los Adaes went, in 1795, to a Frenchman named Pierre (Pedro) Dolet, who, according to the executor, "pulled up Grass, Planted Stakes, and threw dust in the air to show his possession."[13] Another, known as the Los Ormigas Land Grant, spans much of present-day Sabine and DeSoto parishes, and legally undergirds much of their subsequent settlement. Another, known as La Nana Land Grant (1797), went to a settler named Manuel Sanchez for an area where the Camino Real crossed a confluence of Bayou Nana, a convenient stopping site for travels.

Anglo-American settlers later made their way down the old Spanish Camino Real, which they made into the Natchitoches and San Antonio Highway. One of them, John Baldwin, built a double-pen dogtrot log cabin near that confluence crossing on Bayou Nana. He opened Baldwin's Store in one of the cabin pens, which attracted more travelers, and thus more settlers, leading to the blazing of additional roads. In 1843 the state legislature designated this site to become the seat of the newly created Sabine Parish, and named it to honor Colonel James B. Many, the American garrison commander at nearby Fort Jesup. Baldwin's Store spawned a community boasting a "hotel, tavern, general mercantile, post office, city hall, and courthouse."[14]

Today in Many (pronounced *Man-ee,* population 2,500), one is greeted by a stately Spanish Mission–style Catholic church emplaced squarely on the former Camino Real. Along the intersecting San Antonio Avenue, one finds a prominent building designed like the Alamo (only bigger) and a theater named after the Parish of Sabine—the Spanish word for cypress, Louisiana's state tree.[15] Wrote parish historian John G. Belisle of this intersection, "there were two great avenues for travel through Sabine Parish, the road from Natchitoches to San Antonio, opened by St. Denys [Denis], and the highway known as Nolan's Trace . . . between Alexandria and Texas." Writing in 1912, he noted also that "Fallen Springs, four miles south of Many, was a popular camping ground for all who traveled the Nolan road, and in this vicinity many robberies and murders are alleged to have been perpetrated."[16]

Fort Jesup had been established by the Americans in 1822 for the same reason France founded Natchitoches and Spain created Los Adaes: as a defensive garrison and to protect settlers from the sort of frontier bedlam ongoing at Fallen Springs. "The site for the fort is one of the most commanding and picturesque that could have been selected," wrote Belisle. "Located in the center of a reservation two miles square" along the Natchitoches-San Antonio Road, Fort Jesup was "situated on one of the highest elevations in Louisiana and a surrounding country altogether beautiful."[17]

Communities sited for military strategy, however, often die out when

Many, Louisiana, aggregated around a general store founded where the Old Spanish Trail crossed Bayou Nana. Though settled mostly by Anglos, the town retains a Spanish Texan flair, with its Mission-style Catholic church (*left*) on San Antonio Avenue. Nearby is Fort Jesup (*right*), the American military response to the Spanish presence in Texas. Photographs by Richard Campanella.

threats fade, and that's what happened once France, then Spain, then Mexico left the region. "There are no traces of Adios left any more," wrote travel writer Catharine Cole, who understood Los Adaes to be either Adyas or Adios and translated it as "the jumping off place." Once "a village of adobe houses and Spanish inhabitants," all that remained by the time of her 1888 visit was "that mysterious clearing that Nature never forgives nor re-clothes." The nearest population today is the hundred or so people who now live in what Cole described as "the new railroad town of Robeline" a mile away, where the Texas & Pacific Railroad crossed the former Camino Real.[18]

As for Fort Jesup, it remained a stopover on the Natchitoches-San Antonio Road, with a hotel and other services. It even had its own den of iniquity, nearby Shawneetown, where soldiers rendezvoused with locals for "ruffian revelry."[19] The military post served as a concentration point for American troops deployed in the Mexican-American War, but once the war ended and Texas joined the Union, Fort Jesup was abandoned (1846). In 1903, homesteaders were allowed to settle on the larger reservation, giving rise to the few dozen households near the old fort site today, enough to warrant a "Fort Jesup Community" roadside sign.

Los Adaes and Fort Jesup are among Louisiana's best examples of purely military siting stories. They evidence that militarized sites do not necessarily make good urban locations if they have no economic advantages backing them up. As for Fallen Springs, it completely fell off the map—except for treasure hunters seeking booty allegedly buried by frontier bandits.

Fort St. Jean Baptiste, on the other hand, managed to reincarnate into the modern city of Natchitoches, home to over 17,000 people. It avoided the fate of Los Adaes and Fort Jesup because, in addition to being militarily strategic, it was also a head-of-navigation site with trading advantages—which brings our attention back to the Red River.

The Red is rather ordinary at its headwaters, on the Llano Estacado in eastern New Mexico. As it flows eastward past arid Amarillo, its sparse waters attain a growing load of Permian-Age sediment, giving a ruddy color called *Bah Hatínu* by the Caddo, *Rojo* by the Spanish, *Rouge* by the French, and Red by the Americans. As the river wended eastward, its water volume swelled in the verdant Texarkana region, where it attained "one of the largest sediment concentrations of all major rivers in the world," along with a debris load to match—timbers, brush, and roots falling into the channel from soft banks through dense woods.[20] It is in northwestern Louisiana that the Red becomes extraordinary, perhaps unique. Because of the way its waters incised a narrow valley through the state's oldest rock layers—the Paleocene-Epoch Sabine Uplift and Natchitoches Wold, 65 million years old—debris tended to jam the gorge and dam the flow. Making things worse was an avulsion (channel jump) farther downriver, as discussed previously in the siting stories of Simmesport and Melville, which positioned the Red to eventually empty into the Mississippi and discharge down a longer path to the sea. That weakened gradient had the effect of slowing water velocity, causing yet more sediment and organic matter to fall out upstream. Logjams ensued *en masse,* like few other rivers on earth, and they turned Louisiana's Red into a snarl of pent-up hydraulic energy. "This entanglement of logs, vegetation, and sediments remained in place for at least a millennium," wrote geologists Nalini Torres and Danny Harrelson, "causing a complete change in its geomorphic character from a single channel to a series of anastomosing [interconnecting] channels," each with *their* own logjams. Debris heaps merged into what became known as the Red River Raft, and "as the Raft grew, the Red River was forced to seek new lateral channels, making a chain of marginal valley lakes," themselves occluded with mud-caked timbers. "Research has documented very few other known cases where Rafts exist in the world."[21]

Viewed ecologically, the Red's raft lakes were watery Edens teaming with life. But to colonial eyes, they impeded navigation and subsumed fertile fields. The effort to clear them out and push the Red's head of navigation upriver started in 1780, when the Spanish commander at Fort St. Jean Baptiste levied a tax on Natchitoches residents to pay for removing the logjams closest to town. By 1799, that effort opened the Cane and Red rivers up to the Bayou Pierre confluence. The next year, Spain secretly retroceded Louisiana to the French, who in 1803 sold it to the United States. Now the Red was an American river, and the raft became an American problem.

In 1805, John Sibley was able to guide a keelboat to the upper of the two Campti plantation houses, making the area between today's Campti and Powhatan the latest head of navigation—though these communities, with a combined population of 1,200, owe their siting to modern crossroads. Above Campti was more of the Red River Raft: shifting piles of mud-caked debris extending a hundred miles, according to the 1806 Red River Expedition of Thomas Freeman and Peter Custis. Reports from the 1810s and 1820s put the main raft just up from the Coushatta Chute by present-day Coushatta, now a crossroads town with 2,250 residents.[22] There, by one 1828 estimate, "the enormous quantity of brush, trunks of trees, &c . . . [had] gained at least one mile per annum," and backed up "water upon the land for many miles," making "a lake of what was before a prairie. The forests too . . . are often killed by the overflow of water, and [their] trees become rotten and fall."[23] Only a concerted effort could unjam the Red and open up northwestern Louisiana, and it would have to be done by the right man with the latest machinery.

That man was Captain Henry Miller Shreve, a Quaker from New Jersey who became a master riverman and advocate for open navigation. Appointed superintendent of western river improvements in 1826, Shreve was charged with blasting boulders, dredging shoals, and removing snags (tree trunks) and sawyers (bobbing snags), a task for which he designed a special craft equipped with a steam-powered windlass. His boat *Helopolis,* nicknamed Uncle Sam's Tooth-Puller, removed some 2,000 snags on the Ohio and Mississippi rivers, while his crew sheared bankside vegetation to prevent future obstacles. "Flatboats navigating the Mississippi river, from the mouth of the Missouri to New Orleans," reported Shreve in 1831, "now float at night with as much safety as they do in the Ohio river, by which means their passage is now made in one half the time it was three years ago."[24]

Shreve's prowess earned him a daunting new charge from the secretary of war: clear out the Red River Raft and open the channel to commerce. Steaming out of Natchitoches during the high water of April 1833, Shreve piloted his *Archimedes* into the lowermost logjam—literally, like a battering ram. The bash jostled the debris heap, after which crew members fastened a chain to a lodged trunk and extracted it, tooth-like. The subsequent loosening opened new angles to chop logs, pry out roots, and prepare for the next bash. It was dangerous work under brutal conditions, but the progress was palpable, as each clearing released the lake above it and flushed out the channel below, making it navigable. In this manner, Captain Shreve and his crew obliterated fifty-six logjams and pushed the Red's head of navigation upstream by seventy-one miles just during the spring of 1833, followed by another fifty or so miles in 1834. Funding

A snag boat, identified as the US *Aid,* clearing logjams on the Red River in 1873. Photograph by R. B. Talfor/Library of Congress.

irregularities led to delays, but by the spring of 1838 Shreve had removed the last of the Red River's rafts, all within five years, and for a mere $311,130.[25]

In this era prior to railroads, when Louisiana siting stories usually involved waterways, Shreve and his crew substantially reconfigured the state's riverine settlement geography. Annual land sales within the raft region increased thirtyfold in size, from 27,718 acres in 1829 to 894,359 acres in 1836, while their sales value nearly tripled just during 1835–1836, when $976,386 changed hands. The white population more than doubled between 1830 and 1840, after which it tripled to nearly 48,000 by 1860, a pace of increase far steeper than Louisiana's—and on par with the raft region's slave population, which grew sevenfold between 1830 and 1860, to 63,198. Shreve himself marveled how "there was not a trace of a man to be seen" for 115 miles when he started removing the raft in 1833, but by the time he finished in 1838 a "continued line of cotton plantations" fronted every river mile he cleared.[26]

Shreve did not work alone in unleashing this staggering transformation. It happened under the auspices of the federal government, and it paralleled both the national imperative for Indian removal and the southern resolve to spread slavery. Even as Shreve began his work, American speculators and squatters collaborated with the commissioner of Indian affairs to pressure the Caddos to sell their land in 1835 in what historian Robert Gudmestad described as a "hasty buyout" amid misinformation, ambiguity, and veiled threats from Fort Jesup. And then there was Texas, that steadily Americanizing section of Mexico presently under revolt, which in all likelihood would soon adjoin Louisiana as a friendly trading region, accessible via the Texas Road. Additionally, the settlement of Louisiana's Red River Valley could have only happened with the prior development of the steamboat, particularly the flat-hulled varieties designed for shallow western tributaries. Shreve's "removal of the Red River Raft," wrote Gudmestad, "provides great understanding not just for the settlement of northwestern Louisiana and southwestern Arkansas; it helps explain how much of the Old South drew its nourishment from steamboat traffic."[27]

That nourishing traffic drew speculative eyes to the banks of the now free-flowing Red. There were already settlements at Campti and Coushatta Chute, dating to those early years of obstacle-circumvention, and they did well after the clearance. But because Shreve's work progressed so rapidly, settlements did not have time to emerge organically; rather, they happened speculatively, as agents and buyers eagerly leap-frogged to optimal sites, knowing that a good site plan announced early would undercut the emergence of smaller rivals. To this day, there are no bankside towns or villages for nearly fifty river miles up the Red River from Coushatta, a consequence of the speed of Shreve's progress.

As for that optimal site, speculators focused on Coates Bluff, a rise along a hairpin meander where some families had settled and where Natchitoches merchants, knowing their head-of-navigation advantage was about to become history, had recently established a trading post. But they had competition from investors in Bennet's Bluff two miles upriver, one of which was Captain Henry Miller Shreve. In 1836, the Bennet's Bluff team established the Shreve Town Company, purchased former Caddo Indian land on the cheap, and hired Louisville city surveyor E. D. Hobbs to design an urban plat. Why here? Bennet's Bluff had a landing on the Red, yet was high enough to evade flooding—a dry-point site at a port landing, the best of both worlds.[28] It also had a trading post, and its two owners became investors in the company. The bluff was situated near the Texas Road, giving it overland access to points west and east, while also taking advantage of a confluence with Twelve Mile Bayou. Finally, it had commanding access to all those new cotton fields, making it a great situation as well as a fine site. To be sure, Coates Bluff fit that bill too. But Shreve would hear none of it. He pressured locals to dig a cutoff channel to sever the meander on which Coates Bluff was based, leaving it on a useless oxbow lake. The cutoff shortened the river distance to Bennet's Bluff, which made Shreve Town that much more advantageous. That bottomland is still called Shreve's Cutoff today, while Coates Bluff is a neighborhood in the city of Shreveport—the settlement's new name as of 1838, a year before it became the administrative seat of Caddo Parish.[29]

Shreveport blossomed in the years ahead, even as new logjams began to form farther up the Red, leading to panic among cotton-growers. Sporadic

Shreveport developed at the new head of navigation on the Red River following the debris-clearing efforts of Captain Henry Shreve, a key investor in the riverside bluff that would come to host the fourth-largest metro area in Louisiana. Here we see Shreveport's skyline in 1919 and in 2020. Photographs by Grabill Studio and Carol M. Highsmith/ Library of Congress.

clearing efforts helped little until the federal government rejoined the effort after the Civil War, finally removing the Red River Raft in 1873. The clearance begot new problems: water often flowed perilously low in the Red, now that the raft lakes were no longer steadily releasing impounded water. But the continued shipping hindrances helped Shreveport as much as they hurt, because they secured its status as the head of navigation. The city eclipsed both Alexandria and Natchitoches in population as early as the 1840s, as it became a crossroads, a courthouse town, and later a railroad hub, with fully ten railroads crossing here by 1907.[30] Together with its cross-river subsidiary of Bossier City, greater Shreveport is now home to nearly 400,000 people, fourth-largest metropolis in the state—and twenty times the size of the Red's former head of navigation at Natchitoches.

Apart from Shreveport/Bossier City, Alexandria/Pinedale, and Natchitoches, the Red River deterred town formation along its malleable banks, along which plantations effectively substituted for nucleated settlements. Today only a handful of small communities directly front the Red, from the Arkansas border down to the Atchafalaya River. What emerged instead is a parade of hamlets begun as arterial increment sites or intersections near the Red, more terrestrial than riverine in their reasons for being. Those to the east of the Red, along the Highway 71/Louisiana & Arkansas Railroad corridor, include enclaves such as Taylortown, Elmgrove, and Edgefield; the aforementioned towns of Coushatta and Campti; Clarence and St. Maurice; the former steamboat landing of Montgomery (Creole Bluff, 1840); Aloha; and Tioga, a rail junction that has since been subsumed into Pineville. The pattern continues south of Alexandria along arteries down to Melville on the Atchafalaya River, where eleven communities are strung out at a mean interval of six miles, a median and mode of five miles, and a maximum of ten miles—in other words, five-mile and ten-mile towns. Some initially nucleated as bayou-side landings (Lecompte, Meeker, Cheneyville) or crossroads (Lebeau) and were revitalized by the Texas & Pacific Railroad, principally Bunkie, a city of 3,300 people.[31] West of the Red, along the Highway 1 railroad corridor, are Grand Bayou, Harmon, Lake End, Powhatan, Natchez, Lena, and the town of Boyce, which began as Cotile Landing, grew as a train station, and is now within greater Alexandria.

That sequence—from antebellum landing to postbellum railroad to modern highway—describes many siting stories in the Red River Valley, and warrants a closer look at Boyce. Its site grew from a river landing—that is, a small, private wharf used for the transfer of cargo and passengers, usually associated with the plantation fronting it. Landings proliferated along the Red River; there were twenty-two within just one ward in Avoyelles Parish, and most had storage depots, supply stores, ferry service, and sometimes a post office. They also had names, which put them on the map as miniature break-of-bulk sites, with the potential to grow into towns. "River landings were the predecessors of modern ports," wrote historian Mary Ann Sternberg of the same phenomenon along the lower Mississippi. "Plantation town landings served as mooring facilities for loading passengers, crops, firewood for steamboat fuel, and other products and merchandise. The landings were straightforward wooden wharves worked by manual labor, [and] inland planters and farmers paid to use a town or private landing."[32] Foot traffic meant cash flow, which often attracted permanent settlement.

Another example is Calhoun's Landing, a wharf on the Red at the point where the river had cut through the hard sedimentary rock of the Kisatchie Wold, narrowing the valley into what has been called the Colfax Choke. The landing served the plantations of Meredith Calhoun, who once ranked as the state's premier cotton producer, thanks to the toil of 700 slaves.[33] Calhoun's Landing might not have survived the postbellum bust were it not saved by political geography. During Reconstruction, federally backed Republicans sought to augment their control of state government by carving out new parishes from larger existing jurisdictions, particularly in the north and west of the state. Nine new parishes were created between 1868 and 1877, and with them came new seats of governance and justice, usually staffed with political appointees.

When the Republican-dominant state legislature created one such new parish in 1869 and named it for President Ulysses S. Grant, it designated the seat to be the area's largest settlement, Calhoun's Landing, and renamed it for Grant's vice president, Schuyler Colfax.

Such gestures were viewed contemptuously by local Democrats, most of them former Confederates, and they directed their animus at the emancipated population. On Easter Sunday 1873, racial tensions at the Colfax Courthouse exploded into a massacre, leaving scores of mostly Black fatalities—the bloodiest incident during all of Reconstruction, and one that white supremacists would later ride to state power. The incident secured a notorious place for Colfax in the history books—at a site traceable to the landing at Calhoun's slave plantation.

Another example of a Red River landing-cum-community is—or rather, was—Moncla, where, 2,000 years ago, the river carved another gorge through the compacted clays of the Pleistocene Terrace. Through that gap, the Red lunged eastward and eventually merged with the Mississippi, which discharged into the sea through present-day Plaquemines Parish rather than down Bayou Teche. That longer channel and weaker gradient slowed the velocity of the Red, and made it more of the debris-dumping, jam-and-dam river it would become by colonial times. Navigational interventions in the 1830s freed up the Red and opened central Louisiana for development, but they also augmented river flow volumes, leaving overland travelers with a need for safe crossings. The Moncla Gap offered such a site, with enough topography to firm up the banks along this particularly narrow channel. By one account, a ferry operated here as early as 1804, when it was called Glass Landing, later Faulk's Landing (1842) and David's Ferry (1847). A settlement formed in 1859 when French-born Dr. Joseph Thibault Moncla, previously living in nearby Mansura, purchased 320 acres on both banks and took control of the Moncla Ferry. In subsequent decades, Moncla's sons built houses, a store, a steamboat landing, a new ferry, and a stagecoach stop; later came a cotton gin, warehouses, and a sawmill, as well as a church, a school, and in 1896 a post office. What started as a ferry landing became a village, and arguably a "gap town"—a settlement sited at a topographic pass or gorge.[34]

The same topography that attracted Dr. Moncla to this site, however, would subvert Moncla's siting story. During the gubernatorial administrations of Huey P. Long and O. K. Allen, state engineers selected the Moncla Gap for the construction of a modern automobile bridge. Once it opened in 1934, motorists whizzed by Moncla, rendering its siting logic obsolete. In the spring of 1945, unusually high waters came flushing down the Red, and on April 12 the Moncla

The Red River's Moncla Gap (*top*) gave rise to a ferry landing named Moncla, which developed into a community. When a bridge replaced the ferry, Moncla lost its original siting rationale. It endures today as a rural enclave (*bottom*). Photographs by Richard Campanella.

Bridge crashed into the Moncla Gap. A replacement was eventually built a mile upstream, but by then Moncla had become what it is today: a verdant hamlet of some 600 people distributed among forests and fields, with a Catholic church, a community center, and a historic plaque. If it is any consolation, Moncla, Louisiana, has six times as many residents as the French Pyrenees village of Moncla, where Joseph Thibault Moncla had been born in 1806.[35]

Traffic diverted from Moncla helped grow Marksville into the most sizeable city of the lower Red River region. A marvel of siting logic, Marksville sits upon the same topographic feature as Moncla, a grassy upraised terrace dating from the late Pleistocene Epoch. Geographer Milton Newton described it as "an island-like plug of terrace-like land" prone to "side-swiping attacks" by the Red, as the river avulsed and sheared off a portion of the main Attakapas Prairie and eventually incised itself through the Moncla Gap. At the same time, the braided meanders of the much larger Mississippi system swept away soils on the eastern flank of the terrace, making it like an island amid floodplains. What resulted was the Avoyelles (or Marksville) Prairie, a crescent-shaped plateau a dozen miles in length and forty feet higher than surrounding lowlands, with Moncla to the north, Mansura to the south, and Marksville in the middle.[36]

And that's what made Marksville ideal for human habitation—that middling position amid accessible waterways and productive wetlands, yet topographically protected from their deluges. Here, indigenous people 1,500 to 2,000 years ago created what one archaeologist described as "the largest and most complex Middle Woodland site in the lower Mississippi Valley[,] without known parallels," with up to seventy ring-shaped earthworks, most with fire pits in the middle. Their use is uncertain, more likely ceremonial than domestic, but their location was strategic. The Natives sited their mounds atop a forty-foot escarpment overlooking the eastern lowlands, creating the highest points in modern Marksville, which itself occupies the brow of the Avoyelles Prairie.[37]

French colonials noted this grassy plateau as early as 1700, admiring its herds of bison (*boeuf sauvage,* thus the name of nearby Bayou Boeuf), and trading with natives by 1718. Some scribed the tribe's name as Tamoucougoula, and others as Avoyel or Avogel (Avoyelles), meaning "flint people" or "people of the rocks," in reference to their flint-head axes or possibly the escarpment. Accounts from throughout the colonial era tell of friendly relations with the Avoyelles, for their trading as well as their mutual antipathy for the Natchez Indians. Economic interaction with the Avoyelle and nearby Tunica tribes became so valuable by 1780 that Spanish authorities established the Poste Des Avoyelles to prevent encroachment on their prairie territories. Early commanders Noel Soileau (Soilleaux), Jacques Gagnard, Domingo de Apereto, and Estevan de la Morandier initially sited this garrison on those ancient earthworks, and later moved it inland. As a defensive position, the Avoyelles Post had a similar siting story to that of the Opelousas Post, which also began as a Spanish military installation atop a prairie-terrace hillock with a commanding view. Neither site had a waterfront, but both were well-positioned for overland roads to intersect.[38]

Just such a crossroads had formed by 1796, when the Spanish lieutenant governor of the region, Don Carlos de Grandpre, secured a grant for land immediately abutting the military post. Around that time, a Venetian-born peddler of Jewish descent named Marcos Litche (later known as Marc Eliché or Mark Elishe) happened along a road when, the story goes, his wagon broke down, giving him time to assess the Avoyelles Prairie. He decided to stay, obtained a Spanish grant for land near that of Grandpre, and in 1796 married Louisiana-born Julie Carmouche. The couple built a home and opened a trading post that, by 1809, came to be known as Marc's Ville, Marc's Store, or Marc's Village. Their house became the parish's provisional courthouse when the police jury met there in 1817, and their land donation provided space for the present-day courthouse square when the settlement became the seat of Avoyelles Parish. After Marc died around 1821, his widow, Julie, "played an active role in the subsequent development of the town; numerous land transactions show the sale of lots by her," and are "the first documentary evidence in which the name Marksville appears."[39] The community grew as a crossroads, trade center, and administrative center—"a thriving and busy place," according to an 1860 account, sited on "the highest land on the prairie of Avoyelles," with two landings on the nearby Red River for "communication with the outside word in the freight and passenger way."[40] Acadian diffusion from the south made Marksville the northernmost point in the so-called Acadian Triangle, spanning from Lafourche Parish to Cameron Parish and up to Avoyelles Parish. Anglo-Saxon settlers came as well, such that by the time Marksville got its first newspaper it published in both French and English.[41]

Two descriptions of Marksville testify to the racially polarized worlds of nineteenth-century Louisiana. Solomon Northup, the kidnapped freeman from New York who was sold into slavery on a Red River plantation in 1841, endeavored for years to get a letter mailed through Marksville to alert his family of his predicament. When he finally arrived in 1852, he found the town little better than the wretched environs he had endured. "Marksville, although occupying a prominent position, and standing out in impressive italics on the map of Louisiana," wrote Northup in *12 Years a Slave,* "is, in fact, but a small and insignificant hamlet. Aside from the tavern, kept by a jolly and generous boniface, the court house, inhabited by lawless cows and swine in the seasons of vacation, and a high gallows, with its dissevered rope dangling in the air, there is little to attract the attention of the stranger." (Those gallows had been used a year earlier to execute a fellow slave who, while being whipped unjustly, "sprang to his feet, and seizing an ax, literally chopped the overseer in pieces.")[42] Contrast that Marksville to the one seen by the progressive white travel writer Catharine Cole, who in 1891 described "a thrifty, neat, well-appearing little place, having about one thousand inhabitants, supporting two newspapers, several hotels and many stores [around] the courthouse and public square. . . . A neat Catholic Church stands nearby, and pleasant, hospitable residences form the outer margin in all directions. Social life in Marksville is refined and cultivated; a piano is in every house, and an accomplished musician will be its owner."[43]

Whichever Marksville one recognizes, its economic growth was indisputably crimped by the same shortcoming of its cross-prairie sister, Opelousas: it had no direct shipping access. But in both cases, navigable bayous flowed not too far away, and offshoot ports soon developed on their banks. As high, dry

Opelousas on the Attakapas Prairie spun off the port of Washington on Bayou Courtableau, so too did high, dry Marksville on the Avoyelles Prairie spin off its own port, on the lowlands to its south. Named Cottonport, it formed on Bayou Rouge (Bayou des Glaises), flourished commensurately with Washington, and helped activate the confluence site of Simmesport on the Atchafalaya River where it nears the Red River. The halfway point between Marksville and Cottonport gave rise to Mansura, just as Moreauville, Hamburg, and Red Fish formed at four-mile intervals along the road connecting Mansura and Simmesport.

Likewise, navigating around Bayou des Glaises's semicircular "Big Bend," settlements arose at more or less regular intervals. It is ten miles following the bayou from Moreauville to Bordelonville, six miles from Bordelonville down to the community of Bayou des Glaises, fourteen miles from there down to Hamburg, and nine miles to Simmesport. Average interval: around ten miles. A traveler in 1860 emphasized how the spatial relationships among these communities affected their interaction:

> Twelve miles from Simmesport is Moreauville, which stands nearly in the exact center of the parish, and on the banks of Bayou de Glaize. . . . Here the road to Marksville, which is also the road to Alexandria, crosses the bayou . . . by a little "puncheon bridge," [else] by ferriage. . . . The prairie is ten to twelve miles long by five to seven wide, and on it stand the towns of Mansura and Marksville, the former five miles from Moreauville, and the latter twelve miles from that place, and thirty-five from Alexandria. Masura is a pleasant place, and though so near to Marksville, and so far from any navigable stream, considerable business is done there in a retail way.[44]

Modern times have not been generous to the lower Red River region. Centralized as they may have been two centuries ago, major transit arteries now largely circumvent the region, leaving behind diminished opportunities, aging residents, and vestigial places like Moncla. That serene Red River hamlet lost its landing, its ferry, and its bridge to the trade vectors that initially activated the site only to later abandon it. Avoyelles Parish has flatlined in recent decades, at just below 40,000 residents, while every community mentioned above has lost residents, primarily their young. Marksville recently dipped below 5,000 in population, but it remains Avoyelles's largest city and parish seat. As to its whimsical siting story, Marc Eliché's broken wagon wheel still endures, on Marksville's entrance sign and its city logo.

Avoyelles Parish Courthouse in Marksville, a town originally sited as a Spanish post on a series of terrace-top Indian mounds. Like many prairie/terrace settlements, Marksville benefited by being high and dry, but suffered for lack of navigational access. Enter Cottonport (*below*) on nearby Bayou Rouge, which served as a shipping port for Marksville in the same way Washington did for terrace-based Opelousas. Photographs by Richard Campanella.

Of the thirty-two cities, towns, villages, and other communities in the Red River region analyzed in this study, 50 percent had riverine- or water-based primary siting stories (above the state average of 29 percent), while 19 percent were primarily railroad sites, 13 percent were crossroads, and 3 percent were resource extraction or processing sites (compared to state averages of 33 percent, 10 percent, and 13 percent, respectively). The second-oldest colonial region in the state, settlements began forming here in the 1710s, climaxed in the 1840s with the opening of the Red River, and ended in the 1900s. Nearly two-thirds (63 percent) of Red River region settlements emerged organically, the remaining third having been ordained by a founder, compared to the statewide ratio of 49 percent/51 percent emergent/ordained.

12

THE WESTERN HILL COUNTRY

To the west of the Avoyelles Prairie and to the north of the Mamou and Attakapas prairies, elevations rise, topography steepens, soils get older and harder, rivers and bayous flow more like streams and brooks, and biomes shift from prairie grasslands to "the Great Pine Woods."[1] The hills of Beauregard, Allen, northern Evangeline, and particularly Vernon, Sabine and DeSoto parishes, dating from 2 million to 50 million years ago, comprise the Sabine Uplift—a series of sedimentary rock layers pushed upward to the surface and eroded down to a mere dome, today's Dolet Hills near Mansfield. The subterranean layers bowed as they uplifted, stacked "like a tilted deck of cards," as geographers Fred Kniffen and Sam Hilliard put it, each "with younger beds overlaying older layers" and eroding at different rates. What resulted were a series of 300- to 500-foot ridges known as *wolds* (an old English term for wooded uplifts) or *cuestas* (Spanish for inclines) traversing Texas, Louisiana, and Arkansas. The Kisatchie Wold is centered around Vernon and Rapides parishes, while the older Nacogdoches Wold spans from Sabine Parish up to Webster and over to Winn. Down through the middle cut the erosive current of the Red River, as did the Sabine River to the west.[2]

Western Louisiana's ancient wolds and cuestas are strikingly different from what Samuel Clemens described as the "the youthfulest batch of country that lies around there anywhere" along the Mississippi to the east.[3] The siting stories of the western hills, too, differ markedly from those of Louisiana's delta and bayou country. Settlements that materialized here were fewer in number, smaller in size, and later in arising, while the region today remains one of Louisiana's least populated, with no city larger than 10,000 people in the 5,000 square miles bracketed by Shreveport, Alexandria, and Lake Charles. The key to understanding settlement in the western hill country involves its earliest siting story: crossroads.

Prehistoric travelers through this region, home to the "Sunrise People," crossed paths at the Atàkapa Trace Junction, where "foot trails in the Atakapas' homeland that reached [to] present-day Natchitoches, Rapides, and Sabine Parishes," known collectively as the Atakapa-Coushatta Trace, merged with trails extending westward into coastal Texas, home to the "Sunset People."[4] The crossroads was called *wànne tol hokínul,* meaning "roads join together," and it linked six bands of the larger Atakapa-Ishak Nation, including the Teche, Opelousas, and Coushetta bands. This ancient trace loosely followed today's Highway 190 from DeRidder through Merryville and across the Sabine River to the Texas coastal plain. One such trail appears on the 1806 Lafon map, heading southwestwardly from present-day Alexandria, while the 1820 Melish map plots an "Indian Path" westward across the Sabine, where stood a "Village of Coushatta Savages" led by Chief Red Shoes, located near today's Merryville. If this now-gone settlement is indeed related to the prehistoric *wànne tol hokínul,* its siting story was that of a road junction and river crossing linking two halves of a nation across distinct geophysical regimes.[5]

By the 1790s, other nations increasingly made use of such passages for trading (usually illicit) between Spanish subjects to the west and growing American populations to the east. Some twenty miles north of the Merryville "Indian Path" passed another historic artery heading toward the setting sun. Through here came freebooter and smuggler Philip Nolan as he drove Spanish-bred horses from San Antonio over to Natchez on the Mississippi River, earning the road the sobriquet "Nolan's Trace."[6] Other frontier rogues and pioneers followed, calling into need a ferry at what one government survey labeled as the Old Coushatta Crossing.[7] In 1807, an Ohio doctor named Timothy Burr built a cable-strung barge ferry here, and later a gristmill, sawmill, and cotton gin. Burr also provided pasture for the cattle herds driven along the "Beef Road" from Liberty, Texas, to Louisiana markets. The Burr family operated the ferry until around 1840, by which time the landing was sometimes known as Hickman's Ferry, serving the cattle road connecting Zavella in Texas with Opelousas in Louisiana. The ferry settlement became a defensive position during the Civil War and endured until 1937, when the Burr Ferry Bridge was built, after which the community moved inland to the present-day crossroads of Highway 8 and Highway 111. An interpretative sign at the nearby Confederate breastworks historic site calls Burr's Ferry "the Back Door of the United States," as indeed it was in the early 1800s. With a siting story that began as a river crossing and ended as a crossroads, Burr Ferry is now the back door into Vernon Parish, and home to a few hundred rural folk.[8]

As Highway 111 passes through Burr Ferry today, it runs southward to the Beauregard Parish community named Junction—that is, *wànne tol hokínul,* the old Atàkapa Trace junction. At the half-way point on that twelve-mile stretch is Evans, sited on a tributary of the Sabine named Red Bank Creek, which became a post office/school/Sunday town for the surrounding countryside. South of Junction is Merryville, where, as we have seen, indigenous bands passed prehistorically and settled well into the 1800s. They were followed by Europeans en route from Opelousas to Nacogdoches, though it was not until the late 1800s that the community of Merryville was founded.[9]

Merryville's name is a mystery, but its siting story is not. It speaks of the area's abundant longleaf yellow pine, as well as a rare perch thirty feet above the Sabine River floodplain, roughly where the old Indian path crossed.[10] Here, timber cutters hauled logs down to the Sabine River to float them to market, and by 1881, enough workers settled nearby to warrant the opening of a post office, managed by postmaster Moses F. Frazer. "Until 1904, the town consisted principally of only a couple general mercantile stores, a post office, and perhaps a livery stable or physician," wrote historian William T. Block, "until the rails of the Jasper and Eastern (Santa Fe Railroad) arrived from Kirbyville, Texas, in 1905. . . . A great body of virgin long leaf pines, as well as hardwoods, became instantly available for harvesting, and sawmills sprang up everywhere."[11] The timber industry thrived through the 1910s, by which time Merryville had become "the trading and supply town for a large section of the country," and 2,600 people lived there into 1930.[12] But by then the yellow pine had been depleted, and the last of the sawmills closed in 1933. Born as a resource extraction site later energized by a railroad, Merryville downsized to a train stop and crossroads, and now has a population of under 1,000 people.

East of Merryville was another timber-cutting settlement, Miersburg, named for postmaster Elias Miers and established in 1894 for an upcoming railroad. Behind the project was Arthur Stilwell, a New York-born capitalist who aimed to link western Missouri with Gulf Coast cattle and timber via his Kansas City, Pittsburgh & Gulf Railroad. Collaborating with Dutch investors, Stilwell launched a subsidiary called the Kansas City, Shreveport & Gulf Railway Company, laid tracks through Shreveport in 1896, and extended them through Many, Leesville, Miersburg, newly established De Quincy, and into Texas by 1897.

As would later happen in Merryville, Miersburg went from outpost to boomtown, and enthused investors from Holland thrice renamed it with Dutch names—Schovall, DeKidder, and finally DeRidder, the last for Ella de Ridder, sister-in-law of one of Stilwell's financial backers. As for De Quincy, it got its name from the director of the Netherlands-based syndicate, a nobleman named Baron de Quincy. The new community got its post office in 1898, and by the 1910s it became the junction of the Colorado Southern and the Kansas City Southern (KCS) railroads, and home to over 700 people.[13] Its sister city of DeRidder, meanwhile, became a "sawmill hub," where 200 workers produced 34 million board feet annually and shipped out 3,000 boxcars per year on the KCS. The population grew by two-thirds between 1910 and 1920, to 3,500 people, roughly the same size as De Quincy. By this time, DeRidder had become a major turpentine producer as well as the seat for newly designated Beauregard Parish. That administrative status gave the town a safety net when the yellow pine ran out—an advantage not shared by De Quincy, whose population has since flatlined at around 3,000. Tree farming has enabled both a paper and wood industry to persist in DeRidder, now the largest city (population 9,700) between Shreveport and Lake Charles, and, like De Quincy, exemplifies an enduring resource extraction and processing site activated by a railroad.[14]

In this manner, the Kansas City Southern Railway and its spur lines became a premier settlement catalyst in the state's history. The conveyance affected thirty-one named communities throughout rural western Louisiana, from Caddo Parish down to Calcasieu Parish. About two-thirds were formed circa 1897 entirely as a result of KCS stations or flag stops, and survive today as small track-straddling population clusters. Among them is New Llano, which started as a railroad-enabled timber town named Stables and became the unlikely home to a commune of California socialists, lasting from 1917 to 1937.[15] Another is Hornbeck, founded by an agent of the Arkansas Town Site Company who purchased the land around the KCS station, named the community for himself, and presided over an economy boom—until the town's locomotive roundhouse got relocated to Leesville and its lumber-turpentine trade waned, leaving Hornbeck to become today's "Gateway to the Toledo-Bend Reservoir." Ludington would be so lucky: it similarly prospered when the KCS arrived, and busted when the timber ran out—but with no alternative source of income, it has all but disappeared from Beauregard Parish.[16]

The other ten or so stations linked by the KCS were built in preexisting emergent settlements. Each benefited from the new economic lifeline, sometimes to the point of repurposing itself entirely. Mansfield, for example, had been founded in 1843 at the crossing of a backcountry road linking Natchitoches with Caddo and Coushetta Indian villages, and another road heading west to Logan's Ferry (now Logansport) across the Sabine River into Texas.[17] A traveler described that artery as a "ridge road" for stagecoaches, "rough and dusty in the extreme[,] running thus along the high lands."[18] It passed through the geographical center of the newly created DeSoto Parish, which is what got that crossroads designated a seat of justice and made into an administrative center. Named for a Scottish lord admired by a local official, Mansfield soon became a trade center, home to a women's college, and the site of a key battle in the Red River Campaign of the Civil War. Mansfield's economy changed radically once it attained a KCS station and became a junction for the Texas & Pacific Railroad. Lumber, cattle, and agricultural commerce bustled as the population doubled to 1,800 people between 1900 and 1910, and again by 1930. Mansfield has since leveled off at around 5,000 residents, and the town still relies squarely on its dual siting rationales, as a centralized administrative crossroads that became a rail hub.[19]

Leesville also began at a juncture of ridges, along a wilderness road heading west from Alexandria as it approached the Bayou Anacoco swamps. According to one recollection, the spot marked an area of unusually dark, rich soil known as "the Blacklands," good for farming and grazing. "Believe or not," recounted an elderly citizen, "this black soil surrounding Leesville, is largely responsible for the people settling around here."[20] By the 1860s, a doctor named Edmund Ellison Smart was operating a plantation on those fertile soils, including on a bluff above Bayou Castor where he had an office and general store. Its urban transformation became something of a family project, as Edmund's father, John R. Smart, introduced a bill to the state Senate in 1871 to create Vernon Parish. He used his son's donation of bluff-top land positioned near the center of the new parish to justify designating that spot as the parish seat and erecting a courthouse. Edmund Smart named it Leesville, in honor of the recently deceased Confederate general Robert E. Lee, while another family member, John F. Smart, won the contract to build the courthouse.[21]

Like Mansfield, Leesville became an administrative and trade center. But without a navigable waterway, it struggled to develop—until the arrival of the KCS in 1897. The railroad made Leesville into a timber town and helped get it selected for the Louisiana Maneuvers war exercises in 1941, and later for a permanent military base that eventually became Fort Polk. Were it not for the creation of Vernon Parish and Smart's centrally located donation, there would be no Leesville, and if it weren't for the KCS, there'd be no Fort Polk, Louisiana's largest military base. Leesville today has a population of 5,400, while the "garrison town" of Fort Polk, renamed Fort Johnson in 2023, has upward of twice that number of stationed troops.[22]

Another hill country settlement reactivated by the KCS is a marvel of Louisiana siting stories. It emerged along the dusty treads of El Camino Real de

DeSoto Parish Courthouse in Mansfield (*left*) and Vernon Parish Courthouse in Leesville (*right*). Photographs by Richard Campanella.

los Tejas, that network of wilderness roads extending from Mexico City to Los Adaes, the fortified Spanish mission sited in 1717. As the Camino crossing at Bayou Nana had given rise to the town of Many, so too did its crossing of a bayou confluence spawn another settlement ten miles to the north. According to one account, Spanish friars on their way to and from Los Adaes knew this area as Las Cabezas as early as 1767, and established a church in this vicinity, followed by a second one in 1795—Nuestra Señora de Guadalupe, predecessor of today's St. Joseph Catholic Church. Another account puts the founding at 1773, when, following the Spanish takeover of Louisiana, soldiers at Los Adaes who were ordered back to San Antonio instead settled at Las Cabezas, which they named Vallecillo (Little Valley) on account of the sloped terrain around the bayou confluence. Other Spanish soldiers settled four miles to the west at Ybarbo, named for Alcario Ybarbo, a relative of the founder of El Presidio de Nuestra Señora del Pilar at Los Adaes. In the century to come, Vallecillo and Ybarbo remained rural hamlets as this part of Spanish Mexico became the American state of Louisiana. All the while, Castilian Spanish gave way to American English, and Vallecillo got truncated to "Cie," "Cye," "Scie," and "Bayou Scie," while Ybarbo got anglicized to "Ebarb."[23]

Then came the KCS investors, among them a native of Zwolle, Holland, named Jan DeGoeijen. As part of an inspection tour of Dutch financiers, DeGoeijen found charm in Bayou Scie's hilltop St. Joseph Church, in the *bonhomie* of its people, and in their generous gift of ten acres for a train depot. Thus was born Zwolle—or rather reborn, from old Bayou Scie—and by 1913 it was "one of the important lumbering towns that has grown up along the line of the Kansas City Southern R. R. . . . and nearly the entire population is engaged in some form of lumbering industry. It has a bank, a money-order post office and telegraph office, and is the trading and shipping point [extending to] the Sabine River."[24] DeGoeijen's support of the old Spanish mission town continued until

Influential in the siting of a number of early Louisiana settlements, the Camino Real (Royal Road) in some instances comprised a network of backcountry arteries linking Spanish outposts, such as in northwestern Louisiana (highway sign at left). In other cases, Camino Real simply meant the main thoroughfare in a Spanish town or city, such as present-day Decatur Street in New Orleans (*right*). Photographs by Richard Campanella.

his death during the German occupation of World War II. Zwolle, Louisiana, today is an incorporated town of 1,700 residents, while Ebarb is an unincorporated rural population cluster one-fifth the size. Why the difference? Because only Zwolle updated its *raison d'être,* from mission to station and mill.[25]

Among the other stops repurposed by the KCS are Rodessa, formerly Frog Level, originally founded in 1879 as a trading center; Mooringsport, established in 1836 as Timothy Mooring's landing for ferries and steamboats on Ferry (now Caddo) Lake; and Westlake, which began in the 1840s as a timber town named Lisbon until economic activity shifted eastward and spawned Lake Charles. Taken together, these thirty-one western Louisiana communities created by KCS station sites are now home to nearly 150,000 Louisianians, half of whom live in neighborhoods outside downtown Shreveport and Bossier City. The average interval between those thirty-one station sites is 7.3 miles, with most falling in the four- to eleven-mile range.[26]

The KCS was in the business of transportation, and its stations made money by putting passengers and cargo on company cars. The Lake Charles & Leesville Railroad, on the other hand, was exclusively in the lumber business. Planned in 1896 and built by the Bradley-Ramsey Lumber Company, this dedicated tram line ran from Moss Bluff northward thirty-six miles into the piney woods.[27] The main base camp ("log front") gave rise to Longville, named for President R. A. Long of the Long-Bell Lumber Company. By 1906, according to researcher William Theodore Block, seven locomotives pulling 120 cars rolled regularly on the tram to and from the Bradley-Ramsey mills, which produced dimension lumber, ripsaw flooring, fence pickets, railroad ties, trestle beams, and more battleship decking than anywhere in the world. When the timber ran out, both the mills and the trains went silent. But the tram trajectory lives on as today's Highway 171, from Lake Charles/Moss Bluff to DeRidder, along which Longville remains an unincorporated population cluster, and the community of Rigley marks a nearby crossroads.[28]

As the KCS and tram triggered settlements to the north, the Kansas City, Watkins & Gulf Railway did the same to the northeast, skirting the hill country. Behind the project was the same Kansas-born Jabez B. Watkins who in 1883 had purchased 1.5 million acres near Lake Charles and peopled them by recruiting midwesterners to become Louisianians. In 1887, as president of the North American Land and Timber Company, Watkins obtained a charter for a railroad from Lake Charles through Alexandria "to the north line of this State, thence through the States of Arkansas and Missouri," aiming to bring Gulf Coast lumber and cattle up to Kansas City. Advocates in Louisiana hoped the line would also do the reverse, such that "the products of Kansas and the great Northwest will find their way to the markets of the world, [making] Lake Charles . . . one of the safest and most important seaports on the Gulf of Mexico."[29] Grading of the bed and laying of "the Watkins Road" tracks began in 1890 and reached Alexandria in 1892, after which stations opened and settlements formed. The distances between them were mostly around five miles, some ten to fifteen, all in a straight line, and all with midwestern-sounding names: Iowa (named for the state), Woodlawn, Fenton, Edna, Kinder, Oberlin (named for the city in Ohio), Oakdale, Glenmora, Forest Hill, Woodworth, and the Willow Glen suburb of Alexandria. Most were founded wholly on account of KCW&G stations, about half became mill towns, and nearly all have since become highway crossroads. In time, the KCW&G became known as the St. Louis, Iron Mountain & Southern line, and it is now part of Union Pacific.

Some station towns predated the railroad, albeit in elemental form. Kinder, for example, originally emerged at a confluence of the Calcasieu River used to float rafts down to Lake Charles, where it was crossed by a cattle trail up to Alexandria. The arteries drew enough settlers for homesteader James Kinder to open a general store on land he acquired in 1889. As construction on the KCW&G approached, Kinder sold a parcel to Watkins for the tracks and station, around which grew a community bearing his name. That Kinder now lies precisely along the straight track bed, but four miles from the old Calcasieu crossing, shows how the original emergent siting rationale had been superseded by the ordained 1890s station. Now home to 2,000 people at the intersection of three highways, Kinder proudly calls itself "The Crossroads to Everywhere."[30]

The gravitational pull of the railroad explains the next town north of Kinder. It, too, emerged near the Calcasieu, at a bankside spring where Ohio homesteaders settled amid an oak grove. They called the spot Oaklin Springs and built a general store and post office. After Watkins acquired his railroad right-of-way three miles to the east and sold a parcel to the Oberlin Townsite Company to survey streets around the planned station, those residing at Oaklin Springs moved to the new ordained site and named it Oberlin, for the Ohio city from whence they came. Timber mills followed, as did cattle, sheep, and rice industries. In 1912, Oberlin prevailed over Kinder and Oakdale to become the seat of the newly created Allen Parish, thanks to its centralized location. Today, Oberlin is a railroad-straddling crossroads and administrative center of 1,500 people, while all that remains of Oaklin Springs is the cemetery.[31]

Oberlin is not, however, the largest community in Allen Parish; that rank goes to the next settlement north. It originated as Dunnsville in 1890, when W. T. Dunn acquired a homestead here, possibly near an earlier settlement named Bay on the Calcasieu River. Like Oberlin and Kinder, Dunnsville's fulcrum shifted to Jabez Watkins's new station once his tracks came through two years later. Renamed Oakdale, the site roughly marks the midpoint of the KCW&G's eighty-mile run from Iowa to Alexandria, and benefited additionally by becoming a rail junction with the Gulf, Colorado & Santa Fe Railroad and an eight-mile tram line of the Industrial Lumber Company. The three tracks made Oakdale a substantial mill town, while the tram enabled Industrial Lumber to build a classic company town named Elizabeth to the northwest. By the 1920s, Oakdale's mills slowed for lack of timber, and while Industrial practiced more sustainable forestry methods ("Builders, Not Spoilers" was its motto), it too closed in the 1940s. Sited as a tram line company town, Elizabeth is now home to 400 residents, while Oakdale, as Allen Parish's only incorporated city, has

Rocky outcroppings on Kisatchie Wold. Photograph by Richard Campanella.

7,000 residents, four times the population of the parish seat of Oberlin. Taken together, the ten communities initiated or nudged by railroad stations, from Lake Charles to Alexandria, are today home to 25,000 Louisianians.[32]

By the early 1900s, a triangle of interstate railways circumscribed the western Louisiana hill country. On the western flank was Arthur Stilwell's Kansas City Southern Railway; to the east ran Jabez Watkins's Kansas City, Watkins & Gulf (now the Union Pacific); and coming down from the north was the Red River–paralleling Texas & Pacific. Along all three arteries were fifty or so coeval station-stop settlements sited every five to fifteen miles, while inside that triangle were private trams, spur lines, and dirt roads, but no navigable rivers. With such limited transportation access and with hard clay soils on hilly slopes with rocky outcroppings, subsistence farmers had every reason to settle elsewhere. Those few who did cast their lot with this "hog wallow land" tended to settle along the winding roads interconnecting the train-stop towns, or else at timber mills on spur lines. That is, most siting stories in the hilly western interior entailed crossroads, rail stops, resource extraction and processing sites, or some combinations thereof. Most of these agglomerations subsequently lost population once the "cut-out-and-get-out practice" of the timber cutters came to an inexorable end. They left the hills "a blackened stump-waste," at which point the U.S. Forest Service began acquiring and reforesting the land to create Kisatchie National Forest, now a significant source of income for remaining communities.[33]

There are some exceptions to the archetypal hill country siting story, though in the end they tend to prove the rule. One is Sugartown, now a few hundred people in the terrace-to-hill transition between DeRidder and Oakdale. Sugartown began as a ford site on Sugar Creek—that is, a crossable section of a shallow waterway with tapered banks—along a trail that connected key regional endpoints: Alexandria on the Red River to the northeast, Opelousas on the Attakapas Prairie to the east, the Calcasieu Lake area to the southwest, and ferry crossings on the Sabine River into Texas. Remembered today as Old Campground, that shady ford became an overnight waystation. Some travelers chose to settle here as early as 1817, along what a contemporary map labeled as an "Indian Path" into Texas, where cattle herds were driven to Alexandria.[34] By 1841 the former campground had a post office, and by 1861 around 150 families lived within a few square miles—hardly a nucleated urban center, but fairly substantial for this time and place. By one account, the name Sugartown came from an attempt to grow and mill sugarcane here, though cotton, corn, and timber were better suited, as evidenced by the fact that Sugartown had a sawmill, two cotton gins, and a steam-driven gristmill by 1877. Surprisingly, this rural community also became an academy town, the educational equivalent of the Sunday towns we have seen previously. The magnet here was a reputation for fine public education, and starting in 1879 the Sugartown Male and Female Academy. This private coeducational institution trained students from ten parishes plus Texas to become leaders in various fields. Sugartown also had a Sunday town effect in that local Methodists would hold religious and social gatherings here, known as "campground meetings," drawing the faithful from miles around.

What sucked the energy out of Sugartown were all those new rail-accessed sawmills and lumber towns, especially DeRidder and Oakdale. With no tracks and train station of its own, Sugartown lost population to the iron triangle of rails. The only thing keeping Sugartown on the map today is the intersection of Highways 112 and 113 a mile northwest of Old Campground—where, just like Oaklin Springs, all that remains is the cemetery. Though its original river ford siting story was unusual, Sugartown ended up an archetypal hill country crossroads.[35]

Pitkin, north of Sugartown and east of Elizabeth, had its genesis as a water-driven gristmill, a siting story as rare in Louisiana as it was common in the interior South and Northeast. A few streams in hilly parts of the state had just enough hydraulic head to push a paddle geared to a millstone, at least during peak flow. Chief among them was Kisatchie Falls in Natchitoches Parish, where a watermill was built to serve local families. Another example operated in Grant Parish until the creek fork went dry, but not before giving rise to a village named Dry Prong.[36] To one Mr. Milam (Millam), the confluence of the Big and Little Sixmile creeks also seemed to have hydropower potential. There in 1872 he built a gristmill to grind corn meal and probably to saw wood, because the community that formed contiguously was named Slabtown, for the smoothed split logs ("slabs") used to make puncheon floors in log cabins.[37] A merchant from New Jersey named A. Thornton subsequently opened a store at Slabtown, and when the first post office opened, he renamed the community for his daughter, Lydia. Two other post offices opened nearby, at Hillco and Dido, though the dispersion of settlers did not have enough centripetal force to render one single nucleated community. A more powerful locus came, once again, in the form of a railroad—namely the Atchison, Topeka & Santa Fe (Gulf, Colorado & Santa Fe), which in 1905 built tracks from Kirbyville, Texas, to Oakdale and erected a station at Pitkin, named for a deceased company official. Like Sugartown and Oaklin Springs, residents in and around Lydia and Hillco gravitated to Pitkin, which became a timber town as well as a station stop—until the trees, the mill, and the train all disappeared, leaving Pitkin and tiny Dido to become the bucolic Vernon Parish crossroads they are today.[38]

The most exceptional hill country siting story may be found on a river with a long history of thwarting town sitings. Explaining how Logansport became Louisiana's sole incorporated community on the Sabine River requires understanding why other attempts failed. We have previously seen how the border dispute of 1682 to 1821 parried settlement in the "Sabine Free State" (Neutral Ground) for its lack of governance and clear land titles, how the Sabine's banks were either too swampy or too steep, how the river's sinuous and shoal-prone channel frustrated steamboat pilots, and how the river's hinterland offered limited economic promise. By the time those conditions changed, railroads and highways had superseded navigation in providing efficient access to the interior, while the growing Texas cities of Port Arthur and Orange quashed any hope of a river port materializing on the Louisiana side of the lower Sabine.

Logansport's siting rationale on the upper Sabine was just that—a river port (landing), founded in 1830 on the Mexican/U.S. border by one Dr. Logan, and named Logan's Ferry until it got its first post office in 1848.[39] Various reasons explain why Logansport alone prevailed on the Sabine. For one, it was located at the very northern tip of the old Spanish/American Neutral Ground, minimally affected by its liminal status and lingering stigma. Logansport's terrain, meanwhile, was conducive to a port town, being up on a flat bluff with sloping banks, while the Texas side was good enough for a crossing but not enough to nourish a superior rival. All other Louisiana landings on the Sabine lacked these attributes. Regarding the river itself, it flowed in an unusually straight channel here, better for navigators, and while it is true that the Sabine's head of navigation reached as far into Texas as Belzora Landing when conditions were ideal, Logansport was reliably reachable most of the time.[40] Trekkers heading west on stagecoach roads certainly had a need to ferry across the Sabine at this bluff; in fact, Logansport today features a commemorative covered wagon at the town gateway. Finally, DeSoto Parish had plenty of marketable timber to warrant railroad construction through Logansport starting in 1885, which enabled the community to reequip as a rail and mill town.[41] Today, Logansport has 1,300 people, bridges, railroads, and a timber industry; recently it has also become an industrial service center, water provider, and wastewater processor for extensive oil and gas drilling. Dr. Logan never could have known it, but when he sited his ferry two centuries ago, he did so atop the massive Haynesville-Bossier Shale Play, wellspring of the natural gas boom that has put western Louisiana on the world stage—and the Sabine Pass Liquefied National Gas facility on the Louisiana map.

Ten miles downriver of Logansport, another Sabine River energy project had the effect of reconfiguring settlement patterns over hundreds of square

Logansport, the only incorporated community on Louisiana's side of the Sabine River, began as a ferry landing that gained railroad access and became a resource extraction and processing site. Photograph by Richard Campanella.

miles. The idea dawned in the 1930s, when regional interests realized the Sabine River, still "largely untamed and forgotten in the timberlands of East Texas and West Louisiana," according to legal scholar Ryan M. Seidemann, might have more value as a reservoir. "Political rumblings began about converting the River to a water conservation area and a recreational destination," and grew louder after World War II, when industrialists called for a reliable source of freshwater for petrochemical processing on the Texas coast. In 1949–1950, Texas and Louisiana formed twin Sabine River Authorities and gave them sweeping legal powers, including property expropriation.[42] Funding came not from the federal government, which found the project unnecessary for flood control, but from both states and three electrical companies. Louisiana got particularly creative in its financing: politicians noticed the state had millions of dollars in its Confederate Veterans pension fund, but only one surviving Confederate widow, so it passed a constitutional amendment in 1960 to rededicate those monies to the reservoir.[43]

The two state authorities proceeded to purchase or expropriate hundreds of private properties from the banks of the Sabine and its tributaries up to the 172-foot elevation contour. Affecting 206,000 acres, the effort displaced 400 families, eradicated communities with names like Pine Flat, Kites Landing, Richard Neck, and Haddens, and incurred years of litigation and lasting bitterness. (The average compensation amounted to only $97 per acre.) Among the displaced were members of the Choctaw-Apache Tribe, descendants of Choctaw forcibly removed from the east and Apache from the west. Another targeted settlement, known as Toledo, stood on a bend just below the proposed main dam site, home to a few families, a school, and cemetery. Toledo originated on the 1830s land grant of A. M. Bevil, who operated Bevil's Crossing (later Hadden's Ferry) for passage into Haddens, Louisiana. Because engineers

The Toledo Bend Reservoir radically reconfigured the settlement geography of 600 square miles of western Louisiana and eastern Texas, to the point of even un-siting the community whose name it bears. Photograph by Richard Campanella.

had selected this narrow valley for the dam, they dubbed the project Toledo Bend, and the name stuck—even as Toledo and Haddens were destroyed.

The Toledo Bend project had plenty of regional support, particularly in peripheral communities. In addition to electrical production, advocates argued that the stored water could attract resorts and tourism, irrigate farms, keep paper mills and petrochemical plants supplied with water, and stabilize river flow for wastewater discharge. The strongest supporter was Many-based State Representative Cliff Ammons, who had initially opposed the project, as his family stood to lose land holdings. But upon reading forecasts of regional benefits, he advocated for the reservoir, to the point of becoming known as "the Father of Toledo Bend."[44]

In 1964, work began on the 1.6-mile-long earthen dam, and by 1966 the Sabine River began swelling until it covered 186,000 watery acres. Turbines and power facilities were then installed, as were new roads and recreational facilities, and in 1969 Toledo Bend Reservoir opened for public use and electrical generation.[45]

Today, Toledo Bend is the largest manmade reservoir in the South, Louisiana's most draconian transformation of contiguous landscape, and "the only dam and lake of its size ever built without federal funding."[46] The two-state asset generates 205 million kilowatt-hours of electricity annually, along with tens of millions in recreational dollars—"a godsend to this part of the world," according to *Louisiana Sportsman* writer Andy Crawford.[47] The sprawling alligator-shaped reservoir also induced a wholesale reorganization of settlement geography over 600 square miles, reshuffling everything from homes and businesses to roads and transmission lines. Toledo Bend is now integral to the economy and lifestyle of the western hill country, and most locals probably cannot imagine life without it. It may also be said that those who were wrenched from these hills in the early 1960s could never have imagined their own states would drown out their homes, their ancestral communities, and even their cemeteries.

Of the forty-one cities, towns, villages, and other communities in the western hills analyzed in this study, only 7 percent had riverine- or water-based primary siting stories (the lowest in Louisiana, whose statewide average is 29 percent), while 51 percent were primarily railroad sites, 22 percent were crossroads, and 12 percent were resource extraction or processing sites (compared to state averages of 33 percent, 10 percent, and 13 percent, respectively). The data attest to the paucity of navigable waterways and the reliance on roads and railroads for transportation. Settlements began forming in this region in the 1770s, crested in the 1880s with the railroad boom, and ended by the 1940s. Only one-third (34 percent) of settlements in the western hill country emerged organically, the other 66 percent having been ordained by a founder, usually railroad executives. This compares to the statewide average of 49 percent/51 percent emergent/ordained.

13

THE NORTHERN HILL COUNTRY

Greenwood might come across as an ordinary bedroom community of a small American city, strung out indistinctly along the I-20 corridor west of Shreveport. The town's narrow Main Street, only two blocks long and curiously devoid of commercial buildings, furthers the sense that Greenwood was little more than a wooded green not too long ago. In fact, this Caddo Parish community was once deemed a "rival town" and "more promising place than Shreveport."[1] What put Greenwood on the map were westward-oriented roads in a region otherwise traversed by southward-flowing rivers, making this site a jumping-off point to the western frontier.

As we have seen with the Camino Real, the origins and exact routes of these old wagon trails are perfectly murky. Many began as wildlife corridors, or as indigenous trade routes and hunting trails—or vice-versa, or all three. Bison, found in Louisiana through the 1700s, were particularly effective road blazers, "going from the pastures to the drinking places or salt-licks," wrote Nancy Maria Miller Surrey in 1916. "Year after year the herds passed over the same path, [in] an astonishingly direct line. . . . The paths were worn deep, and the earth was packed so hard that no vegetation ever grew upon them. . . . The buffalo 'trace,' as it was called by the pioneer, was spacious enough for two wagons to go abreast, [sometimes] wider than ordinary public highways are today."[2] Natives pursued game along these traces, and both man and beast knew to head uphill when waters swelled, and downhill if quenching thirst. Colonial explorers followed in their footsteps, on paths of least resistance through briar-strewn thickets, especially when they led to villages and trade opportunities. So too came settlers, and the pathways widened and multiplied as more travelers had more places to go, guiding livestock, riding horses, driving stagecoaches, and leading ox carts. Maps from the early 1800s show, however inconsistently, multitudinous routes wending toward fords and bridgeheads, some with stopovers and crossroads, few with names. Settlements emerged upon this migrant road network, and undergirding it were prehistoric indigenous trails and hamlets. The village of Shongaloo in Webster Parish, for example, now sits at a modern crossroads, but it initially arose along a Choctaw trail, at the site of a natural spring (the origin of the name) and a mound called the Wauhoo Ridge. The name "Shongaloo" remained in the cultural memory long after the Choctaws departed, the spring dried, and the old Indian trail became today's Highway 2. Today, Shongaloo has 150 residents, roughly the size of its prehistoric antecedent.[3]

Starting in 1811, as Congress made lands of the Louisiana Purchase into the Territory of Orleans, it legislated that 5 percent of revenue from parcel sales would fund the construction of roads and levees. Following statehood in 1812, those funds flowed into state coffers and out to projects, growing to the point that, in 1826, the state legislature created the forerunner of today's Department of Transportation and Development, called the Board of Internal Improvements. In 1833, legislators created an affiliated Board of Public Works and staffed it with surveyors and engineers to build "roads, levees, bridges, canals and ditches. In case of emergency," noted geographer Keumsoo Hong, "the engineers could mobilize male slaves of 15 to 60 years of age from nearby plantations."[4] State contractors crossed paths with private builders clearing out their own roads, some of which formed intersections and seeded settlements. In this manner, the old Indian and colonial paths grew into a web of public and private turnpikes, some treaded with wooden boards ("plank roads"), others with toll gates or bridges, each with varying levels of engineering and maintenance. The main stagecoach route from Monroe to Shreveport, pieced together from Indian trails and costing $15 for the jarring thirty-hour trip, helped sprout a number of lasting communities. Among them were Forksville, Vienna, Arcadia, Mt. Lebanon, Minden, Bellevue, Fillmore, and Red Chute. The artery connecting them got nicknamed the Wire Road when telegraph lines were strung along it in 1857.[5]

On such roads trekked pioneers across northern Louisiana bound for Texas and points west. Growing Anglo-American migration and rising tension with the Mexican government triggered fighting in 1835–1836 and launched the Republic of Texas, which drew additional migration through Louisiana. Those years also brought Indian removal policies to the region, in which federal authorities forced the Caddo tribe, through cunning and cross-cultural confusion, to relinquish their land in Arkansas and Louisiana and move to the Brazos River in Texas.[6] To white interests, the 1835 displacement cleared the way for a

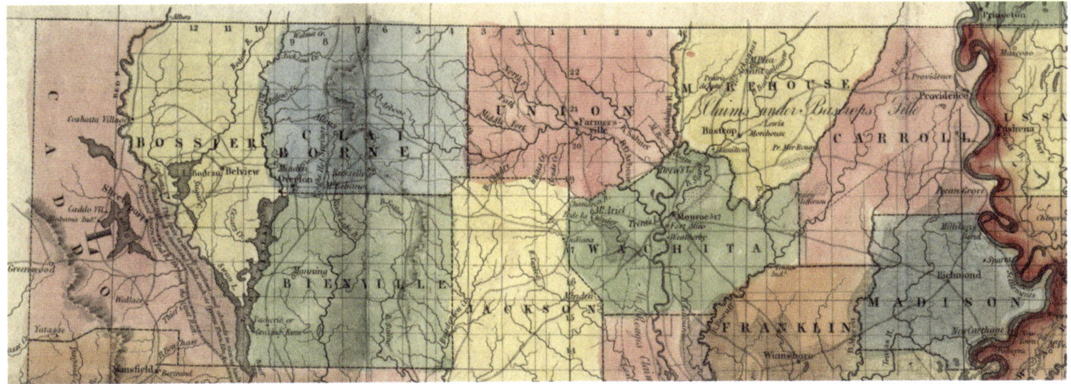

This detail of the Tanner map (1851) shows how east/west-oriented stagecoach roads interacted with north/south-oriented rivers in influencing the settlement geography of northern Louisiana. Library of Congress.

constant flow of pioneer stagecoaches heading west and cotton wagons heading east. The main west-bound road passed through nascent Shreveport and followed a slight ridge as it neared the international border. There, at a crossroads, a post office opened where mail was marked "Hold for Texas," since the Republic of Texas had no postal service. Its citizens had to come to Louisiana for their correspondence. While there, they might have seen on doors or signposts the hastily scrawled initials "G.T.T."—Gone to Texas.[7]

The lively frontier outpost attracted commercial attention. In 1839, William Littlejohn and nine other investors acquired land at the main crossroads, and two years later they launched the Greenwood Town Company to devise a plat. They tried the old tactic of donating land for a courthouse in the hope that Greenwood would become the seat of newly designated Caddo Parish (1838). But while the state legislature never concurred, it did authorize, in 1844, the construction of an improved twenty-foot-wide toll turnpike from Shreveport to Greenwood. The proscribed rates: "a loaded wagon (10 cents per mile), a loaded cart and team (8 cents), an empty wagon and team (5 cents), an empty cart and team (4 cents), each man and horse (3 cents), cattle, horses, or mules (2 cents), hogs or sheep (1 cent), and each footman (1 cent)."[8] By that time, a judge in Greenwood had his workers complete the first brick home in Caddo Parish, most others being rustic dogtrot log cabins—testimony to Greenwood's siting story as a frontier jumping-off point.[9]

Pioneers arrived from South Carolina, Georgia, Alabama, Tennessee, and elsewhere, and by the 1850s Greenwood catered to the Texas-bound traffic with a saddlery and tanning yard, a wagon and plow factory, blacksmiths, tinsmiths, foundries, machine shops, and brickyards, along with "seven stores, a Mason lodge, two two-story schools, a Methodist church, five doctors, three saloons, and a hotel" with fifteen rooms and a ballroom.[10] In effect, Greenwood had become a forerunner to today's standard interstate highway community, sited at a crossroads exit and functioning as a through-traffic service center. An 1864 wartime map by Helmuth Holtz shows as much, depicting Greenwood as a regional hub, with six roads and three railroads unifying here, commensurate to Shreveport. The momentum persisted enough after the Civil War for Greenwood to be incorporated as a town in 1876.

But by then the community had been steadily losing its siting advantages, and regretted the one it never got—the parish courthouse. Texas joined the Union, developed its own infrastructure, and attracted settlers through various new routes—now including railroads, only one of which would pass through Greenwood. In 1896, the town of Greenwood let its incorporated status lapse, though in the early 1900s it regained some momentum, becoming "the junction of the Missouri, Kansas & Texas and the Texas & Pacific . . . in the western timber district, [with] saw mills, etc., . . . and a population of 200."[11] Greenwood came back in the century ahead, when modern highways once again made it an interstate community. It reincorporated as a town and now functions as a bedroom community to its former rival, Shreveport. Greenville's frontier road siting story may explain its curious Main Street, surely among the narrowest in all of Louisiana at only one lane wide, possibly a vestige of that twenty-foot-wide turnpike of 1844.

Greenwood's westward turnpike forked to the north to access three remnant indigenous villages pertaining to the Alabama, Caddo, and Coushatta tribes.[12] The Coushatta village marked where an old Indian trail (labeled as the Quachatta Path in an 1816 map) approached the Red River. Following the federal removals, a man named Philo Alden settled here in 1843 and built a steam-operated sawmill to harvest the dense stands in Cypress Bayou. Over one particular tributary was built a bridge named after the Alden property, becoming today's Alden Bridge, sited as among the first of many resource extraction sites in northwestern Louisiana. Most, such as Plain Dealing to the north, would become timber towns; one, Oil City to the west, was eponymic of its siting story.[13]

To the east and south of Alden Bridge emerged two antebellum settlements with dueling siting rationales. Along the road heading east toward Overton and Minden was a crossing of two old Dauchite Indian trails, where formed a hamlet first known as Freedonia, then Society Hill, and finally Bellevue. Nearby Bayou Badcau and its tributaries were just deep enough to float barges to Shreveport, giving Bellevue a port economy.[14] In 1843, the state legislature created Bossier Parish with the stipulation that its seat of justice be sited within five miles of its geographical center. Bellevue thence landed the parish courthouse, despite the fact that its accessibility diminished once the old Indian trails gave way to better access elsewhere. By 1860, the remote seat of justice had, according to a visiting journalist, 115 or so inhabitants and "one store, two bar-rooms, and a church, which . . . they don't run 'regularly.' The courthouse is a fine building, however, and it is rumored that its being there is about all that retains Bellevue as the seat of the parish, its location not being a very convenient one."[15]

Meanwhile, south of Alden Bridge, a road was blazed in the 1820s courtesy of Missouri senator Thomas Hart Benton, an advocate of internal improvements who sought to connect Lewisville in Arkansas with the roads crossing northern Louisiana. Traversing an elevated tongue of land before dropping down into bottomlands, Benton's road passed near enough to a landing on the Red River to foster the formation of a hamlet named Benton. What revitalized the settlement was the postbellum reconfiguration of Bossier Parish, carried out at a time when political operatives seeking patronage eyed oversized parishes as ripe for redistricting. In 1871, legislators created Webster Parish out of portions of Bossier, Bienville, and Claiborne, all of which jostled the geographical centers on which courthouse locations had been based. Bossier Parish's new shape shifted its center away from Bellevue and toward Benton—bad news for Bellevue, but good for most other parish residents, who struggled to get to Bellevue. Benton was hardly nodal, but at least it was on a decent road near a river. In 1872, a fire destroyed most of Bellevue and damaged its courthouse, further weakening residents' argument to remain the seat of justice. After years of controversy and contested referendums, officials in 1890 finally relocated the Bossier Parish courthouse from Bellevue to Benton. With it went all the benefits of an administrative center, including a new railroad and station. Benton today is an incorporated town of 2,000 residents, while all that remains of Bellevue is a cemetery and historical plaque.[16]

Heading east from Benton through Bellevue got you to the largest waterway this side of the Red River, Bayou Dorcheat (or Dauchite, the Caddo word for "people") at the headwaters of Lake Bistineau ("big broth"). Navigability on Bayou Dorcheat has long been fraught, subject to weather conditions and judicial rulings affecting ownership to this day.[17] But 200 years ago, certain craft could navigate this unusually long bayou connecting Arkansas with Louisiana. One settler, a gunsmith from middle Tennessee named Newitt Drew, came down Bayou Dorcheat and in 1819 settled with kin and kith where the bayou widened into Lake Bistineau. This site had a number of advantages: terrestrial road access, plenty of water, lake resources, navigability by light steamboats, timber aplenty, gravel pits, and salt deposits, long used by Natives and later becoming the Bistineau Salt Works. Drew opened a sawmill and gristmill at the confluence of Cooley Creek and Bayou Dorcheat, and in 1825 the growing community gained the name Overton, in honor of a presiding judge. In the years ahead, the Overton area became a crucible of siting factors, having intermodal break-of-bulk points, vessel landings, a ferry and bridge, depots, stores, mills, resources for extraction and processing, and a church and post office. It even had centrality within the newly created Claiborne Parish (1828), for which it was designated the seat of justice, making Overton also an administrative center.

Overton's siting bonanza soon began to unravel. Captain Henry Shreve's clearing of the Red River killed steamboat traffic on Lake Bistineau and Bayou Dorcheat—which quieted Overton's landings, which diverted overland traffic, which quelled local commerce. When Bossier Parish was carved out of Claiborne, it changed parish centrality and, like Bellevue, cost Overton its courthouse—which went to Athens in 1846. Outbreaks of yellow fever and malaria in 1839 and 1841 killed as many as 350 residents, while high water occasionally inundated the area. An exodus ensued uphill to Minden, and Overton became a ghost town. "Today nothing remains of this former parish seat," noted the curators of the Dorcheat History Museum in Minden, "but a few graves in a cemetery atop a hill, isolated among gravel pits along Dorcheat Bayou."[18]

Whereas Overton initially enjoyed water-based siting advantages, Minden began inauspiciously, as a roadside stopover. It started at a hilltop inn opened by a New Yorker named Charles Veeder in 1835, who named the spot for the home of his German ancestors. Minden benefitted from its elevated perch, distant from the flood-prone bottomlands, and yet close enough to access three landings on Bayou Dorcheat. As Overton's siting pros became cons, Minden looked better by comparison. It became the largest community in Claiborne Parish, and the main crossroads between Shreveport and Monroe. Known for its churches and academies, Minden incorporated as a town in 1850, became the seat of justice for the newly created Webster Parish in 1871, and got a railroad in 1898, after which its population doubled to 3,000 and continued to grow with the subsequent timber boom.[19]

Bolstering Minden's growth was the formation of a religious commune led by the self-styled "Countess of Leon," Elisa Leon, who in 1833 guided fellow Utopians on a peregrination from southern Germany all the way to northern Louisiana—specifically, seven miles northeast of Veeder's inn. Known as Germantown (1836), Leon's settlement endeavored to be communal in its organization, and therefore did not need the sort of siting rationales apropos of a capitalistic economy. Like most communes, it worked until it didn't, and its irrational site did not help. Germantown steadily lost members and closed in 1871, leaving its people to resettle in Minden.[20]

Mural in downtown Homer. Photograph by Carol M. Highsmith/ Library of Congress.

Minden, meanwhile, benefitted from the rise of automotive highways, whose routes roughly followed the old stagecoach roads. Better yet, Minden's site marked a convenient driving interval for I-20 motorists. It is roughly thirty miles from Monroe to Ruston, from Ruston to Minden, from Minden to Shreveport, etc., making the modern city, now with 12,000 people, still a roadside stopover and hill country crossroads. Germantown, on the other hand, is now an outdoor museum.

Minden and Overton occur on a triangle of antebellum roads connecting settlements with similar siting rationales and aspirational names: Athens, Homer, Sparta, Arcadia, and Mt. Lebanon, as well as Russellville. The classical allusions reflected an American fascination with archaeological discoveries made in Greece, coupled with the lingering veneration of Hellenism that started with the Enlightenment and resonated in the Old South. If there is a standard siting formula for these and other hill country communities in northern Louisiana, including Bellevue and Overton, it goes something like this: (1) founded in the second quarter of the nineteenth century, mainly the 1840s, at (2) a stopover, crossroads, or break-of-bulk site along an overland road, which turned out to be (3) centrally positioned vis-à-vis parish boundaries, qualifying the settlement to be a seat of justice, which (4) enabled it to become an administrative and trade center. The corollary: if that designation was later lost due to parish boundary changes, and if no railroad were to be built in subsequent years, the community would wither and die. But if the community was able retain or gain the parish courthouse, and/or land a railroad or highway, it would survive.

At the happier end of that spectrum is "picturesque and pleasant" Homer, founded in 1849 and "a very prosperous town of seven or eight hundred inhabitants" by 1860, which got both a courthouse and a railroad and now has over 2,500 people. Another is Arcadia, which originated as a stagecoach stop in the 1820s and became a town in 1854. While it never had a courthouse, it benefitted by being the highway midpoint between Monroe and Shreveport, and now has 2,650 residents.[21] Farmerville, on the other hand, never got railroad but managed to remain the seat of Union Parish since its designation in 1839, allowing the old crossroads and 1790 Spanish land grant to endure today as a centralized administrative town with a population of 3,300. Variations of the same formula apply to the town of Haynesville (founded north of Homer at a crossroads in 1843, shifted to meet the railroad in 1898, now home to 1,900 people), and Vienna, which was founded to the east of Athens in 1838 as a main stop and crossroads on the Monroe-Shreveport stagecoach road ("Wire Road") and became the Lincoln Parish seat in 1873—only to lose both the courthouse and a perch on the railroad to nearby Russ Station. Vienna still has nearly 500 inhabitants, mostly because of its proximity to the city that grew around that train station: today's Ruston, now the seat of Lincoln Parish, population 22,000.

At the other end of that spectrum are Russellville (founded 1828), Mt. Lebanon (1836), Athens (1846), and Sparta (1849). Three of those communities were once parish seats, only to later lose the honor, and not one got a railroad. Sparta seemed doomed as early as 1860, when a visitor rued it had been "unhappily located far from any navigable watercourse" and built "in a regular old-fashioned sand-bed, the base of which could scarcely be reached by an artesian bore," making Sparta a town with a bad situation *and* a lousy site. "It would not be surprising," the visitor jested, "if, two or three generations hence, Spartans were born splay-footed." Instead, Spartans voted with their feet and departed after they lost the courthouse, and nature has since reclaimed their sandy-bottomed site.[22] Russellville and Sparta are now completely gone, as is the original site of Athens, which was abandoned after a new highway opened two miles to the east. Mt. Lebanon and the new community known as Athens hang on with a few hundred residents—but only because they reconstituted around highway intersections. Only the Old Athens Cemetery remains at Athens's original site.

Louisiana's triangle of classical communities is intriguing for its parallels across the globe. As Claire D'Artois Leeper pointed out, "Arcadia, La., is located between Sparta, in Bienville parish, and Athens, in Claiborne parish, just as Arcadia in Greece is located between Athens and Sparta." Given that their post offices were all established during 1850–1851, around the peak of the Classical Revival, Leeper contended "this geographical parallel . . . is no coincidence," reflecting instead an explicit homage to antiquity.[23] Relatedly, most of the surviving antebellum buildings in these communities exhibit the Greek Revival architectural idiom and remain majestic today. More so, the original site of Athens—at the time the highest community in Louisiana, at 415 feet above sea level—may have been named because its hilltop site brought to mind the setting of the Acropolis in Athens, Greece. Both locales had flowing springs, suggesting, in a very distant way, that they share a similar siting story.[24]

As we saw in the western hills and southern prairies, railroads would thoroughly reconfigure northern Louisiana, inverting its settlement-making processes from emergent forces to ordained choices. Rails superseded stagecoach roads, just as stagecoach roads had done to Indian paths and buffalo traces—though rarely did they completely erase their antecedents.

In 1853, the state legislature approved the incorporation of the Vicksburg, Shreveport & Texas Railroad Company, and from the outset, roadside settlements in Louisiana understood that their propinquity to this upcoming line would make or break their future. It did not bode well that, despite the fact that the company was chartered in Louisiana and domiciled in Monroe, the only Louisiana town cited in the company's name was the *river* town of Shreveport. Advocates in the Concordia Parish town of Vidalia "thought the selection of Vicksburg as the eastern terminus [was] a 'suicidal policy,'" wrote historian Marshall Scott Legan, "and extolled the more advantageous position of Vidalia," while pointedly questioning why "'the vast and wealthy Parish of Concordia . . . is entirely to be left out of the Railroad enterprise.'"[25] After final routing decisions were made at a Monroe meeting in July 1852, construction began at Delta Point across from Vicksburg in 1853 and proceeded erratically, beleaguered by floods, epidemics, engineering challenges, and revenue shortfalls. The Delta-to-Monroe section opened just as southern states began seceding from the Union, leading to the Civil War and the Confederate commandeering of the line. Its destruction in subsequent fighting was followed by two decades of intermittent rebuilding, corporate reorganizations, piecemeal acquisitions, name changes, and finally full service. Maps of the era show the main trunk of what became the Vicksburg, Shreveport & Pacific line running from Delta straight across to Greenwood, after which intersecting north-south lines were built separately through Shreveport, Minden, Monroe, and Tallulah.[26]

By the 1880s, a transfigured hill country settlement geography fell into place. Track routes and station stops birthed new communities, while those solely dependent on stagecoaches withered. Remote stands of "merchantable" timber suddenly became accessible, birthing resource extraction and processing towns, which thence became intersections for new roads. What became the largest of the new northern Louisiana railroad towns started in a time-honored way: a land subsidy offered by a plantation owner, in this case Robert E. Russ, to the Vicksburg, Shreveport & Pacific Railroad, in exchange for a commitment to build a station and create a town around it. VS&P officials agreed in 1884,

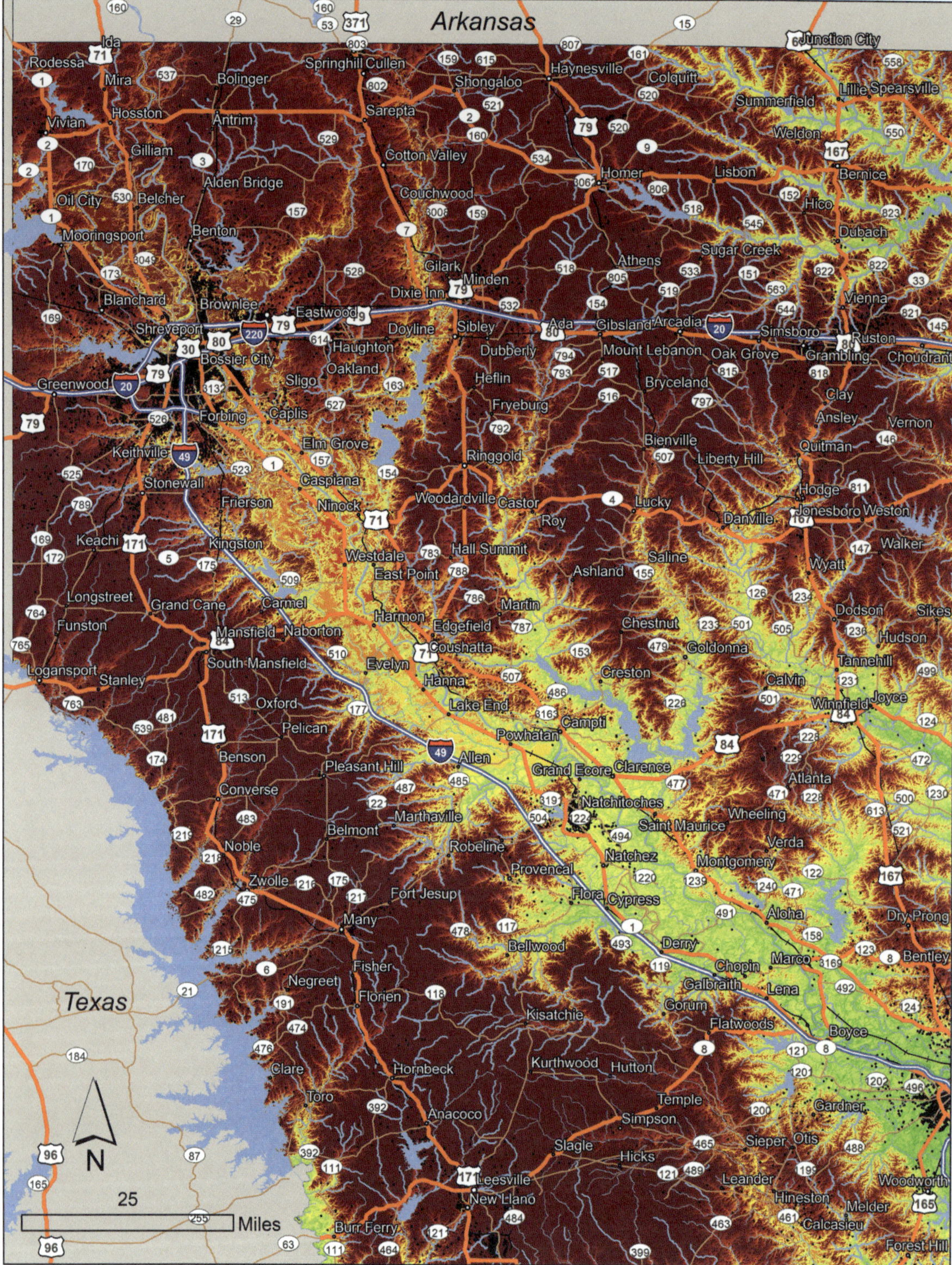

Arkansas
Texas
Junction City
Rodessa
Ida
Mira
Bolinger
Springhill
Cullen
Shongaloo
Haynesville
Colquitt
Summerfield
Lillie
Spearsville
Vivian
Hosston
Antrim
Sarepta
Weldon
Gilliam
Cotton Valley
Homer
Lisbon
Bernice
Alden Bridge
Couchwood
Hico
Oil City
Belcher
Dubach
Mooringsport
Benton
Sugar Creek
Athens
Gilark
Minden
Blanchard
Brownlee
Dixie Inn
Vienna
Eastwood
Shreveport
Doyline
Sibley
Ada
Gibsland
Arcadia
Simsboro
Ruston
Bossier City
Haughton
Dubberly
Mount Lebanon
Oak Grove
Grambling
Choudrant
Greenwood
Oakland
Sligo
Heflin
Bryceland
Clay
Forbing
Caplis
Fryeburg
Ansley
Vernon
Elm Grove
Bienville
Keithville
Ringgold
Liberty Hill
Quitman
Stonewall
Caspiana
Hodge
Frierson
Ninock
Woodardville
Castor
Lucky
Jonesboro
Weston
Roy
Danville
Keachi
Kingston
Hall Summit
Walker
Westdale
Wyatt
East Point
Ashland
Saline
Longstreet
Grand Cane
Carmel
Martin
Dodson
Sikes
Funston
Harmon
Edgefield
Chestnut
Mansfield
Naborton
Coushatta
Goldonna
Hudson
Tannehill
Logansport
South Mansfield
Evelyn
Creston
Stanley
Hanna
Calvin
Oxford
Lake End
Winnfield
Joyce
Pelican
Campti
Powhatan
Benson
Allen
Pleasant Hill
Grand Ecore
Clarence
Atlanta
Converse
Natchitoches
Marthaville
Belmont
Saint Maurice
Wheeling
Noble
Robeline
Verda
Natchez
Provencal
Montgomery
Zwolle
Fort Jesup
Flora
Cypress
Aloha
Dry Prong
Many
Bellwood
Derry
Marco
Bentley
Fisher
Chopin
Negreet
Galbraith
Lena
Florien
Gorum
Kisatchie
Flatwoods
Boyce
Clare
Hornbeck
Kurthwood
Hutton
Toro
Temple
Simpson
Gardner
Anacoco
Slagle
Sieper
Otis
Hicks
Leesville
Leander
Woodworth
New Llano
Hineston
Melder
Calcasieu
Burr Ferry
Forest Hill
N
25
Miles

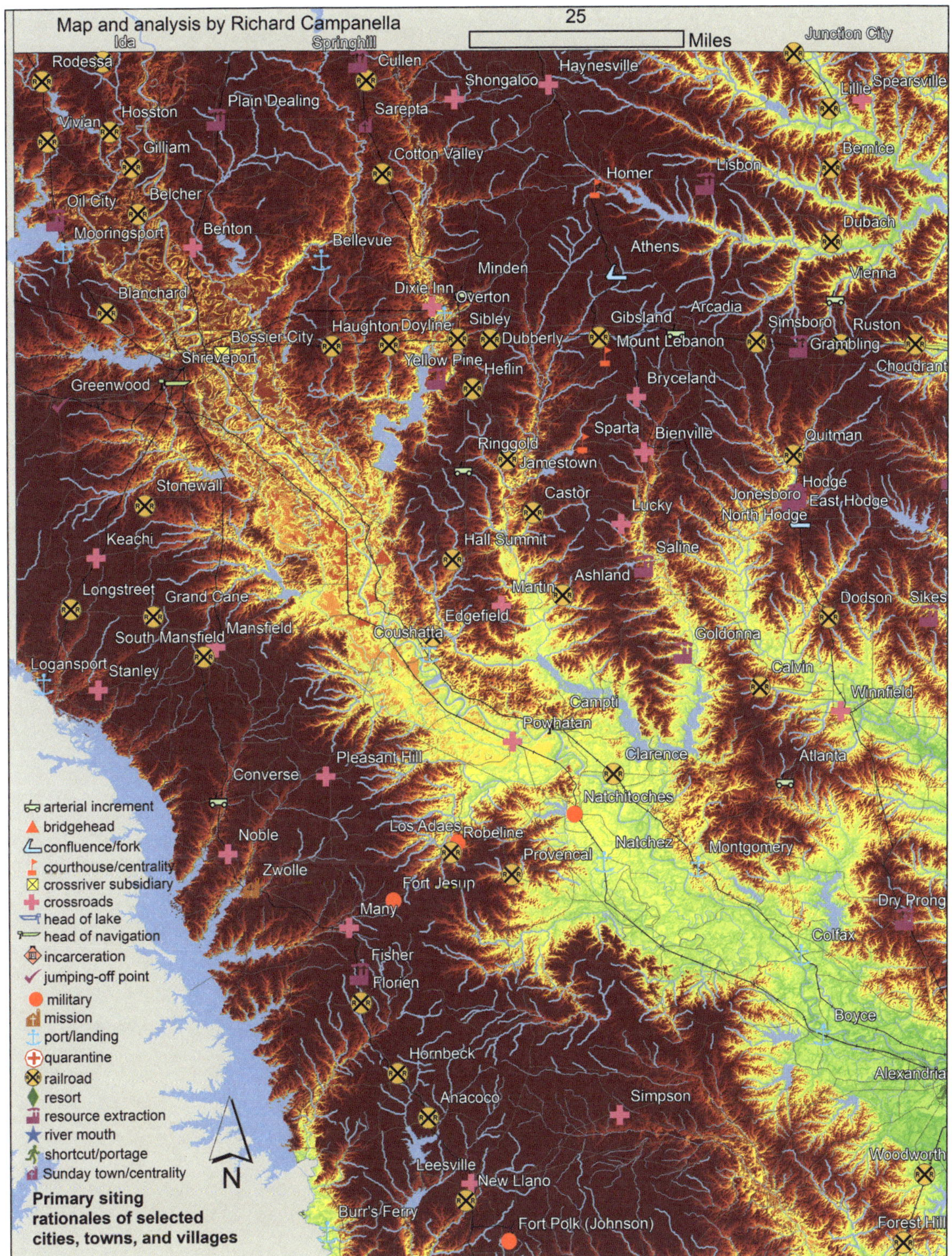

Map and analysis by Richard Campanella
25
Miles
arterial increment
bridgehead
confluence/fork
courthouse/centrality
crossriver subsidiary
crossroads
head of lake
head of navigation
incarceration
jumping-off point
military
mission
port/landing
quarantine
railroad
resort
resource extraction
river mouth
shortcut/portage
Sunday town/centrality
N
Primary siting rationales of selected cities, towns, and villages

hiring a surveyor to lay out streets of "unusual width and symmetry" and naming it Russ Town. Residents from Vienna and Old Trenton (now West Monroe) quickly started to migrate to what folks pronounced as "Ruston," making it a trade center and, in 1886, Lincoln Parish's seat of justice. Ruston "literally took the courthouse from Vienna," noted Clare D'Artois Leeper, when "trustees paid a contractor $601.18 to move the building" to the new site. Another source, writing in 1892, stated plainly that "the removal of the parish [seat] to Ruston," following the denial of railroad access, "added the death blow to Vienna."[27] In 1900, the Chicago, Rock Island & Pacific Railroad was built through Ruston, making it a rail hub and the home to repair shops, trainmen headquarters, and growing timber-milling and cotton-ginning industries. Its population went from zero in 1880 to over 3,300 by 1910, and with the help of Louisiana Tech University, Ruston has been one of the few regional cities to register steadfast growth, to over 22,000 inhabitants today. Vienna, now with under 500 in population, lost everything to Ruston—its people, its courthouse, even its past. A historic plaque at a cottage on West Alabama Avenue reads, "Oldest house in Ruston. Built in Vienna in 1876, dismantled, and moved to Ruston in 1884. . . . First child in Ruston born here."[28]

The VS&P sited its next station by the homestead of James Monroe Sims, who in 1848 had settled along an overland road to build a store and mill. What became known as Old Simsboro gave way to present-day Simsboro at the new train station, to the east of which were extensive timberlands now accessible to sawyers. There, in 1900, Ruston resident Judd Grambling opened a sawmill, which in turn motivated railroad officials to erect a station for mill workers housed nearby, many of whom were African American. With the help of the North Louisiana Colored Agriculture Relief Association, the Black workers organized a school for their children and contacted famed Tuskegee Institute president Booker T. Washington to recommend a schoolmaster. Charles P. Adams came to town with that charge, got the school up and running, and leveraged donations as well as parish support to grow the institution into the Lincoln Parish Training School. With state funding in the 1930s, the school became the Louisiana Negro Normal and Industrial Institute, and in 1946 the Grambling sawmill family donated additional land for campus expansion. The institute was renamed Grambling College, and after three decades of further growth the institution became Grambling State University. Credit for Grambling goes squarely to Charles Adams and his colleagues, but its siting was the product of the same railroad and timber industries that transformed this entire region at the turn of the twentieth century.[29]

Gibsland, too, began as a station site on the VS&P and became a rail crossing with the construction of the Louisiana & Northwest Railroad. The junction became "the shipping point for a large cotton and timber area[,] several manufacturing concerns, among which is a furniture factory," and home to Coleman College, for a while a rival of Grambling.[30] Much like Ruston and Vienna, Gibsland's rail-based vibrancy came at the expense of the older community of Mt. Lebanon, bypassed by three miles, which subsequently diminished to a few dozen inhabitants living along a section of Highway 154 still known as Stagecoach Trail. Likewise, Sibley, west of Gibsland, was born of the VS&P line where it was later crossed by the Louisiana & Arkansas and the Shreveport, Alexandria & Southwestern lines. All three vectors spurred an extensive timber industry, benefitting Sibley and sending Overton on the same downward path as Vienna and Mt. Lebanon.[31]

A story is told that a pioneer from Georgia driving cattle to Texas in 1840 had been chased by Indians out of the area south of Overton. Upon returning weeks later to round up his herd, he found the cattle feeding contently among the soaring pines just east of Lake Bistineau. Seeing no reason to leave, he became the first settler of what would later become Yellow Pine. If the story is true, the outpost might be the only one in Louisiana sited by cows. What truly put the community on the map, however, was its namesake timber—stands of old-growth trees up to 120 feet high—and men desirous of the beautiful wood. In 1891, representatives of the Lake Bistineau Lumber Company bought up timberland for a mill plus a five-mile-long right-of-way to Sibley, along which they built the Sibley, Lake Bistineau & Southern (SLB&S) Railway to connect with the VS&P. By the early 1900s, the operation came under the control of the Missouri-based Long-Bell Lumber Company, which turned Yellow Pine into a quintessential company town: over 2,000 people living in 154 abodes plus a boarding house, hotel, doctor's office, school, and church. Residents worked at the sprawling Globe Lumber Mill plus a dry kiln, storage depots, a commissary with a butcher and ice house, and a drinking water plant. The town even had its own electrical power plant and telephone system.[32]

Yellow Pine's lifeline was the SLB&S, which was later extended southward, galvanizing the settlements of Ringgold, Hall Summit, Whiskey Junction, and Davis Switch, with spurs out to Gidden, Madden Spur, and Lesche Crossing, and logging camps as far away as Natchitoches Parish. Similarly, the Louisiana & Arkansas line was built southward from Gibsland, and it left behind mill towns at Fryeburg, Castor, Roy, Ashland, Chestnut, Goldonna, and Calvin, at which point the tracks tied in with the Kansas City Southern line and led into Winnfield. Correspondingly, the Chicago, Rock Island & Pacific line headed south from Ruston, accounting for Clay, Quitman, Jonesboro, Wyatt, Dodson,

Tannehill, and Winnfield. All along these tracks, stations were opened, mills were built, workers were housed, trees came down, lumber was milled and shipped, and money was made—though little of it stayed locally.

Among this cavalcade of rail-catalyzed resource extraction sites are some interesting exceptions. Ringgold, for example, formed two generations earlier, in 1836, when two Georgians named Simon Manning and Phillip Purser Brinson settled at the stagecoach crossroads of the Military Road and Sparta Road. There they opened a tavern, built houses, and operated a sawmill hewing "slabs," smoothed logs used for the puncheon floors of log cabins—thus "Slabtown," the original name for Ringgold. Into the 1950s, the old Manning dogtrot log cabin stood on Manning and Mill Street, presumably with slab floors, and Ringgold itself remains on Military Road, an example of a settlement with both emergent and ordained siting stories. Renamed to honor either a blazer of the Military Road or the place in Georgia from which the Mannings hailed, Ringgold today is an incorporated town of more than 1,300 people.[33]

Yellow Pine, among the shortest-lived of those rail/mill towns, had no such luck. It took only fifteen years, 1898 to 1913, for Long-Bell's Globe Lumber Company to clearcut 63,000 acres, lay off workers, uproot their facilities, and depart for Texas and Washington, leaving behind not even a reforestation plan. "Her fair forests have been cut down," wrote a former denizen in 1930; "the mill is gone, most of the residences and the hotel have been torn down and removed, and the busy worker gone into new fields."[34] Yellow Pine is barely on the map today, home to a handful of houses, no railroad, dense thickets full of ruins, and pastures with herds of cows—still apparently contented.

Of the aforementioned mill towns, some like Yellow Pine have disappeared, others persevere as country crossroads, and only Jonesboro and Winnfield boast more than a few thousand people. The reason: both hedged their siting bets by diversifying their economies. Take Jonesboro, which began a generation prior to the rail-and-mill era. In 1860, settlers Joseph and Sarah Pankey Jones established a homestead by the Dugdemona River and Caney Creek and built a grist mill. By one account, the area gained the nickname Coon Town because "raccoons were so numerous and destructive that grain could not be left overnight at the Joseph Jones Grist Mill."[35] The Joneses also helped established the Macedonia Baptist Church, giving Coon Town the more dignified moniker of Macedonia. As railroad officials sized up the community in 1900, they honored its founders by naming the new station "Jonesboro," with service to Ruston on the Arkansas Southern line (later Chicago, Rock Island & Pacific), and shortly thereafter, with service to Sikes on the Tremont & Gulf line. In time, Macedonia officially became known as Jonesboro, and its railroad junction bustled with freights of logs and milled lumber. After the boom, however, Jonesboro became a trade center with sustainable silviculture and value-added industries for wood and agricultural byproducts. It grew to the point that it was able to win a 1911 parish-wide referendum to relocate Vernon's courthouse and become the new Jackson Parish seat of justice. The town benefitted additionally from the paper mill jobs in three nearby communities named Hodge. The original Hodge had been founded in 1899 by the Hodge-Hunt Lumber Company on the Arkansas Southern Railroad; its offshoots, North Hodge and East Hodge, were separately incorporated in 1953 and in 1968. Having germinated from the Joneses' raccoon-infested gristmill back in 1860, greater Jonesboro now endures with a combined population of nearly 5,000 people, the largest urbanized area within twenty miles. Vernon, founded in 1846 "on a knobby, knolly, hilly piece of ground" for its parish centrality and incorporated in 1859, never recovered from its loss of its courthouse, and today is a rural crossroads.[36]

Winnfield began like Vernon, centralized within Winn Parish when it was carved out of neighbors in 1852. The name honored attorney Walter O. Winn, who was "instrumental in handling legislation" to create the parish and designate its seat. Evidence suggests Winnfield was not sited solely on grounds of jurisdictional centrality; an 1806 map plots a road passing through future Winnfield, and an 1820 map shows a crossroads as well as a salt works by Saline Lake fifteen miles to the west.[37] What the salt inferred was a rare and valuable resource known as the Cockfield Formation, a 150-foot-thick layer of bedrock comprising silty sediments and a low grade of coal known as lignite shale ("asphalt lands"), along with "valuable deposits of salt[,] kaolin, gypsum, limestone, iron, fire and potter's clay [and] a variegated stone . . . which when burned makes excellent lime."[38] Winnfield became a key salt provider and the sole source of limestone and lime in the region, home to Louisiana's only true rock quarry, plus a wide range of other derivative industries enabled by railroad transport. While crossroads and parish centrality are the original siting rationales for Winnfield, there is no question that railroad-based resource extraction and processing empowered Winnfield to grow twentyfold in population during 1880–1910 and peak at 7,300 residents by 1980, though the population has since dropped to 4,100.[39]

In fact, the northern Louisiana hill country as a whole witnessed a commensurate reconfiguration, as railroads supplanted tortuous trails and twisting rivers for transportation. It all happened within a generation, 1880s to 1900s, and even those prone to romanticize the days of yore, such as narrative historian Alcée Fortier, swiftly accepted the new order, as revealed in his 1914 description of Claiborne Parish:

> Transportation and shipping facilities are provided by the Louisiana & Northwest R. R., which traverses the western part of the parish, from north to south, passing through Homer. This road has direct connections with the Cotton Belt, the Vicksburg, Shreveport & Pacific R. R., the Louisiana Railway & Navigation company and the Texas & Pacific R. R., while the Shreveport & Northeastern R. R. runs southwest from Homer to Minden, in Webster parish, connecting with the Louisiana & Arkansas R. R. Homer and Athens, the two most important towns of the parish, are located on the Louisiana & Northwest R. R.[40]

Where tracks were laid in the late 1800s, automobile roads followed in the 1900s. The route selected at that 1852 convention of VS&T Railroad Company executives, for example, is today's I-20 corridor, and all transecting tracks are now also paralleled by highways. Asphalt ribbons have superseded iron rails as siting vectors, just as rails had superseded stagecoach roads following old Indian paths and game trails. Settlements' fates depended on their ability to adapt to each reconfiguration. Gibsland, for instance, was born of the railroad but declined upon being narrowly bypassed by I-20, sending motorist dollars to Arcadia to the east and Minden to the west. Sibley, too, was bypassed by the federal interstate, but because it lies closer to Minden and Shreveport, it has managed to grow modestly.

The new siting logic of northern Louisiana is that of the arterial increment, in which geographical distance fuels travelers' demand for services. Consider those regularly spaced communities along the VS&P/I-20 corridor: Haughton is midway between Sibley and Shreveport, Doyline is midway between Haughton and Sibley, Gibsland is roughly midway between Minden/Sibley and Arcadia—which is midway between Minden and Ruston, itself the halfway point across all of northern Louisiana. Each site has attracted interconnecting rails or roads, each with *their* own incremental communities. The result: dozens of population clusters dispersed among the hills, at intervals dictated by the needs of machines and people on the move.

The new spatial girding begot novel sites previously unfathomable for settlement. One station-stop community ordained by railroad officials had zero prior advantages: no navigable rivers; no fertile soils; no oil, salt, limestone, or springs; no Indian trails or overland roads, much less a crossroads; and no jurisdictional centrality. Quite the opposite: the town founded here landed *on* boundaries, lots of them, making it anything but centralized. What activated the site was political geography. Railroad companies in this era won support by serving elected officials' constituents. So long as railroad tracks were already destined for a certain direction, why not nudge them to cross multiple divisions, and make the most friends? In this case, the Arkansas Southern Railway, founded in 1892, steered its tracks southward toward one such jurisdictional juncture, and in 1894 established a station named Junction on the Arkansas state line. Three years later, the Alexandria, Junction City & Shreveport Railway Company continued those rails southward to Ruston and Winnfield, and in 1899 merged with its Arkansas counterpart. By that time, the renamed Junction City had become the only place in the world sited "at the junction of 2 states, 1 county, 2 parishes, and 3 congressional districts." With half its footprint in Arkansas's Union County, and the other half split between Louisiana's Claiborne and Union parishes, Junction City is the southernmost community in Arkansas and the northernmost in Louisiana. While separately incorporated, the two halves of Junction City today share a school district and fire department serving 1,000 people—half Arkansans, half Louisianians.[41]

And speaking of halves, approximately halfway between Junction City and Ruston is the town of Bernice, midway between Ruston and Bernice is the town of Dubach, halfway between Dubach and Ruston is Vienna, and midway between Junction City and Bernice is the enclave of Lillie. Half these hamlets are spatial byproducts of the other half, and without the marvelously arbitrary Junction City, the rail-based settlement geography of the northern hill country would look very different today.

In Lincoln Parish. Photograph by Richard Campanella

Of the sixty-nine cities, towns, villages, and other communities in the northern hills region analyzed in this study, 9 percent had riverine- or water-based primary siting stories (well below the state average of 29 percent), while 42 percent were primarily railroad sites, 20 percent were resource extraction or processing sites, and 16 percent were crossroads (compared to state averages of 33 percent, 10 percent, and 13 percent, respectively). Settlements began forming in this region in the 1820s, crested during the railroad heyday of the 1890s, and ended by 1940. About 35 percent of settlements in the northern hill country emerged organically, the other 65 percent having been ordained (mostly by railroad and timber companies), compared to a statewide split of 49 percent/51 percent emergent/ordained.[42]

14

THE OUACHITA RIVER VALLEY

A hundred million years ago, the crust of the North American continent warped downwardly through present-day eastern Louisiana, Arkansas, and Missouri on one side, and western Mississippi, Tennessee, and Kentucky on the other. Seawater intruded this embayment up to southern Illinois, and in the eons ahead, as global temperatures cycled through cooling and warming trends, sea levels fell and rose accordingly, each leaving behind depositions of sediment within this syncline.

As cooler temperatures prevailed approximately 2 million years ago, ice sheets augmented, sea levels dropped, the Mississippi Embayment emptied out, and the edge of the continent prograded southwardly. But starting around 20,000 years ago, temperatures began to rise, melting ice sheets and sending outwash southward to the Gulf. The former embayment refilled with sediment to become a broad alluvial valley, and through it coursed rivers and tributaries with braided channels, among them the Ouachita, Boeuf, Tensas, and Mississippi rivers of modern-day northeastern Louisiana.[1]

Bordering the valley to the west were the ancient uplifts of the Kisatchie Wold, while to the east were an equally undulating but softer and younger topographic feature known as loess bluffs. These reddish hillocks formed as winds mobilized post-glacial deposits of silt and dropped them a few hundred miles downwind. Those particles that fell on the Pleistocene Terrace gave rise to the sloping terrain of the Feliciana parishes and southwestern Mississippi; those that fell within the lower Mississippi Valley mostly got swept away, except for some island-like formations, such as Crowley's Ridge, the Bastrop Hills, and Maçon Ridge. Surrounded by rich alluvial bottomlands, accessible via waterways yet protected from floods, the Maçon Ridge was particularly ideal for settlement.

Mound A at Poverty Point. Photograph by Richard Campanella

What occurred here ranked among the largest early sustained concentrations of humans on the North American continent, arguably its first "city." Beginning around 3,700 years ago, this rendezvous site served indigenous peoples of various subcultures for more than half a millennium, before being abandoned and later partly reoccupied around 1,300 years ago. "Some came to exchange goods and news or to meet people," wrote the curators of this UNESCO World Heritage Site. "Others were attracted by the site's natural resources. Still others came to create the site's mounds and ridges or to take part in ceremonies. Most probably had deep family ties in the area."[2] The site has some of the largest prehistoric earthworks in the nation, particularly for people who were hunter-gatherers and not agriculturalists. At the time of their construction, they were the largest anthropogenic structures in the Western Hemisphere, taking 27 million basket-fills of soil to build over 300 years. "Simply extraordinary" is how archaeologists describe the Maçon Ridge site, in a spot so spare by the nineteenth century that its owners dubbed it Poverty Point.[3]

We have learned much about Poverty Point since its rediscovery in the 1830s, especially after aerial photographs in the 1950s revealed its striking concentric ridges. Yet it remains shrouded in mystery—its construction, uses, societies, transformations, abandonment, and, most fundamentally, its siting rationale: why here? Consider the advantages: a topographic upland (the Maçon Ridge, the first "high ground below the confluence of all the trade routes") immediately abutting a navigable waterway (Bayou Maçon) and tributary (Harland Bayou), surrounded by fertile bottomlands, and accessible via the Ouachita and Boeuf rivers to the west and by the Tensas and Mississippi rivers to the east.[4]

But those attributes may be found elsewhere on the Maçon Ridge, not to mention the Bastrop Hills, Crowley's Ridge, and other loess bluffs. As geographer Milton B. Newton noted, while Poverty Point is unique for its size, "it is not the only such earthen construction dating from that time. [Other] clusters occur in the Yazoo Basin, on the Maçon Ridge, near Lake Catahoula, [and] around Baton Rouge, New Iberia, and around the mouth of the Pearl River." Whatever Poverty Point's siting rationale, its occupants apparently made a good decision, because the community they created lasted longer than any other human settlement in present-day Louisiana.[5]

While the fate of Poverty Point's inhabitants is unknown, that of their descendants is all too familiar. Decimated by disease since the 1540s, Native peoples endured additional pressure from French and Spanish efforts to establish interior posts, giving rise to Natchitoches, Opelousas, New Iberia, Alexandria, and Marksville. Left vacant on colonial maps was the valley of the Ouachita River, extending from its hilly headwaters in present-day Arkansas, past the Bastrop Hills and Maçon Ridge, down to the Tensas confluence and its eventual joining with the Black and Red rivers.

Spanish lieutenant governor Don Francisco Bouligny aimed to fill that vacancy. In 1778, he issued a report describing the Ouachita River Valley as fertile, healthful in climate, abundant in game, only occasionally hunted by amicable Natives, and ideal for settling 1,000 Spanish families. Governor Bernardo de Gálvez rejected the settlement recommendation, sensing potential danger with the Osage Indians, and in time those immigrant families instead ended up in today's New Iberia, Gonzales, and St. Bernard Parish. But just before he was transferred to Mexico, Gálvez decided to act on the District of Ouachita, and recruited former soldier Don Juan (Sieur Jean Baptiste) Filhiol to serve as its commandant. Governor *ad-interim* Esteban Miró officially commissioned Filhiol to establish alliances and trade relations with the Natives, deter "Englishmen, Americans, and vagabonds" from the region, and establish settlements for Spanish subjects, starting with a fortified military post.[6]

In early 1782, Filhiol struggled up the Mississippi, Red, Black, and Ouachita rivers in a keelboat, seeking a site for his fort far into present-day Arkansas. He selected a riverside perch known as Écore à Fabri, used by French travelers since the 1740s. "Fabre's Bluff" afforded commanding views of the river valley and marked the crossroads of Caddo and Quapaw Indian trails. It was a fine fort site, but not an ideal settlement situation. Floodwaters often swamped the bottomlands, and being isolated from the main Louisiana colony, the Écore à Fabri region failed to attract settlers. In 1784–1785, Filhiol headed downriver to establish a better-situated primary post at a confluence he had known previously, called Prairie des Canots (Prairie of the Canoes), while retaining the Écore as a secondary position.[7]

As was the case upriver, Filhiol was hardly the first colonial in Prairie des Canots. Over a hundred rather roguish hunters and traders circulated around the Bayou de Siard confluence where various Indian trails intersected, serving the Caddo to the west, the Osage to the north, the Tunica to the east, and the Choctaw to the south.[8] Filhiol established the Ouachita Post to bring order to the backcountry traders, and in late 1790 began work on his main charge, the military installation he would name Fort Miró. Positioned on the east bank of the Ouachita River and built by volunteer labor, the stockade covered 150 feet by 190 feet, with a blockhouse on each corner, and a commissary, two houses (his own and a priest's), and a jail inside.

At first blush, Filhiol's selection of this particular site might seem arbitrary. It was not to guard the confluence or the crossroads, which were both a distance away, nor was it for its topographic perch, as there were more salient bluffs upstream. But Filhiol's site was sufficiently elevated to evade flooding while also commanding a clear view of one of the few straight channel segments (three miles in length) on the otherwise sinuous Ouachita, should an enemy approach on the river. If attacked on land—most likely by the British from the east—Fort Miró was positioned to face them, being on the east bank.[9]

Though enemies never attacked, the military reasoning behind Fort Miró's siting proved prudent for settlement as well. "The fort accomplished what Filhiol could not do himself," wrote parish historian Gordon E. Harvey. Fort Miró "create[d] a center of activity, commercial and otherwise, for the area[.] Court, commerce, and communication were all hosted at the fort, forcing the local residents to gather there and creating a sense of community." Spanish land grants, including one for Filhiol and his family, led people to settle around the fort and make it the nerve center of the Ouachita District. Following a muddled interregnum period, the stockade became an American garrison in 1805, at which point a street grid was surveyed around it. Explorer George Hunter visited Fort Miró around this time and described its transition to a civilian settlement: "The Spanish old stockade fort has been torn down, & a new small one without cannon or port holes erected by the Americans under Leuit Bowman. it is only a defense against the Indians being unfinished & scarcely [secure]. . . . There is but an Infant settlement here; The land hitherto . . . being only habitable here & there immediately on the river banks[,] the rest being greatest part swamp overflowed every year."[10] Fort Miró became the seat of the original Ouachita Parish in 1807, and in 1819 the steamboat *Monroe* ventured this far up the Ouachita for the first time, a moment so auspicious that, in 1820, the

At top, the original location of Fort Miró, the Spanish military site on the Ouachita River that became Monroe. At bottom, a mural in downtown Monroe and a view of Trenton Street in the Cotton Port district across the Ouachita River. Photographs by Richard Campanella.

settlement's old Spanish name was changed to the more American-sounding name of the steamboat.[11]

Monroe, Louisiana, grew steadily as a river port, crossroads, and trading and administrative center. A visitor in 1860 rhapsodized on its siting, describing Monroe as "situated in the garden spot of the Ouachita valley, [at] a central point of business, of resort, and of general interest to the surrounding country. . . . The town crowns the high and, at this point, never-overflowed banks of the beautiful Ouachita [and] is just now receiving a strongly stimulating 'lick ahead' on the proximate completion . . . of the Vicksburg and Shreveport railroad."[12] That line and subsequent railroads, followed by roadways, enabled Monroe's population to double every fifteen years through the 1960s. Now with 47,000 city dwellers in a metro area double that number, Monroe is the largest population center within a seventy-mile radius, and by far the largest in northeastern Louisiana. The footprint of old Fort Miró lies by the present-day Ouachita Parish Courthouse in downtown Monroe, while its older sister a hundred miles upriver, at Fabre's Bluff, is now the city of Camden, Arkansas. Monroe's siting story is traceable to an overland crossroads on a bluff near a river confluence that became a trade and administrative center. But first and foremost, this was a fort site, with artillery positioned to answer enemy incursions. Had it been just a garrison, like that of the Spanish post at Avoyelles or Opelousas, Filhiol likely would have selected a different site, perhaps on the west bank. Yet upon transitioning to a civilian role, Fort Miró made for a fine urban locale nonetheless, something that cannot be said of other military sites in Louisiana, such as Fort Jesup or Los Adaes.

Monroe's adjacent settlements present a potpourri of siting stories. The port function, for example, happened not initially at Fort Miró, but at a more suitable bankside site known as Trent's Landing, two miles upriver on the west bank. It was here at William Trent's ferry landing that the steamer *Monroe* actually docked in 1819, and it was the consequent town of Trenton that became the Ouachita's premier cotton port. Trenton incorporated in 1870, intensifying a cross-river rivalry with Monroe, even as it endured a fire in 1873 and a flood in 1874. What it could not endure, however, was losing out to Monroe in getting the new Vicksburg, Shreveport & Pacific Railroad station in 1882. Port activity shifted southward to abut the new train bridge, giving rise to Cottonport, located straight down Trenton Street from old Trenton and directly across the river from Monroe. Because Avoyelles Parish already had a town named Cottonport, the new landing in 1884 changed its name to West Monroe, which eventually subsumed old Trenton and another west bank town called Byron. Today the city of West Monroe, population 12,500, is a cross-river subsidiary to Monroe, and the dual municipalities have a relationship akin to that of Port Allen/Baton Rouge, Pineville/Alexandria, and Bossier City/Shreveport. Both cities expanded outwardly to form a conurbation, a process that subsumed a number of enclaves with their own siting stories. For example, a shortcut road extending eastward to Bayou De Siard, today's Desiard Street, gave rise to Sicard and Edgewater, both now suburbs of Monroe. Likewise, railroads and roads extending westward toward Ruston precipitated the formation of Brownville, Cheniere, and Claiborne, all of which are now suburbs of West Monroe.[13]

In antebellum times, the Monroe/Trenton perch on the Ouachita became northern Louisiana's premier transportation junction, with at least eight overland roads intersecting here by 1851. They pointed in every direction, and each spawned settlements where they split, merged, crossed waterways, or accessed resources. One road heading west from Monroe to Vienna forked off to a Choctaw village, leaving behind today's Forksville and Indian Village. That road continued through Vernon to the salt and limestone deposits where Winnfield and Goldonna would arise as resource extraction sites, and eventually to Campti and Natchitoches along the Red and Cane rivers. Another road heading northwest from Monroe led to Farmerville, itself a crossroads, which

The Bastrop Hills (*in the distance*) rise just a few dozen feet above the broad alluvial valley of the Mississippi River, but the topographic change underscores substantial differences in soils, land use, transportation, and settlement geography. Photograph by Richard Campanella.

found itself centrally positioned within newly created Union Parish in 1839 and gained designation as its seat of justice. Perched on a series of hills, Farmerville remains chiefly an administrative center today, still linked to Monroe by that road, and still the main crossroads within Union Parish.[14]

Heading northeast from Monroe got travelers into the loess bluffs of Bastrop, a town whose siting story has an unusual prologue and epilogue. Bastrop may seem to have originated in a typical manner, as an administrative center ordained when Morehouse Parish was created in 1844. But if spatial centrality were the rationale, the courthouse ought to have gone to a preexisting settlement born on an old Spanish land grant, which partly became the property of Colonel Abraham Morehouse and later Josiah Davenport. Both men had settled their families on this land, specifically a place known as Mer Rouge, named by an earlier French traveler who noted the area's "sea" of "red" sedges. Because Abraham Morehouse led the effort to carve out a parish for the area's growing population, the new jurisdiction took on his name, and its borders were drawn in a manner that centrally positioned Mer Rouge as the logical seat. But a "bitter rivalry" broke out over who should get the courthouse, "and the contending towns agreed to give the seat to a new place" to be named Bastrop. "In 1846 a town site was laid out on 192 acres [near] Bayou Bartholomew," seven miles to the west and up upon the Bastrop Hills. Although the new site was less centralized, its waterway "enabled steamboats to carry cotton to market," while its topography protected from high water.[15] A visitor in 1860 described Bastrop as "a very pleasant little town [which] will compare favorably with a majority of parish seats in the State," sited near "Bayou Bartholomew, a branch of the Ouachita," whereby "the merchants of Bastrop receive their goods and the majority of the planters ship their produce. . . . A flourishing business is done at Bastrop, and the town wears a lively aspect at all times. Its population is about four hundred and fifty."[16]

At left, a mural in Mer Rouge depicts the cotton-growing and -ginning industry that minted "Red Sea Gold." At right is the Morehouse Parish Courthouse in the city of Bastrop, an uncommon example of an administrative site that managed to diversify its economy with industry. Photographs by Richard Campanella.

How Bastrop got its name intimates the unusual prologue of this siting story, one that dovetails with Monroe's origins as Fort Miró. The commonality was Spain's plan to people the *barrera*—that is, to settle loyal subjects in Louisiana as a barricade to British antagonism, while also installing a productive workforce. In the late 1770s, the *dons* behind Fort Miró had hoped to bring Spanish immigrants to the Ouachita District, until the governor judged the remote region to be not quite ready for families. But much changed over next twenty years, and by the late 1790s, with Fort Miró now established and the British threat transformed to a potential American threat, another immigration-settlement proposal arose—a rather peculiar one.

It came from one Philip Hendrik Nering Bögel, a Dutch national born in Surinam who fled Holland for tax evasion, found his way to Spanish Louisiana, reinvented himself as "the Baron de Bastrop," and convinced Governor Héctor de Carondelet (a real baron, originally from Belgium) of his plan to settle 300 Dutch families to grow wheat in Ouachita. Contracts were signed, lands were granted (or so they thought), money changed hands, and in 1797 the frontier empresario sailed down the Mississippi with ninety-nine prospective farmers. The newcomers hailed not from across the Atlantic Ocean but from up the Ohio River—Kentucky, to be precise—and helping him with the recruitment was a Kentucky colonel by the name of Abraham Morehouse, namesake of the future parish.

The project soon began to unravel. Costs rose, funds depleted, the Ouachita region proved unsuitable for wheat, and skeptics were alarmed that Bastrop was importing the very people the Spanish were guarding against—Protestant Americans.

Bastrop reworked his brand of entrepreneurial colonization and pedaled it to Spanish authorities elsewhere, each time meeting with rejection. When he attempted to cash out his Ouachita land grant in 1799 by selling it to his Kentucky collaborator, Abraham Morehouse, it came to light that the king of Spain had never formally approved the grant in the first place. Lawsuits ensued just as news broke of Spain's retrocession of Louisiana to the French, followed by France's sale to the United States.[17]

Once again, Bastrop found himself a man without a country—and not a moment too soon. He abandoned his legal entanglements in Louisiana and took his bag of tricks to Texas, where he found kindred spirits eager to recruit Anglo-American settlers. He died in 1827, and while he remained loyal to Spanish Mexico, Bastrop is remembered positively in Texas today, as evidenced by a city and county bearing his name. His reputation in Louisiana is that of a colorful rapscallion—and neither the first nor last phony royal. He left behind ongoing turmoil in the titling of land, such that into the 1850s a prominent map had the words "*Claims under Bastrop Title*" superscripted over the area, as if in warning. Another dubious grant, known as the Maison Rouge Land Claim, disrupted titling in the area north of Monroe. But the land sale made to Abraham Morehouse had sufficient legal legitimacy to enable the formation of Morehouse Parish, and by nature of its shape, it gave rise to today's city of Bastrop.[18]

Thus ends the unusual prologue of Bastrop's otherwise common siting story. As for the epilogue, Bastrop completely rewrote its reason for being, in a manner rare for administrative centers. It became a key junction for two railroads traversing the Ouachita River Valley, making Bastrop a transshipment point for cargo shipped by vessel. Investors capitalized on the intermodal access, and in doing so they transformed the city. Wrote a researcher in 1941, "Bastrop is almost alone among northeast Louisiana towns in that its prosperity is based not upon cotton but upon industry: paper making from wood pulp, manufacturing carbon black from natural gas, brick making, and lumbering. The presence of low-priced natural gas fuel," which had been discovered in 1916, "has been largely responsible for the town's industrial development," and along with the pulp paper mills established in 1920, exuded "a potent and inescapable reminder of Bastrop's industrial character[:] the pungent odor."[19] Unpleasant perhaps, but the smoky industries created jobs that supported 10,000 residents. The village of Mer Rouge, Bastrop's former rival to the east, has only one-twentieth of that population, but it has managed to endure nonetheless as a trade center for cotton—"Red Sea Gold," according to a mural on West Davenport Avenue, named for the village's founder.

A third artery heading south of Monroe paralleled the Ouachita River, fronting a sequence of cotton plantations. About ten terrestrial miles (twenty river miles) downstream was the land grant made by the Spanish government to Don Juan Filhiol for his founding of Fort Miró. The site had previously been a Choctaw village recorded as "the Olivets" by two earlier explorers. In 1847, Filhiol's grandson built a Federal-style plantation house on his inherited portion of the parcel and named it Logtown.[20] The river landing of the Logtown Plantation served cotton plantations and possibly timber cutters, which may account for its name. Too close to Monroe and Trenton to grow any larger, Logtown faded as a landing wharf and refueling stop. Yet the toponym remains on the map, and its namesake plantation house still stands, descendants of the Filhiol family having owned it until 1999.[21]

A more substantial Ouachita River port formed farther down the Monroe road, at a spot where in 1827 North Carolina-born John Humphries established a homestead—"for the sole purpose of hunting bear," it is said, "and to raise a family. From all accounts, he did both in a big way," leaving the area with few bears and numerous progeny.[22] What made Humphries's homestead into a busy port was a quintuple siting advantage, with an aspirational name to match: Columbia. For one, this site marked the midpoint between Monroe/Trenton to the north and the Tensas River confluence to the south. That made it a convenient refueling and loading wharf for cotton shipments to New Orleans, as well as a favored home for steamboat captains, much like Washington in St. Landry Parish and St. Francisville in West Feliciana Parish. The site itself slopes down to a flat landing fronting a straight channel segment of the Ouachita, all good for docking, cargo transfer, and ferry crossings. During low water, the river here was fordable by ox carts, and during high water another advantage came into relief: a series of bluffs rising 125 feet up a prairie terrace. Atop emerged the settlement of Columbia Heights, a dry-point site replicating the under-the-hill/on-the-hill geographies seen at other river bluff towns. Columbia and Columbia Heights thenceforth became a crossroads, the main artery of which passed through a gap in the bluffs and accessed the famous Harrisonburg Road connecting Natchez and the Natchez Trace with Natchitoches and the Camino Real. "Columbia is perched on the lofty banks of the Ouachita," wrote a visitor in 1860, "a lively and thriving little place[,] beautifully situated." Those advantages positioned Columbia centrally within Caldwell Parish when it was carved out of Ouachita and Catahoula parishes in 1838, making it suitable for the courthouse. John Humphries's bear hunting lair thus became the Caldwell Parish seat of justice, and has served as an administrative center ever since.[23]

The other candidate for parish seat, located just down the road to Harrisonburg, was originally known as Prairie du Cote and came to be known as Copenhagen for its Scandinavian settlers. Its post office, named New Kentucky, was established in 1834, the first in the area. But because Copenhagen had been

Initially blessed by multiple siting rationales, Columbia (*left*) declined as Ouachita River traffic shifted to rails and then to highways; now it is mostly its administrative role, as seat of Caldwell Parish, that sustains the scenic riverside town.

Like Columbia, Harrisonburg (*left*) had many siting advantages on the Ouachita, including a beautiful hillside perch to protect it from floodwaters. But the same changes that befell Columbia also made Harrisonburg dwindle down to a reliance on its administrative role, as the seat of Catahoula Parish. Photographs by Richard Campanella.

sited only on account of a roadside store, it declined as overland transit shifted to river navigation, giving the advantage to Columbia.

Once river traffic gave way to railroads, and railroads to highways, Columbia too found itself isolated amid antiquated siting rationales. Columbia's population peaked at 1,000 people in 1960 and has since dropped to 277, making it one of the state's smallest parish seats. Were it not for its courthouse, Columbia might have gone the way of Copenhagen, which today, with a few dozen people, barely hangs on the map.[24]

Monroe had another antebellum road that headed southeastwardly, across the Boeuf River, to a place that had only one of Columbia's siting advantages—but one with endurance. When American authorities first began delineating parishes in Louisiana, the least-populated regions naturally got the largest jurisdictions. Ouachita Parish in 1807, for example, initially comprised the entire northeastern corner of the future state. As settlers arrived and populations grew, legislators delineated new parishes and designated seats of justice at their centers. By 1814, Louisiana's northeastern corner had three parishes. A generation later it had eight, most recently Franklin, created in 1843 from portions of Ouachita, Catahoula, and Madison parishes, thanks to the advocacy of State Senator John Winn. Settlement within Franklin Parish tended to be along its riverine eastern and western borders, leading to a debate over where to site the seat. "The issue was settled," wrote Clare D'Artois Leeper, "when John Willis donated 160 acres of land, situated virtually in the center of the parish, and stipulated that the parish seat be named Winnsboro in honor of Senator John Winn."[25] Originally spelled Winnsborough, the community had no siting advantage other than administrative convenience. Turkey Creek was hardly navigable, and there were no roads, posts, portages, or resources to justify a town. But that rationale has served Winnsboro well, and today it is a city of 5,000 people, twenty times the size of Columbia and the largest city within thirty miles. Aside from being parish seats, and despite their different sizes, Columbia and Winnsboro share a commonality in their siting stories: both initially came to attention as "a favorite campsite of bear hunters."[26]

Heading southward, all transit funneled through an important node in the antebellum era, a place called Harrisonburg. Analogous to Columbia, Harrisonburg had rich soils for cotton and high bluffs against floods, as well as a sloped landing down to the Ouachita, not far from its confluence with the Tensas River. Regionally, it was well-situated to be a stopover and transshipment point—between Monroe and New Orleans by boat, overland between Natchez and Natchitoches, or from Vicksburg or Port Gibson to Alexandria. Natives had been active here, as evidenced by two nearby 2,000-year-old mounds, and their hunting trails probably explain the crossroads that formed here. Stories are told of a French fur-trading post operating here in 1712–1714, leading local advocates to claim their village is nearly the oldest in Louisiana ("Founded 1714," reads its entrance sign, "Home of the Bulldogs"). Other sources trace Harrisonburg's colonial origins to a land grant made to John Hamberlain in the late 1700s, followed by the designation of this riverside bluff as seat of the newly created Catahoula Parish in 1808. Hamberlain "subsequently sold it to John Harrison, and in 1818 the latter employed Edward Dorsey to survey and make a plat of the town site, and it was from Mr. Harrison that the town derived its name."[27]

What made the courthouse town of Harrisonburg economically vital was its role as a hub of north-south river traffic intersecting east-west overland travel along the famed Harrisonburg Road. Blazed around 1800, made into an official public road in 1825, and served by stagecoaches starting in 1849, this key artery connected more than just Natchez and Natchitoches. It enabled economic and cultural interaction among (1) the Anglo-American region of southwestern Mississippi and (2) its feeder artery, the Natchez Trace leading up to Nashville and the Ohio Valley, with (3) the French Creole region of the Red and Cane rivers, and to its west, (4) the Camino Real into Spanish Texas and Mexico.[28] The Harrisonburg Road helped spawn at least six lasting settlements (Vidalia, Harrisonburg, Jena, Georgetown, Atlanta, and St. Maurice), and earned Harrisonburg its first post office in 1822, just as steamboat traffic began calling regularly at its landing. The town benefitted additionally by being the low-water head of navigation on the Ouachita during a time of year (autumn) that coincided with the cotton harvest, which meant great numbers of bales came into Harrisonburg for export to New Orleans. Wrote an admiring visitor in 1860, "Harrisonburg is a handsomely built and thriving town of some three or four hundred inhabitants, and is beautifully situated on a high bluff, but at the foot of a still loftier hill . . . coated with . . . a lusty growth of forest trees[—]a very prosperous commercial point."[29] Indeed, Harrisonburg is truly spectacular, the closest thing Louisiana has to a genuine hillside community, with bluffs rising steeply behind the courthouse and peaking at the Civil War–era Fort Beauregard, nearly 200 feet above the Ouachita River. Harrisonburg also has Louisiana's most topographically rugged burial grounds, Cedar Ridge Cemetery, from which views of the horizon may be gained.

Despite similar advantages, Harrisonburg was handicapped by the same problems as Columbia. Their respective catchments were low in population and high in poverty, their cotton industries shifted westward, and their stagecoaches and steamboats lost customers to trains and automobiles. Harrisonburg never landed a railroad, nor even a four-lane highway, and its population, which peaked at 750, has recently fallen by two-thirds. Once again, the only siting rationale keeping Harrisonburg on the map is the parish centrality that earned it the courthouse back in 1808. Contrast that with Bastrop, also born as a courthouse town, but one that diversified its economy and now has a population twenty times that of Harrisonburg and Columbia *combined.* Their siting stories are reminders that geographical advantage is ultimately defined by human need.

By hydrology alone, the next twenty miles down the Ouachita present an ideal situation for a city. Three rivers (the Ouachita, Tensas, and Little) merge to become the Black River, and eventually join a major tributary (the Red) of the continent's greatest river, the Mississippi. From here one could, in theory, navigate from the Ouachita Mountains of Arkansas, to the Alleghenies of Pennsylvania, to the foothills of the Rockies, down to New Orleans and beyond. What this situation did *not* have, however, was an adequate site. All the wind-blown silt (loess) that fell here got swept away by the aforementioned rivers, leaving only a broad floodplain, sans the bluffs that shored up Harrisonburg, Columbia, Monroe, and Bastrop. Natives during AD 400–700 addressed the problem by building terraced platform mounds, the largest of which was located right at the confluence, 160 feet by 250 feet at its base and rising eighty-two feet high.[30]

The ancient earthworks became useful to colonials in need of the same flood protection. One, a ferry operator named Monsieur Cades (Cadi), met the explorers Dunbar and Hunter during their expedition to document the lands of the Louisiana Purchase. Cades served travelers between Natchez and Fort Miró, and, according to Hunter writing in October 1804, "lives on an Indian mound about an acre in extent which is the only place near him that is not overflowed in the great freshes, & he seems to express a satisfaction that he has no bad neighbors. The ground here[,] if it were to be defended by a dike or Bank would be inexhaustibly fertile."[31] A ferry landing settlement developed around the mound and came to be called Trinity, for the triple confluence. But inadequate flood protection stunted growth, as did a bitter family feud during the 1850s and 1860s. In 1871, Laura Stewart Jones, the titleholder of an old Spanish land grant who had been left widowed by feud violence, had a section platted across from the older settlement of Trinity, fronting the fourth named river resulting from the triple confluence, the Black. The new community was officially named Troyville in 1878, reinvigorated by the Natchez & Red River Railroad in 1883, and renamed Jonesville in 1888. By 1914, the town had "a bank, several stores, 2 hotels, good schools, a saw and shingle mill, a money order post office, and a population of 287."[32]

Jonesville and Trinity are textbook examples of confluence settlements, and they might have grown into a sizeable city were it not for the very rivers

Jonesville's logo—"Where Four Rivers Meet"—is essentially the town's siting story. The Catahoula Parish seat might have grown into a sizeable city were it not for high waters on the Ouachita—which Natives evaded by building mounds, one of which has been reconstructed at the entrance of town. Jonesville is now protected by a ring levee. Photographs by Richard Campanella.

that attracted settlers in the first place.[33] In 1946, Jonesville's 2,000 residents finally got the white man's answer to the Indians' mounds: a ring levee encircling the town. But by then, the four rivers had lost their commercial importance, and highways supplanted railroads for terrestrial travel—including one rammed right through the ancient heart of Jonesville. In 1931, Smithsonian archaeologist Winslow M. Walker had been working in the area when he heard of construction activity around the Troyville Earthworks. "When I got there I found the largest and most important mound leveled by highway workers. What was left in the debris indicates that the loss to science was inestimable."[34] Today only three vertical feet remain of the ancient earthworks on Mound Street, while a more salient mound survives on nearby Front Street, long used as the Old Methodist Church Cemetery. Now home to 1,650 people living within its ring levee, Jonesville proudly touts its siting rationale. "Where Four Rivers Meet," reads its entrance sign, behind which are Four Rivers Park, Four Rivers Masonic Lodge, Four Rivers Insurance, and Four Rivers Home Health. Also at the entrance to town, Jonesville citizens constructed a "Great Mound Replica of the Ancient Troyville Site, the 2nd Tallest Mound in America Before It Was Torn Down to Build the Black River Bridge Approach."[35]

In the last third of the nineteenth century, railroads reconfigured the Ouachita River Valley with new trade and settlement vectors. We have already seen how, from 1853 through the 1870s, the Vicksburg, Shreveport & Pacific Railroad connected Monroe latitudinally with Vicksburg and Shreveport, spawning station-stop settlements such as Delhi, Rayville, Ruston, and Arcadia. What followed in the 1880s and 1890s was the construction of a triangle of new track beds running longitudinally along the valley, each poised to compete with Ouachita River shipping.

The eastern leg of that triangle began as the New Orleans & Northwestern (later the St. Louis, Iron Mountain & Southern) Railway, and ran from Arkansas

Photograph by Richard Campanella.

through Bastrop, Rayville, and Winnsboro down to Vidalia. Along the way, it activated a series of station-stop settlements at regular increments, including the still-existing communities of Mangham, Gilbert, Wisner, Sicily Island, and Clayton. (A community named Sicily Island had been created in 1881, when 151 Russian Jewish refugees were brought here by the Hebrew Emigrant Aid Society. Sited arbitrarily on available real estate, the agricultural colony failed by 1885, and had hardly any influence on the later railroad-based village of Sicily Island, now home to 330 people.)[36]

The western leg of the triangle comprised the Houston, Central Arkansas & Northwestern (later the St. Louis & Iron Mountain and the Alabama, Louisiana & Gulf) Railroad, connecting Bastrop with Monroe, Columbia, Georgetown, and Alexandria, and spinning off station-stop settlements at Fairbanks, Riverton, Grayson, Kelly, Olla, Urania, Tullos, and Pollock. Finally, across the base of the triangle, ran the Natchez & Red River (later Western) Railroad, which ran from Vidalia to Jonesboro, and was later extended through Jena and Georgetown as the Louisiana & Arkansas line. It spawned Minorca, Concordia, and Frogmore—site of an indigenous village from AD 700 to 1200, whose remnant ceremonial mound still stands.

Only half of these Ouachita Valley railways still operate, such that the iron triangle of a century ago traces the shape of an X today, with the Union Pacific crossing the Kansas City Southern at Monroe and heading to Bastrop, Vicksburg, Alexandria, and Shreveport in each cardinal direction.[37] People continued to live at the settlements they precipitated, and because modern highways often parallel old track beds, those rural population clusters have since become arterial increment or crossroads sites. In the cases of Rayville and Jena, both were station sites that became seats of justice, as new parishes (Richland Parish in 1868; La Salle Parish in 1910) were delineated in a manner that positioned them centrally. Still other station settlements became resource extraction sites, usually for timber (such as Urania) or oil (for example, Tullos).

Olla's siting story has a number of interesting chapters. The settlement began not in its current location but two miles away on Bayou Castor (Castor Creek), a navigable tributary of the Little and Ouachita rivers, where a ferry landing and loading dock operated in late antebellum times. After the Civil War, the site got a wholesale repurposing. On account of underlying petroleum wells, sulfurous minerals dissolved into a spring and bubbled to the surface by the bayou. The medicinal understanding of the day held that such waters had curative properties for afflictions of the skin, muscle, and bone. Larger springs had the potential to become health resorts, as we saw in places like Krotz Springs, Greenwell Springs, and Abita Springs. Thus arose the community of Castor Sulphur Springs, home to a two-story hotel, guest cottages, two stores, a post office, picnic areas, fishing holes, and an ornamented octagon pavilion shading the main attraction known as Big Spring. Visitors came from far and wide "to bathe in the blue sulfur mud to relieve them from arthritis and all other muscle pains," wrote local historian L. H. Taylor. "After wallowing . . . for ten days, crutches were thrown away, arms were released from slings, and once again they were able to enjoy the fruits of God's world."[38]

Castor Sulphur Springs prospered during the 1870s and 1880s. But as railroads gave health-seekers other options, such as Arkansas's Hot Springs and Eureka Springs, small resorts like Castor lost their appeal. In 1891, the Houston, Central Arkansas & Northwestern Railroad decided to build its station two miles to the east, making Castor inconvenient, while a new iron bridge killed the ferry traffic. The railroad usurped river traffic, and in 1893 the post office relocated next to the train station, as had most folks in Castor. The new site gained the name Olla, for "a well-educated, attractive and accomplished young lady" named Olla Mills, "who was instrumental in community activities." Another prominent local figure, Riley Joe Wilson, launched the Olla Military Institute, which became known for its sharp gray uniforms, rigorous curriculum, and excellent faculty—including Olla Mills, who taught music and drama. "The school soon had more students than the entire population of the town," wrote L. H. Taylor, making Olla into something of an academy town. But after only six years the Olla Institute burned down, and for lack of insurance it never reopened. The town of Olla, however, continued to reinvent itself. It tapped its abundant natural springs to become a water-bottling center in the 1920s, and transformed to a petroleum town following the 1938 discovery of the Olla Oil Field—the source, it came to be understood, of those sulfurous waters. Today, Olla, population 1,300, is a forestry products town, crossroads, and midway point for motorists between Monroe and Alexandria—and still on the same railroad line that altered the community's locale and rationale. What remains of old Castor Sulphur Springs lies beneath a dammed section of Castor Creek, utterly indiscernible today.

Of the thirty-three cities, towns, villages, and other communities in the Ouachita River Valley analyzed in this study, 21 percent had riverine- or water-based primary siting stories (compared to the state average of 29 percent), while 36 percent were primarily railroad sites, 18 percent were resource extraction or processing sites, and 12 percent were crossroads (compared to state averages of 33 percent, 13 percent, and 10 percent, respectively). Settlements began forming in this region in the 1780s, peaked in the 1870s, and ended in the 1900s. Roughly 39 percent of Ouachita River region settlements emerged organically, the other 61 percent having been ordained by a founder, compared to the statewide split of 49 percent/51 percent emergent/ordained.

15

THE UPPER DELTA COUNTRY

The Tensas flows through a part of northeastern Louisiana adjacent to the watershed of the Ouachita, but that's about all the two river systems have in common. Whereas the Ouachita drains 25,000 square miles between mountainous central Arkansas and silty central Louisiana, the Tensas draws water from the nearly flat meander belt of the lower Mississippi. Formerly the main channel of the Father of Waters and now an active lateral channel, the Tensas originates as a bayou outflowing from oxbow-shaped Lake Providence, becomes a river around Tallulah, merges with the Ouachita at Jonesville to form the Black, and discharges into the Red, Atchafalaya, and Mississippi. The braided channels within the Tensas/Mississippi floodplain, be they active or abandoned, each produced natural levees, ridges, alluvial fans, meander cutoffs, and other features useful to human movement—and germane to regional siting stories.[1]

That region goes by many names, among them the upper delta, the delta parishes, the Louisiana delta, and the Miss-Lou-Ark delta, for the three states it intersects. Use of the term "delta" might seem colloquial in this context, more the language of culture than science. "In a strict definition," wrote geologist Randel Tom Cox, "a 'delta' is a pile of gravel, sand, and mud that is being dumped at a continent's edge at the mouth of a major river," like the Nile in Egypt. Thus "it may seem a misnomer to call the Mississippi River lowlands in their entirety a 'delta,' rather than just a 'flood plain' or 'bottom lands.'" But Cox acknowledged that a saltwater embayment once intruded up to Illinois and, starting 90 million years ago, gradually filled with alluvium "dumped at a continent's edge at the mouth of a major river"—a delta by strict geological definition, again like the Nile. (Thus the American cities named Memphis and Cairo, in a region dubbed "Little Egypt.") To distinguish this interior region from the Mississippi River Deltaic Plain of southeastern Louisiana, we will refer to the bottomlands of northeastern Louisiana as the upper delta, spanning from East Carroll Parish down to Concordia Parish.[2]

Three factors induced settlement siting in the upper delta. One was river travelers' need for food, fuel, supplies, services, and rest at regular increments. Conversely, residents needed landings to export local produce (principally cotton) and receive imports. Thirdly, topographic ridges, meager though they were, enabled roads to be blazed to elevated banks. Put together, these three variables yielded precious few options and left the upper delta sparsely populated and highly impoverished, despite its fertile soils and continental-scale river. In fact, one of those options, today's Lake Providence, ended up ranking as "the poorest place in America."[3]

Yet Lake Providence is also the epitome of an emergent settlement, selected because people saw hope and opportunity here. Being in former Caddo and Tunica indigenous territory, it sits amid scores of archaeological sites in a region that has been humanized for millennia. Being on a segment of the Mississippi navigated by both De Soto and La Salle, it was one of the first Louisiana places to be seen by European eyes. Being on a salient cutoff meander, it hosted early colonial transients, trappers, and traders who camped here. What led to permanent settlement was the convergence of those three factors.

By the late 1780s, Americans increasingly began moving down the Ohio and Mississippi Valleys and venturing to New Orleans. Ever more flatboats and keelboats navigated the river, passing through the upper delta in need of supplies. Around the same period, Don Juan Filhiol established Fort Miró and planned to add to the 200 or so Spanish subjects in the vicinity, who themselves needed landings on the Mississippi. Then the Baron de Bastrop brought those ninety-nine Kentuckians to his putative land claim, furthering the need for river access. When word spread of the Spanish denial of Americans' right to deposit cargo at New Orleans in 1795, American boatmen began using a particular island to warehouse cargo, earning it the name Stack (or Stock) Island. Frontiersmen blazed a crude path to connect Fort Miró (future Monroe) with present-day Bastrop and Oak Grove straight east toward Stack Island. It terminated at a suitable bankside site, where the natural levee of a meander had broken off from the main channel, creating an oxbow (cutoff) lake, akin to False River. The crescent-shaped waterbody discharged into Tensas Bayou, which flowed south and created its own natural levee. Oxbow lakes made for attractive town sites in the upper delta, offering high ground, freshwater, fisheries, and a harbor-like waterbody. This particular oxbow adjoined the Mississippi along a relatively straight channel segment, making it easier for docking. And halfway into the channel, only two miles away, was Stack Island, with more than its share of cargo-wielding smugglers and outlaws. According to legend, so perilous was navigation around the roguish island that traders "were wont to say, '[if] we reach the lake below Stack Island, it is Providence.'" More likely, the inspiring name aimed to attract residents and traders. Either way, the name stuck, and eventually became Lake Providence.[4]

During the first decade of American dominion, 1803–1813, Anglo-Saxon settlers with names like Floyd, Culfield, Collins, Bruit, White, Hood, Barker, Demsey, and Millikin began claiming tracts by Lake Providence. Bottomlands were cleared for cotton cultivation, and with the rise of steamboats in the 1820s Lake Providence became a portal to world markets. The growing town also became the gateway to northern Louisiana, via public stagecoach roads connecting Monroe, Shreveport, Greenwood, and the Texas frontier. In 1832, the state legislature created Carrol Parish and designated Lake Providence as the seat of justice, with its courthouse subsequently built on donated land. But as in-migration over the next twenty years shifted settlement in Carroll Parish westward, the new inhabitants found Lake Providence inconvenient. In 1855, voters elected to move the courthouse to donated land in a more centrally located place on Bayou Maçon, called Floyd.[5]

Nevertheless, Lake Providence remained the most important and populous town in the parish, even after the turmoil of war and the subsequent rise of railroads. Redesignated the seat of East Carroll Parish when it was separated from West Carroll in 1877, Lake Providence's population surpassed 1,500 by the early 1900s, by which time it had "two banks, a number of good stores, hotels, lodges of various secret and benevolent orders [and] a good municipal government." It also had three river landings, ferry service, mills for lumber and cotton seed oil, and a station on the St. Louis, Iron Mountain & Southern Railroad, making "it a good shipping and distributing point [for] a profitable wholesale business, especially in groceries."[6]

Lake Providence peaked in 1980 with 6,300 people and has since fallen precipitously. The site advantages that made economic sense in the early 1800s now left the community isolated in a rural region, with no bridge, no more ferries, no major highway, and hardly any through traffic. Now with fewer than 3,200 residents, of whom half are indigent and four-fifths are African American, Lake Providence retains one last siting rationale: the administrative role it first realized in 1832.

As for Floyd, which became the seat of justice for Carroll Parish starting in 1855, it kept that status when West Carroll Parish was created in 1877. But when a spur of the St. Louis, Iron Mountain & Southern bypassed Floyd in 1906,

Lake Providence (*top*) exemplifies a strategic site that, over the course of the twentieth century, lost all but one of its rationales—that of an administrative center, seat of East Carroll Parish. At right, Oak Grove's siting story went from cotton field to train stop to administrative center, all within a decade in the early 1900s. Photographs by Richard Campanella.

the railroad spawned new station stops at Kilbourne, Oak Grove, Pioneer, and Epps, some of which built wood mills or cotton gins. Floyd became inconvenient, and in 1912 the state legislature allowed the parish police jury to select a more centralized seat. A rivalry erupted between the two best-positioned candidates, and in 1915 Oak Grove prevailed over Pioneer to land the West Carroll Parish courthouse. Today, Oak Grove is home to 1,400 people, ten times the population of Pioneer and a hundred times more than "Old Floyd."[7] Oak Grove's siting story is one of the few that went from cotton field to station stop to administrative center, all well into the twentieth century.

If Lake Providence epitomizes an emergent town, Tallulah, like Oak Grove, exemplifies the opposite. This Madison Parish city, now with 5,800 residents, was ordained by officials of the Vicksburg, Shreveport & Texas Railroad, who opened a station here in 1857, sixteen miles west of the line's origin at Delta (itself the cross-river subsidiary of Vicksburg). Settlers gravitated to the new conveyance, as they would throughout Louisiana in the decades ahead, and the community gained the indigenous-sounding name of Tallulah.[8]

Alas, this siting story has a charming contingency. Tallulah, in fact, had a predecessor that was anything but arbitrarily ordained. It was called Richmond, and it emerged at the confluence of Brushy and Roundaway bayous, whereupon it developed into a regional crossroads on par with Columbia and even Monroe. In 1839, the state legislature designated Richmond as the seat of Madison Parish, giving the community a third siting advantage. Maps from the 1850s

Roundaway Bayou (*right*) hosted the busy confluence town of Richmond until the Vicksburg, Shreveport & Texas Railroad decided to put its station at Tallulah (*left*) in 1857. Union troops torched Richmond in 1863, after which Tallulah developed into the main city and seat of Madison Parish. Photographs by Richard Campanella.

suggest it was Richmond that dominated the region west of Vicksburg. But when the VS&T sketched out its rail corridor in 1852, company engineers decided to skirt Richmond two miles to the north and place their station at a stop they called Tallulah. This was not unusual; railroad companies often bypassed towns, even courthouses, to avoid messy expropriations and minimize right-of-away acquisition costs. But locals tell a more romantic reason for the bypass.

According to a recollection published in 1927, a VS&T engineer had initially planned for the tracks to go through Richmond—until he fell under the sway of "a charming widow, the possessor of large plantations," who discreetly pointed out to "the gallant engineer, [who] was unmarried at the time," that "if the line could be changed a little to pass some miles to the north, it would traverse her properties and greatly enhance their value. Could not the change be considered?" And so he redrew the route to bypass Richmond in favor of the widow's "fertile fields." Once the tracks were laid and plans for the station were finalized in 1857, however, "her interest in the kind engineer suddenly and permanently waned." She got what she wanted, and it wasn't the gallant engineer. But it was he who got the last laugh. "At this turn of fortune," the story continues, "the railroad man apparently began harking back in memory to a former love; for when he established a little station where the line crossed Brushy Bayou, he named that station for the sweetheart of his younger days—Tallulah—and the town which grew around it was destined in later years to become the parish seat."

Richmond's rivalry with Tallulah would only last six years. During the Vicksburg Campaign of 1863, Federal troops demolished some of Richmond's houses to build a bridge over Roundaway Bayou, and burned the rest to the ground. In the years ahead, Tallulah gained every siting advantage once claimed by Richmond—transportation access, crossroads, courthouse—demonstrating that, in geography as in life, all is fair in love and war.[9]

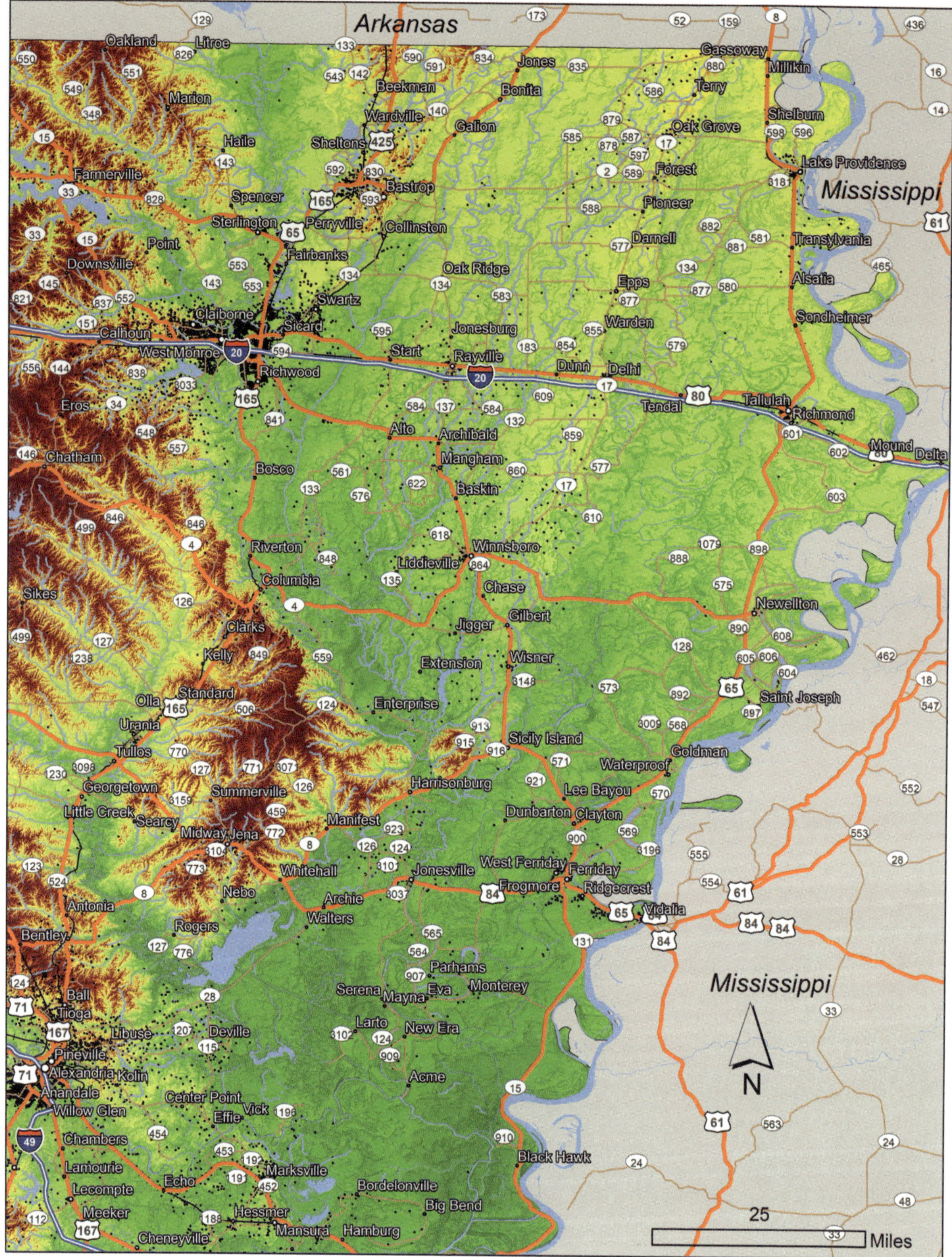
Arkansas
Mississippi
Mississippi
Oakland
Litroe
Marion
Haile
Farmerville
Spencer
Sterlington
Point
Downsville
Claiborne
Calhoun
West Monroe
Richwood
Eros
Chatham
Sikes
Beekman
Wardville
Sheltons
Bastrop
Perryville
Collinston
Fairbanks
Swartz
Sicard
Jones
Bonita
Galion
Oak Ridge
Jonesburg
Start
Rayville
Dunn
Delhi
Tendal
Tallulah
Richmond
Mound
Delta
Gassoway
Millikin
Terry
Shelburn
Oak Grove
Forest
Pioneer
Lake Providence
Darnell
Transylvania
Alsatia
Epps
Warden
Sondheimer
Alto
Archibald
Mangham
Baskin
Bosco
Riverton
Columbia
Winnsboro
Liddieville
Chase
Gilbert
Jigger
Extension
Wisner
Clarks
Kelly
Olla
Standard
Urania
Tullos
Georgetown
Little Creek
Searcy
Summerville
Midway
Jena
Enterprise
Sicily Island
Harrisonburg
Waterproof
Goldman
Lee Bayou
Dunbarton
Clayton
Newellton
Saint Joseph
Manifest
Whitehall
Jonesville
West Ferriday
Ferriday
Frogmore
Ridgecrest
Vidalia
Nebo
Archie
Walters
Antonia
Bentley
Rogers
Ball
Tioga
Libuse
Deville
Pineville
Alexandria
Kolin
Anandale
Willow Glen
Center Point
Effie
Vick
Chambers
Lamourie
Lecompte
Meeker
Echo
Marksville
Hessmer
Mansura
Cheneyville
Hamburg
Bordelonville
Big Bend
Black Hawk
Parhams
Serena
Mayna
Eva
Monterey
Larto
New Era
Acme
N
25
Miles

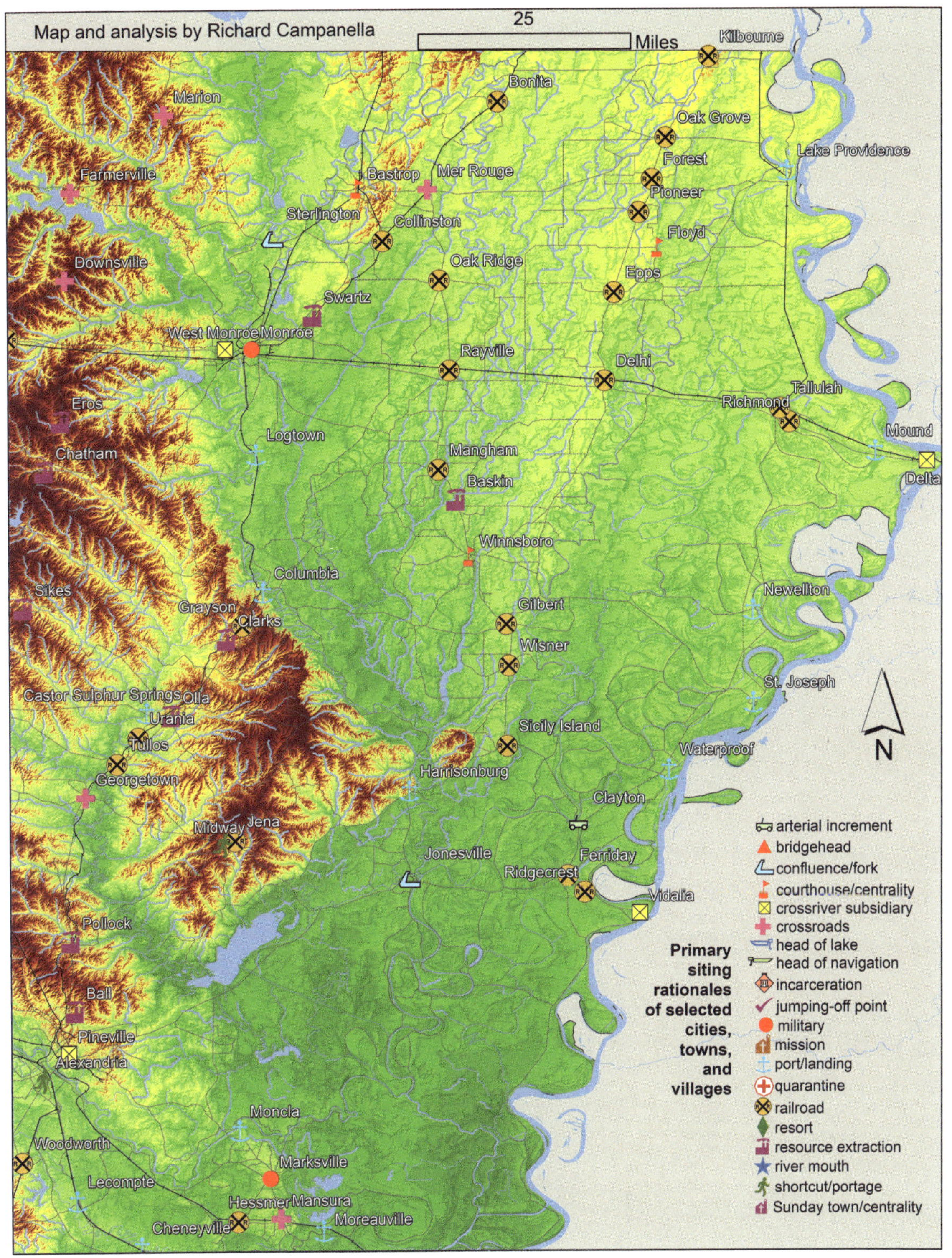
Map and analysis by Richard Campanella
25
Miles
Kilbourne
Bonita
Marion
Oak Grove
Lake Providence
Forest
Farmerville
Bastrop
Mer Rouge
Pioneer
Sterlington
Collinston
Floyd
Downsville
Oak Ridge
Epps
Swartz
West Monroe
Monroe
Rayville
Delhi
Tallulah
Richmond
Eros
Mound
Logtown
Chatham
Mangham
Delta
Baskin
Winnsboro
Columbia
Newellton
Sikes
Grayson
Gilbert
Clarks
Wisner
St. Joseph
Castor Sulphur Springs
Olla
Urania
Tullos
Sicily Island
Waterproof
Georgetown
Harrisonburg
N
Clayton
Midway
Jena
arterial increment
Jonesville
Ferriday
bridgehead
Ridgecrest
confluence/fork
courthouse/centrality
Vidalia
crossriver subsidiary
Pollock
crossroads
head of lake
Primary siting rationales of selected cities, towns, and villages
head of navigation
incarceration
Ball
jumping-off point
military
Pineville
mission
Alexandria
port/landing
quarantine
Moncla
railroad
resort
Woodworth
Marksville
resource extraction
river mouth
Lecompte
shortcut/portage
Hessmer
Mansura
Sunday town/centrality
Moreauville
Cheneyville

In 1882, the Mississippi Valley Railroad released a map envisioning tracks laid from eastern Arkansas through the upper delta down to West Baton Rouge. Floods, finances, and other woes delayed and fragmented the effort into a series of disparate sub-projects. Among them were the New Orleans, Natchez & Fort Scott Railroad linking Vidalia and Bastrop, commenced in 1899; the Memphis, Helena & Louisiana Railroad, linking Ferriday with McGehee, Arkansas, in 1901; and the Texas & Pacific Railroad, linking Port Allen to Concordia Parish, also in 1901. By the 1910s, most main lines through the upper delta became part of the St. Louis, Iron Mountain & Southern system, which later became the Missouri Pacific.[10] Tallulah became the key railroad junction in the upper delta, and the tracks became place-makers from Lake Providence down to Ferriday. Railroad officials ordained station-stop communities at the standard five- to ten-mile increment, and in doing so they opened a right-of-way for a modern roadway to follow, today's Highway 65—which in turn bolstered arterial communities. What resulted was a crop of tiny settlements, all in a row, as if planted by Johnny Appleseed.

In 1937, a field researcher with the Works Progress Administration drove across the upper delta taking notes on these arterial increment hamlets and their struggle to remain viable. To the north of Lake Providence were Gassoway, Millikin, and Shelburn; to the south was Willman, described as "a small collection of shacks" unlabeled on most maps, where a "sign indicates that it has given itself a name and hopes to become a town. There is a gin on the left (east) and a store on right (west). . . . Merely serves farmers." Next was Transylvania, a "crossroads" leading to the "parish prison farm," with "not good" roads. Next south, Lakeside Station, was home to little more than a cotton gin; then Alsatia—"a café on the right of road, store on left and a few houses"—next, Bomer Spur ("not a town listed on any map . . . cotton gin on right, store, few houses"), and Roosevelt, where a peeved local wielding a big stick led the fleeing researcher to dub the place Grand Baton. Originally named O'Hara's Switch, this rail-side stopover was renamed for President Theodore Roosevelt, who hunted bear in the vicinity in 1907 and wrote about his experiences "In the Louisiana Canebrakes." A bit more substantial was Sondheimer, the next settlement south, which had a manufacturing mill and "numerous poor tenant houses," but little more. Enoka, Talla Bena, and Mansford had even less, as did those south of Tallulah, including Turntable (its main store "burns down periodically"), Alligator, Quimby, and Somerset, leading finally to Newellton.[11]

Newellton marks the point where the Tensas and Mississippi rivers draw close enough for their dueling fluvial dynamics to intermesh, like two arms with hands cupped, each scooping up sediment and mounding up earth. What resulted was a dizzying splay of crescent-shaped natural levees, formed either by the Tensas, by the Tensas when it hosted the Mississippi, by the present-day Mississippi, and/or by past channels that have since broken off as oxbow lakes. By hopscotching from ridge to ridge, traders and travelers made this narrow neck of alluvial bottomlands into a perigee portal between the Anglo-American frontier to the east and the Franco-Spanish borderlands to the west. "The principal nucleus for the settlement of the Tensas Basin," stated geographer Yvonne Phillips in her 1953 dissertation, "was Natchez," the century-old bluff-top fort site that had become a jumping-off point to the southwestern frontier. A constellation of settlements came into being on account of this passage, from Newellton and St. Joseph down to Waterproof, Ferriday, and Vidalia on the eastern side, and from Winnsboro down to Harrisonburg and Jonesville on the western flank.[12]

Newellton arose on the natural levee of the oxbow Lake St. Joseph, where it had once formed a confluence with another relict channel called the Black River. Though not particularly accessible, "Newell's Ridge" marshaled enough topography to rise about the fertile bottomlands, relatively safe from inundations. Settlers began arriving in the late Spanish period from the Natchez area, starting with the Routh family and followed by the Newells, who in the 1830s acquired land at the western bend of the lake and soon founded Newellton as a trade and ginning site. There was much lint to gin: "If King Cotton reigned anywhere," wrote historian Jeffrey Alan Owens, "Lake St. Joseph was the place. Twenty plantations lined its banks[;] their combined cotton crop in 1860 was 12,246 bales, which was greater than the separate totals for thirty entire Louisiana parishes. . . . Most of the owners were members of the cultured and confident Routh clan," and most of the labor came from 2,166 slaves.[13] Resenting their opulence, Union troops engaged in the Vicksburg Campaign destroyed the plantation houses by Newellton, leaving only Winter Quarters, which had been built by the Routh family circa 1803 on the last of the old Spanish land grants. Disparate as it had been, prosperity would never return to Newellton, though the railroad imbued new life in the early 1900s, as would Highway 65 later. Newellton's reason for being today, for its 850 residents, remains its original siting story—as an agricultural services and trade center. Members of the Newell family had invented a cotton press here in the 1830s, and to this day cotton ginning is a key local industry.[14]

As Newellton predated the station-stop communities to its north, the two riverside towns of Vidalia and St. Joseph predate Newellton, having emerged at advantageous sites late in the colonial era. The founder was Don José Vidal, a captain who served in the Spanish Navy fighting the British during the Amer-

Vidalia's siting story has many chapters, among them river landing, ferry crossing, land grant, fort site, administrative center, crossroads, jumping-off point, and terminus of roads and railroads. But above all, Vidalia (*above*) is a cross-river subsidiary, born of the larger and older city of Natchez. Cotton gins (*below*), as resource processing sites, often helped catalyze settlements in the upper delta country. Photographs by Richard Campanella.

ican Revolution and became commandant at Natchez at the time Spain relinquished that bluff-top city to the Americans. Seeking a new duty back in Spanish Louisiana, Vidal in 1798 accepted for himself and his two sons a grant of 1,800 arpents in Concordia, across the Mississippi from Natchez, along with a charge to act as its military and civil commandant. "Concordia" derived from the name of Governor Manuel Gayoso's mansion in Natchez, and came to mean the southern end of the Tensas/Mississippi delta. In the same manner that Spanish military posts spawned the cities of Opelousas, New Iberia, Monroe, and Marksville, so too would the post of Concordia produce a city—Vidalia.[15]

Vidalia's site, on a promontory (point bar) known as Waverly Point, resulted from a grant stipulation that three arpents be reserved as a riverfront commons and town site, which Vidal positioned where ferries had long accessed Natchez. Initially called Nueva Concordia, the commons became the site for the military installation, known as Fort Concord. Its defensive role became muddled as news circulated of the Spanish retrocession of Louisiana to France, followed by the French sale of the territory to the United States. Vidal became an American citizen, prominent and admired on both sides of the Mississippi, in part because he operated the main ferry. Vidal donated land for New Concordia to host the courthouse for the new Concordia Parish, around which a street grid was surveyed. In 1811, Vidal's fellow citizens elected him to the state legislature, and it was that body that renamed New Concordia to honor Vidal.[16]

Vidalia's siting story has many chapters: river landing, ferry crossing, land grant, fort site, administrative center, crossroads, jumping-off point, terminus of the old Harrisonburg Road and numerous railroad lines, among others. But were it not for Natchez, these functions could have been located elsewhere. As one geographer pointed out, "the natural levees on the cut bank sides of the meanders north and south of Waverly Point were preferred to the Vidalia site" in terms of land-granting for plantations.[17] This leaves us to conclude that Vidalia's siting story is that of a cross-river subsidiary, its fundamental advantage being a corollary to Natchez, itself established by Bienville in 1716 as a bluff-top defensive site.

Unprotected by such topography, Vidalia has endured its share of water woes, having been inundated periodically, sometimes severely, and in 1938–1939 forced to shift inland for levee realignments and navigation improvements. But Vidalia retains its geographical relevance, and while its current population of 3,900 residents represents a one-third decline since 1980, it remains the largest city and seat of Concordia Parish, and still very much a cross-river subsidiary to Natchez.[18]

Once Vidalia had been established, additional land grants were made during the interregnum years of 1800–1803 "from very near Red River," wrote Phillips, "into Tensas Parish around Lakes St. Joseph, Bruin, St. John, and Concordia." Apropos to the incoming regime, most recipients were "of Anglo-Saxon stocks, with a sprinkling of French or Spanish[;] most of these people had come from the eastern states . . . then crossed the river," indicating Natchez's role as a jumping-off point and Vidalia's as a gateway. "In all, one hundred seventy grants were made along the Mississippi in Tensas Basin during or before 1803, thirty on Lake Concordia, seven on Tensas River, six on Bayou Vidal, four on Lake St. Peter, and five on Lake St. Joseph." Each grant capitalized on those upraised crescents enabling passage through quagmire. "Roads followed the 'line of least resistance,'" wrote Phillips, "and meandered through the backswamp to make use of the ridges or abandoned natural levees."[19]

Where no raised topography existed, roads had to be blazed across bottomlands—not ideal, but not impossible, at least during dry conditions. One such connector may explain the siting of St. Joseph, eleven miles south of Newellton and originally fronting the Mississippi. Here, around 1803, John Densmore built a riverside house, store, and wharf that developed into Densmore's Landing, serving boatmen in need of supplies and services. Interior cotton planters, meanwhile, needed access to the river to export bales, so a road was built from ridge to ridge, in that path-of-least-resistance manner, to connect to Densmore's Landing. In the years ahead, that road would be paved with planks and

Much of the upper delta country appears depressed in spirit. Not St. Joseph. Sited as a river landing accessed by a plank road, the settlement became an agricultural services node and seat of Tensas Parish, and today it has a vibrant main street (still named Plank Road, *top*) and a New England–style courthouse green (*bottom right*), a rarity in Louisiana. Photographs by Richard Campanella.

opened to public use for a toll, creating inland access that made Densmore's Landing into the main trade and population center within a hundred square miles. The community came to be known as St. Joseph, likely renamed by a Jesuit priest in honor of the patron saint of Don José Vidal, the man who founded Vidalia and enkindled regional settlement.

As riverine Vidalia became the ideal parish seat for Concordia, so too did riverine St. Joseph become the seat of Tensas Parish, created by the state legislature in 1843. Improbably, the town was laid out in the New England tradition, in which "the use of an axial green running from the levee to the Courthouse shows a level of Baroque city planning almost unknown in small towns in Louisiana, most of which grew on an expanding grid." Sited as a trade center and river landing with a road intersection, St. Joseph became an administrative center and agricultural services node, even as the river edged away and left an inundated forest fronting its levee. While St. Joseph's population has halved in the past generation, a recent civic revival has uplifted the spirit of this picturesque town of 800 inhabitants, laid out along a main street that is still called Plank Road. It is one of the very few downtowns in the region where most storefronts are active, and some are vivacious.[20]

Waterproof's siting story rhymes with that of St. Joseph. Both towns originally fronted the Mississippi, at landings where entrepreneurs opened stores (Densmore's Landing for St. Joseph; Goldman's Landing for Waterproof), and both became villages as roads were blazed to their rears (Plank Road for St. Joseph; the "old Texas Road" for Waterproof). Like Vidalia, Waterproof also had ferry service to and from Rodney in Mississippi, on which came as many as fifty covered wagons per day bound for Texas.[21] As regards the ironic name, various folk etymologies circulate, one of which tells of a flood report declaring that "everything in their whole region was under water 'except one waterproof knoll.' When the flood subsided, the community moved itself to the knoll, and the town acquired the name of Waterproof." If so, both the initial settlement and the subsequent deluge must have happened prior to 1841, because New Orleans newspapers that year started advertising steamboat service via Natchez to Waterproof.[22]

Unfortunately, Waterproof could not live up to its name. It had to be relocated twice due to flooding, bank scouring, levee realignments, and channel modifications. The village has occupied its present location since 1880, nearly a mile from its original site and substantially set back from the main river channel. Like St. Joseph, Waterproof no longer depends on the Mississippi, but rather on Highway 55 and the croplands behind it. In the past fifty years, the town's population has declined from over 1,400 to under 550 people, while Tensas Parish has only 4,000 residents, down 78 percent since 1900 and now Louisiana's least-populated parish. It's a somber reminder that riverine siting rationales in the upper delta did not age well over the twentieth century.

South of Waterproof brings us to the narrow neck of bottomlands separating the Tensas and Mississippi rivers. We have already seen how Vidalia became a cross-river subsidiary to Natchez and a gateway to north Louisiana. That access increased in the railroad era, as westward-reaching lines created station-stop enclaves at Minorca, Ridgecrest, and Ferriday. Famous as the birthplace of the heaven-and-hell-raising cousins Jimmy Lee Swaggart, Jerry Lee Lewis, and Mickey Gilley, Ferriday has quite a siting story as well. It occupies the natural levee of Lake Concordia, a cousin of the other oxbow (cutoff meander) sites of Lake Providence, Newellton, Spokane, Lake Bruin, Quimby, and New Roads. Ferriday also has a confluence, where Bayou Cocodrie unites two tributaries skirting the southern edge of town. A portage traces a line of least distance between the Mississippi and Tensas, the likes of which usually attract shortcutting. But because overland travelers had already found passage on the Texas Road through Waterproof, or on the Harrisonburg Road through Vidalia (both of which had ferry access to the Natchez area), no settlement aggregated on Lake Concordia's natural levee, and the land instead became cotton plantations.

One such plantation, formerly named Helena, belonged to the Ferriday family, and it was here, under subsequent ownership, that the advantageous site finally became activated by that most common of circa 1900 settlement-makers. "The town of Ferriday," wrote the geographer Phillips, was "a direct result of railroad construction. When both the Texas and Pacific and the Iron Mountain systems chose the spot as a terminal point, the town sprang up on what had been part of Helena Plantation." In 1903, the Realty Investment Company, which stewarded the deal, envisioned a town at the station and named it for former land owner and parish leader J. C. Ferriday. One writer described nascent Ferriday in autumn 1903 as "a town being built overnight," where the company "simply borrowed the same cookie cutter so often used on small towns and cut the area into blocks [running] up from the train depot. . . . In came the railroad workers, the real estate speculators, the businessmen[;] up went the hotels, the saloons, the nightclubs, the gambling joints [and] the brothels."[23] Ferriday incorporated in 1906 and developed industries including "a hoop mill, cooperage, cotton compress, compression plant, and sawmills."[24] Population doubled each decade through 1930 and peaked in 1970, with over 5,000 people.

Recent declines do not inhibit residents from expressing fierce hometown pride. Boosters describe Ferriday as having "produced in its short history more famous people per square mile than any other town in the country,"[25] and show it with Hollywood-style Hall of Fame sidewalk stars at Mickey Gilley Plaza—by the Delta Blues Museum, formerly the post office. Like so many other places throughout Louisiana, Ferriday proves how siting stories germinate remarkable communities, and so long as human willpower can summon people in passage to stay a spell and settle, those stories will continue to blossom.

Ferriday prides itself on its outsized role in American musical history, and demonstrates that remarkable communities can arise from even routine siting stories—in this case, an early 1900s railroad town in an agricultural region. Photograph by Richard Campanella.

Of the nineteen cities, towns, villages, and other communities in the upper delta analyzed in this study, 37 percent had riverine- or water-based primary siting stories (above the state average of 29 percent), while 53 percent were primarily railroad sites, above the 33 percent figure for the state. The upper delta was the only region that had zero crossroad or resource extraction/processing sites, two rationales that accounted for 10 percent and 13 percent of sites statewide, respectively. Settlements began forming in this region in the 1790s, crested in the 1870s, and ended in the 1900s. Roughly 42 percent of upper delta settlements emerged organically, the other 58 percent having been ordained by a founder, compared to 49 percent/51 percent emergent/ordained statewide.

CONCLUSION

TRENDS AND PATTERNS IN THE SITING OF LOUISIANA CITIES, TOWNS, AND VILLAGES

Crossroads, cutoffs, and confluences; ports, portages, and perigees; forts, fords, and ferries: the paradox of siting stories is their cryptic pertinence. They spawn our cities, towns, and villages, even as they fade from memory. They hide in plain sight as they recede from relevance, yet they affect our homes, emplace our lives, and inform our daily movements in the most literal sense. What ultimately determines community outcomes, however, are the chapters that residents add to those siting stories: whether they can overcome adversity, make prudent decisions, secure needed resources, and adapt to changing times. Siting stories are pertinent enough to explain our spatial lives, but it's those successive chapters that shape the quality of our lives. And it takes a village to write them.

This paradox makes it difficult to assess siting outcomes without indulging in presentism—that is, judging the past through the lens of the present. Maybe that's not entirely problematic; after all, we are talking about not just interesting artifacts but the spatial fate of millions of people. Outcomes are fair game. How, then, do we assess the settlement decisions of the past three centuries?

Consider St. Denis, who, I would argue, acted sensibly when he sited Natchitoches as a military outpost at a far-inland head of navigation, enabling the French to trade with tribes while countering Spanish threats to the west. A century later, however, all three rationales became obsolete, and Shreveport leapfrogged ahead of Natchitoches. This does not mean that Henry Shreve wielded superior site-surveying skills than St. Dens; it only means that history by 1836 had repositioned "Shreve's port" within a superior geographical situation compared to what St. Denis had to work with in 1714. Today, greater

Bronze depictions of the founding of Natchitoches and New Orleans, on a door in the Louisiana State Capitol. Photograph by Carol M. Highsmith/Library of Congress.

Shreveport is twenty times the size of Natchitoches and the third-largest metropolis in the state: kudos to Shreve. Then again, Natchitoches is 122 years older than Shreveport, persevering longer than any Louisiana community, and remains a sizable city with beautiful architecture, a fine university, and a stable economy. Kudos to St. Denis.

Likewise, Bienville, I contend, acted judiciously in siting New Orleans in 1718. Had he located the city too far downriver, it would have been that much more flood-prone, and if he went too far upriver, it would have inhibited oceangoing access. But, like St. Denis, Bienville had no way of knowing that railroads would change that dynamic in the mid-1800s, that containerization would change world shipping in the mid-1900s, and that by the early 2000s, coastal erosion, soil subsidence, and sea level rise would make his selected site increasingly precarious. Today, pundits are more likely to question Bienville's sanity than praise his acumen. And yet Bienville's city was, for well over a century, the largest in the South—and in 1840 the third-largest in the nation—for reasons directly related to Bienville's reckoning. New Orleans still hosts one of the world's busiest port systems, and it remains the largest municipality and largest metropolitan area in both Louisiana and the central Gulf Coast. No pundit could have done better.

Assessed on similar standards, Hammond stands out as a siting success. It was born along a railroad, like so many other communities, but initially as a shoe-manufacturing center and only later as a station. Surrounded by fine farmland and plenty of freshwater (but not too much!), Hammond also became an agricultural center for Tangipahoa Parish, where dairy, strawberries, and vegetables grow well, and where rails provided access to big urban markets. In the 1920s, Hammond attained an asset that would become a key ingredient for community success: an institution of higher learning, today's Southeastern Louisiana University, the state's third-largest public academy. In the 1960s, the asphalt "rivers" of I-55 and I-12 were built through Hammond, giving it a travel and distribution economy in all four cardinal directions. The interstates also positioned Hammond within commuting reach of both greater New Orleans and Baton Rouge, making it almost an exurb, all while being on relatively high ground and inland from the worst hurricane effects. And, unlike most other Louisiana railroad towns, passenger trains still stop daily in Hammond, at its historic station centered in a vibrant downtown. No wonder Hammond is the only railroad siting story in Louisiana ranked by the U.S. Census Bureau to be among the state's nine Metropolitan Statistical Areas, with 134,758 residents in 2020—and hardly any of them still manufacture shoes.

Other Louisiana communities also managed to revamp their siting rationales. Places like Houma and Lafayette, for example, emerged in the early nineteenth century at waterway confluences or navigation heads. But only by pivoting to petroleum were they able to grow ten- to thirtyfold during the twentieth century. Whether they and other petrochemical communities can adapt to looming changes in the global fossil fuel economy will determine whether their siting stories will ultimately have happy outcomes. This pending re-rationalization looms ominously over Louisiana. But if Houma and Lafayette have adapted to change before, they can do it again.

Many other communities have adapted as well, re-rationalizing their siting stories. Mandeville, for example, began in 1836 as a resort site, remained a small weekend getaway for a century, and had only 1,300 residents into the 1950s. Then, overnight, it repurposed itself as a bridgehead site, at the northern terminus of the Lake Pontchartrain Causeway, benefitting anew from its historical propinquity to New Orleans. Today, Mandeville has ten times its 1950s population, and incoming families now tend to leapfrog into Covington (originally a confluence site), Abita Springs (also a former resort site), or Hammond (see above). Each adapted to changing times like their futures depended on it, and came out bigger and better as a result.

Long is the list of communities that did not, falling victim to their obsolete siting stories. The militarized sites of Los Adaes, Fort Jesup, and Galveztown lost their enemies, and thus their purpose. The settlers at the Burlington ferry landing on the Amite could not adapt to the new bridge over the Amite. The timber town of Yellow Pine lost all its yellow pine and had no Plan B. The administrative site of Bellevue could not survive the loss of its courthouse, because it offered no other opportunities outside the courthouse. The spring from which Oaklin Springs sprung could not outdraw the train station that opened in nearby Oberlin—which is why Oberlin now has 1,700 residents and Oaklin Springs has only a cemetery. The many siting advantages that birthed Port Hudson all died in an epic Civil War battle, leaving it with only one "site" left in its story—Port Hudson State Historic Site. The resort site of Isle Dernière could not overcome geophysical adversity, a fate that awaits other coastal Louisiana communities in the face of sinking soils, eroding wetlands, changing climates, and rising seas.

Regardless of outcomes, so many Louisiana siting stories are downright fascinating for their unexpected sequence of chapters. Take Zwolle in the northwestern hill country, which emerged in the 1700s as a stopover and confluence crossing along a Spanish frontier road, attained a Spanish church and mission, became an American railroad and mill town thanks to a kindly Dutch patron, and today is part timber town, part crossroads, and part recreational site, home to 1,800 Louisianians—and the Zwolle Tamale Festival. The siting stories of Gramercy, Bogalusa, Newellton, and Morgan City are striking because their original *raisons d'être* are still the most important industries in town, and in the case of Gramercy's sugar mill and Bogalusa's wood and paper mill, they still dominate the skyline.

Morgan City's siting story ranks among the most complex. The city's underlying geography may be described as an island, a peninsula, a strait, a natural levee of a bayou, or the bank of a great river. It is set among a dizzying array of delta bays, lakes, swamps, marshes, bayous, rivers with multiple channels, passes, cutoffs, canals, and a spillway. Its siting stories, meanwhile, tell of a river port, a bayou fork, a train station, a rail junction, a crossroads, a basin bypass, and a jumping-off point to resource extraction sites.

Contrast Morgan City's all-of-the-above complexity to those siting stories that are idiosyncratic, involving quarantine (Carville), incarceration (Angola), and Utopian communal living (Germantown, Sicily Island, and New Llano). In a handful of cases, animals have played an inadvertent role in siting settlements, including path-blazing deer, wallowing bison, thirsty livestock, salt-licking cows, and bears pursued by hunters. For what it's worth, those settlements all fared better than those sited by Utopians.

Louisiana siting stories trace meaningful trends in time and space, marking rises, peaks, and lulls. The challenge in discerning them lies in converting nuanced qualitative information (i.e., all previous chapters of this book) into discrete quantitative data, a process that entails vexing categorization decisions but yields informative numerical findings. Readers will find in the appendix my best effort to encapsulate 418 Louisiana siting stories by their primary and secondary rationales, along with each community's foundation year, its emergent or ordained genesis, and the community's current status as a city, town, village, Census-Designated Place, population cluster, or ghost town.

Once we accept the costs of categorization, we reap the benefits of trend detection. Spatially, for example, we learn that Louisiana's two largest swamp basins, the Bayou Manchac/Maurepas and the Atchafalaya, saw the most spontaneous community formation—and, conversely, the least amount of ordained place-making. Fully 78 percent and 88 percent of their settlements, respectively, emerged from the bottom up by folks on the move. The corollary is that these regions also had the highest percentages of riverine- and water-based siting rationales (78 percent and 82 percent), and the fewest terrestrial ones, namely railroads (only 11 percent and 12 percent). Compare these figures to state averages, where emergent sites made up 49 percent of our 418 cases, where riverine/water sites made up 29 percent, and where railroads made up 33 percent. We may surmise that, in the aggregate, low-lying topographical regions abetted organic settlement emergence, whereas higher inland regions tended to invite ordainers of settlements. An inspection of a modern-day map of the Maurepas and Atchafalaya basins reveals settlement geography in its most populist form, where humans made space into place through their everyday movements, with minimal authoritative intervention. You have to go uphill and inland to see where authorities made most siting decisions: the Florida parishes, west and east, were 67 percent and 88 percent ordained in their settlement geography, followed by the western hills (66 percent) and Ouachita Valley (61 percent) regions. Railroad-related rationales accounted for most of those settlement sites, and railroad executives made most of the decisions.

Most of Louisiana's jumping-off sites fell within the southernmost tier of the state, because that peri-coastal region possesses most of our big basins, lakes, and bays where resources were abundant in their cores but were only reachable from their perimeters. Similarly, all river-mouth sites fell in or near the southern coast, which of course is where all rivers discharge. If there's any surprise here, it's the relative paucity of river-mouth sites, namely Madisonville, Lacombe, Cameron, Grand Chenier, and arguably Morgan City. Why so few? The answer is physical geography: a fluvial delta offers very few opportunities for stable urban footing along its coastal fringe. Just ask the folks in Chênière Caminada or Isle Dernière, if you can find any.

Likewise, most of Louisiana's Sunday towns are in the south, not because southern Louisiana was more pious, but because Catholics were the original churchgoers at the time that most of the population was in the south. The ecumenical nature of Catholicism precluded offshoot congregations, quite unlike Protestantism, and therefore its parish churches were more likely to draw the faithful from afar, thus instigating settlements. Resort sites were also mostly in the southeastern quadrant of the state, not because that's where most springs and swimming holes were, but because that's where most Louisianians lived to seek a refreshing weekend getaway.

Shortcuts and portage sites were highly prevalent along rivers and bayous in the older alluvial and deltaic regions to the south and east, because that's where early overland-trekking and pirogue-paddling settlers sought such spatial assists. These siting stories were wholly absent in the hills of the north and west, because settlers arrived there later, because sinuous rivers were fewer, and because railroads were more likely to undercut the advantages of shortcutting.

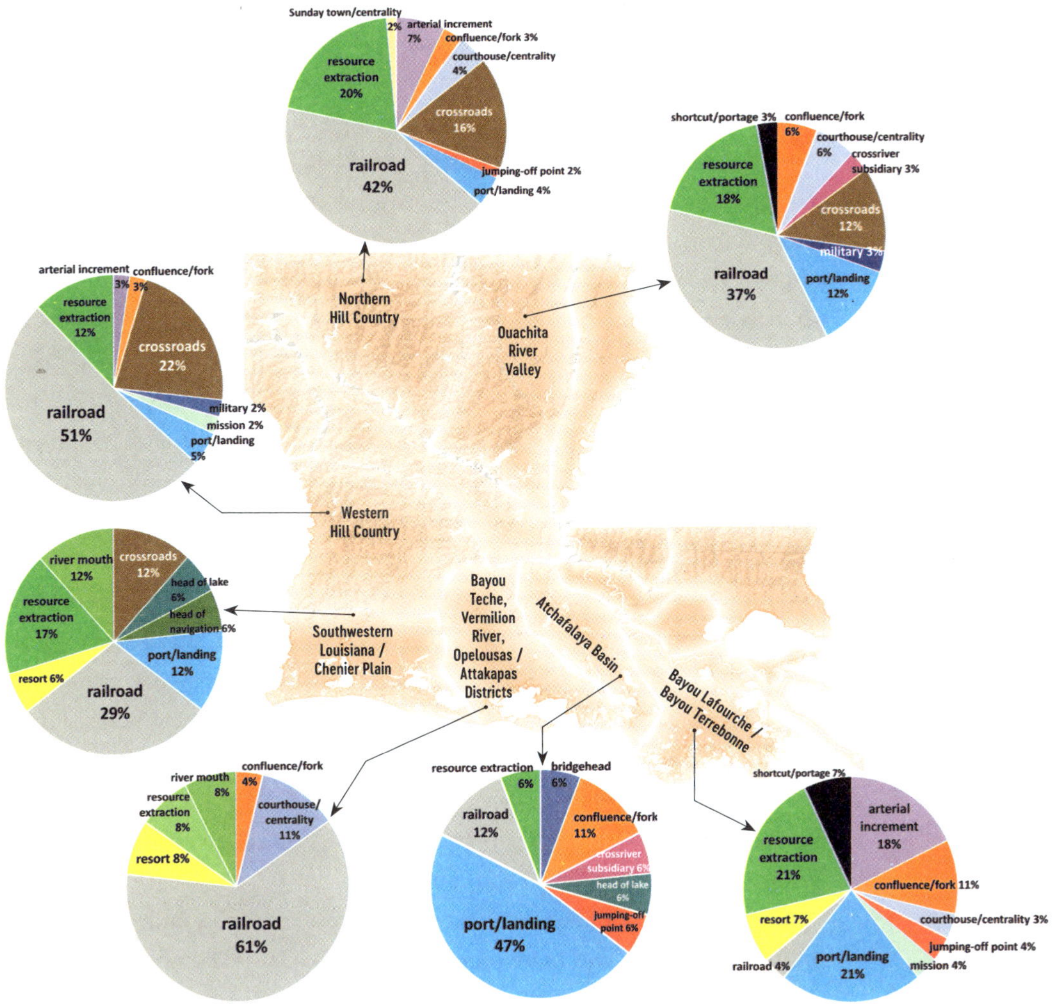

Military sites, on the other hand, were disproportionately in the northern half of the state, because that's where French, Spanish, and American imperial interests needed to stake their claims and position their weapons. This was Louisiana's frontier in both senses of the word, as borderlands and as wilderness, and both called for militarization, however symbolic.

Resource extraction and processing sites have an unusually bifurcated geography, with many in the west and north, and just as many clustered in the south and east. The reasons: timber and oil. Voids appear in the prairie region and the upper delta. Why? No timber, no oil.

The most spatially dispersed siting stories were railroads, crossroads, and arterial increment sites—all seemingly ubiquitous, until we look closely and see voids. They mark where lithosphere gives way to hydrosphere—and that is precisely where our many riverine sites prevail.

Now let's look at temporal trends. Since colonization, settlements formed in Louisiana over roughly 225 years, starting in 1714 and petering out around 1940, arguably the last one being Port Fourchon in 1981. The time line of siting stories is not evenly distributed or bell-shaped, but bimodal, with a slow ramp-up and a gradual ramp-down across two distinct peaks.

The first rise lagged behind the initial settlements (Natchitoches in 1714, Los Adaes in 1717, New Orleans in 1718, and Algiers in 1719) because most French exertions through the 1750s went into plantation development rather than interior expansion.[1] That changed over the next half-century as the Spanish regime cast its eyes inland and, through its military, immigration, and land-granting policies, more than quintupled the settlement-making of the French period. This analysis enumerated twenty-five communities forming from 1763 to 1803, the core of the Spanish period, compared to only four during the French regime (one of which, Los Adaes, was entirely a Spanish project, overseen from Mexico).[2] Most of the Spanish-era settlements were riverine in their setting, due to the few roads and wild terrain. The Spanish years also saw more military and missionary siting efforts than any period.

Community-making escalated steadily through the antebellum period, as the number of new settlements doubled every two decades. Twenty-one places formed during the 1800s–1810s, followed by forty-three in the 1820s–1830s, and eighty-four during the 1840s–1850s. The antebellum decades also marked the heyday of emergent settling processes, as Louisianians spread inland on vessels, and as Americans elsewhere made their way westward overland, clustering at stopovers, crossroads, shortcuts, fords, ferries, bridgeheads, landings, and heads of navigation. Communities continued to emerge in this bottom-up fashion into the 1920s, but would never match their circa 1850 peak. Yet this

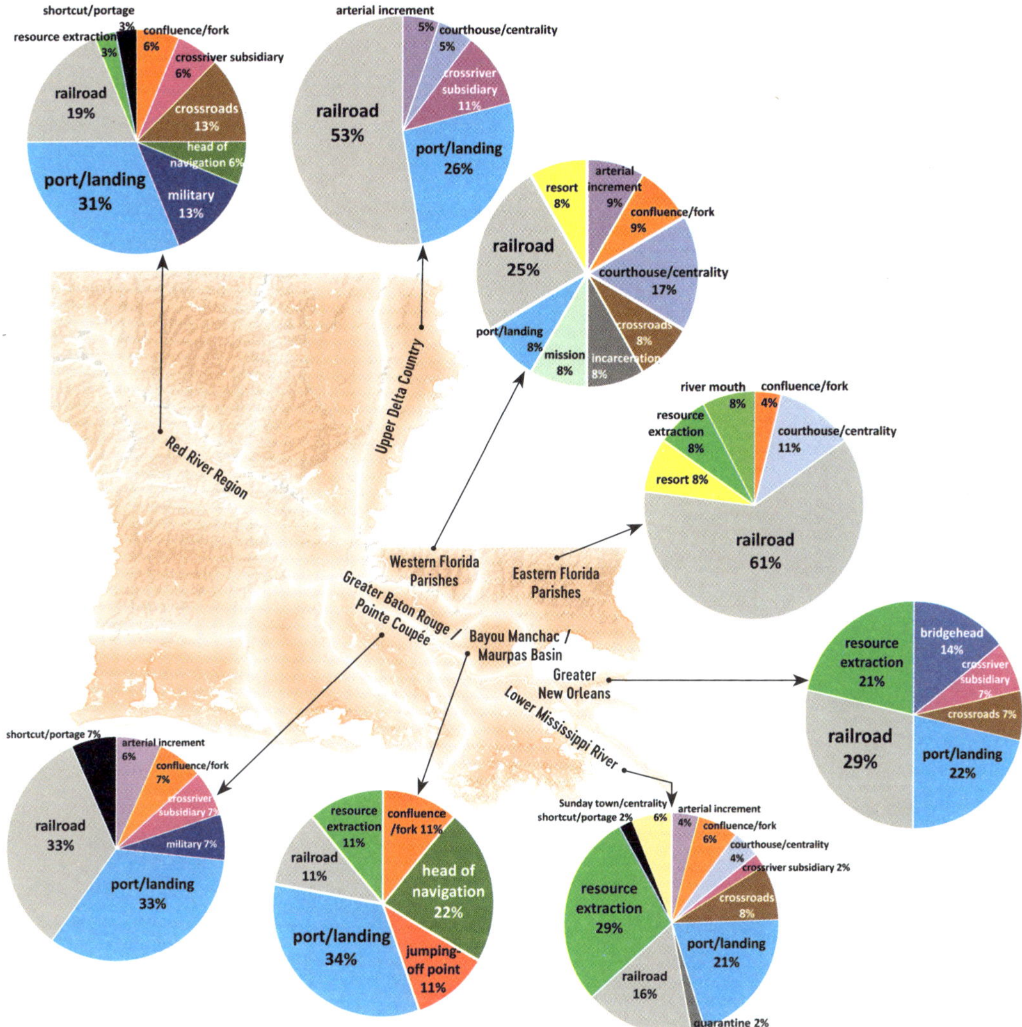

era also saw a gradual increase in ordained siting, some on grounds of administrative centrality as new parishes were created, and others birthed by early railroads in need of stations at regular increments.

The most frequent siting stories of the 1800s–1810s, be they primary or secondary, were riverine—ports along rivers and landings on bayous, particularly at confluences or forks. Water represented the path of least resistance to interior opportunities, and communities amassed wherever bulk could be broken and access could be gained. The waterway trend continued across the antebellum decades, as rivermen pushed heads of navigation farther upriver (a siting story that peaked in the 1820s–1830s), as steamboats plied farther up tributaries and down distributaries, and as planters came to rely on exporting their produce. But concurrently, terrestrial drivers gained ground, as more

Frequency of ordained and emergent settlements (*top*), and all Louisiana settlements (*bottom*). Graphs by Richard Campanella.

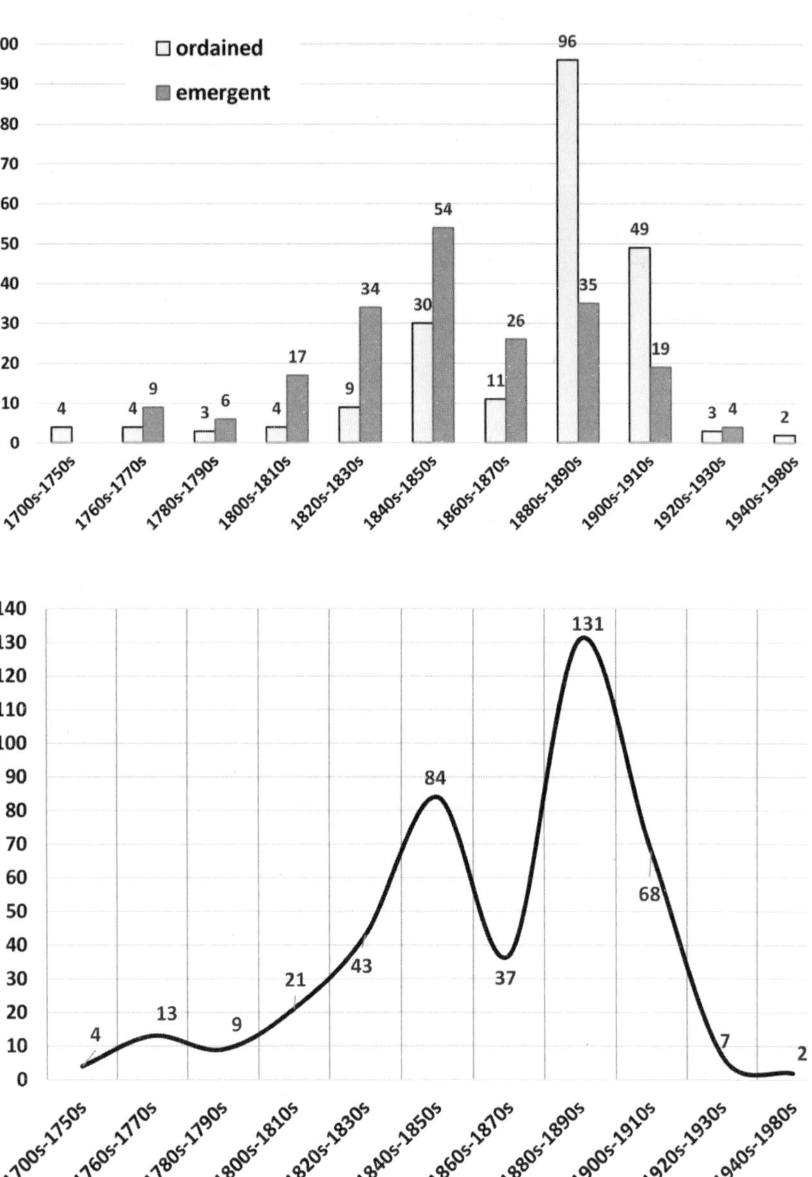

roads, parish seats, and railroads came into being, to the point that, by the 1850s, while port/landing sitings retained their plurality status, they no longer accounted for the majority of new settlements. Places primarily or secondarily sited at crossroads, for example, surged from only three in the 1800s–1810 to nine during the 1820s–1830s, and to twenty-two in the 1840s–1850s, while railroad sites rose from three to nineteen between 1833 and 1857. Louisianians had effectively learned to become landlubbers, and in the decades ahead rails and roads would draw ever more of them away from rivers and bayous.

Detail above main entrance to the U.S. Post Office and U.S. Courthouse in Monroe, Louisiana. Photograph by Carol M. Highsmith/ Library of Congress.

The Civil War brought a complete halt to Louisiana settlement formation, and through Reconstruction our time line shows a 50 to 70 percent drop from peak levels. But soon, two siting stories conspired to become the most productive settlement-makers in state history: railroads stations and resource extraction/processing operations, mostly for timber, later for petroleum. During the 1880s and 1890s, nearly 100 settlements materialized around railroad stations, and another thirty-two at resource sites, as either primary or secondary rationales. In the two subsequent decades, an additional sixty-six settlements so formed, such that the total number of new settlements in Louisiana roughly doubled from 1880 to 1920. The same period saw the demise of new riverine settlements. Port/landing sites, for example, plummeted from twenty-seven to only six over the turn of the century, and went extinct after 1920. That same era saw a dramatic rise of the arterial increment site. At least forty-six such settlements arose at regular distances along railroads and early automobile roads between 1880 and 1920, birthed because of the effect of travel upon human and vehicular needs.

Railroad towns, timber towns, and oil towns usually happen when decisions are made by railroad men, timber tycoons, and oil barons. It is no coincidence, then, that the turn of the century marked the heyday of the ordained siting story, peaking around 1890, forty years after the circa 1850 peak of emergent siting stories. The decades in between witnessed the end of the slaveholding regime, the closing of the frontier, the rise of corporate America, a shift from river to rail transit, and an agrarian economy becoming more industrialized, nationalized, and globalized.

The fall of slavery and the rise of railroad-based industry set the stage for a significant change in Louisiana's settlement geography. Slavery had skewed population distributions, making them mostly rural statewide and highly urbanized in only one spot, with relatively few small cities and towns in between. Typically, the largest city in a state or nation has roughly twice the population of the second-largest city, three times the third-largest, four times the forth, and so on—a relationship so standard it's been called the Rank-Size Rule, or the Law of the Primate City. But Louisiana's primate city, New Orleans, had in 1860 over fourteen times the population of its second-largest city (not Baton Rouge, not Shreveport, but nearby Donaldsonville), and fully thirty-three times more than each of the next three largest cities (two of which were immediately adjacent to New Orleans). Compared to free northern states or border regions, antebellum Louisiana had a striking paucity of small cities, towns, and villages, most of them relatively small, and only one true metropolis.[3]

The reason for the skew: slave plantations. With 47 percent of the state's population in bondage, the plantation system tied hundreds of thousands of people to rural crop production operations—physically, socially, and economically. Plantations became surrogates for towns: they had "residential" areas (slave cabins, overseers' quarters, the master's house), commercial and industrial areas (workshops, warehouses, gins, mills, kilns), services (the office, kitchen, infirmary, church, cemetery), and infrastructure (roads, levees, drainage ditches, conveyances, and a wharf at the river landing). These town-like qualities explain the old southern custom of ascribing names to plantations, as one would a town. And if the plantation's landing later became a siting story, its name usually became the name of the town.

Of course, this still left hundreds of thousands of free people to establish towns and villages—and they did, by the score, as we have seen throughout this book. But what resulted were far fewer and smaller communities than were found in free states. To wit, the compendium volume of the 1860 census needed only half a page to tabulate the populations of Louisiana's "Cities, Towns, &c," wherein the figures showed that greater New Orleans had six times more people than all sixteen other municipalities *combined,* their median population being only 966 residents. That same source used twenty-six full pages to tabulate Ohio's hundreds of cities and towns, most of which were at least double Louisiana's median town size, and which collectively dwarfed the population of the state's largest city, Cincinnati.[4] This disparity occurred throughout antebellum America, where freedom tended to catalyze more "aspirational towns, their sights set on becoming wholesaling complexes for surrounding farms [and] manufacturing start-ups," and where slavery suppressed such aspirations.[5]

As if to prove the point, Louisiana caught up on its town-making in the decades following the Civil War. Many emancipated families became sharecroppers or leaseholders of small farms, and settled in tiny linear hamlets on the flanks of former plantations—hardly municipalities, but agglomerated communities nonetheless, usually with a rustic church and country store.

Brick slave dwellings on the Magnolia Plantation in Natchitoches Parish. Photograph by Richard Campanella.

Dozens of such communities may be found today up and down rivers and bayous, particularly the River Road. They tend to be entirely Black, largely impoverished, rarely incorporated, and mostly arranged along a single artery perpendicular to the waterway—just like the old French long lots from which they were subdivided. Other African Americans migrated to existing towns and cities, where they might find services, resources, and jobs. Black urban populations grew substantially. Those in New Orleans, for example, doubled from 25,423 to 50,456 during 1860–1870. Still other rural Black migrants found new homes in all those newly ordained communities arising at railroad stations, timber mills, and processing plants, for this was also the era when Louisiana's premier economic sector shifted from agriculture to industry. More often than not, they ended up settling on the other side of the tracks—literally.

This "post-emancipation micropolitanization"[6] had the effect of increasing both the number and size of Louisiana's villages, towns, and cities while reducing the sheer dominance of New Orleans. Whereas the census tabulated only twenty-one Louisiana "cities, towns, &c." in 1860, the 1890 and 1900 censuses listed seventy-five and 104 "cities, towns, and villages," respectively, with a dozen of them having at least triple the circa 1860 median town population. The shift from rural plantations to agglomerated communities explains why the state legislature felt a need to pass the Lawrason Act in 1898, clarifying the criteria for municipal incorporation and setting definitions for what constituted a "city" (over 5,000 population), "town" (1,000 to 5,000) and "village" (under 1,000).[7] Louisiana through the 1900s and 2000s has since seen its settlement geography even out somewhat, and its ten largest cities now come closer to limning the curve of the Rank-Size Rule. Yet striking differences remain between Louisiana's modern-day settlement geography and those of northern or border states, with their intricate dispersions of sizeable cities, towns, and villages.[8]

* * *

Judging from sheer numbers, one may infer that the 1890s shift practically rewrote the story of settlement siting in Louisiana, and that captains of industry were its new authors. Railroads are indeed Louisiana's most common siting story, accounting for 179 settlements (43 percent of those analyzed statewide) as their primary or secondary rationale. Add to that the seventy-eight settlements originating primarily or secondarily as resource extraction and processing sites, nearly all of which relied on rails. But most station sites were born rural and remote, and most railroad towns remain exactly that, with anemic economies and diminishing demographics. The same may be said of most resource extraction sites, especially former timber towns. Train stations and lumber mills may have been the most fruitful progenitors of Louisiana settlements, but they were not the best parents. The trains lost passengers to automobiles, and the timber companies cut and ran. Their siting stories may dominate our map, but they do not explain our distribution.

What *does* explain where we live are the older, emergent siting stories of the Bayou State. Millions of Louisianians today remain grounded in communities traceable to the organic settlements of 200–300 years ago, where history was made along waterways. Even when rails outcompeted rivers, rivers remained relevant.[9] Many bankside settlements managed to modernize their maritime métier by reequipping themselves with rails, roads, industry, and/or as administrative and knowledge centers. The outcome: our old waterside settlements remain our largest cities, despite the fact that they no longer rely on waterways as they once did. They adapted.

This is true no matter how we measure it. If we look at the ten largest municipalities, home to 1,257,592 Louisianians (27 percent of the state population) in 2020, every one of those ten cities had a waterborne siting rationale, most as the primary factor, and most of them emerged in their formation, without an ordainer. All but one were founded in colonial or antebellum times, mostly during the 1710s–1830s. Only one (Kenner) began as a railroad site, and only Bossier City was founded after the Civil War.

Alternately, if we look at metropolitan statistical areas—of which Louisiana has nine, home to 3,914,867 people, or 84 percent of its population—the trend grows stronger. One hundred percent of them formed during colonial or antebellum times; 89 percent had a waterborne siting story, most of them primary and emergent; and only the smallest of the nine (greater Hammond) originated as a railroad town.

Returning to our original question, then, we conclude with an answer. *Why are we here?* Because Louisianians found that the Bayou State's myriad waterways provided, as Richard M. Hurd would have said, "convenient points of contact with the outer world along lines of least resistance, and at points where a break in transportation occurs—harbors, heads of rivers, confluences, obstructions, and where ocean and river meet."[10]

ACKNOWLEDGMENTS

A book about the origins of Louisiana's cities, towns, and villages is really a book about all Louisianians, past and present, and it is to them that I express my deepest gratitude. I specifically acknowledge all those diligent researchers—academic historians and geographers as well as parish record keepers, city archivists, village storytellers, and indefatigable history buffs—who documented the earliest days of Louisiana communities. Among them are parish historians such as Henry Skipwith, Sidney Albert Marchand, Frederick S. Ellis, William J. Sandoz, and Harry Lewis Griffin; academics such as Richard M. Hurd, Gilbert C. Din, Milton B. Newton Jr., Fred B. Kniffen, Sam B. Hilliard, Yvonne Phillips, Donald J. Millet, and Lawrence N. Powell; and narrative historians such as Alcée Fortier, William Henry Perrin, Claire D'Artois Leeper, Mary Ann Sternberg, and Shane K. Bernard. I thank the institutions that provided me access to primary sources, documents, maps, and books, including libraries, archives, and museums in scores of parishes and cities, as well as the Howard-Tilton Library at Tulane University, the Louisiana Collection of the Earl K. Long Library at the University of New Orleans, the Louisiana Division of the New Orleans Public Library, the Main Branch of the Jefferson Parish Library, the Louisiana Research Collection at Tulane University, the Louisiana Endowment for the Humanities, the Louisiana State Land Office, the Louisiana State Library, the Louisiana State Museum, The Historic New Orleans Collection, the U.S. Census Bureau, and the U.S. Library of Congress. Special gratitude goes to historian Lawrence N. Powell for his insightful review of my manuscript, to fellow backroads explorer Louis N. Ritten, and to Iñaki Alday and Scott Bernhard, dean and associate dean of the Tulane University School of Architecture, where I hold a faculty appointment and serve as associate dean for research. I am grateful to Jean and Saul A. Mintz for the professorship that, along with the Carol Lavin Bernick Faculty Grant Program, provided subvention funds for this publication. I express gratitude to Derik Shelor, of Shelor and Son Publishing, for his thorough editorial review of the manuscript. I especially would like to thank the staff of the Louisiana State University Press, including editor in chief Rand Dotson, managing editor Catherine L. Kadair, production manager and book designer Barbara Bourgoyne, marketing manager James Wilson, and director Alisa Plant, among others. Finally, I thank my wife, Marina Campanella, and our son, Jason Campanella, for their love, support, and interest in Louisiana siting stories.

APPENDIX

ORIGINS OF 418 LOUISIANA CITIES, TOWNS, AND VILLAGES

The table below lists the 418 Louisiana communities considered in this book, along with their region; status as a city, town, village, Census-Designated Place (CDP), unincorporated population cluster, or ghost town; main foundation year; whether the settlement emerged through human movement or was ordained by an empowered agent; and the settlement's primary and secondary siting rationales. While in the text I took pains to parse numerous complex rationales, the synopses listed below necessitated the collapsing of all those nuances into twenty discrete categories, a task in which subjectivity abounded, and judgment calls had to be made.[1] Foundation years presented a similar challenge, as many settlements got restarted, renamed, relocated, and/or re-rationalized over decades, or had differing time lines for their first settler, post office, street grid, or incorporation. I did my best in identifying the most reliably recognized year in which the settlement sprouted to become the community we recognize today. Finally, I note that the focus of this book has been on nucleated settlements, that is, those with downtowns or equivalent nuclei; not included are scattered rural populations and tract housing subdivisions without discernible cores. The data in the table below enabled the computation of the trends and patterns in Louisiana siting stories presented in the conclusion.

NAME	REGION	STATUS	ERA	TYPE	PRIMARY	SECONDARY
Abbeville	Teche/Vermilion	city	1843	emergent	Sunday town/centrality	confluence/fork
Abita Springs	Eastern Florida	town	1853	ordained	resort	resource extraction/ processing
Addis	Lower Mississippi	town	1894	ordained	railroad	n/a
Albany	Manchac/Maurepas	village	1907	ordained	railroad	resource extraction/ processing
Alexandria	Red River Valley	city	1789	emergent	shortcut/portage	head of navigation
Algiers	Greater New Orleans	pop cluster	1719	ordained	cross-river subsidiary	port/landing
Ama	Lower Mississippi	CDP	1891	emergent	arterial increment	n/a
Amelia	Atchafalaya Basin	CDP	1883	emergent	port/landing	railroad
Amite City	Eastern Florida	town	1854	ordained	railroad	courthouse/centrality
Anacoco	Western Hills	village	1875	ordained	railroad	crossroads
Angie	Eastern Florida	village	1907	ordained	railroad	n/a
Angola	Western Florida	pop cluster	1880	ordained	incarceration	port/landing
Arabi	Lower Mississippi	CDP	1848	ordained	resource extraction/ processing	port/landing
Arcadia	Northern Hills	town	1854	emergent	arterial increment	n/a
Arnaudville	Atchafalaya Basin	town	1870	emergent	confluence/fork	head of navigation
Ashland	Northern Hills	village	1891	ordained	railroad	resource extraction/ processing
Athens	Northern Hills	village	1846	emergent	confluence/fork	crossroads
Atlanta	Northern Hills	village	1858	emergent	arterial increment	n/a
Avondale	Lower Mississippi	CDP	1880	ordained	railroad	resource extraction/ processing
Baker	Greater Baton Rouge	city	1884	ordained	railroad	n/a
Baldwin	Teche/Vermilion	town	1867	emergent	arterial increment	confluence/fork
Ball	Red River Valley	town	1893	ordained	resource extraction/ processing	railroad
Barataria	Greater New Orleans	CDP	1870	emergent	resource extraction/ processing	jumping-off point
Basile	Teche/Vermilion	town	1896	ordained	railroad	arterial increment
Baskin	Ouachita Valley	village	1890	ordained	resource extraction/ processing	railroad
Bastrop	Ouachita Valley	city	1846	ordained	courthouse/centrality	port/landing
Baton Rouge	Greater Baton Rouge	city	1770	ordained	military	port/landing
Bayou Cane	Lafourche/Terrebonne	CDP	1822	ordained	courthouse/centrality	port/landing
Bayou Gauche	Lower Mississippi	CDP	1900	emergent	port/landing	jumping-off point
Bayou Sara	Western Florida	ghost	1799	emergent	confluence/fork	port/landing
Bayou Vista	Teche/Vermilion	CDP	1890	emergent	port/landing	shortcut/portage

NAME	REGION	STATUS	ERA	TYPE	PRIMARY	SECONDARY
Belcher	Northern Hills	village	1898	ordained	railroad	port/landing
Belle Chasse	Lower Mississippi	CDP	1888	emergent	shortcut/portage	port/landing
Belle Rose	Lafourche/Terrebonne	CDP	1847	emergent	arterial increment	port/landing
Bellevue	Northern Hills	pop cluster	1840	emergent	port/landing	courthouse/centrality
Benton	Northern Hills	town	1830	emergent	crossroads	courthouse/centrality
Bernice	Northern Hills	town	1899	ordained	railroad	resource extraction/ processing
Berwick	Atchafalaya Basin	town	1840	emergent	cross-river subsidiary	port/landing
Bienville	Northern Hills	village	1890	emergent	crossroads	arterial increment
Blanchard	Northern Hills	town	1895	ordained	railroad	crossroads
Bogalusa	Eastern Florida	city	1906	ordained	resource extraction/ processing	railroad
Bonita	Ouachita Valley	village	1892	ordained	railroad	port/landing
Boothville	Lower Mississippi	CDP	1840	emergent	resource extraction/ processing	jumping-off point
Bossier City	Red River Valley	city	1883	emergent	cross-river subsidiary	port/landing
Boutte	Lower Mississippi	CDP	1866	emergent	crossroads	n/a
Boyce	Red River Valley	town	1887	emergent	port/landing	railroad
Breaux Bridge	Atchafalaya Basin	city	1829	emergent	bridgehead	port/landing
Bridge City	Greater New Orleans	CDP	1935	ordained	bridgehead	n/a
Broussard	Teche/Vermilion	town	1884	ordained	railroad	n/a
Brusly	Lower Mississippi	town	1901	ordained	railroad	n/a
Bryceland	Northern Hills	village	1890	emergent	crossroads	n/a
Bunkie	Red River Valley	city	1882	ordained	railroad	arterial increment
Buras-Triumph	Lower Mississippi	CDP	1840	emergent	resource extraction/ processing	jumping-off point
Burlington	Greater Baton Rouge	ghost	1840	emergent	port/landing	n/a
Burr's Ferry	Western Hills	pop cluster	1807	emergent	port/landing	jumping-off point
Bush	Eastern Florida	town	1907	ordained	railroad	arterial increment
Calvin	Northern Hills	village	1891	ordained	railroad	resource extraction/ processing
Cameron	SW La/Chenier Plain	CDP	1845	emergent	river mouth	port/landing
Campti	Red River Valley	town	1805	emergent	head of navigation	port/landing
Cankton	Teche/Vermilion	village	1900	emergent	crossroads	arterial increment
Carencro	Teche/Vermilion	city	1872	emergent	arterial increment	n/a
Carlyss	SW La/Chenier Plain	CDP	1907	ordained	railroad	crossroads
Carville	Lower Mississippi	pop cluster	1868	ordained	quarantine	shortcut/portage
Castor	Northern Hills	village	1891	ordained	railroad	crossroads

NAME	REGION	STATUS	ERA	TYPE	PRIMARY	SECONDARY
Castor Sulphur Springs	Ouachita Valley	ghost	1870	emergent	port/landing	resort
Cecilia	Atchafalaya Basin	CDP	1840	emergent	port/landing	crossroads
Chackbay	Lower Mississippi	CDP	1873	emergent	crossroads	n/a
Chalmette	Lower Mississippi	CDP	1848	ordained	resource extraction/ processing	courthouse/centrality
Charenton	Teche/Vermilion	CDP	1779	emergent	jumping-off point	port/landing
Chataignier	Teche/Vermilion	village	1856	emergent	crossroads	n/a
Chatham	Northern Hills	town	1903	ordained	resource extraction/ processing	railroad
Chauvin	Lafourche/Terrebonne	CDP	1875	emergent	arterial increment	n/a
Cheneyville	Red River Valley	town	1835	emergent	port/landing	n/a
Chênière Caminada	Lafourche/Terrebonne	pop cluster	1870	emergent	resource extraction/ processing	jumping-off point
Choudrant	Northern Hills	village	1900	ordained	railroad	arterial increment
Church Point	Teche/Vermilion	town	1843	emergent	port/landing	Sunday town/centrality
Clarence	Red River Valley	village	1898	ordained	railroad	arterial increment
Clarks	Ouachita Valley	village	1902	ordained	resource extraction/ processing	railroad
Clayton	Upper Delta	town	1890	emergent	arterial increment	n/a
Clinton	Western Florida	town	1833	ordained	courthouse/centrality	n/a
Cocodrie	Lafourche/Terrebonne	pop cluster	1900	emergent	resource extraction/ processing	jumping-off point
Colfax	Red River Valley	town	1855	emergent	port/landing	courthouse/centrality
Collinston	Ouachita Valley	village	1902	ordained	railroad	crossroads
Columbia	Ouachita Valley	town	1827	emergent	port/landing	courthouse/centrality
Convent	Lower Mississippi	pop cluster	1809	emergent	Sunday town/centrality	port/landing
Converse	Western Hills	village	1905	emergent	arterial increment	n/a
Cotton Valley	Northern Hills	town	1896	ordained	railroad	crossroads
Cottonport	Red River Valley	town	1830	emergent	port/landing	n/a
Coushatta	Red River Valley	town	1820	emergent	port/landing	crossroads
Covington	Eastern Florida	city	1816	emergent	confluence/fork	courthouse/centrality
Creole	SW La/Chenier Plain	pop cluster	1880	emergent	crossroads	n/a
Crowley	Teche/Vermilion	city	1887	emergent	confluence/fork	railroad
Cullen	Northern Hills	town	1894	ordained	railroad	resource extraction/ processing
Cut Off	Lafourche/Terrebonne	CDP	1860	emergent	shortcut/portage	port/landing
Darrow	Lower Mississippi	pop cluster	1846	emergent	cross-river subsidiary	port/landing

NAME	REGION	STATUS	ERA	TYPE	PRIMARY	SECONDARY
DeRidder	Western Hills	city	1898	ordained	railroad	resource extraction/ processing
Delcambre	Teche/Vermilion	town	1877	emergent	port/landing	arterial increment
Delhi	Upper Delta	town	1883	ordained	railroad	n/a
Delta	Upper Delta	village	1853	emergent	cross-river subsidiary	n/a
Denham Springs	Greater Baton Rouge	city	1856	emergent	confluence/fork	resort
DeQuincy	Western Hills	city	1897	ordained	railroad	n/a
Des Allemands	Lower Mississippi	CDP	1850	emergent	port/landing	bridgehead
Destrehan	Lower Mississippi	CDP	1770	emergent	Sunday town/centrality	port/landing
Dixie Inn	Northern Hills	village	1940	emergent	crossroads	military
Dodson	Northern Hills	village	1900	ordained	railroad	n/a
Donaldsonville	Lower Mississippi	city	1806	emergent	confluence/fork	port/landing
Downsville	Northern Hills	village	1850	emergent	crossroads	n/a
Doyline	Northern Hills	village	1885	ordained	railroad	arterial increment
Dry Prong	Ouachita Valley	village	1875	emergent	resource extraction/ processing	crossroads
Dubach	Northern Hills	town	1901	ordained	railroad	resource extraction/ processing
Dubberly	Northern Hills	village	1885	ordained	railroad	n/a
Dulac	Lafourche/Terrebonne	CDP	1872	emergent	jumping-off point	resource extraction/ processing
Duson	Teche/Vermilion	town	1880	ordained	railroad	n/a
East Hodge	Northern Hills	village	1899	ordained	resource extraction/ processing	railroad
Edgard	Lower Mississippi	CDP	1770	emergent	Sunday town/centrality	courthouse/centrality
Edgefield	Red River Valley	village	1898	ordained	railroad	n/a
Elizabeth	Western Hills	town	1890	ordained	resource extraction/ processing	n/a
Elmwood	Greater New Orleans	CDP	1935	emergent	bridgehead	n/a
Elton	Western Hills	town	1906	ordained	railroad	crossroads
Empire	Lower Mississippi	CDP	1890	emergent	port/landing	resource extraction/ processing
Epps	Upper Delta	village	1906	ordained	railroad	n/a
Erath	Teche/Vermilion	town	1884	ordained	railroad	n/a
Eros	Northern Hills	town	1898	ordained	resource extraction/ processing	n/a
Estelle	Greater New Orleans	CDP	1880	emergent	crossroads	n/a
Estherwood	Teche/Vermilion	village	1901	ordained	railroad	n/a
Eunice	Teche/Vermilion	city	1894	ordained	railroad	arterial increment

NAME	REGION	STATUS	ERA	TYPE	PRIMARY	SECONDARY
Evergreen	Red River Valley	town	1869	emergent	confluence/fork	n/a
Farmerville	Ouachita Valley	town	1839	emergent	crossroads	courthouse/centrality
Fenton	Western Hills	village	1890	ordained	railroad	arterial increment
Ferriday	Upper Delta	town	1903	ordained	railroad	n/a
Fisher	Western Hills	village	1899	ordained	resource extraction/ processing	railroad
Florien	Western Hills	village	1897	ordained	railroad	n/a
Floyd	Upper Delta	pop cluster	1855	ordained	courthouse/centrality	port/landing
Folsom	Eastern Florida	village	1904	ordained	resource extraction/ processing	railroad
Fordoche	Greater Baton Rouge	town	1854	emergent	port/landing	arterial increment
Forest	Upper Delta	village	1906	ordained	railroad	n/a
Forest Hill	Western Hills	village	1890	ordained	railroad	arterial increment
Fort Jesup	Red River Valley	pop cluster	1822	ordained	military	n/a
Fort Polk (Johnson)	Western Hills	CDP	1941	ordained	military	n/a
Franklin	Teche/Vermilion	city	1808	emergent	port/landing	shortcut/portage
Franklinton	Eastern Florida	town	1823	ordained	courthouse/centrality	n/a
French Settlement	Manchac/Maurepas	village	1800	emergent	port/landing	crossroads
Galliano	Lafourche/Terrebonne	CDP	1795	emergent	arterial increment	port/landing
Galveztown	Manchac/Maurepas	ghost	1778	emergent	confluence/fork	military
Gardere	Greater Baton Rouge	CDP	1905	ordained	railroad	n/a
Garyville	Lower Mississippi	CDP	1903	ordained	resource extraction/ processing	railroad
Georgetown	Ouachita Valley	village	1891	emergent	crossroads	railroad
Gibsland	Northern Hills	town	1890	ordained	railroad	crossroads
Gilbert	Ouachita Valley	village	1890	ordained	railroad	arterial increment
Gilliam	Northern Hills	village	1898	ordained	railroad	port/landing
Glenmora	Western Hills	town	1890	ordained	railroad	n/a
Golden Meadow	Lafourche/Terrebonne	town	1931	emergent	resource extraction/ processing	jumping-off point
Goldonna	Northern Hills	village	1891	ordained	resource extraction/ processing	railroad
Gonzales	Manchac/Maurepas	city	1887	emergent	port/landing	crossroads
Grambling	Northern Hills	town	1900	ordained	resource extraction/ processing	railroad
Gramercy	Lower Mississippi	town	1894	ordained	resource extraction/ processing	railroad
Grand Cane	Western Hills	village	1881	ordained	railroad	n/a
Grand Chenier	SW La/Chenier Plain	pop cluster	1845	emergent	river mouth	n/a

NAME	REGION	STATUS	ERA	TYPE	PRIMARY	SECONDARY
Grand Coteau	Teche/Vermilion	town	1821	emergent	arterial increment	crossroads
Grand Isle	Lafourche/Terrebonne	town	1795	ordained	resort	jumping-off point
Grand Terre	Lafourche/Terrebonne	ghost	1795	emergent	port/landing	jumping-off point
Gray	Lafourche/Terrebonne	CDP	1911	emergent	arterial increment	n/a
Grayson	Ouachita Valley	village	1891	ordained	railroad	n/a
Greensburg	Eastern Florida	town	1832	ordained	courthouse/centrality	n/a
Greenwell Springs	Western Florida	city	1855	ordained	resort	n/a
Greenwood	Northern Hills	town	1839	emergent	jumping-off point	crossroads
Gretna	Greater New Orleans	city	1836	emergent	port/landing	cross-river subsidiary
Grosse Tete	Atchafalaya Basin	village	1880	emergent	port/landing	n/a
Gueydan	Teche/Vermilion	town	1896	ordained	railroad	n/a
Hackberry	SW La/Chenier Plain	CDP	1894	emergent	port/landing	n/a
Hahnville	Lower Mississippi	CDP	1843	ordained	courthouse/centrality	railroad
Hall Summit	Northern Hills	village	1906	ordained	railroad	n/a
Hammond	Eastern Florida	city	1854	ordained	railroad	n/a
Harahan	Greater New Orleans	city	1914	ordained	railroad	n/a
Harrisonburg	Ouachita Valley	village	1818	emergent	port/landing	crossroads
Harvey	Greater New Orleans	CDP	1840	emergent	port/landing	cross-river subsidiary
Haughton	Northern Hills	town	1881	ordained	railroad	arterial increment
Haynesville	Northern Hills	town	1843	emergent	crossroads	railroad
Heflin	Northern Hills	village	1882	ordained	railroad	n/a
Henderson	Atchafalaya Basin	town	1935	emergent	jumping-off point	n/a
Hessmer	Red River Valley	village	1902	ordained	railroad	crossroads
Hodge	Northern Hills	village	1899	ordained	resource extraction/ processing	railroad
Holly Beach	SW La/Chenier Plain	pop cluster	1925	ordained	resort	n/a
Homer	Northern Hills	town	1849	ordained	courthouse/centrality	railroad
Hopedale	Lower Mississippi	pop cluster	1885	emergent	resource extraction/ processing	jumping-off point
Hornbeck	Western Hills	town	1897	ordained	railroad	n/a
Hosston	Northern Hills	village	1905	ordained	railroad	n/a
Houma	Lafourche/Terrebonne	city	1834	emergent	port/landing	confluence/fork
Ida	Northern Hills	village	1877	ordained	railroad	n/a
Ile de Jean Charles	Lafourche/Terrebonne	pop cluster	1830	emergent	resource extraction/ processing	jumping-off point
Independence	Eastern Florida	town	1854	ordained	railroad	n/a
Iota	Teche/Vermilion	town	1896	ordained	railroad	n/a

NAME	REGION	STATUS	ERA	TYPE	PRIMARY	SECONDARY
Iowa	SW La/Chenier Plain	town	1890	ordained	railroad	n/a
Isle Derniere	Lafourche/Terrebonne	ghost	1850	ordained	resort	n/a
Jackson	Western Florida	town	1816	ordained	courthouse/centrality	port/landing
Jamestown	Northern Hills	village	1891	ordained	railroad	crossroads
Jean Lafitte	Greater New Orleans	town	1900	emergent	resource extraction/ processing	jumping-off point
Jeanerette	Teche/Vermilion	city	1878	emergent	port/landing	arterial increment
Jena	Ouachita Valley	town	1906	ordained	railroad	courthouse/centrality
Jennings	SW La/Chenier Plain	city	1888	ordained	railroad	n/a
Jonesboro	Northern Hills	town	1860	emergent	confluence/fork	railroad
Jonesville	Ouachita Valley	town	1871	emergent	confluence/fork	railroad
Junction City	Northern Hills	village	1897	ordained	railroad	n/a
Kaplan	Teche/Vermilion	city	1902	ordained	railroad	arterial increment
Keachi	Western Hills	town	1858	emergent	crossroads	arterial increment
Kenner	Greater New Orleans	city	1854	ordained	railroad	port/landing
Kentwood	Eastern Florida	town	1854	ordained	railroad	n/a
Kilbourne	Upper Delta	village	1906	ordained	railroad	n/a
Killian	Manchac/Maurepas	village	1900	emergent	port/landing	n/a
Killona	Lower Mississippi	CDP	1890	emergent	port/landing	arterial increment
Kinder	Western Hills	town	1889	emergent	confluence/fork	railroad
Krotz Springs	Atchafalaya Basin	town	1900	emergent	resource extraction/ processing	resort
Labadieville	Lafourche/Terrebonne	CDP	1843	ordained	mission	arterial increment
Lacombe	Eastern Florida	CDP	1770	emergent	river mouth	head of lake
Lafayette	Teche/Vermilion	city	1821	emergent	head of navigation	n/a
Lafitte	Greater New Orleans	CDP	1900	emergent	resource extraction/ processing	jumping-off point
Lake Arthur	SW La/Chenier Plain	town	1840	emergent	head of lake	port/landing
Lake Charles	SW La/Chenier Plain	city	1852	emergent	port/landing	head of lake
Lake Providence	Upper Delta	town	1830	emergent	port/landing	n/a
Laplace	Lower Mississippi	CDP	1890	ordained	railroad	crossroads
Larose	Lafourche/Terrebonne	CDP	1890	emergent	port/landing	shortcut/portage
Lecompte	Red River Valley	town	1880	emergent	port/landing	railroad
Leesville	Western Hills	city	1871	emergent	crossroads	courthouse/centrality
Leonville	Atchafalaya Basin	town	1898	emergent	port/landing	shortcut/portage
Lillie	Northern Hills	village	1897	ordained	railroad	arterial increment
Lisbon	Northern Hills	village	1849	emergent	resource extraction/ processing	crossroads

NAME	REGION	STATUS	ERA	TYPE	PRIMARY	SECONDARY
Livingston	Manchac/Maurepas	town	1915	ordained	resource extraction/ processing	courthouse/centrality
Livonia	Greater Baton Rouge	town	1846	emergent	port/landing	head of navigation
Lockport	Lafourche/Terrebonne	town	1841	emergent	confluence/fork	port/landing
Logansport	Western Hills	town	1830	emergent	port/landing	resource extraction/ processing
Logtown	Ouachita Valley	pop cluster	1855	emergent	port/landing	n/a
Longstreet	Western Hills	village	1891	ordained	railroad	crossroads
Loreauville	Teche/Vermilion	village	1870	emergent	port/landing	shortcut/portage
Los Adaes	Red River Valley	ghost	1717	ordained	military	mission
Lucky	Northern Hills	village	1910	emergent	crossroads	n/a
Luling	Lower Mississippi	CDP	1890	ordained	railroad	port/landing
Lutcher	Lower Mississippi	town	1889	ordained	resource extraction/ processing	railroad
Lydia	Teche/Vermilion	CDP	1875	emergent	crossroads	arterial increment
Madisonville	Eastern Florida	town	1813	emergent	river mouth	head of lake
Mamou	Teche/Vermilion	town	1909	ordained	railroad	arterial increment
Mandeville	Eastern Florida	city	1834	ordained	resort	head of lake
Mangham	Ouachita Valley	town	1890	ordained	railroad	arterial increment
Manila Village	Lafourche/Terrebonne	ghost	1873	ordained	resource extraction/ processing	n/a
Mansfield	Western Hills	city	1843	emergent	crossroads	courthouse/centrality
Mansura	Red River Valley	town	1850	emergent	crossroads	arterial increment
Many	Red River Valley	town	1840	emergent	crossroads	courthouse/centrality
Maringouin	Atchafalaya Basin	town	1890	emergent	port/landing	arterial increment
Marion	Ouachita Valley	town	1839	emergent	crossroads	railroad
Marksville	Red River Valley	city	1780	ordained	military	crossroads
Marrero	Greater New Orleans	CDP	1880	ordained	railroad	port/landing
Martin	Northern Hills	village	1910	emergent	crossroads	n/a
Mathews	Lafourche/Terrebonne	CDP	1910	emergent	arterial increment	port/landing
Maurice	Teche/Vermilion	village	1870	emergent	crossroads	arterial increment
McNary	Western Hills	village	1913	ordained	resource extraction/ processing	railroad
Melville	Atchafalaya Basin	town	1880	emergent	port/landing	arterial increment
Mer Rouge	Ouachita Valley	village	1844	emergent	crossroads	n/a
Meraux	Lower Mississippi	CDP	1910	emergent	resource extraction/ processing	port/landing
Mermentau	SW La/Chenier Plain	village	1840	emergent	head of navigation	port/landing

NAME	REGION	STATUS	ERA	TYPE	PRIMARY	SECONDARY
Merryville	Western Hills	town	1890	emergent	resource extraction/ processing	crossroads
Midway	Ouachita Valley	CDP	1833	emergent	shortcut/portage	crossroads
Minden	Northern Hills	city	1835	emergent	arterial increment	crossroads
Moncla	Red River Valley	pop cluster	1859	emergent	port/landing	n/a
Monroe	Ouachita Valley	city	1785	ordained	military	port/landing
Montegut	Lafourche/Terrebonne	CDP	1883	emergent	confluence/fork	arterial increment
Montgomery	Red River Valley	town	1840	emergent	port/landing	n/a
Montpelier	Eastern Florida	village	1812	ordained	courthouse/centrality	crossroads
Montz	Lower Mississippi	CDP	1905	emergent	port/landing	n/a
Mooringsport	Northern Hills	town	1836	emergent	port/landing	n/a
Moreauville	Red River Valley	village	1855	emergent	port/landing	arterial increment
Morgan City	Atchafalaya Basin	city	1845	emergent	port/landing	river mouth
Morganza	Greater Baton Rouge	village	1847	emergent	port/landing	shortcut/portage
Morse	Teche/Vermilion	village	1896	ordained	railroad	arterial increment
Moss Bluff	SW La/Chenier Plain	CDP	1896	ordained	resource extraction/ processing	railroad
Mound	Upper Delta	village	1872	emergent	port/landing	shortcut/portage
Mt. Lebanon	Northern Hills	town	1836	ordained	courthouse/centrality	arterial increment
Napoleonville	Lafourche/Terrebonne	village	1813	emergent	port/landing	shortcut/portage
Natalbany	Eastern Florida	CDP	1854	ordained	railroad	arterial increment
Natchez	Red River Valley	village	1803	emergent	port/landing	shortcut/portage
Natchitoches	Red River Valley	city	1714	ordained	military	head of navigation
New Iberia	Teche/Vermilion	city	1779	emergent	head of navigation	port/landing
New Llano	Western Hills	town	1898	ordained	railroad	resource extraction/ processing
New Orleans	Greater New Orleans	city	1718	ordained	port/landing	shortcut/portage
New Roads	Greater Baton Rouge	city	1822	emergent	shortcut/portage	n/a
New Sarpy	Lower Mississippi	CDP	1875	ordained	railroad	port/landing
Newellton	Upper Delta	town	1835	emergent	port/landing	shortcut/portage
Noble	Western Hills	village	1896	emergent	crossroads	n/a
Norco	Lower Mississippi	CDP	1916	ordained	resource extraction/ processing	n/a
North Hodge	Northern Hills	village	1899	ordained	resource extraction/ processing	railroad
North Vacherie	Lower Mississippi	CDP	1770	emergent	port/landing	shortcut/portage
Norwood	Western Florida	village	1884	ordained	railroad	arterial increment
Oak Grove	Upper Delta	town	1906	ordained	railroad	courthouse/centrality

NAME	REGION	STATUS	ERA	TYPE	PRIMARY	SECONDARY
Oak Ridge	Ouachita Valley	village	1879	ordained	railroad	crossroads
Oakdale	Western Hills	city	1890	ordained	railroad	crossroads
Oberlin	Western Hills	town	1890	ordained	railroad	courthouse/centrality
Oil City	Northern Hills	town	1895	ordained	resource extraction/ processing	n/a
Old Jefferson	Greater Baton Rouge	CDP	1900	emergent	arterial increment	n/a
Olla	Ouachita Valley	town	1891	ordained	resource extraction/ processing	railroad
Opelousas	Teche/Vermilion	city	1765	ordained	military	shortcut/portage
Overton	Northern Hills	ghost	1819	emergent	port/landing	courthouse/centrality
Paincourtville	Lafourche/Terrebonne	CDP	1840	emergent	port/landing	crossroads
Palmetto	Atchafalaya Basin	village	1871	ordained	railroad	arterial increment
Paradis	Lower Mississippi	CDP	1900	ordained	railroad	arterial increment
Parks	Atchafalaya Basin	village	1900	emergent	port/landing	shortcut/portage
Patterson	Teche/Vermilion	city	1835	emergent	port/landing	shortcut/portage
Pearl River	Eastern Florida	town	1883	ordained	railroad	n/a
Pierre Part	Atchafalaya Basin	CDP	1810	emergent	head of lake	n/a
Pine Prairie	Western Hills	village	1909	ordained	railroad	n/a
Pineville	Red River Valley	city	1805	ordained	cross-river subsidiary	railroad
Pioneer	Upper Delta	village	1906	ordained	railroad	arterial increment
Pitkin	Western Hills	pop cluster	1905	ordained	resource extraction/ processing	crossroads
Plain Dealing	Northern Hills	town	1839	ordained	resource extraction/ processing	railroad
Plaquemine	Lower Mississippi	city	1817	emergent	confluence/fork	port/landing
Plaucheville	Red River Valley	village	1845	emergent	crossroads	shortcut/portage
Pleasant Hill	Western Hills	village	1846	emergent	crossroads	n/a
Pointe à la Hache	Lower Mississippi	pop cluster	1815	ordained	courthouse/centrality	port/landing
Pollock	Ouachita Valley	town	1891	ordained	resource extraction/ processing	railroad
Ponchatoula	Eastern Florida	city	1854	ordained	railroad	n/a
Port Allen	Greater Baton Rouge	city	1798	emergent	cross-river subsidiary	n/a
Port Barre	Atchafalaya Basin	town	1820	emergent	confluence/fork	jumping-off point
Port Fourchon	Lafourche/Terrebonne	pop cluster	1981	ordained	resource extraction/ processing	jumping-off point
Port Hudson	Greater Baton Rouge	pop cluster	1833	ordained	railroad	port/landing
Port Sulphur	Lower Mississippi	CDP	1933	ordained	resource extraction/ processing	n/a
Port Vincent	Manchac/Maurepas	village	1839	emergent	head of navigation	confluence/fork

NAME	REGION	STATUS	ERA	TYPE	PRIMARY	SECONDARY
Powhatan	Red River Valley	village	1887	emergent	crossroads	head of navigation
Poydras	Lower Mississippi	CDP	1848	ordained	railroad	crossroads
Provencal	Red River Valley	village	1880	ordained	railroad	crossroads
Quitman	Northern Hills	village	1900	ordained	railroad	arterial increment
Raceland	Lafourche/Terrebonne	CDP	1853	emergent	shortcut/portage	railroad
Rayne	Teche/Vermilion	city	1884	ordained	railroad	crossroads
Rayville	Ouachita Valley	town	1883	ordained	railroad	courthouse/centrality
Reeves	Western Hills	village	1906	ordained	railroad	arterial increment
Reggio	Lower Mississippi	pop cluster	1890	emergent	crossroads	resource extraction/ processing
Reserve	Lower Mississippi	CDP	1855	ordained	resource extraction/ processing	port/landing
Richmond	Upper Delta	village	1857	ordained	railroad	port/landing
Ridgecrest	Upper Delta	town	1903	ordained	railroad	arterial increment
Ringgold	Northern Hills	town	1836	emergent	arterial increment	resource extraction/ processing
Robeline	Red River Valley	village	1886	ordained	railroad	n/a
Rodessa	Northern Hills	village	1879	ordained	railroad	crossroads
Rosedale	Atchafalaya Basin	village	1875	ordained	railroad	port/landing
Roseland	Eastern Florida	town	1854	ordained	railroad	arterial increment
Rosepine	Western Hills	town	1902	ordained	railroad	resource extraction/ processing
Ruston	Northern Hills	city	1883	ordained	railroad	courthouse/centrality
Saline	Northern Hills	village	1904	ordained	resource extraction/ processing	railroad
Sarepta	Northern Hills	town	1869	emergent	Sunday town/centrality	railroad
Schriever	Lafourche/Terrebonne	CDP	1855	ordained	railroad	port/landing
Scotlandville	Greater Baton Rouge	pop cluster	1884	ordained	railroad	crossroads
Scott	Teche/Vermilion	city	1907	ordained	railroad	n/a
Shongaloo	Northern Hills	village	1850	emergent	crossroads	resource extraction/ processing
Shreveport	Red River Valley	city	1836	emergent	head of navigation	port/landing
Sibley	Northern Hills	town	1890	ordained	railroad	crossroads
Sicily Island	Ouachita Valley	village	1881	ordained	railroad	port/landing
Sikes	Northern Hills	village	1900	ordained	resource extraction/ processing	n/a
Simmesport	Red River Valley	town	1836	emergent	confluence/fork	shortcut/portage
Simpson	Western Hills	village	1850	emergent	crossroads	n/a
Simsboro	Northern Hills	village	1848	ordained	railroad	resource extraction/ processing

NAME	REGION	STATUS	ERA	TYPE	PRIMARY	SECONDARY
Singer	Western Hills	pop cluster	1898	emergent	crossroads	arterial increment
Slaughter	Western Florida	village	1884	ordained	railroad	n/a
Slidell	Eastern Florida	city	1883	ordained	railroad	n/a
Sorrento	Manchac/Maurepas	town	1905	emergent	jumping-off point	resource extraction/ processing
S. Mansfield	Western Hills	village	1905	ordained	railroad	n/a
South Vacherie	Lower Mississippi	CDP	1850	emergent	crossroads	shortcut/portage
Sparta	Northern Hills	ghost	1849	ordained	courthouse/centrality	n/a
Spearsville	Northern Hills	village	1845	emergent	crossroads	n/a
Springfield	Manchac/Maurepas	town	1763	emergent	head of navigation	port/landing
Springhill	Northern Hills	city	1894	ordained	resource extraction/ processing	railroad
St. Francisville	Western Florida	town	1775	ordained	mission	port/landing
St. Gabriel	Lower Mississippi	town	1770	emergent	port/landing	shortcut/portage
St. Joseph	Upper Delta	town	1803	emergent	port/landing	courthouse/centrality
St. Martinville	Teche/Vermilion	city	1811	emergent	Sunday town/centrality	port/landing
St. Rose	Lower Mississippi	CDP	1889	emergent	port/landing	n/a
Stanley	Western Hills	village	1850	emergent	crossroads	n/a
Starks	SW La/Chenier Plain	pop cluster	1860	emergent	crossroads	resource extraction/ processing
Sterlington	Ouachita Valley	town	1845	emergent	confluence/fork	port/landing
Stonewall	Western Hills	town	1880	ordained	railroad	crossroads
Sugartown	Western Hills	pop cluster	1840	emergent	crossroads	arterial increment
Sulphur	SW La/Chenier Plain	city	1865	ordained	resource extraction/ processing	railroad
Sun	Eastern Florida	village	1907	ordained	railroad	arterial increment
Sunset	Teche/Vermilion	town	1880	ordained	railroad	n/a
Supreme	Lafourche/Terrebonne	CDP	1895	emergent	port/landing	n/a
Swartz	Ouachita Valley	CDP	1890	ordained	resource extraction/ processing	railroad
Taft	Lower Mississippi	CDP	1905	emergent	arterial increment	n/a
Talisheek	Eastern Florida	pop cluster	1907	ordained	railroad	arterial increment
Tallulah	Upper Delta	city	1854	ordained	railroad	n/a
Tangipahoa	Eastern Florida	village	1854	ordained	railroad	n/a
Thibodaux	Lafourche/Terrebonne	city	1820	emergent	confluence/fork	port/landing
Tickfaw	Eastern Florida	village	1854	ordained	railroad	n/a
Tullos	Ouachita Valley	town	1891	ordained	railroad	resource extraction/ processing
Tunica	Western Florida	pop cluster	1820	emergent	port/landing	n/a

NAME	REGION	STATUS	ERA	TYPE	PRIMARY	SECONDARY
Turkey Creek	Western Hills	village	1909	ordained	railroad	arterial increment
Urania	Ouachita Valley	town	1891	ordained	railroad	crossroads
Varnado	Eastern Florida	village	1907	ordained	railroad	arterial increment
Venice	Lower Mississippi	CDP	1840	emergent	resource extraction/ processing	jumping-off point
Vidalia	Upper Delta	town	1798	emergent	cross-river subsidiary	military
Vienna	Northern Hills	town	1838	emergent	arterial increment	courthouse/centrality
Ville Platte	Teche/Vermilion	city	1824	emergent	crossroads	arterial increment
Vinton	SW La/Chenier Plain	town	1888	ordained	railroad	resource extraction/ processing
Violet	Lower Mississippi	CDP	1875	emergent	confluence/fork	port/landing
Vivian	Northern Hills	town	1898	ordained	railroad	crossroads
Waggaman	Lower Mississippi	CDP	1880	emergent	port/landing	railroad
Wakefield	Western Florida	pop cluster	1838	emergent	arterial increment	n/a
Walker	Greater Baton Rouge	town	1876	emergent	port/landing	n/a
Wallace	Lower Mississippi	CDP	1885	emergent	port/landing	arterial increment
Washington	Teche/Vermilion	town	1820	emergent	head of navigation	confluence/fork
Waterproof	Upper Delta	town	1835	emergent	port/landing	shortcut/portage
Welsh	SW La/Chenier Plain	town	1890	ordained	railroad	arterial increment
West Monroe	Ouachita Valley	city	1819	emergent	cross-river subsidiary	port/landing
Westlake	SW La/Chenier Plain	city	1845	ordained	resource extraction/ processing	port/landing
Westwego	Greater New Orleans	city	1870	ordained	railroad	port/landing
Weyanoke	Western Florida	pop cluster	1905	emergent	crossroads	arterial increment
White Castle	Lower Mississippi	town	1885	ordained	resource extraction/ processing	port/landing
Wilson	Western Florida	village	1884	ordained	railroad	arterial increment
Winnfield	Northern Hills	city	1852	emergent	crossroads	courthouse/centrality
Winnsboro	Ouachita Valley	city	1843	ordained	courthouse/centrality	n/a
Wisner	Ouachita Valley	town	1890	ordained	railroad	arterial increment
Woodworth	Western Hills	town	1890	ordained	railroad	arterial increment
Yellow Pine	Northern Hills	pop cluster	1891	ordained	resource extraction/ processing	railroad
Yscloskey	Lower Mississippi	pop cluster	1848	ordained	resource extraction/ processing	jumping-off point
Zachary	Greater Baton Rouge	city	1884	ordained	railroad	n/a
Zwolle	Western Hills	town	1773	ordained	mission	railroad

NOTES

Introduction

1. Robert E. Dickinson, "The Scope and Status of Urban Geography: An Assessment," *Land Economics* 24, no. 3 (August 1948): 223.

2. Richard M. Hurd, *Principles of City Land Values* (1903; reprint, New York: The Record and Guide, 1924), 13–24.

3. B. J. Garner, "Models of Urban Geography and Settlement Location," in *Socio-Economic Models in Geography,* ed. R. J. Chorley and P. Haggett (London: Methuen, 1967), 304–305.

4. Griffith Taylor, *Urban Geography: A Study of Site, Evolution, Pattern and Classification in Villages, Towns and Cities* (New York: Dutton, 1946), 233–242.

5. Leslie J. King, *Central Place Theory* (India: SAGE Publications, 1984), 44–49.

6. Milton B. Newton Jr., *Louisiana: A Geographical Portrait,* 2nd ed. (Baton Rouge: Geoforensics, 1987), 106.

7. For an overview of the emergence of Louisiana's civil parishes and courthouse site selection and architecture, see Carl A. Brasseaux, Glenn R. Conrad, and R. Warren Robison, *The Courthouses of Louisiana—USL Architecture Series No. 1* (Lafayette: Center for Louisiana Studies, University of Southwestern Louisiana, 1980), particularly 15–18.

8. Zachary Howser, "A Binding and Perpetual Obligation: Protecting Louisiana's Sixteenth Section Land as a Natural Resource," *LSU Journal of Energy Law and Resources* 2, no. 2 (Spring 2014): 363.

9. Fourteen communities investigated in this book coincide with Sixteenth Section land, including Raceland, Mansfield, Baldwin, Brusly, Labadieville, Melville, St. Joseph, Leonville, Waterproof, Montgomery, Hornbeck, Georgetown, Delta, and Taft. GIS analysis by author, using section data from the Louisiana State Lands Office.

10. René-Robert Cavelier, Sieur de La Salle, as quoted by Francis Parkman in *La Salle and the Discovery of the Great West* (Boston, MA: Little, Brown, 1896), 286–287.

11. Happily, siting stories often appear in town logos, welcome signs, or downtown murals, likely because their spatial nature makes them conducive to illustration.

12. Assessing cities by their functions, the authors of one such text wrote that "Oxford, England is a university town; Rochester, Minnesota is a health-care town; Norfolk, Virginia is a military town; Canberra, Australia is a government town; and Cancún, Mexico is a tourist town." However, if we assessed their initial siting rationales, Oxford would be deemed a confluence site; Rochester, a stagecoach stop; Norfolk, a port and harbor; Canberra, a farming and ranching center; and Cancún, a resource extraction (fishing) site. Such is the difference between urban function and siting story. Stanley D. Brunn, Donald J. Zeigler, Maureen Hays-Mitchell, and Jessica K. Graybill, eds., *Cities of the World: Regional Patterns and Urban Environment* (Lanham, MD: Rowman and Littlefield, 2020), 17–18.

13. Overview, Lawrason Act, Louisiana Revised Statutes, January 2019, https://app.lla.state.la.us/llala.nsf/BC353E94C499B01086257AB800697A27/$FILE/Lawrason%20Act%20FAQ.pdf (accessed September 23, 2022).

1. Greater New Orleans

1. *Ouquódky* was documented in the 1707 account and map of Lamhatty, as interpreted by David I. Bushnell Jr., "The Account of Lamhatty," *American Anthropologist,* New Series 10, no. 4 (October–December 1908): 571.

2. C. C. Robin, *Voyage to Louisiana, 1803–1805,* abridged translation of 1807 publication by Stuart O. Landry Jr. (New Orleans: Pelican, 1966), 31.

3. Samuel R. Brown, *The Western Gazetteer or Emigrant's Directory, Containing a Geographical Description of the Western States and Territories* (Auburn, NY: H. C. Southwick, 1817), 117 and 141.

4. Adam Mandelman, *The Place with No Edge: An Intimate History of People, Technology, and the Mississippi River Delta* (Baton Rouge: Louisiana State Univ. Press, 2020), 100.

5. M. Cavelier de La Salle, "Memoir of M. Cavelier de La Salle," in *On the Discovery of the Mississippi,* ed. Thomas Falconer (London: 1844, translation of 1680s original), page 4 of appendix; Joseph G. Tregle Jr., "The Lower Mississippi," in *The Rivers and Bayous of Louisiana,* ed. Edwin Adams Davis (Baton Rouge: Louisiana Education Research Association, 1968), 146.

6. M. Cavelier de La Salle, "Memoir of M. Cavelier de La Salle," in *On the Discovery of the Mississippi,* ed. Thomas Falconer (London: 1844, translation of 1680s original), appendix: 3–4, 24–27.

7. Daniel H. Usner, "American Indians in New Orleans: Native Communities Were Integral to the City's Foundation," in *New Orleans and the World: The Tricentennial Anthology,* ed. Nancy Dixon (New Orleans: Louisiana Endowment for the Humanities, 2017), 13–16; Fred B. Kniffen, Hiram F. Gregory, and George A. Stokes, *The Historic Indian Tribes of Louisiana, from 1542 to the Present* (Baton Rouge: Louisiana State Univ. Press, 1987), 52–57, 123; presentations at "Indigenous Spaces, French Expectations: Exploring Exchanges Between Native and Non-Native Peoples in Louisiana," New Orleans Center for the Gulf South Symposium, March 14, 2018.

8. Tristram R. Kidder, "Making the City Inevitable: Native Americans and the Geography of New Orleans," in *Transforming New Orleans and Its Environs: Centuries of Change,* ed. Craig Colten (Pittsburgh, Pennsylvania: Univ. of Pittsburgh Press, 2000), 13; Kniffen, Gregory, and Stokes, *The Historic Indian Tribes of Louisiana,* 20. See also "Indian Economies" in Fred B. Kniffen and Sam Bowers Hilliard, *Louisiana: Its Land and People* (Baton Rouge: Louisiana State Univ. Press, 1988), 107.

9. Spanish surveyor Carlos Trudeau, 1803, as quoted in Betsy Swanson, *Terre Haute de Barataria: An Historic Upland on an Old River Distributary Overtaken by Forest in the Barataria Unit of the Jean Lafitte National Historic Park and Preserve* (Harahan, LA: Jefferson Parish Historical Commission Monograph XI, 1991), 17.

10. Pierre Le Moyne, Sieur d'Iberville, quoted in Le Cercle Historique, *French Colonial Foundations of Pointe Coupée: 1680s–1740s,* conference proceeding of the First Annual Forum of the Foundations of Community, Pointe Coupée et Environs Series, October 14, 2006, 33.

11. Pierre Le Moyne, Sieur d'Iberville, *Iberville's Gulf Journals,* ed. Richebourg Gaillard McWilliams (Tuscaloosa: Univ. of Alabama Press, 1991, translation of 1700 journal), 52–54.

12. d'Iberville, *Iberville's Gulf Journals,* 57.

13. Charles N. Elliott, "A Geography of Power: French and Indian Alliances on the Southeast Louisiana Frontier," in *A Fierce and Fractious Frontier: The Curious Development of Louisiana's Florida Parishes, 1699–2000,* ed. Samuel C. Hyde Jr. (Baton Rouge: Louisiana State Univ. Press, 2004), 24–27; Clare D'Artois Leeper, *Louisiana Place Names: Popular, Unusual, and Forgotten Stories of Towns, Cities, Plantations, Bayous, and Even Some Cemeteries* (Baton Rouge: Louisiana State Univ. Press, 2012), 156.

14. d'Iberville, *Iberville's Gulf Journals*, 111.

15. Tregle, "The Lower Mississippi," 145.

16. Lawrence N. Powell, *The Accidental City: Improvising New Orleans* (Cambridge, MA: Harvard Univ. Press, 2011), 28.

17. Quoted in Marc de Villiers du Terrage, "A History of the Foundation of New Orleans (1717–1722)," *Louisiana Historical Quarterly* 3, no. 2 (April 1920): 174 (emphasis in original). The September 1717 date is obscured in the register, but ancillary information indicates it was September 9.

18. Jonathan Darby, "New Orleans, The Capital of the Colony and the Seat of Government and the Courts of Justice," translated by Rev. Conrad M. Widman, S.J., and published in "Some Southern Cities (in the U.S.) about 1750," *Records of the American Catholic Historical Society of Philadelphia* 10 (1899): 202; Jonathan Darby, quoted in Shannon Lee Dawdy, *Madame John's Legacy (160R51) Revisited: A Closer Look at the Archeology of Colonial New Orleans* (New Orleans: Friends of the Cabildo, 1998), 26–29; *Journal Historique Concernant l'Establissement de la Louisiane, tiré des Mémoires Originaux par le Chevalier de Beaurain, géographe ordinaire du Roy,* as quoted in the *Relation de Pénicaut,* in Pierre Margry, *Découvertes et Établissements Des Français Dans L'Ouest et Dans Le Sud de L'Amérique Septentrionale, 1614–1754,* vol. 5 (Paris, France: D. Jouaust, 1875), 549, footnote.

19. "Instruction Pour M. Perrier, Ingenieur en Chef de la Louisiane, 14 Avril 1718," in Pierre Margry, *Découvertes et Établissements Des Français Dans L'Ouest et Dans Le Sud de L'Amérique Septentrionale (1614–1754)—Mémoires et Documents Originaux* (1875), 605.

20. Richard Campanella, "A Year After Foundation, New Orleans' First Flood—and Levees," *Times-Picayune,* April 7, 2019.

21. Le Blond de La Tour, quoted in Samuel Wilson Jr., *The Vieux Carre, New Orleans—Its Plan, Its Growth, Its Architecture* (New Orleans: City of New Orleans, 1969), 1; Richard Campanella, *Bourbon Street: A History* (Baton Rouge: Louisiana State Univ. Press, 2014), 10–14.

22. Marc de Villiers du Terrage, "A History of the Foundation of New Orleans (1717–1722)," *Louisiana Historical Quarterly* 3, no. 2 (April 1920): 223.

23. Villiers du Terrage, "A History of the Foundation of New Orleans (1717–1722)," 222–229.

24. Letter, Bienville to the Council, February 1, 1723, *Mississippi Provincial Archives 1704–1743: French Dominion,* vol. 3, ed. Dunbar Rowland and Albert Godfrey Sanders (Jackson: Mississippi Department of Archives and History, 1932), 343–44.

25. Richard Campanella, *Bienville's Dilemma: A Historical Geography of New Orleans* (Lafayette: Univ. of Louisiana Press, 2008).

26. M. Perrin Du Lac, *Travels Through the Two Louisianas . . . in 1801, 1802, & 1803* (London, 1807), 87–88 plus asterisked footnote. Despite his defense, Du Lac was not impressed with the city. "New Orleans," he wrote, "does not merit a favourable description."

27. Friedrich Ratzel, *Sketches of Urban and Cultural Life in North America,* trans. and ed. Stewart A. Stehlin (New Brunswick, New Jersey: Rutgers Univ. Press, 1988, translation of 1876 publication), 196 (emphasis added).

28. Erin M. Greenwald, "Arriving Africans and a Changing New Orleans," in *New Orleans in the Founding Era,* ed. Erin Greenwald and trans. Henry Colomer (New Orleans: The Historic New Orleans Collection, 2018), 104.

29. Mark Ballard, "Bills Would Allow Algiers to Secede from City of New Orleans; Here's What's Next," *Baton Rouge Advocate,* May 15, 2015, http://www.theadvocate.com/baton_rouge/news/politics/legislature/article_aa9ddc81-1442-56f9-a9ae-4dcc171811ae.html (accessed September 29, 2018).

30. Richard Campanella, *The West Bank of Greater New Orleans: A Historical Geography* (Baton Rouge: Louisiana State Univ. Press, 2020). Population figures reflect the 2020 U.S. Census.

31. Richard Campanella, "Today's Lafitte Greenway Was Spanish New Orleans' Carondelet Canal," *Times-Picayune,* November 17, 2017; Richard Campanella, "185-Year-Old New Basin Canal Continues to Affect Thousands of New Orleanians," *Times-Picayune,* December 8, 2017.

32. Thomas A. Becnel, *The Barrow Family and the Barataria and Lafourche Canal: The Transportation Revolution in Louisiana, 1829–1925* (Baton Rouge: Louisiana State Univ. Press, 1989).

33. William D. Reeves, *Harvey: The Canal, the Family, the Community, Written in Honor of the 100th Anniversary of the Harvey Canal Limited Partnership* (Harvey, LA: Harvey Land and Improvement Co., 1998); William D. Reeves, "Destrehan/Harvey History Manuscript-Binder 1" (manuscript, Farnet Family Collection), chapter 2, "Nicholas Noel Destrehan: from Destrehan to Harvey," 15.

34. David Fritz and Sally K. Reeves, *Algiers Point: Historical Ambience and Property Analysis of Squares Ten, Thirteen, and Twenty, with a View Toward Their Archaeological Potential* (New Orleans: U.S. Army Corps of Engineers, June 1984), 60.

35. R. Christopher Goodwin and Associates, *Cultural Resources Survey of Gretna Phase II Levee Enlargement Item M-99.4 to 95.5-R, Jefferson Parish, Louisiana* (New Orleans: U.S. Army Corps of Engineers, 1990), 28.

36. "Ferries," *A. Mygatt & Co.'s New Orleans Business Directory for 1858* (New Orleans: A. Mygatt and Co., 1858), xxxix.

37. Richard Campanella, "Electric Avenue: Our Own Champs-Élysées [Elysian Fields] Was Once Extraordinary—and Could Be Again," *Times-Picayune,* June 10, 2018.

38. J. Ben Meyer Sr., "Railroads of the Delta," in *Plaquemines: The Empire Parish* (New Orleans: LaBorde Printing Company, 1981), 75–77; J. H. Colton's maps from 1855 and 1863 and other cartographic sources courtesy of the Library of Congress.

39. Richard Campanella, "Lost Coastal Communities of Eastern New Orleans," *Times-Picayune,* January 5, 2020.

40. Richard Campanella, "Bucktown and the Lost Bayous of East Jefferson," *Times-Picayune,* February 3, 2020.

41. 1896 Rand McNally Company map of Louisiana, courtesy of the Library of Congress.

42. Craig A. Bauer, *An Untractable Country: The History of Kenner, Louisiana* (Lafayette: Univ. of Louisiana Press, 2016), 66–70; Craig A. Bauer, "From Burnt Canes to Budding City: A History of the City of Kenner, Louisiana," *Louisiana History* 23, no. 4 (Autumn 1982): 353–381, quote on 371.

43. "Kenner Project—The Nation's Greatest Asset," *Manufacturer's Record,* March 27, 1913, 197; Richard Campanella, *Draining New Orleans: The 300-Year Quest to Dewater the Crescent City* (Baton Rouge: Louisiana State Univ. Press, 2023).

44. Walter Pritchard, "A Forgotten Louisiana Engineer: G. W. R. Bayley and His 'History of the Railroads of Louisiana,'" *Louisiana Historical Quarterly* 30, no. 4 (October 1947): 1262–1271.

2. The Lower Mississippi River

1. David Goldfield, *Region, Race, and Cities: Interpreting the Urban South* (Baton Rouge: Louisiana State Univ. Press, 1997), 45.

2. Newton, *Louisiana: A Geographical Portrait,* 134.

3. Richard Campanella, *Time and Place in New Orleans: Past Geographies in the Present Day* (Gretna, LA: Pelican, 2002); Richard Campanella, "Why Prytania Jogs at Joseph," *Preservation in Print,* October 2013, 18–19.

4. J. W. Dorr, "A Tourist's Description of Louisiana in 1860," ed. Walter Pritchard, *Louisiana Historical Quarterly* 21 (January–October 1938): 1113.

5. That flatboatman was Abraham Lincoln, recalling his 1828 voyage to New Orleans from Rockport, Indiana. Abraham Lincoln, "Autobiography Written for John L. Scripps," June 1860, *Collected Works,* vol. 4, ed. Roy P. Basler (New Brunswick, New Jersey: Rutgers Univ. Press, 1953), 62.

6. Maps courtesy of the Library of Congress.

7. Charter of the Company of the West, 1717, quoted in Mary Ann Sternberg, *Along the River Road: Past and Present on Louisiana's Historic Byway* (Baton Rouge: Louisiana State Univ. Press, 2001), 29.

8. Pierre Clément de Laussat, *Memoirs of My Life* (1831; trans. Baton Rouge: Louisiana State Univ. Press and The Historic New Orleans Collection, 1978), 67. The church in question was today's St. Louis Cathedral in New Orleans.

9. The confusing dual system lasted until 1845, when counties were abandoned; Louisiana has had parishes only ever since. Richard Campanella, "A Mysterious Switch: Louisiana's Change from Counties to Parishes," *Louisiana Cultural Vistas* (Spring 2017): 58–59.

10. Alcée Fortier, *Louisiana—Comprising Sketches of Parishes, Towns, Events, Institutions, and Persons, Arranged in Cyclopedia Form,* vol. 2 (1914), 317–318.

11. "Croatian President to Celebrate Opening of New Cultural Center," *Times-Picayune,* September 20, 2023, 2G (Crescent City section).

12. René Le Conte, "The Germans in Louisiana in the Eighteenth Century," 1924 article trans. by Glenn R. Conrad, *Louisiana History* 8, no. 1 (Winter 1967): 77; Charles R. Maduell Jr., *The Census Tables for the French Colony of Louisiana from 1699 to 1732* (Baltimore, MD: Genealogical Pub. Co., 1972), vii, 39; Ellen C. Merrill, *Germans of Louisiana* (Gretna, LA: Pelican, 2005), 24.

13. Quoted in Lubin F. Laurent, "History of St. John the Baptist Parish," *Louisiana Historical Quarterly,* ed. Henry P. Dart, 7 (January-October 1924): 317–321.

14. Dorr, "A Tourist's Description of Louisiana in 1860," 1116–1117; Mary Ann Sternberg, *Along the River Road: Past and Present on Louisiana's Historic Byway* (Baton Rouge: Louisiana State Univ. Press, 2013), 294–295.

15. William de Marigny Hyland, *Tour of Historic Saint Bernard Parish* (St. Bernard Parish/Los Isleños Museum Complex, 2012), 44–45.

16. William S. Ward, *Diary* [of Flatboat Trip from New Albany, Indiana to New Orleans, Louisiana, 1839], The Historic New Orleans Collection, Accession Number 2009.0139, 64–69. Historically, "Bonnet Quarre" (Bonnet Carré) referred to today's Reserve, while "Bonnet Quarre Church" was across the river, down from today's Edgard. The term once broadly connoted the resemblance of this bend of the river to a woman's square bonnet, and today is exclusively used to refer to the Bonnet Carré Spillway.

17. Sternberg, *Along the River Road,* 306–308.

18. The term "Arcady" was used regularly by Catharine Cole (a.k.a. Martha R. Field), who toured the state by buggy, boat, and train and wrote numerous dispatches for the *Daily Picayune* in the 1880s and 1890s. Martha R. Field, *Louisiana Voyages: The Travel Writings of Catharine Cole,* ed. Joan B. McLaughlin and Jack McLaughlin (Jackson: Univ. Press of Mississippi, 2006).

19. Field, *Louisiana Voyages,* 46.

20. Alcée Fortier, *Louisiana—Comprising Sketches of Parishes, Towns, Events, Institutions, and Persons,* vol. 1 (Century Historical Association, 1914), 284; Marie McDowell Pilkington Campbell, *Nostalgic Notes of St. James Parish, Then and Now* (Baton Rouge: Instant Print Centers, 1981); Sternberg, *Along the River Road*; and other sources.

21. *Plaquemine* comes from *placminier,* the French Creole derivation of the Illinois indigenous word *piakimin,* meaning "persimmon," the fruit of a tree native to Louisiana. Claire D'Artois Leeper, "Plaquemine," March 20, 1960, in *Louisiana Places—A Collection of the Columns from the Baton Rouge Sunday Advocate, 1960–1974* (Baton Rouge: Legacy Pub. Co., 1976), 186.

22. d'Iberville, *Iberville's Gulf Journals,* 64

23. Thomas Ashe, 1806, quoted in Sidney Albert Marchand, *The Story of Ascension Parish, Louisiana* (Donaldsonville, LA: J. E. Ortlieb, 1931), 49; *Biographical and Historical Memoirs of Louisiana,* vol. 1 (Chicago, IL: Goodspeed Pub. Co., 1892), 135.

24. "Iberville," *New-Orleans Daily Chronicle,* September 13, 1819.

25. Richard L. Forstall, *Population of States and Counties of the United States, 1790–1990* (Washington, D.C.: Department of Commerce, U.S. Bureau of the Census, Population Division, 1996), 71.

26. *Biographical and Historical Memoirs of Louisiana,* 1:134–135.

27. "Iberville," *New-Orleans Daily Chronicle,* September 13, 1819; Atchafalaya Water Heritage Trail, "Bayou Plaquemine—Plaquemine Lock State Historic Site" interpretative display, Plaquemine Lock State Historic Site, Plaquemine, Louisiana, visited July 18, 2019.

28. Based on the research of D. E. Frazier and others, as reviewed by Roger T. Saucier, *Geomorphology and Quaternary Geologic History of the Lower Mississippi Valley,* vol. 1 (Vicksburg, MS: U.S. Army Engineer Waterways Experiment Station, 1994), 141, 255, 276–286.

29. Thomas Ashe, 1806, quoted Marchand, *The Story of Ascension Parish, Louisiana,* 49.

30. *Barthélemy Lafon in New Orleans, 1792–1820,* report by Jay D. Edwards, Ina Fandrich, and Gabriele Richardson (Baton Rouge: Louisiana Division of Historic Preservation, 2019), 58, 62, 231; Leeper, *Louisiana Place Names,* 82; Fortier, *Louisiana—Comprising Sketches of Parishes, Towns, Events, Institutions, and Persons,* 1:45; Marchand, *The Story of Ascension Parish, Louisiana,* 49.

31. Marchand, *The Story of Ascension Parish, Louisiana,* 49–99.

32. "New River Post office is on the left bank of the river, eight miles above Donaldsonville and 90 miles from New Orleans," wrote J. W. Dorr in 1860. "At New River, there is a Presbyterian Church," quoted in Sternberg, *Along the River Road,* 185.

33. The Malagueños and Granadinos, so named because they were Iberian *peninsulares* as opposed to islanders, would eventually settle in New Iberia in south-central Louisiana.

34. Hyland, *Tour of Historic Saint Bernard Parish,* 23.

35. Gilbert C. Din, *Populating the Barrera: Spanish Immigration Efforts in Colonial Louisiana* (Lafayette: Univ. of Louisiana Press, 2014), 153–159.

36. Meyer, "Railroads of the Delta," 75–77; J. H. Colten's maps from 1855 and 1863 and other cartographic sources courtesy of the Library of Congress

37. Louisiana—Hahnville/Luling Topographic Map, U.S. Geological Survey, 1892 through 1983, and other cartographic sources; "Luling Town History," from *L'Observateur,* in *River Current Magazine* (January 2000), posted on St. Charles Parish Virtual Museum, https://scphistory.org/luling-town-history/ (accessed August 27, 2022.

38. Laurent, "History of St. John the Baptist Parish," 329. Sixty years after the flood, the Army Corps of Engineers installed the Bonnet Carré Spillway within the crevasse, designed to release excess river water into the lake—a remedy to the problematic "levees only" policy.

39. Louisiana—Bonnet Carré Topographic Map, U.S. Geological Survey, 1892 (surveyed in 1890), and other cartographic sources; Sternberg, *Along the River Road,* 133–134.

40. Frank M. Lovrich, "The Social System of a Rural Yugoslav-American Community: Oysterville" (Ph.D. diss., South Dakota State University, 1963), 3. Lovrich coined the name Oysterville to protect the privacy of his subjects.

41. Frank M. Lovrich, "The Dalmatian Yugoslavs in Louisiana," *Louisiana History* 8, no. 2 (Spring 1967): 160–161; William Richard Stringfield, *Le Pays Des Fleurs Oranges (The Land of Orange Blossoms): A Genealogical Study of Eight Creole Families of Plaquemines Parish* (Plaquemines Parish, LA: Gateway Press, 1989), excerpted online, http://files.usgwarchives.net/la/plaquemines/history/book/chapter4a.txt (accessed August 31, 2022).

42. Leeper, "Venice," January 14, 1973, in *Louisiana Places,* 244; sign at the end of the road in Venice, visited December 31, 2023.

43. J. Ben Meyer Sr., "The Sulphur Story," in *Plaquemines: The Empire Parish,* 84–85, and other sources.

44. Donna Fricker, "Historic Context: The Louisiana Lumber Boom, c. 1880–1925," report published by Fricker Historic Preservation Services LLC, available at https://www.crt.state.la.us (accessed September 1, 2022); Paul Wallace Gates, "Federal Land Policy in the South 1866–1888," *Journal of Southern History* 6, no. 3 (August 1940): 303–330, https://www.jstor.org/stable/2192139.

45. "Lutcher Town: An Example of the Growth of Louisiana," *Daily Picayune,* December 30, 1895, 10; Fricker, "Historic Context: The Louisiana Lumber Boom, c. 1880–1925," 15; and other sources.

46. Shelley N. C. Holl, "A Shrine to Woodier Times in Garyville," *Times-Picayune,* September 2, 1994.

47. Laurent, "History of St. John the Baptist Parish," 330–331; Holl, "A Shrine to Woodier Times in Garyville"; Sternberg, *Along the River Road,* 142–143.

48. Peter M. Wolf, *The Sugar King: Leon Godchaux: A New Orleans Legend, His Creole Slave, and His Jewish Roots* (Xlibris: Peter M. Wolf, 2022), 125–135.

49. Wolf, *The Sugar King,* 176.

50. Gerald J. Keller, quoted in Wolf, *The Sugar King,* 179.

51. R. Christopher Goodwin and Associates, *Historic Resources Survey of Reserve Historic District* (Jefferson, LA: R. Christopher Goodwin and Associates, 2018), 9–16.

52. George P. Meade, quoted in Campbell, *Nostalgic Notes of St. James Parish, Then and Now,* 266; "The Gramercy Refinery. Golden Grove Plantation the Site Selected," *Daily Picayune,* May 22, 1895.

53. "Longer than Any City Block: Cares and Responsibilities of the Man Who Directs Great Transfer Barge at Harahan," *Times-Picayune,* May 14, 1916, 52; Federal Writers' Project of the Works Progress Administration, *New Orleans City Guide* (Boston, MA: Houghton Mifflin, 1938); U.S. Department of the Interior, U.S. Geological Survey, *Louisiana—New Orleans Quadrangle, N.W. Quarter and N.E. Quarter* (1932).

54. "Buy Bridge-Head Lots at Belt City," *New Orleans States,* March 14, 1926, 20.

55. René Pierre Meric Jr. and Philip J. Meric, *Avondale, A Model for Success: The Story of a Great American Shipyard* (New Orleans: Philip J. Meric Consulting, 2015), xi–3.

56. Darin Acosta, "The Petrochemical Industrial Complex of the St. Charles Parish Industrial Corridor and Its Influence on Urbanization Patterns" (Master's thesis, University of New Orleans, 2010), 2.

57. Barbara Allen, "The Popular Geography of Illness in the Industrial Corridor," and Raymond J. Burby, "Baton Rouge: The Making (and Breaking) of a Petrochemical Paradise," both in *Transforming New Orleans and Its Environs: Centuries of Change,* ed. Craig E. Colten (Pittsburgh, Pennsylvania: Univ. of Pittsburgh Press, 2000), 160–201, and other sources.

58. Sternberg, *Along the River Road,* 122–124; Acosta, "The Petrochemical Industrial Complex," 31; Adrien Persac, *Norman's Chart of the Lower Mississippi River* (New Orleans: B. M. Norman, 1858).

59. "Black residents of Diamond Win Fight with Shell Chemical for Relocation 1989–2002—Case Study Detail," Global Nonviolent Action Database, https://nvdatabase.swarthmore.edu (accessed September 7, 2022).

60. Norco and Diamond population figures computed by author using block-level data from the 2020 U.S. Census.

61. Edward McPherson, "Judicial Decisions and Opinions: The Louisiana Slaughter-House Cases," *Hand-Book of Politics for 1874: Being a Record of Important Political Action, National and State, from July 15, 1872 to July 15, 1874* (Washington, D.C., 1874), 41.

62. This was the *Canal des Pecheurs,* or Fishermen's Canal, which at the time formed the parish line. In 1875, the state legislature passed an act to redraw the Orleans/St. Bernard Parish line, from "Canal des Pecheurs, or Fishermen's canal, (to) the lower line of the property known and used as the United States Barracks"—that is, Jackson Barracks, where the parish line remains today.

63. Ronald M. Labbé and Jonathan Lurie, *The Slaughterhouse Cases: Regulation, Reconstruction, and the Fourteenth Amendment* (Lawrence: Univ. Press of Kansas, 2003), 120–22, 163.

64. Hyland, *Tour of Historic Saint Bernard Parish,* 7–8; *St. Bernard Parish: Its Natural Resources and Advantages* (St. Bernard Parish, LA: Parish Immigration League, 1906).

65. Alcée Fortier, *Louisiana—Comprising Sketches of Parishes, Towns, Events, Institutions, and Persons,* vol. 3 (Century Historical Association, 1914), 504–505.

66. *Report of the Sanitary Commission of New Orleans on the Epidemic Yellow Fever of 1853* (New Orleans: City Council of New Orleans, 1854), viii. This leper colony had existed at least since the 1790s,

when the Carondelet Canal was cut near "the high lands of the Lepers," along the Metairie or Gentilly Ridge by Bayou St. John. François-Xavier Martin, *Orleans Term Reports, or Cases Argued and Determined in the Superior Court of the Territory of Orleans,* vol. 2 (New Orleans: Roche Brothers, 1813), 12.

67. "Louisiana's Lepers—A New Colony Where All the Afflicted Are to Be Segregated," *Catholic Standard,* February 1895, article exhibited at the National Hansen's Disease Museum, Carville, Louisiana, visited December 21, 2022.

68. Drawn from documents and exhibits at the National Hansen's Disease Museum, Carville, Louisiana, visited December 21, 2022.

69. "Louisiana's Lepers," *Catholic Standard,* February 1895.

3. Bayou Lafourche, Bayou Terrebonne, and the Barataria-Terrebonne Basins

1. Iberville (1699) quoted in Elliott, "A Geography of Power," 23; Elisée Reclus, "An Anarchist in the Old South: Elisée Reclus' Voyage to New Orleans, Part II," trans. Camille Martin and John Clark, in *Mesechabe: The Journal of Surre(gion)alism,* no. 12 (Winter 1993–1994) (New Orleans, LA), 19; John McPhee, *The Control of Nature* (New York: Farrar, Straus and Giroux, 1989), 5.

2. Saucier, *Geomorphology and Quaternary Geologic History of the Lower Mississippi Valley,* 1:141, 255, 276–286.

3. Field, *Louisiana Voyages,* 81.

4. Harnett T. Kane, *The Bayous of Louisiana* (New York: Bonanza Books, 1943), 143.

5. Kane, *The Bayous of Louisiana,* 147.

6. This is today's Jackson Street in downtown Thibodaux. David D. Plater, "The Builders: Master Carpenters of the Ante-Bellum Lafourche," draft manuscript reviewed by Richard Campanella for David D. Plater of Thibodaux, Louisiana, introduction and first chapter, June 2023.

7. Tanya B. Ditto, *The Longest Street: A Story of Lafourche Parish and Grand Isle* (Baton Rouge: Moran Publishing, 1980), 42; Janis Meyer Lasseigne, "Thibodaux Timelines, 1803–1969," in *The Lafourche Country III: Annals and Onwardness,* eds. John P. Doucet and Stephen S. Michot (Thibodaux, LA: Lafourche Heritage Society, 2010), 84–85; Plater, "The Builders," introduction and first chapter.

8. Louisiana Historical Records Survey—Service Division, Work Projects Administration, *Inventory of the Municipal Archives of Louisiana—Town of Thibodaux* (Baton Rouge: Department of Archives, Louisiana State University, 1942), 1 to 6.

9. Field, *Louisiana Voyages,* 85–86.

10. Kane, *The Bayous of Louisiana,* 144.

11. Michael Caron, "The Chinese," *Mississippi Delta Ethnographic Overview* (Baton Rouge: National Park Service and National Council for the Traditional Arts, 1979, 365; Betsy Swanson, *Historic Jefferson Parish: From Shore to Shore* (Gretna, LA: Pelican, 1975), 137–138.

12. "New Orleans' Chinese Captains of Industry," *Daily Picayune,* July 2, 1911, 14.

13. Lafcadio Hearn, "Saint Maló: A Lacustrine Village in Louisiana," quoted in S. Frederick Starr, *Inventing New Orleans: Writings of Lafcadio Hearn* (Jackson: Univ. Press of Mississippi, 2001), 85–86.

14. "A Chinese Colony on the Swampy Lands Bordering the Gulf, That Lives by Drying Shrimp," *Daily States,* November 12, 1899.

15. R. Christopher Goodwin and Associates, *Cultural Resources Survey of Bayou Dularge Disposal Areas, Terrebonne Parish, Louisiana* (New Orleans, LA: U.S. Army Corps of Engineers—New Orleans District, 1998), 15.

16. Christopher Everette Cenac and Claire Domangue Joller, *Eyes of an Eagle: Jean-Pierre Cenac, Patriarch—An Illustrated History of Early Houma-Terrebonne* (Houma, LA: JPC, 2011), 81–87.

17. Lynn M. Alperin, *History of the Gulf Intracoastal Waterway* (Washington, D.C.: National Waterways Study, U.S. Army Engineer Water Resources Support Center/Institute for Water Resources, January 1983), U.S. Census Bureau statistics, and other sources.

18. Hurd, *Principles of City Land Values,* 13–24.

19. Jeffrey J. LeBlanc, *The Story of Lockport* (Lockport, Louisiana, 1959), 10.

20. Ditto, *The Longest Street,* 52–55; Becnel, *The Barrow Family and the Barataria and Lafourche Canal,* 1–3; Campanella, *The West Bank of Greater New Orleans.*

21. "Notice . . . The Harang Canal," *Daily Picayune,* January 31, 1877.

22. Leeper, *Louisiana Place Names,* 55; Lafourche Heritage Society historic plaques, "Larose, Circa 1846" and "Our Lady of the Rosary Catholic Church," Larose, Louisiana; U.S. Geological Survey, Cut-Off Sheet, 1892; and other sources.

23. Ditto, *The Longest Street,* 57.

24. Philip S. Rose, "Lifting Farms Out of Water: Beginning a Big New Series About Power Farming in the South," *Country Gentleman: A Journal for the Farm, the Garden and the Fireside* 84, no. 24 (June 14, 1919): 3–4, 29.

25. *Annual Report of the Board of Swamp Land Commissioners to the Legislature of the State of Louisiana, January 1860* (Baton Rouge: J. M. Taylor, 1860), letter from Civil Engineer Joseph Gorlinski dated July 15, 1859, 75; Roland Guidry and Lou Anna Guidry, "The Cut Off Canal and the War of 1812," in *The Lafourche Country III: Annals and Onwardness,* eds. John P. Doucet and Stephen S. Michot (Thibodaux, LA: Lafourche Heritage Society, 2010), 82–83.

26. As per sources cited by Leeper in "Cut Off," December 26, 1971, in *Louisiana Places,* 74; Ditto, *The Longest Street,* 60–61.

27. According to an 1863 map of the Atchafalaya Basin, the Attakapas Canal was actually a natural distributary rendered into a navigation canal, more so than a manmade canal dug to connect with a distributary. This Civil War–era chart shows the Attakapas Canal as a wending waterway with hardly any straight segments, starting from Napoleonville and terminating at what is now Attakapas Landing in Lake Verret. Henry L. Abbot, Department of the Gulf Map No. 8, Atchafalaya Basin, February 8, 1863.

28. Field, *Louisiana Voyages,* 92; Sam F. Gilbert, *History of the Town of Napoleonville* (Napoleonville, Louisiana, 1936), 1–9; Leeper, "Napoleonville," June 2, 1968, in *Louisiana Places,* 167.

29. Residents of Thibodaux rejected the railroad over concerns of noise and grime. Company officials instead routed the tracks south of town, activating new station-stop settlements at Theriot, Ewing, Rousseau, Thibodaux Junction, and Donner, and new crossroads communities at Lafourche Crossing, Schriever, Chacahoula, and Gibson.

30. Kane, *The Bayous of Louisiana,* 215; Ditto, *The Longest Street,* 48–51; Martin Lynn Cortez and Lee Roy Rybiski, *Memories: A Story of Raceland and Bowie* (Raceland, LA: Raceland Jaycees, 1980), 1–20; U.S. Geological Survey topographic maps, Lac des Allemands Sheet, 1891–1892; and other sources.

31. Donald W. Davis, *Washed Away? The Invisible People of Louisiana's Wetland* (Lafayette: Univ. of Louisiana Press, 2010), 255.

32. Jeanne Rome, "A History of Golden Meadow," in *The Lafourche Country II: The Heritage and Its Keepers,* eds. Stephen S. Michot and John P. Douchet (Lafourche Heritage Society, 1996), 71–73, and other sources.

33. A. J. Liebling, *The Earl of Louisiana* (New York: Ballantine Books, 1960), 69.

34. J. Daniel D'Oney, "The Houma Nation: A Historiographical Overview," *Louisiana History* 47, no. 1 (Winter 2006): 64–65.

35. "Our History—Dulac Community Center," http://www.dulaccommunitycenter.org/about-us.html (accessed October 20, 2022); Davis, *Washed Away?,* 253.

36. Démé Naquin Jr., interview with Tristan Baurick, "Louisiana Tribe Forced to Leave 'Paradise,'" *Times-Picayune,* January 21, 2024. Built in Schriever between Houma and Thibodaux, "New Isle, the country's first federally funded resettlement site for a community threatened by climate change," opened in 2022 with free homes for tribal members displaced from Isle de Jean Charles

after Hurricane Isaac in 2012, and is currently slated for expansion. Not coincidentally, Cocodrie's Louisiana Universities Marine Consortium (LUMCON) is also gradually relocating its operations to Houma. Tristan Baurick, "Climate Resettlement Site Grows Beyond First Batch of Homes," *Times-Picayune,* November 18, 2023.

37. Lawrence N. Powell, *The Accidental City: Improvising New Orleans* (Cambridge, MA: Harvard Univ. Press, 2011), 101.

38. William C. Davis, *The Pirates Laffite: The Treacherous World of the Corsairs of the Gulf* (New York: Harcourt, 2005), 56–57; Robert C. Vogel, "The Patterson and Ross Raid on Barataria, September 1814," *Louisiana History* 33, no. 2 (Spring 1992): 160; William D. Reeves and Daniel Alario Sr., *Westwego: From Cheniere to Canal* (Harahan, LA: Jefferson Parish Historical Series, Monograph XIV, 1996), 5; Davis, *Washed Away?,* 219–200.

39. Vogel, "The Patterson and Ross Raid on Barataria, September 1814," 168; Sally Kittredge Evans, Frederick Stielow, and Betsy Swanson, *Grand Isle on the Gulf—An Early History* (Metairie, LA: Jefferson Parish Historical Commission, 1979), 20, 30–32.

40. Evans, Stielow, and Swanson, *Grand Isle on the Gulf,* 11–19, 31, quotes from 82 and 93.

41. Loulan J. Pitre, "A Late Nineteenth-Century Coastal Cajun Community: Chênière Caminada *Avant L'Ouragan,*" in *The Lafourche Country II: The Heritage and Its Keepers,* eds. Stephen S. Michot and John P. Douchet (Lafourche Heritage Society, 1996), 53–56; Evans, Stielow, and Swanson, *Grand Isle on the Gulf,* 21.

42. Field, *Louisiana Voyages,* 18.

43. Rose C. Falls, *Cheniere Caminada, or, The Wind of Death: The Story of the Storm in Louisiana* (New Orleans: Hopkins Printing Office, 1893), 8–17, 57; "The State Engineers Make a Full Report," *Daily Picayune,* April 30, 1894, 8.

44. Jason Theriot, "Building America's First Offshore Oil Port: LOOP," *Journal of American History* 99 no. 1 (May 2012): 190.

45. "Port Fourchon," https://portfourchon.com/seaport/ (accessed October 22, 2022).

4. Greater Baton Rouge and Pointe Coupée

1. "An Inland Seaport," exhibit at Louisiana State Museum, Baton Rouge, visited October 28, 2023.

2. Newton, *Louisiana: A Geographical Portrait,* 241. Wrote Newton on the changing character of Baton Route: "only with the first election of Gov. [Edwin] Edwards," a Cajun from Avoyelles Parish who took office in 1972, "did the people of the capital begin to adopt French pretensions, such as Mardi Gras, fleur d'lis on street signs, and the serving of jambalaya and gumbo at Chamber of Commerce promotions."

3. Le Cercle Historique, *French Colonial Foundations of Pointe Coupée, 1680s–1740s,* conference proceeding of the First Annual Forum of the Foundations of Community, Pointe Coupée et Environs Series, October 14, 2006, 22, 27; Rose Meyers, *A History of Baton Rouge, 1699–1812* (Baton Rouge: Louisiana State Univ. Press/Baton Rouge Bicentennial Corporation, 1999), 7–21.

4. Fabel, "Boom in the Bayous," 47–57.

5. Meyers, *A History of Baton Rouge,* 21–41.

6. To this day, Baton Rouge is a head of navigation for oceangoing vessels, thanks to river conditions as well as the limited air draft of its two bridges.

7. Meyers, *A History of Baton Rouge,* 42–51.

8. Richard Campanella, "Grandeur on Government Street: Baroque Urban Planning in Louisiana's Capital," *Louisiana Cultural Vistas* (Summer 2018): 52–53; Vicente Sebastián Pintado, Map of Louisiana, Spanish West Florida, 1805, courtesy of the Library of Congress.

9. "Some miles below the mouth of the Red River," wrote François Marie Perrin Du Lac in 1802, "is a small fort of Baton-rouge, occupied by some Spanish soldiers, under the command

of a sub-lieutenant. This fort is of so little importance, and the number of inhabitants so small, that I shall not delay the time in mentioning it." Fourteen years later, a flatboatman jotted in his journal, "Tuesday Oct. 22[d]., Got under way at daylight, and passed *Baton rouge* at 8 oclock. This is a village and Military post on the Left bank. . . . It is a mean [crude] village, irregularly built [by] the ruins of the old fort." M. Perrin Du Lac, *Travels Through the Two Louisianas . . . in 1801, 1802, & 1803* (London: Richard Phillips, 1807), 85; Edwin Adams Davis and John C. L. Andreassen, "From Louisville to New Orleans in 1816: Diary of William Newton Mercer," *Journal of Southern History* 2, no. 3 (August 1936): 401–402.

10. Richard Campanella, "How 'Forward Thrust' Reshaped Southern Geography," *Louisiana Cultural Vistas* (Winter 2014–2015): 42–43; Richard Campanella, "'Oft-forgotten Florida Purchase,' 200 Years Ago This Month, Gave Louisiana Its Distinctive Boot Shape," *Times-Picayune/New Orleans Advocate,* February 10, 2019, 1.

11. Vadim Rossman, *Capital Cities: Varieties and Patterns of Development and Relocation* (London: Routledge Research in Planning and Urban Design, 2017); Campanella, "How 'Forward Thrust' Reshaped Southern Geography," 42–43.

12. Gleaned from various historical maps, including the circa 1840s Public Lands Survey map on file with the Louisiana State Land Office, accessible through the online SONRIS mapping system; *Norman's Chart of the Lower Mississippi River* ("Persac Map") of 1858, courtesy of the Library of Congress; *Map of the Region East and North of Baton Rouge, Showing Batteries on the Mississippi North of Port Hudson* of 1863, also from the Library of Congress; and the Baton Rouge quadrangle of the U.S. Geological Survey, surveyed in 1906.

13. Annabelle M. Armstrong, *Historic Neighborhoods of Baton Rouge* (Charleston, SC: History Press, 2010), 18–19, 76–77, as well as previously cited maps.

14. Livingston Parish American Revolution Bicentennial Committee, *The Free State—A History and Place-Names Study of Livingston Parish* (Livingston Parish Police Jury and the Louisiana American Revolution Bicentennial Commission, 1976), http://files.usgwarchives.net/la/livingston/history/placename/bentonsf.txt (accessed September 23, 2022); "Historical Timeline of Denham Springs," Denham Springs Main Street, https://www.denhamspringsmainstreet.org/ (accessed September 23, 2022).

15. Gleaned from various historical maps, including the circa 1840s Public Lands Survey map on file with the Louisiana State Land Office, accessible through the online SONRIS mapping system; *Norman's Chart of the lower Mississippi River* ("Persac Map") of 1858, available through the Library of Congress; *Map of the Region East and North of Baton Rouge, Showing Batteries on the Mississippi North of Port Hudson* of 1863, also from the Library of Congress; and the Baton Rouge quadrangle of the U.S. Geological Survey, surveyed in 1906, which depict the identified enclaves.

16. Samuel H. Lockett, "Report of the Topographical Survey of Part of Louisiana, Made During the Months of July and August 1869," in *Biennial Report of the Louisiana State University and Agricultural and Mechanical College to the General Assembly of the State of Louisiana* (New Orleans: J. O. Nixon, State Printer, 1869), 68.

17. As recounted in "April Meeting of Historical Society Held; Rise and Fall of Greenwell Springs is Discussed," *Baton Rouge States-Times,* April 28, 1917, 2, transcribed by the Louisiana Works Progress Administration.

18. Public Lands Survey map (1840s) on file with the Louisiana State Land Office, accessible through the online SONRIS mapping system; *Map of the Region East and North of Baton Rouge, Showing Batteries on the Mississippi North of Port Hudson* of 1863, Library of Congress; Baton Rouge and adjacent quadrangles of the U.S. Geological Survey, surveyed in 1906; Richard Campanella, "The Ozone Belt: How St. Tammany Parish Turned 'Ecological Services' into Good Business—But for the Wrong Reasons," *Times-Picayune,* July 10, 2015; and other sources.

19. Richard Campanella, "The Flow and Ebb of Bayou Metairie," *Times-Picayune,* March 10, 2017.

20. Quoted in Olivia McClure, "Ten Years After Becoming a City, Central Is Growing but Getting by with 2% Sales Tax, 3 City Employees," *Baton Rouge Advocate,* originally published in 2015, updated January 9, 2018.

21. Carl L. Bankston III and Stephen J. Caldas, *Controls and Choices: The Educational Marketplace and the Failure of School Desegregation* (Landham, MD: Rowman and Littlefield, 2015), 42–44; City of Central website, www.centralgov.com/page/why-central (accessed September 16, 2022); U.S. Census Bureau; and other sources.

22. The same may soon be said of St. George, which in April 2024 finally won legal approval to incorporate. "The new city of St. George will include at least 86,000 residents between Essen Lane and the southeast parish line, making it one of the largest cities in the state. It will also be East Baton Rouge Parish's fifth city, along with Baton Rouge, Central, Baker and Zachary." Lara Nicholson and Charles Lussier, "With Louisiana Supreme Court Ruling Paving the Way for City of St. George, How Will It Operate?," *Baton Rouge Advocate,* April 27, 2024.

23. "The Bridge at Benton's Ferry," *Baton Rouge Daily Comet,* June 25, 1856.

24. "Hotels—Amite Springs," *Daily Picayune,* August 7, 1856.

25. "Historical Timeline of Denham Springs," https://www.denhamspringsmainstreet.org/denham-springs-timeline (accessed September 23, 2022).

26. A 1732 map places Ste. Reyne on a bend of the Mississippi that aligns more with the mouth of Thompson's Creek. If accurate, then Ste. Reyne, which most sources associate with St. Francisville, may in fact be the antecedent of Port Jackson. Jean-Baptiste Bourguignon d'Anville, *Carte De la Louisiane par Le Sr. D'Anville Dressee en Mai 1732, publiee en 1752,* map of Louisiana made in 1732 and published in 1752, courtesy of the Library of Congress

27. V. Elaine Thompson, *Clinton, Louisiana: Society, Politics, and Race Relations in a Nineteenth-Century Southern Small Town* (Lafayette: Univ. of Louisiana Press, 2014), 12–14; "Map of Louisiana" in *Morse's North American Atlas* (New York: Harper and Brothers, 1842), courtesy of the Library of Congress.

28. Stanley Clisby Arthur, *The Story of The West Florida Rebellion* (Baton Rouge: Claitor's, 1975), 28; Virginia Lobdell Jennings, *The Plains and The People: A History of Upper East Baton Rouge Parish* (Baton Rouge: Claitor's, 1974), 42–44; Henry Skipwith, *East Feliciana, Louisiana Past and Present: Sketches of the Pioneers* (New Orleans: Hopkins' Printing Office, 1892), 5, 8; James A. Greene Jr., "Where Was the Town of Port Jackson?," *Louisiana Archaeological Society Newsletter* 37, no. 2 (2009): 13.

29. Milledge L. Bonham Jr., *Man and Nature at Port Hudson, 1863, 1917,* booklet reprinted for the Preservation of the Port Hudson Battlefield, January 1, 1965, 1–2.

30. Jennings, *The Plains and the People,* and other sources.

31. Jennings, *The Plains and the People,* 1.

32. Zachary Bicentennial Committee, *Zachary Faces and Places: A History of the City of Zachary, Louisiana* (Zachary, LA: Zachary Bicentennial Committee, 1976), 3–4.

33. Richard Campanella, "Baker's Long-Lost Leland College Was Uptown's First University," *Times Picayune/New Orleans Advocate,* December 7, 2020; Lawrence E. Estaville Jr., "A Small Contribution: Louisiana's Short Rural Railroads in the Civil War," *Louisiana History* 18, no. 1 (Winter 1977): 87–103; and various cartographic sources.

34. "No Valid Complaint," *Daily Picayune,* February 21, 1914, 5, quoting in part Governor Luther Hall; Charles Vincent, *A Centennial History of Southern University and A&M College, 1880–1980* (Baton Rouge: Moran Publishing, 1981), 13–14, 78–80.

35. Exhibit, "Port Allen: 100 Years of Progress," West Baton Rouge Museum, Port Allen, Louisiana; "300 Years of History—New Settlements," West Baton Rouge Museum, https://wbrparish.org/957/New-Settlements (accessed December 12, 2023); Quinn Welsch, "Museum Showcases the History of the City," *West Side Journal,* September 15, 2016, https://www.thewestsidejournal.com/ (accessed September 17, 2022); National Register of Historic Places Registration Form, "Stone

Square Lodge No. 8 (Port Allen, Louisiana)" (Washington, D.C.: U.S. Department of the Interior, National Park Service, 2021); and other sources.

36. Exhibit, "Port Allen: 100 Years of Progress," West Baton Rouge Museum, Port Allen, Louisiana; historical marker, "Sunrise," erected at site.

37. Fortier, *Louisiana—Comprising Sketches of Parishes, Towns, Events, Institutions, and Persons,* 2:625–627 (West Baton Rouge Parish entry); "City of Port Allen—History," https://www.portallen.org/history/ (accessed August 9, 2022).

38. Hilgard O'Reilly Sternberg, "A Contribution to the Geomorphology of the False River Area, Louisiana" (Ph.D. diss., Louisiana State University, 1956), ix; Brian J. Costello, *A History of Pointe Coupée Parish, Louisiana* (Donaldsonville, LA: Margaret Media, 2010), 12–15.

39. Costello, *A History of Pointe Coupée Parish, Louisiana,* 18–27.

40. Roger Baudier, *The Catholic Church in Louisiana* (1939), quoted in Le Cercle Historique in *Foundations of Pointe Coupée: 1738–1769,* conference proceeding of the Second Annual Forum of Foundations of Community, Pointe Coupée et Environs Series, October 6, 2007, 18.

41. D'Anville, *Carte De la Louisiane*; Costello, *A History of Pointe Coupée Parish, Louisiana,* 18–34.

42. Captain Philip Pittman, *Present State of the European Settlements on the Mississippi,* written in 1764, published in 1770, and quoted in Le Cercle Historique in *Foundations of Pointe Coupée, 1738–1769,* conference proceeding of the Second Annual Forum of Foundations of Community: Pointe Coupée et Environs Series, October 6, 2007, 35.

43. Costello, *A History of Pointe Coupée Parish, Louisiana,* 18–34, 63–66; Jack D. L. Holmes, *A Guide to Spanish Louisiana 1762–1806* (New Orleans: Louisiana Collection Series of Books and Documents on Colonial Louisiana, 1970), 4–5; Gwendolyn Midlo Hall, "The 1795 Slave Conspiracy in Pointe Coupée: Impact of the French Revolution," *Proceedings of the Meeting of the French Colonial Historical Society* 15 (1992): 130–141; Ulysses S. Ricard Jr., "The Pointe Coupée Slave Conspiracy of 1791," *Proceedings of the Meeting of the French Colonial Historical Society* 15 (1992): 118.

44. Costello, *A History of Pointe Coupée Parish, Louisiana,* 63.

45. Based on my field research and conversations with residents in June–July 2023.

46. J. H. Colton map of 1855, courtesy of the Library of Congress; U.S. Geological Survey, Fordoche Quadrangle (1935), which labels "Head of Navigation" at Livonia; "Livonia Mounds," historical plaque in Livonia, https://www.hmdb.org/m.asp?m=112094 (accessed May 30, 2023).

47. Railroad communities, many now surviving in name only, gleaned from 1906 to 1935 U.S. Geological Survey quadrangles; see also Costello, *A History of Pointe Coupée Parish, Louisiana,* 159–161; Reid Wilson, "Each State's Population Center, Visualized," *The Hill,* December 30, 2021, https://thehill.com/homenews/state-watch/587666-each-states-population-center-visualized/ (accessed May 31, 2023); False River Park visited by author in 2017 and 2023.

5. The Western Florida Parishes

1. *Wold* is an old English term for a wooded uplift, also known as a *cuesta* (incline) in Spanish. Both terms are used in Louisiana geography.

2. Edward Teas, Julia Ideson, and Sanford W. Higginbotham, "A Trading Trip to Natchez and New Orleans, 1822: Diary of Thomas S. Teas," *Journal of Southern History* 7, no. 3 (August 1941): 388–389.

3. Samuel C. Hyde Jr., "Introduction," in Hyde, ed., *A Fierce and Fractious Frontier,* 2.

4. Richard Campanella, "'Oft-forgotten Florida Purchase,' 200 Years Ago This Month, Gave Louisiana Its Distinctive Boot Shape," *Times-Picayune,* February 10, 2019.

5. D'Anville, *Carte de la Louisiane* (Map of Louisiana), made in 1732 and published in 1752; Coastal Environments, *The Lost River Town: History and Archeology of Bayou Sara* (Baton Rouge: Federal Emergency Management Administration, 2019), 1.

6. Louise Butler, "West Feliciana: A Glimpse of Its History," *Louisiana Historical Quarterly* 7, no. 1 (January 1924): 97.

7. The D'Anville map of 1732 places Ste. Reyne closer to the mouth of Thompson's Creek, in which case it might have been the future Port Jackson, which later disappeared with the creation of Port Hudson—itself also practically a ghost town today. D'Anville, *Carte de la Louisiane* (Map of Louisiana), made in 1732 and published in 1752; Costello, *A History of Pointe Coupée Parish, Louisiana,* 19.

8. Gilbert C. Din, "The Irish Mission to West Florida," *Louisiana History* 12, no. 4 (Autumn 1971): 315, 320; Butler, "West Feliciana," 92–93; Arthur, *The Story of The West Florida Rebellion.*

9. Edwin Adams Davis, *Plantation Life in the Florida Parishes of Louisiana, 1836–1846, as Reflected in the Diary of Bennet H. Barrow* (New York: AMS Press, 1967), 55–56; John Whitling Hall, "Louisiana Survey Systems: Their Antecedents, Distribution, and Characteristics" (Ph.D. diss., Louisiana State University, 1970), 67–80.

10. Brown, *The Western Gazetteer or Emigrant's Directory,* 123.

11. Davis and Andreassen, "From Louisville to New Orleans in 1816: Diary of William Newton Mercer," 401; Teas, Ideson, and Higginbotham, "A Trading Trip to Natchez and New Orleans, 1822," 389–390; Arthur, *The Story of The West Florida Rebellion*; Coastal Environments, *The Lost River Town,* 1.

12. *Louisiana Journal,* October 22, 1825, quoted Davis, *Plantation Life in the Florida Parishes of Louisiana, 1836–1846,* 7–8.

13. "The Historic West Feliciana Railroad," exhibit at Bayou Sara, and Wilkinson County Museum in Woodville, visited on July 4–5, 2023.

14. Earle D. Ross, "A Travelogue of 1849," *Mississippi Valley Historical Review* 27, no. 3 (December 1940): 438.

15. Davis, *Plantation Life in the Florida Parishes of Louisiana, 1836–1846,* 8.

16. Coastal Environments, *The Lost River Town,* 8.

17. Tradition holds that Jackson camped at Buncombe en route back to Tennessee following the victory, and locals returned the honor by renaming their town for him. But historian Powell A. Casey makes the case that Jackson and his entourage took their victory procession from New Orleans up the River Road to Natchez, not through Buncombe. Jackson did, however, later advocate to blaze roads through the area. Powell A. Casey, "Military Roads in the Florida Parishes of Louisiana," *Louisiana History* 15, no. 3 (Summer 1974): 234–236; Skipwith, *East Feliciana, Louisiana Past and Present,* 5–8

18. Village elders writing in 1889 implied that early Jackson had a general store known as Cochran & Rhea's as well as "old Fort [and] Mission House," but it appears their memories referred to the separate settlement of Port Jackson, located fifteen miles down Thompson's Creek, where it emptied into the Mississippi. Port Jackson disappeared following the rise of Port Hudson, and its exact site is something of a mystery today. Skipwith, *East Feliciana, Louisiana Past and Present,* 5–8; Greene, "Where Was the Town of Port Jackson?," 13.

19. Skipwith, *East Feliciana, Louisiana Past and Present,* 23–24. Emphasis in the original.

20. Skipwith, *East Feliciana, Louisiana Past and Present,* 5–8; National Register of Historic Places Nomination, "Jackson Historic District" (Washington, D.C.: U.S. Department of the Interior, National Park Service, 1980); Leeper, *Louisiana Place Names,* 131.

21. Skipwith, *East Feliciana, Louisiana Past and Present,* 59.

22. "Town History," Town of Clinton, https://www.townofclintonla.com/town-history (accessed April 21, 2023); Leeper, *Louisiana Place Names,* 68; Henry Schenck Tanner map of 1851, courtesy of the Library of Congress.

23. Skipwith, *East Feliciana, Louisiana Past and Present,* 60.

24. Skipwith, *East Feliciana, Louisiana Past and Present,* 18.

25. Fortier, *Louisiana—Comprising Sketches of Parishes, Towns, Events, Institutions, and Persons,*

2:632; Bayou Sara Quadrangle Map, U.S. Geological Survey, 1906; National Register of Historic Places Registration Form, "Weyanoke" (Washington, D.C.: U.S. Department of the Interior, 1990), 2–6; National Register of Historic Places Inventory—Nomination Form, "Live Oak, Weyanoke, Louisiana" (Washington, D.C.: U.S. Department of the Interior, 1977), 5–6.

26. Marianne Fisher-Giorlando and Chris Turner-Neal, "Angola: Fact and Fiction," *64 Parishes*, https://64parishes.org/angola-fact-and-fiction (accessed April 26, 2023).

27. Joanne Ryan and Stephanie L. Perrault, *Angola: Plantation to Penitentiary* (New Orleans: U.S. Army Corps of Engineers, 2007), 8.

28. New Roads has been Louisiana's population centroid at least since the 2000 census, after which researchers placed a medallion in a local park to mark this theoretical center of balance of all Louisianians. Reid Wilson, "Each State's Population Center, Visualized," *The Hill*, December 30, 2021, https://thehill.com/homenews/state-watch/587666-each-states-population-center-visualized/ (accessed April 27, 2023).

29. Ryan and Perrault, *Angola*; National Register of Historic Places Nomination, "Red Hat Cell Block, Louisiana State Penitentiary" (Washington, D.C.: U.S. Department of the Interior, 2003); "History of the State Penitentiary," Louisiana Prison Museum and Cultural Center, https://www.angolamuseum.org/history-of-angola (accessed April 25, 2023).

30. Skipwith, *East Feliciana, Louisiana Past and Present*, 12–13; *Biographical and Historical Memoirs of Louisiana*, 1:236; Leeper, *Louisiana Place Names*, 231.

31. Skipwith, *East Feliciana, Louisiana Past and Present*, 18.

32. Fortier, *Louisiana—Comprising Sketches of Parishes, Towns, Events, Institutions, and Persons*, 1:232–233.

33. Quoted from an Illinois Central brass medallion mounted on a rock by the train station in Hammond, Louisiana.

6. Bayou Manchac and the Maurepas Basin

1. Elliott, "A Geography of Power," 16.

2. "Instruction Pour M. Perrier, Ingenieur en Chef de la Louisiane, 14 Avril 1718," in Pierre Margry, *Découvertes et Établissements Des Français Dans L'Quest et Dans Le Sud de L'Amérique Septentrionale (1614–1754)—Mémoires et Documents Originaux* (Paris, France: Imprimerie D. Jouaust, 1875), 605, translation by author.

3. Fabel, "Boom in the Bayous," 47–57.

4. Gilbert C. Din, *Francisco Bouligny: A Bourbon Soldier in Spanish Louisiana* (Baton Rouge: Louisiana State Univ. Press, 1993), 94–95.

5. Gilbert C. Din, *The Canary Islanders of Louisiana* (Baton Rouge: Louisiana State Univ. Press, 1999), 28–45; Marchand, *The Story of Ascension Parish, Louisiana*, 41–42; Leeper, "Galveztown," March 18, 1962, in *Louisiana Places*, 105.

6. Marchand, *The Story of Ascension Parish, Louisiana*, 42–44.

7. H. Thompson Brown, *Ascension Parish, Louisiana: Her Resources, Advantages and Attractions* (Donaldsonville, LA: Donaldsonville Chief Print, 1888), 19.

8. Livingston Parish American Revolution Bicentennial Committee, *The Free State—A History and Place-Names Study of Livingston Parish*, as quoted and supplemented by Mercy Cambre, Pam Lass, and Jonnie Doris and republished in "Village of Port Vincent History," https://portvincent-la.gov/history/ (accessed October 1, 2022).

9. The community of Amite appears as "Amita" on the 1814 Mathew Carey map of Louisiana, Library of Congress.

10. John Snead, Richard P. McCulloh, and Paul V. Heinrich, *Landforms of the Louisiana Coastal Plain* (Baton Rouge: Louisiana Geological Survey, 2019), 27.

11. Brown, *Ascension Parish, Louisiana,* 6–7; "The Houmas Land Claim: A Letter from John Claiborne, Esq., to the Hon. C. T. Bemiss Accompanied by a Letter from the Hon. John Slidell to Mr. Claiborne" (New Orleans: Delta Mammoth Job Office, 1859).

12. Emilie Katherine Johnson, "'System, Papa, in Everything': Plantation Networks in the late Antebellum Deep South" (Ph.D. diss., University of Virginia, 2013), 55 (footnote).

13. Marchand, *The Story of Ascension Parish, Louisiana,* 117.

14. See map, "Examples of Road Networks—Section Line Roads on Regular Sections," in Milton B. Newton Jr, *Atlas of Louisiana—A Guide for Students* (Baton Rouge: School of Geoscience, Louisiana State University, 1972), unpaginated.

15. Marchand, *The Story of Ascension Parish, Louisiana,* 103, 167; "Prairieville Cemetery," Ascension Parish historic marker at Prairieville Cemetery, https://www.hmdb.org/m.asp?m=86105 (accessed April 20, 2023).

16. Brown, *Ascension Parish, Louisiana,* 17–18.

17. "Railroad Development Great; Three Roads Building This Way," *Daily Picayune,* September 1, 1905.

18. That law is what made the Yazoo & Mississippi Valley Railroad change the name of its New River station to Geismar, the latter being the name of the community's post office. Marchand, *The Story of Ascension Parish, Louisiana,* 158.

19. Marchand, *The Story of Ascension Parish, Louisiana,* 158–163.

20. Marchand, *The Story of Ascension Parish, Louisiana,* 117.

21. "Celebration of the Advent of Another Louisiana Red Cypress Company," *American Lumberman,* April 29, 1911, 43–44, 54; Betty Simoneaux, town clerk of Sorrento, interviewed by Clare D'Artois Leeper and published in *Louisiana Places,* 221; Marchand, *The Story of Ascension Parish, Louisiana,* 168; "Sorrento History," Town of Sorrento, http://www.sorrentola.gov/about-us.html (accessed October 5, 2022).

22. Newton, *Louisiana: A Geographical Portrait,* 304.

23. Statistical analysis by Richard Campanella, based on information in text and data in appendix; see the final chapter for more synoptical analyses of Louisiana siting stories.

7. The Eastern Florida Parishes

1. Frederick S. Ellis, *St. Tammany Parish: L'Autre Côté Du Lac* (Gretna, LA: Pelican, 1981), 30–31; David I. Bushnell Jr., *The Choctaw of Bayou Lacomb, St. Tammany Parish, Louisiana* (Washington, D.C.: Smithsonian Institution, Bureau of American Ethnology, Bulletin 48, 1909), 1–7.

2. Elliott, "A Geography of Power," 18–19.

3. Bushnell, *The Choctaw of Bayou Lacomb, St. Tammany Parish, Louisiana,* 1–7 and plate 1 (Ross map); "Indian Village," historical plaque in Slidell, Louisiana https://www.hmdb.org/m.asp?m=127953 (accessed April 29, 2023).

4. Bayou Lacombe Bicentennial Commission, *Bayou Lacombe* (Lacombe, LA: 1976), 2–4.

5. Le Page du Pratz, *The History of Louisiana,* 1774 English translation of 1758 original republished in 1976 by Louisiana State Univ. Press, 217; Ellis, *St. Tammany Parish,* 33–41.

6. Jacob Blackwell, *Observations on West Florida* (1766), quoted Ellis, *St. Tammany Parish,* 45.

7. Blackwell, *Observations on West Florida,* quoted Ellis, *St. Tammany Parish,* 43–47; see also 58.

8. Brown, *The Western Gazetteer or Emigrant's Directory,* 125–126; Ellis, *St. Tammany Parish,* 58–60, 65–67, 87.

9. Ellis, *St. Tammany Parish,* 69.

10. National Register of Historic Places Inventory—Nomination Form, "Division of St. John History District—Covington Historic District" (Washington, D.C.: U.S. Department of the Interior, National Park Service, 1981), 7; C. Howard Nichols, "Covington History," City of Covington, https://

www.covla.com/covington-history/ (accessed May 10, 2023); C. Howard Nichols, ed., *Stories of a River Town: Covington, Louisiana at Two Hundred Years* (Covington, LA: Red Bluff Press, 2014), 128–129.

11. Casey, "Military Roads in the Florida Parishes of Louisiana," 229–230.

12. "About 1856 it was observed that some of the wells and springs in and around Covington possessed medicinal qualities. Since then the town has been the resort of invalids, not only the water but the climate and atmospheric conditions being conducive to health." Billed as the "heart of the Ozone Belt," Covington's health-tourism economy lasted well into the twentieth century. *Biographical and Historical Memoirs of Louisiana,* 2:203.

13. William Darby, *A Geographical Description of the State of Louisiana, the Southern Part of the State of Mississippi, and the Territory of Alabama* (New York: James Olmstead, 1817), 96; Casey, "Military Roads in the Florida Parishes of Louisiana," 235–241; Robert W. Hastings, *The Lakes of Pontchartrain: Their History and Environments* (Jackson: Univ. Press of Mississippi, 2009), 53; exhibits at the Maritime Museum of Louisiana (formerly the Lake Pontchartrain Basin Maritime Museum) in Madisonville, visited in December 2015 and July 2023.

14. Brown, *The Western Gazetteer or Emigrant's Directory,* 125–126.

15. Sara Pagones, "Longtime Madisonville Mayor Dies," *Times-Picayune,* November 30, 2023, Living section, 1; exhibits at the Maritime Museum of Louisiana (formerly the Lake Pontchartrain Basin Maritime Museum) in Madisonville, visited in December 2015 and July 2023; and other sources.

16. Hyde, "Introduction," 2–3.

17. Casey, "Military Roads in the Florida Parishes of Louisiana," 229–241.

18. That same 1820 map marks "Walkers Mill" to the northwest of the old courthouse, not too far from General Carroll's Road, indicating that the topography near present-day Franklinton had enough hydraulic head to power a mill to grind corn—though the mill was not enough to attract a settlement. John Melish map of 1820, courtesy of the Library of Congress; Ellis, *St. Tammany Parish,* 78–81; Tracy O. Joseph, Richard D. Lamb III, Lisha C. Landry, Shayna B. Morvant, Kimberly R. Silas, and Amani C. Perkins, "Louisiana's Historic Courthouses: A Look at the Past and Present," *Louisiana Bar Journal* 64, no. 1 (June/July 2016): 32–33.

19. John Melish map of 1820 and Finley map of 1827, courtesy of the Library of Congress.

20. Leeper, *Louisiana Place Names,* 236.

21. John Melish map of 1820, courtesy of the Library of Congress; "Montpelier," historic plaque in Montpelier, Louisiana, https://www.hmdb.org/m.asp?m=94882 (accessed May 13, 2023); "William Kendrick Square," historic plaque in Greensburg, Louisiana, https://www.hmdb.org/m.asp?m=88217 (accessed May 20, 2023); National Register of Historic Places Inventory—Nominal Form, "Greensburg Land Office" (Washington, D.C.: U.S. Department of the Interior Heritage Conservation and Recreation Service, 1980), 2–3.

22. Quoted in Hastings, *The Lakes of Pontchartrain,* 54.

23. This is evidenced by the contours on the 1935 U.S. Geological Survey's Covington Quadrangle topographical map (1:24,000 scale).

24. "For Mandeville and Madisonville," *Daily Picayune,* August 14, 1841.

25. "Christy Springs," *Daily Picayune,* June 2, 1855.

26. Hammond Centennial Committee, *Centennial Souvenir: A Hammond History Source Book, 1889–1989,* ed. C. Howard Nichols (Hammond, LA: Carr Office Environments, 1989), 145, 3–4.

27. "A Trip on the Grand Trunk Railroad," *Daily Picayune,* September 16, 1855; J. H. Colton maps of 1855 and 1864, and Helmuth Holtz map of 1864, all courtesy of the Library of Congress.

28. J. F. Merry, "Railroad Companies as Town Buildings," *Illinois Central Magazine* 2, no. 10 (March 1911), reproduced in Hammond Centennial Committee, *Centennial Souvenir,* 41–42, 145.

29. J. F. Merry, *Twenty-Five Years' Growth of Tangipahoa Parish, Louisiana* (Manchester, Iowa: Illinois Central Railroad Company, 1910), 3–5 and 18.

30. Letter from C. H. Hummell to Captain J. F. Merry, Hammond, Louisiana, September 28, 1903, reproduced in Hammond Centennial Committee, *Centennial Souvenir,* 45.

31. Merry, *Twenty-Five Years' Growth of Tangipahoa Parish, Louisiana,* 3–7.

32. Ginger Romero, *Hungarian Folklife: The Sweet Taste of Yesterday in the Florida Parishes of Southeast Louisiana* (Hammond Center for Regional Studies, Southeastern Louisiana University, 1987), 1–5; "Hungarian Settlement," historic plaque in Albany, Louisiana; and other sources.

33. Campanella, "The Ozone Belt: How St. Tammany Turned Ecology into Business."

34. Ellis, *St. Tammany Parish,* 166–191.

35. Fortier, *Louisiana—Comprising Sketches of Parishes, Towns, Events, Institutions, and Persons,* 2:463.

36. Carol Saunders Jahncke, *Mr. Kentzel's Covington, 1878–1890* (Covington, LA: Legacy Pub. Co., 1979), 49–51; advertisement in pamphlet for Covington, St. Tammany Parish, Louisiana, February 19, 1910, https://tammanyfamily.blogspot.com/2016/06/the-world-famous-ozone-belt.html (accessed May 2, 2023).

37. Ellis, *St. Tammany Parish,* 189–191; National Park Service National Register of Historic Places Registration Form, "New Orleans & Northeastern/New Orleans & Great Northern Railroad Depot, Slidell, Louisiana" (Washington, D.C.: U.S. Department of the Interior, 1996), https://npgallery.nps.gov/NRHP/GetAsset/a01c99c8-97c8-4a90-8134-2f23607fd4d2 (accessed May 4, 2023); and other sources.

38. Brown, *The Western Gazetteer or Emigrant's Directory,* 127–128. Lima, Gordon Town, Violin, and/or Lee's Creek appear on the 1855 and 1863 Colton maps, the 1864 Holtz map, the 1865 and 1876 General Land Office maps, and the 1896 Rand McNally map, all courtesy of the Library of Congress.

39. Hawkins Rails, "New Orleans Great Northern Railroad—The Ozone Route," https://hawkinsrails.net/mainlines/nogn/nogn.htm (accessed May 24, 2023); Fortier, *Louisiana—Comprising Sketches of Parishes, Towns, Events, Institutions, and Persons,* 1:113–114

40. "Bogalusa's Birthplace," reads a historical plaque on Cumberland Street at Willis Avenue, "City was born in 1906 just west of here on Bogue Lusa Creek bank when tents were set for 1st campsite of Great Southern Lumber Co. Portable sawmill was erected to cut lumber to build town and what became world's largest sawmill."

41. Fortier, *Louisiana—Comprising Sketches of Parishes, Towns, Events, Institutions, and Persons,* 1:113–114; Map, Great Southern Lumber Company—Bogalusa, Louisiana (1911).

42. Ad for the Great Southern Hotel in the *Daily Picayune,* September 1, 1909, featured in "Luxury, 1909 Style," by Mike Scott, *Times-Picayune,* November 18, 2023, InsideOut section, 4–6.

43. Goodyear Plaque, Bogalusa, Louisiana, visited December 30, 2022.

44. "In Honor of John Bickham, Founder of Franklinton," historical plaque in Franklinton, Louisiana, https://www.hmdb.org/m.asp?m=110278 (accessed May 14, 2023); "History of Franklinton," Town of Franklinton, https://www.townoffranklinton.com/blank-page-3 (accessed May 15, 2023); "Parish Courthouse," historical marker on Highway 16 south of Franklinton, https://www.hmdb.org/m.asp?m=127957 (accessed May 15, 2023); "Old Choctaw Trail," https://www.hmdb.org/m.asp?m=110277 (accessed May 24, 2023).

45. Hawkins Rails, "New Orleans Great Northern Railroad–The Ozone Route," https://hawkinsrails.net/mainlines/nogn/nogn.htm (accessed May 24, 2023).

8. The Atchafalaya Basin

1. Malcolm Louis Comeaux, "Settlement and Folk Occupations of the Atchafalaya Basin" (Ph.D. diss., Louisiana State University and Agricultural & Mechanical College, 1969), 1. Other sources describe "Atchafalaya" as a Chitimachan word meaning "those who have pots." Morgan City Historical Society, *A History of Morgan City, Louisiana* (Morgan City, LA: Morgan City Historical Society, 1960), 10.

2. Amos Stoddard, writing in 1812, quoted in Comeaux, "Settlement and Folk Occupations of the Atchafalaya Basin," 12.

3. Thomas Ashe, 1806, quoted in Marchand, *The Story of Ascension Parish, Louisiana,* 49; *Biographical and Historical Memoirs of Louisiana,* 1:135.

4. "Iberville," *New-Orleans Daily Chronicle,* September 13, 1819

5. *Baton Rouge Gazette,* April 10, 1852, quoted in Comeaux, "Settlement and Folk Occupations of the Atchafalaya Basin," 12.

6. Henry L. Abbot, Department of the Gulf Map No. 8, Atchafalaya Basin, February 8, 1863; U.S. Coast Survey Office, "Map of a part of Louisiana and Mississippi, Illustrating the Operations of the U.S. Forces in the Department of the Gulf," 1863; and other sources.

7. Cheryl Bihm Myers, *The History of Port Barre (1765–1950),* as cited by the Town of Point Barre, Louisiana, "Town History," https://www.townofportbarre.com/town-history (accessed November 21, 2022); "Welcome to Port Barre" information sign on the banks of Bayou Courtebleau, visited January 2, 2024; Henry L. Abbot, Department of the Gulf Map No. 8, Atchafalaya Basin, February 8, 1863; U.S. Coast Survey Office, "Map of a part of Louisiana and Mississippi, Illustrating the Operations of the U.S. Forces in the Department of the Gulf," 1863.

8. Comeaux, "Settlement and Folk Occupations of the Atchafalaya Basin," 36.

9. Baron Héctor de Carondelet, quoted in Morgan City Historical Society, *A History of Morgan City, Louisiana,* 11.

10. Becnel, *The Barrow Family and the Barataria and Lafourche Canal,* 1–3.

11. Morgan City Historical Society, *A History of Morgan City, Louisiana,* 10–15.

12. A. G. Blanchard, "Report of the Preliminary Survey of the Algiers & Opelousas Railroad," *Louisiana Acts* (Baton Rouge, Louisiana, 1853), 115–23, quoted in Mark Reutter and J. Parker Lamb, "Crescent City Bound," *Railroad History,* no. 193 (Fall–Winter 2005–2006): 12.

13. Augustus S. Phelps, "New-Orleans and Opelousas Rail-Road Engineer's Report," December 29, 1851, in *De Bow's Review of the Southern and Southwestern States* 12, New Series 5 (1852): 435; Campanella, *The West Bank of Greater New Orleans.*

14. Morgan City Historical Society, *A History of Morgan City, Louisiana,* 15–16.

15. "Morgan's Louisiana and Texas Railroad and Steamship Company," *Daily Picayune,* April 16, 1884, 2; "Morgan's Louisiana and Texas Railroad," *Galveston Weekly News,* November 18, 1880, 4; Ernst von Hesse-Wartegg, *Travels on the Lower Mississippi, 1879–1880: A Memoir by Ernst von Hesse-Wartegg,* trans. and ed. Frederic Trautmann (Columbia: Univ. of Missouri Press, 1990), 144.

16. Quoted in the Morgan City Historical Society, *A History of Morgan City, Louisiana,* 29.

17. Oliver A. Houck, "Atchafalaya Floodway: A Memoir," *Tulane Environmental Law Journal* 34, no. 87 (2021): 88–89.

18. Comeaux, "Settlement and Folk Occupations of the Atchafalaya Basin," 43–46.

19. Emanuel Bowen, *A New Map of Georgia with a Part of Carolina, Florida and Louisiana,* 1748.

20. Corinne L. Saucier, *A History of Avoyelles Parish* (Gretna, LA: Pelican, 1943), 310.

21. Quoted in Hazel Bar, "A History of Simmesport," from "Town of Simmesport—About Us," https://simmesportla.com/about/ (accessed November 30, 2022).

22. Henry L. Abbot, Department of the Gulf Map No. 8, Atchafalaya Basin, February 8, 1863; U.S. Coast Survey Office, "Map of a part of Louisiana and Mississippi, Illustrating the Operations of the U.S. Forces in the Department of the Gulf," 1863; Rev. Herman Cope Duncan, *The Diocese of Louisiana: Some of Its History, 1838–1888* (New Orleans: A. W. Hyatt, 1888), 198.

23. McPhee, *The Control of Nature,* 3–92; Army Corps of Engineers, New Orleans District, *Old River Control,* agency booklet, 1999.

24. Henry L. Abbot, Department of the Gulf Map No. 8, Atchafalaya Basin, February 8, 1863; U.S. Coast Survey Office, "Map of a part of Louisiana and Mississippi, Illustrating the Operations of the U.S. Forces in the Department of the Gulf," 1863.

25. "Melville Progressive and in Fertile Land; Something About a Historic and Yet Modern Region and Its Ambitious Metropolis," *Times-Picayune,* May 8, 1904; "Melville, La. One of the Thriving and Enterprising Towns in St. Landry Parish," *Daily Picayune,* March 26, 1902; Fortier, *Louisiana—Comprising Sketches of Parishes, Towns, Events, Institutions, and Persons,* 2:143; Comeaux, "Settlement and Folk Occupations of the Atchafalaya Basin," 64–65.

26. Leeper, "Melville," June 4, 1972, in *Louisiana Places,* 157, and other sources.

27. "Town History," Town of Krotz Springs, https://krotzsprings.org/town-history (accessed December 1, 2022).

28. "Krotz Springs Project to Give Louisiana Another Health Resort," *Daily Picayune,* July 30, 1910.

29. Leeper, "Krotz Springs," September 22, 1974, in *Louisiana Places,* 135; "Town History," Town of Krotz Springs, https://krotzsprings.org/town-history (accessed December 1, 2022); Carola Lillie Hartley, "A Man Named Krotz," *The Daily World,* June 30, 2017, https://www.dailyworld.com/story/life/2017/06/30/man-named-krotz/440738001/ (accessed December 1, 2022).

9. Bayou Teche, the Vermilion River, and the Opelousas and Attakapas Districts

1. Shane K. Bernard, *Teche: A History of Louisiana's Most Famous Bayou* (Jackson: Univ. Press of Mississippi, 2016), 9–11; Kim Walden, Chitimachan tribal historic preservation office, quoted by Stephen Marcantel in "How Did Bayou Teche Come by Its Name," *Times-Picayune,* November 27, 2022.

2. Robert M. Crisler, "Bayou Teche," in Davis, ed., *The Rivers and Bayous of Louisiana,* 105–112; Bernard, *Teche,* 15–22.

3. The true name of this nation was *Isháк,* "the people." But rival Choctaws disparaged their enemy with the slur of man-eater, which colonials unknowingly adopted and propagated in communiques. The tribe today identifies themselves as the Atakapa-Ishak Nation, and describes themselves as "a Southwest Louisiana/Southeast Texas tribe of ancient Indians who lived in the Gulf of Mexico's northwestern crescent and called ourselves Ishak. The name means The People." Atakapa-Ishak Nation, https://www.are.na/block/3654946 (accessed February 10, 2023); see also "The Atakapa-Coushette Trace," historical interpretative sign, posted in Beauregard Parish and online at https://www.hmdb.org/m.asp?m=211081 and https://www.hmdb.org/m.asp?m=136964 (accessed January 29, 2023).

4. Din, *Francisco Bouligny,* 94–99; Bernard, *Teche,* 40–41.

5. This portage would have been along or parallel to today's Jane Street or Daspit Road.

6. Bernard, *Teche,* 41–42; William Darby, *View of the United States, Historical, Geographical, and Statistical,* vol. 1 (Philadelphia, Pennsylvania: Henry Schenck Tanner, 1828), 268; Din, *Francisco Bouligny,* 94–99.

7. Bernard, *Teche,* 61–63; Gilbert C. Din, "Lieutenant Colonel Francisco Bouligny and the Malagueño Settlement at New Iberia, 1779," *Louisiana History* 17, no. 2 (Spring 1976): 187–202; City of New Iberia, "Becoming New Iberia," historical plaque on East Main Street, https://www.hmdb.org/m.asp?m=98640 (accessed November 15, 2022).

8. Quotation from Dr. Alfred Duperier, *New Iberia Enterprise,* March 25, 1899; steamboat data based on figure of 116 Bayou Teche vessels out of 337 steamboats docking at New Orleans, as cited in interpretative materials at Bayou Teche Museum in New Iberia, Louisiana, visited on January 4, 2024.

9. Bernard, *Teche,* 61–62, 48; Leeper, *Louisiana Place Names,* 223–224.

10. First quote from "St. Martinville" historic plaque, visited January 4, 2024; second quote from "Our Church History," Saint Martin de Tours Catholic Church, https://saintmartindetours.org/full-history (accessed March 14, 2023).

11. Leeper, *Louisiana Place Names,* 103; Bernard, *Teche,* 62–69; and local sources.

12. Bernard, *Teche,* 15–16.

13. Leeper, *Louisiana Place Names,* 45; J. A. Reynolds, "Louisiana Placenames of Romance Origin" (Ph.D. diss., Louisiana State University, 1942), 77; Kiwanis Club of Breaux Bridge, "The Bridge of 1852," historical plaque, https://www.hmdb.org/m.asp?m=129778 (accessed November 17, 2023); "Scholastique Picou Breaux (1796–1846)" and "Breaux Bridge—Crawfish Capital of the World," historical plaques, visited January 1, 2024.

14. Frederick Law Olmsted, *The Cotton Kingdom: A Traveller's Observations on Cotton and Slavery in the American Slave States,* vol. 2 (New York: Mason Brothers and Sampson Low, Son & Co., 1862), 30.

15. Newton, *Louisiana: A Geographical Portrait,* 68; Charles Robert Goins and John Michael Caldwell, "Geological Formations," in *Historical Atlas of Louisiana* (Norman: Univ. of Oklahoma Press, 1995), 9–10; Kniffen and Hilliard, *Louisiana,* 34–44.

16. Nancy Tucker Baker, *Hydrological Features and Processes of the Vermilion River, Louisiana* (Baton Rouge: U.S. Geological Survey Water Resources Investigation Report 88-4019, 1988), 3–8.

17. William J. Sandoz, "A Brief History of St. Landry Parish," *Louisiana Historical Quarterly* 8, no. 1 (January 1925): 225–226.

18. William Henry Perrin, ed., *Southwest Louisiana: Biographical and Historical* (New Orleans: Gulf Pub. Co., 1891), 28.

19. Sandoz, "A Brief History of St. Landry Parish," 225–226.

20. Harry Lewis Griffin, *The Attakapas Country: A History of Lafayette Parish* (1959; reprint, Gretna, LA: Pelican, 1999), 13–15.

21. Sandoz, "A Brief History of St. Landry Parish," 227.

22. "Washington" historic plaque at entrance of town, visited January 2, 2024.

23. *St. Landry Democrat,* October 23, 1880, quoted in Donald J. Millet, "Southwest Louisiana Enters the Railroad Age: 1880–1900," *Louisiana History* 24, no. 2 (Spring 1983): 174; Donald J. Millet, "Town Development in Southwest Louisiana, 1865–1900," *Louisiana History* 13, no. 2 (Spring 1972): 155–156, 165; Perrin, ed., *Southwest Louisiana,* 52.

24. Griffin, *The Attakapas Country,* 15.

25. Preservation Alliance of Lafayette, *The History of Downtown Lafayette, Louisiana* (Lafayette, LA: Preservation Alliance of Lafayette, 2014), 4–8.

26. Preservation Alliance of Lafayette, *The History of Downtown Lafayette, Louisiana,* 9.

27. Griffin, *The Attakapas Country,* 27–30; and other sources.

28. *Biographical and Historical Memoirs of Louisiana,* 1:240; Reynolds, "Louisiana Placenames of Romance Origin," 279; and other sources. Regarding the renaming of Vermilionville, "Lafayette" as a city name had already been taken by an incorporated community outside of New Orleans. But when the city of New Orleans annexed that municipality in 1852, "Lafayette" became available again as a city name—though it would not be until 1884 that Vermilionville officially claimed it, thus matching its parish name. Robin Miller, "Why Was Vermilionville Renamed Lafayette," *Times-Picayune,* January 22, 2023.

29. Lafayette Consolidated Government, Lafayette, Louisiana Historic Register (undated pamphlet), 13.

30. Griffin, *The Attakapas Country,* 27.

31. St. Charles Borromeo Catholic Church informational pamphlet and materials, visited January 2, 2024; Reynolds, "Louisiana Placenames of Romance Origin," 235.

32. Millet, "Southwest Louisiana Enters the Railroad Age: 1880–1900," 179–180; and other sources.

33. Douglas L. Villien Sr., *Between the Crossroads: A Centennial History of Maurice, Louisiana* (Maurice, LA: Villien Publishing, 2012), 3–10; Reynolds, "Louisiana Placenames of Romance Origin," 2–3, 340; "Welcome to Abbeville—City History," City of Abbeville, https://cityofabbeville.net/about-abbeville/ (accessed December 30, 2022); Père Antoine Désiré Mégret statue inscription in downtown Abbeville, visited January 1, 2024.

34. M. B. Hillyard, May 8, 1886, and an anonymous reporter from *The Lake Charles Echo,* February 7, 1885, quoted in Millet, "Town Development in Southwest Louisiana, 1865–1900," 139–141.

35. M. B. Hillyard, May 8, 1886 (emphasis added), quoted in Millet, "Town Development in Southwest Louisiana, 1865–1900," 139.

36. Millet, "Town Development in Southwest Louisiana, 1865–1900," 140–141.

37. Millet, "Southwest Louisiana Enters the Railroad Age: 1880–1900," 182.

38. Fortier, *Louisiana—Comprising Sketches of Parishes, Towns, Events, Institutions, and Persons,* 3:137.

39. Leeper, *Louisiana Place Names,* 163–164; "Rayne Depot Square" and "Pouppeville" historical plaques, in and near Rayne, Louisiana, visited January 3, 2024.

40. Fortier, *Louisiana—Comprising Sketches of Parishes, Towns, Events, Institutions, and Persons,* 3:137.

41. Millet, "Town Development in Southwest Louisiana, 1865–1900," 156–160; *Opelousas Courier,* December 23, 1886, as quoted in "History—Acadia Parish Clerk of Court," https://acadiaparishclerk.com/about-us/history/ (accessed January 7, 2023).

42. Perrin, ed., *Southwest Louisiana,* 237.

43. Fortier, *Louisiana—Comprising Sketches of Parishes, Towns, Events, Institutions, and Persons,* 1:20.

44. Fortier, *Louisiana—Comprising Sketches of Parishes, Towns, Events, Institutions, and Persons,* 3:138.

45. *Opelousas Courier,* December 17, 1907, quoted in Leeper, *Louisiana Place Names,* 155; see also 93.

46. See "Ancient Roads, Based Mainly on Lafon, 1806," in Newton, *Atlas of Louisiana—A Guide for Students,* unpaginated map.

47. Robert Gahn Sr., *A History of Evangeline: Its Land, Its Men and Its Women Who Made It a Beautiful Place to Live* (Baton Rouge: Claitor's, 1972 republication of a 1941 thesis), 41–42.

48. See the maps of John Melish (1820), Henry Schenck Tanner (1851), and J. H. Colton (1855 and 1863), courtesy of the Library of Congress, as well as the Public Land Survey System maps (1840s) of the Louisiana Office of State Lands, Division of Administration, for the network of roads connecting these settlements. See also "Ville Platte," historical plaque posted in Ville Platte, Louisiana, https://www.hmdb.org/m.asp?m=86740 (accessed January 29, 2023); Reynolds, "Louisiana Placenames of Romance Origin," 534.

49. Leeper, *Louisiana Place Names,* 135; "Kaplan, Louisiana," Encyclopedia of Southern Jewish Communities, https://www.isjl.org/louisiana-kaplan-encyclopedia.html (accessed January 9, 2023).

50. Anita G. Guidry, *La Pointe de l'Eglise: A History of Church Point, Louisiana, 1800–1973* (Lafayette, LA: Tribune Printing Plant, 1973), 11–13. One road appears on the 1814 Matthew Carey map; the other on the 1820 John Melish map. Both maps are courtesy of the Library of Congress.

51. Mary Alice Fontenot and Rev. Paul B. Freeland, *Acadia Parish, Louisiana: A History to 1900* (Lafayette: The Center for Louisiana Studies, University of Southwestern Louisiana, 1976), 142–146.

52. Kane, *The Bayous of Louisiana,* 274–275.

53. Leeper, *Louisiana Place Names,* 66; and other sources.

10. Southwestern Louisiana and the Chenier Plain

1. Donald Joseph Millet Sr., "The Economic Development of Southwest Louisiana: 1865–1900" (Ph.D. diss., Louisiana State University and Agricultural & Mechanical College, 1964), 7.

2. R. J. Russell and H. V. Howe, "Cheniers of Southwestern Louisiana," *Geographical Review* 25, no. 3 (July 1935): 449–461; Richard B. Crowell, *Chenier Plain* (Alexandria, LA: Roseau Company, 2015), 12–17.

3. See "Ancient Roads, Based Mainly on Lafon, 1806," in Newton, *Atlas of Louisiana—A Guide for Students,* unpaginated map.

4. Griffin, *The Attakapas Country,* 9.

5. Fontenot and Freeland, *Acadia Parish, Louisiana,* 166–167; maps courtesy of the Library of Congress. See also Leeper, *Louisiana Place Names,* 163–164.

6. Perrin, ed., *Southwest Louisiana,* 29.

7. Donald J. Millet, "Cattle and Cattlemen of Southwest Louisiana, 1860–1900," *Louisiana History* 28, no. 3 (Summer 1987): 327; Donald J. Millet, "The Saga of Water Transportation into Southwest Louisiana to 1900," *Louisiana History* 15, no. 4 (Autumn 1974): 347; Leeper, "Mermentau," June 11, 1972, in *Louisiana Places,* 158.

8. Jedidiah Morse, *The American Universal Geography,* vol. 1 (Charlestown, South Carolina: Lincoln and Edmands, 1819), 670.

9. Darby, *A Geographical Description of the State of Louisiana,* 150. Both names appear on the John Melish map of 1820; only "Mermentau" appears on the Colton map of Louisiana of 1855. Both maps courtesy of the Library of Congress.

10. Calvin Dale Smith and Allen Fitzgerald, *History of Lake Arthur* (Baton Rouge: Pettengill and Hood, 1960), 1–4.

11. J. H. Colton's Map of the State of Louisiana and Eastern Part of Texas (1863), courtesy of the Library of Congress.

12. "Lake Arthur—A New Town and a Lively One," *Daily Picayune,* November 30, 1888

13. Perrin, ed., *Southwest Louisiana,* 164.

14. Olmsted, *The Cotton Kingdom,* 2:29.

15. Cited from interpretations at Los Adaes State Historic Site, El Camino Real de los Tejas National Historic Trail.

16. J. V. Haggard, "The Neutral Ground between Louisiana and Texas, 1806–1821," *Louisiana Historical Quarterly* 28 (October 1945): 1001–1028.

17. Perrin, ed., *Southwest Louisiana,* 123.

18. "Treaty of Amity, Settlement, and Limits Between the United States of America and His Catholic Majesty. 1819," The Avalon Project, Yale Law School, https://avalon.law.yale.edu/19th_century/sp1819.asp (accessed January 12, 2023).

19. Richard Campanella, "Neutral Ground: Political Geography of Imperialism," *Louisiana Cultural Vistas* (Autumn 2015): 66–67; Richard Campanella, "'Oft-forgotten Florida Purchase,' 200 Years Ago This Month, Gave Louisiana Its Distinctive Boot Shape," *Times-Picayune,* February 10, 2019.

20. Sources for this road include the John Melish map of 1820, courtesy of the Library of Congress; the circa 1840s original Public Land Survey System maps of the Louisiana Office of State Lands, Division of Administration; and the 1851 Henry Schenck Tanner map, also courtesy of the Library of Congress. See also Perrin, ed., *Southwest Louisiana,* 123.

21. Also annoying to Olmsted were the bridges crossing the bayous, "so rudely built of logs that the traveller, where possible, left them for a ford," as well as locals' reckoning of distances, which ranged anywhere between 40 to 120 miles for the actual 70 miles between Lake Charles and Opelousas. Olmsted, *The Cotton Kingdom,* 2:30–31.

22. Olmsted, *The Cotton Kingdom,* 2:30.

23. John Dimitry, *Lessons in the History of Louisiana, to Which Are Appended Lessons in Its Geography and Products* (New York, Chicago: A. S. Barnes, 1877), 172–173.

24. Millet, "Town Development in Southwest Louisiana, 1865–1900," 147–149; 1851 Henry Schenck Tanner map, courtesy of the Library of Congress; "History of Lake Charles," Lake Charles, Louisiana, https://www.cityoflakecharles.com/ (accessed January 18, 2023); "History of Calcasieu Parish," Calcasieu Parish Government, https://www.calcasieu.gov/government/parish-history (accessed January 18, 2023).

25. A. Michal McMahon, "Mill Town: Prostitution and the Rule of Lumber in Lake Charles, Louisiana, 1867–1918," *Louisiana History* 45, no. 2 (Spring 2004): 151.

26. These and other Sabine ferry crossings appear on the Henry Schenck Tanner map of 1851, courtesy of the Library of Congress.

27. Annotations in *Map of the River Sabine from its mouth on the Gulf of Mexico in the sea to Logan's Ferry* (1840), courtesy of the Library of Congress.

28. Public Land Survey System maps of the Louisiana Office of State Lands, Division of Administration.

29. Perrin, ed., *Southwest Louisiana,* 163.

30. Ryan M. Seidemann, "Water and Power: The Sabine River Authority of Louisiana—A Review of Property Disputes, Hydropower, and Water Sales," *Tulane Environmental Law Journal* 25, no. 389 (2012): 391.

31. North American Land and Timber Company, advertisement in Chamber of Commerce of Lake Charles and Calcasieu Parish, *Facts and Photographs of Calcasieu Parish (a County of Louisiana) and the City of Lake Charles the Parish Seat,* forty-first page of unpaginated 1916 promotional pamphlet (author's collection).

32. Gleaned from U.S. Geological Survey topographic maps from 1932 and 1945. The 1820 John Melish map depicts the cheniers as islands surrounded by "salt marsh" and labeled as "live oak" for their dominant flora. Many chenier communities would later embed *Île* or "Island" in their names. Map courtesy of the Library of Congress.

33. A congressional record from 1852 notes a "petition of . . . settlers on the Grand Chenier, praying that the right of preemption be granted to them," and few if any were declined. *Journal of the House of Representatives of the United States, Second Session of the Thirty-Second Congress, Volume 1* (Washington, D.C.: Robert Armstrong, Printer, 1852), 50; "About Cameron Parish," Cameron Parish Police Jury, https://cameronpj.org/parish-history/ (accessed January 27, 2023).

34. Perrin, ed., *Southwest Louisiana,* 170–174; *Biographical and Historical Memoirs of Louisiana,* 1:224; Millet, "The Economic Development of Southwest Louisiana: 1865–1900," 199–200.

35. Perrin, ed., *Southwest Louisiana,* 173–175.

36. Commissioner of Immigration of Louisiana, pamphlet, quoted in Perrin, ed., *Southwest Louisiana,* 169–170.

37. Millet, "The Economic Development of Southwest Louisiana: 1865–1900," 160–161.

38. Millet, "Town Development in Southwest Louisiana, 1865–1900," 161–162.

39. Chamber of Commerce of Lake Charles and Calcasieu Parish, *Facts and Photographs of Calcasieu Parish (a County of Louisiana) and the City of Lake Charles the Parish Seat,* illustration on third page of unpaginated 1916 promotional pamphlet.

40. Fred B. Kniffen, "Louisiana House Types," *Annals of the Association of American Geographers* 26, no. 4 (December 1936): 185–190; Millet, "Town Development in Southwest Louisiana, 1865–1900," 162.

41. Sylvester Cary, speaking in 1891, quoted in Millet, "Town Development in Southwest Louisiana, 1865–1900," 162.

42. Leeper, "Iowa," October 2, 1960, in *Louisiana Places,* 126.

43. All of this was fully fifteen years before the Jennings gusher of 1901, which is widely recognized as the birth of the state's petroleum industry. "City of Sulphur—History," City of Sulphur, Louisiana, https://www.sulphur.org/ (accessed January 21, 2023); Perrin, ed., *Southwest Louisiana,* 134, 145–146.

44. 1896 Rand McNally Company map of Louisiana, courtesy of the Library of Congress.

45. Chamber of Commerce of Lake Charles and Calcasieu Parish, *Facts and Photographs of Calcasieu Parish (a County of Louisiana) and the City of Lake Charles the Parish Seat,* fifth and eighteenth pages of unpaginated 1916 promotional pamphlet.

46. Thom Trahan, executive director of Sulphur's Brimstone Museum, as quoted by Robin Miller in "How Did Sulphur, Louisiana Get Its Name?," *Times-Picayune,* April 14, 2024; Leeper, "Sulphur," August 26, 1973, in *Louisiana Places,* 229.

47. See, for example, Chamber of Commerce of Lake Charles and Calcasieu Parish, *Facts and Photographs of Calcasieu Parish (a County of Louisiana) and the City of Lake Charles the Parish Seat,* seventeenth page of unpaginated 1916 promotional pamphlet.

48. See Barthélémy Lafon, *Carte Générale du Territoire D'Orleans,* 1806, courtesy of the Library of Congress; "Ancient Roads, Based Mainly on Lafon, 1806," in Newton, *Atlas of Louisiana—A Guide for Students,* unpaginated map.

49. Perrin, ed., *Southwest Louisiana,* 162–163.

50. Millet, "The Economic Development of Southwest Louisiana: 1865–1900," xiii, 64–70; Leeper, *Louisiana Place Names,* 258–259; Mark Hare, "History of Vinton: The Early Years of The Town," City of Vinton, Louisiana, https://cityofvinton.com/history-of-vinton/ (accessed January 22, 2023).

51. See Knapp Memorial Arch and plaque honoring Seaman Knapp in Washington, D.C., https://www.hmdb.org/m.asp?m=134589 (accessed January 22, 2023).

11. The Red River Region

1. Katherine Bridges and Winston De Ville, trans. and eds., "Natchitoches and the Trail to the Rio Grande: Two Early Eighteenth-Century Accounts by the Sieur Derbanne," *Louisiana History* 8, no. 3 (Summer 1967): 244–245.

2. Patsy K. Barber, *Above the Falls, and Historic Cotile* (Lecompte, LA: Bayou Boeuf Publishing, 1994), 1–3.

3. "We may assume," wrote historian Winston De Ville, "that within the French period, perhaps shortly after 1722, the first colonists began to establish themselves near the 'grand rapide.'" Winston De Ville, *Rapide Post—1799: A Brief Study in Genealogy and Local History* (Baltimore, MD: Genealogical Pub. Co., 1968), xi.

4. Dorr, "A Tourist's Description of Louisiana in 1860," 1154–1155.

5. Circumvention portages go around obstacles. Examples usually involve waterfalls, such as the Great Falls of the Ohio River, where Louisville formed in Kentucky. Shortcut portages connect two waterbodies with a line of minimum distance. Examples include Bayou Road at New Orleans and the Chicago Portage in Illinois.

6. Based on interpretative materials on display at the Northern Louisiana History Museum, Louisiana State Museum, and the Fort St. Jean Baptiste State Historic Site, Louisiana State Parks, Natchitoches, Louisiana.

7. Newton, *Louisiana: A Geographical Portrait,* 106, 118.

8. Based on a sketch of the original fort made by Ignace François in 1733 and rediscovered in Paris in 1938 by architectural historical Samuel Wilson Jr., state historians were able to build a convincing replica of Fort St. Jean Baptiste in 1979–1981. The affiliated visitors' center describes it as "the only full scale fully replicated French fort in the United States."

9. This is now the American Cemetery in Natchitoches.

10. Ignace François Broutin, *Carte Particuliere des Natchitoches* (1733), courtesy of Cammie G. Henry Research Center at Watson Memorial Library, Northwestern State University, Natchitoches, Louisiana. Information in this section was derived from various sources and interpretations on display at the Fort St. Jean Baptiste State Historic Site, Louisiana State Parks.

11. Louisa R. Stark, "Notes on a Dialect of Spanish Spoken in Northern Louisiana," *Anthropological Linguistics* 22, no. 4 (April 1980): 163–164.

12. Din, *Populating the Barrera,* 1–22.

13. Cited from interpretations at Los Adaes State Historic Site, El Camino Real de los Tejas National Historic Trail.

14. Cited from a historic marker for Baldwin's Store on San Antonio Avenue in Many, Louisiana, visited July 27, 2022; Leeper, *Louisiana Place Names,* 158; Newton, *Louisiana: A Geographical Portrait,* 309.

15. Based on my field work in July 2022, including research materials and interpretations at Los Adaes State Historic Site, El Camino Real de los Tejas National Historic Trail, and Fort Jesup State Historic Site.

16. John G. Belisle, *History of Sabine Parish: From the First Explorers and Settlers to the Present* (Many, LA: Sabine Banner Press, 1912), 61–62.

17. Belisle, *History of Sabine Parish,* 79.

18. Field, *Louisiana Voyages,* 59, 155; original Public Land Survey System map for Sabine and Natchitoches parishes, State Lands Office.

19. Belisle, *History of Sabine Parish,* 81–89.

20. Nalini Torres and Danny W. Harrelson, "The Great Red River Raft and Its Sedimentological Implications," in *Reconstructing Human-landscape Interactions,* vol. 1, *Interpreting Desert and Fluvial Environments,* ed. Brett T. McLaurin, Aileen C. Elliott, and Nalini Torres (Paris: SpringerBriefs in Earth System Sciences, 2012), 36, https://www.researchgate.net/publication/278665972_The_Great_Red_River_Raft_and_its_Sedimentological_Implications, visited July 31, 2022.

21. Torres and Harrelson, "The Great Red River Raft and Its Sedimentological Implications," 36.

22. Jacques D. Bagur, *A History of Navigation on Cypress Bayou and the Lakes* (Denton: Univ. of North Texas Press, 2001), 66–70.

23. "The Raft of Red River," *Baltimore Gazette and Daily Advertiser,* October 17, 1828, 2.

24. Henry M. Shreve, "Ohio and Mississippi Rivers: Annual Report of work done in improving the navigation of the Ohio and Mississippi rivers in the present year, ending 30th September 1831," as reproduced in *Daily National Intelligencer* (Washington, D.C.), December 17, 1831, 2; Robert Gudmestad, "Steamboats and the Removal of the Red River Raft," *Louisiana History* 52, no. 4 (Fall 2011): 400.

25. Gudmestad, "Steamboats and the Removal of the Red River Raft," 401–402.

26. Quoted in Gudmestad, "Steamboats and the Removal of the Red River Raft," 408; figures drawn from tables on pages 415–416. Land sale figures dropped in 1837 on account of the financial panic that year, but subsequently rebounded.

27. Gudmestad, "Steamboats and the Removal of the Red River Raft," 392, 402–403.

28. Newton, *Louisiana: A Geographical Portrait,* 308.

29. Eric J. Brock, "The Shreve Town Company," *64 Parishes* (Louisiana Endowment for the Humanities), https://64parishes.org/entry/shreve-town-company-adaptation (accessed August 1, 2022); Gudmestad, "Steamboats and the Removal of the Red River Raft," 404; and other sources.

30. "10 Railroads Came Through Shreveport in 1907," diagram from 1907 on display at Louisiana State Exhibit Museum, visited July 29, 2022.

31. With the 1853 publication of *12 Years a Slave,* this cotton-growing region became nationally notorious for the particularly brutal brand of slavery experienced here.

32. Sternberg, *Along the River Road,* 49; see also Randy DeCuir, *Moncla and the Prairie Communities of Ward Two, 1809–2009* (1979; reprint, Marksville, Louisiana, 2009).

33. Newton, *Louisiana: A Geographical Portrait,* 7–8; LeeAnna Keith, "Colfax Massacre," *KnowLA Encyclopedia of Louisiana,* ed. Joyce Miller (Louisiana Endowment for the Humanities, 2011).

34. Corrine Saucier, "Moncla: Glass Landing, David Landing, Moncla Landing," article written in 1938 and reproduced by DeCuir in *Moncla and the Prairie Communities of Ward Two, 1809–2009,* 67.

35. Drawn from historic and interpretative signs and other sources in Moncla and in the Ben Routh Recreation Area of the Red River Waterway Commission, located across the Red River from Moncla; visited on July 26, 2022.

36. Newton, *Louisiana: A Geographical Portrait,* 30–31; Torres and Harrelson, "The Great Red River Raft and Its Sedimentological Implications," 37–44; Kniffen and Hilliard, *Louisiana,* 51–52.

37. Chip McGimsey, "The Rings of Marksville," *Southeastern Archaeology* 22, no. 1 (Summer 2003): 47–62; measurements from LIDAR elevation data and U.S.G.S. topographic maps.

38. Corinne L. Saucier, *History of Avoyelles Parish, Louisiana* (Corinne L. Saucier, 1943), 1–5; *Biographical and Historical Memoirs of Northwest Louisiana* (Nashville: Southern Pub. Co., 1890), 606–607; "Poste Des Avoyelles" historical marker, Marksville, Louisiana, https://www.hmdb.org/m.asp?m=97870 (accessed February 2, 2023).

39. Leeper, *Louisiana Place Names,* 160; *Biographical and Historical Memoirs of Northwest Louisiana,* 608; historic plaque, "Founding of Marksville," posted in downtown Marksville, https://www.hmdb.org/m.asp?m=99098 (accessed February 2, 2023); "City of Marksville History," City of Marksville, https://www.cityofmarksville.com/work-gallery (accessed February 2, 2023).

40. Dorr, "A Tourist's Description of Louisiana in 1860," 1147.

41. Perhaps the most informative map depicting the Acadian Triangle, without actually using that term, is Milton B. Newton's compilation of "divergent opinions" of fellow geographers plotted in a graphic titled "Defining the North-South Contrast." It first appeared in Newton's *Atlas of Louisiana* (1970) and was republished in his *Louisiana: A Geographical Portrait* (1987), 133. All participants agreed that Marksville marks the apex of the state's southern cultural region, corresponding spatially to the Acadian Triangle.

42. Solomon Northup, *12 Years a Slave—Narrative of Solomon Northup, A Citizen of New-York Kidnapped in Washington City in 1841 and Rescued in 1853, from a Cotton Plantation Near the Red River, in Louisiana* (New York: Miller, Orton, and Mulligan, 1855), 294, 224. Marksville was also where Solomon Northup found an honorable lawyer and judge who arranged for his release in 1853.

43. Field, *Louisiana Voyages,* 39.

44. Dorr, "A Tourist's Description of Louisiana in 1860," 1146–1147.

12. The Western Hill Country

1. This was the term used by Solomon Northup throughout *12 Years a Slave.*

2. Kniffen and Hilliard, *Louisiana,* 34–44; Newton, *Louisiana: A Geographical Portrait,* 6–8; Goins and Caldwell, "Geological Formations," in *Historical Atlas of Louisiana,* 8–10.

3. Samuel L. Clemens (Mark Twain), *Life on the Mississippi* (1883; reprint, New York: Viking, 1958), 4.

4. Atakapa-Ishak Nation, https://www.are.na/block/3654946 (accessed February 10, 2023); "The Atakapa-Coushette Trace," historical interpretative sign, posted in Beauregard Parish, https://www.hmdb.org/m.asp?m=211081 and https://www.hmdb.org/m.asp?m=136964 (accessed February 10, 2023).

5. Barthélémy Lafon, *Carte Générale du Territoire D'Orleans,* 1806; John Melish map of 1820; Henry Schenck Tanner map of 1851; all courtesy of the Library of Congress. See also Merryville Historical Society, "Site of the Coushatta Indian Village," historical marker in Merryville, Louisiana, https://www.hmdb.org/m.asp?m=136681 (accessed February 11, 2023).

6. Belisle, *History of Sabine Parish,* 61–62.

7. *Map of the River Sabine from its mouth on the Gulf of Mexico in the sea to Logan's Ferry* (1840), courtesy of the Library of Congress.

8. Interpretative signs at Burr's Ferry, including "Burr's Ferry—Back Door to the United States," "Legends of the Burr Ferry Road," "The Infamous Burr Ferry Road," and "Burr's Ferry Earthworks" on the Louisiana side, and "Site of Burr's Ferry" on the Texas side, visited July 27, 2022. See the Henry Schenck Tanner map of 1851 for a reference to Hickman's Ferry.

9. This according to the John Melish map of 1820, courtesy of the Library of Congress.

10. An 1840s state lands map indicates the Sabine had previously flowed much closer to present-day Merryville, but later shifted westward to its current channel, leaving behind a waterbody called Black Lake.

11. William Theodore Block Jr., "A Glimpse of Merryville, Louisiana Between 1906–1908," Calcasieu Parish LaGenWeb, http://theusgenweb.org/la/calcasieu/block/merryville.html (accessed February 11, 2023); Leeper, "Merryville," June 25, 1972, in *Louisiana Places,* 158.

12. Fortier, *Louisiana—Comprising Sketches of Parishes, Towns, Events, Institutions, and Persons,* 2:146; Leeper, "Merryville," January 2, 1972, in *Louisiana Places,* 77.

13. Leeper, *Louisiana Place Names,* 80; Fortier, *Louisiana—Comprising Sketches of Parishes, Towns, Events, Institutions, and Persons,* 1:319.

14. Leeper, *Louisiana Place Names,* 80, 164; "History of DeRidder," City of DeRidder, https://www.cityofderidder.org/229/History-of-DeRidder (accessed February 12, 2023); "DeRidder—The Sawmill Hub," interpretative signage posted in DeRidder, Louisiana, https://www.hmdb.org/m.asp?m=109521 (accessed February 12, 2023).

15. Museum of the New Llano Colony, https://www.newllanocolony.com/index.html (accessed February 14, 2023).

16. Hornbeck Centennial Committee, "Hornbeck, Louisiana," historic plaque, Hornbeck, Louisiana, visited July 27, 2022; William Theodore Block Jr., "Ludington, Louisiana: A Ghost Town of Beauregard Parish," Calcasieu Parish LaGenWeb, http://theusgenweb.org/la/calcasieu/block/ludington.html (accessed February 15, 2023).

17. This road is clearly marked on the John Melish map of 1820, and the Mansfield crossroads is equally clear on the H. S. Tanner map of 1851. Courtesy of the Library of Congress.

18. Dorr, "A Tourist's Description of Louisiana in 1860," 1170.

19. Fortier, *Louisiana—Comprising Sketches of Parishes, Towns, Events, Institutions, and Persons,* 2:125. It is worth noting that Mansfield falls within the Sixteenth Section of its respective township, where, according to federal law, land had to be leased or sold to fund public schools. Zachary Howser, "A Binding and Perpetual Obligation: Protecting Louisiana's Sixteenth Section Land as a Natural Resource," *LSU Journal of Energy Law and Resources* 2, no. 2 (Spring 2014): 381–387.

20. John T. Cupid, *A Brief History of Vernon Parish* (Rosepine, LA, 1963), 33; see also Newton, *Louisiana: A Geographical Portrait,* 309.

21. National Register of Historic Places Nomination, "Smart, Edmond Ellison, House, Leesville, Vernon Parish, LA" (Washington, D.C.: U.S. Department of the Interior, National Park Service, 2002), 7.

22. John Melish map of 1820; General Lands Office map of 1876; Fortier, *Louisiana—Comprising Sketches of Parishes, Towns, Events, Institutions, and Persons,* 2:54–55; Newton, *Louisiana: A Geographical Portrait,* 309.

23. Barthélémy Lafon's 1806 map marks the waterway as "Grand Bayou Scie"; John Melish's 1820 map labels "Bayou Scie," as do most subsequent charts for the remainder of the century.

24. Fortier, *Louisiana—Comprising Sketches of Parishes, Towns, Events, Institutions, and Persons,* 2:667.

25. Stark, "Notes on a Dialect of Spanish Spoken in Northern Louisiana," 163–164; Leeper, *Louisiana Place Names,* 275–276; St. Joseph Catholic Church and St. Ann Chapel, "Parish History," https://stjosephzwolle.org/parish-history (accessed February 14, 2023); Carl Dilbeck, "Early Bayou Scie History, Sabine Parish," Sabine Index, Many, Louisiana (1999), http://files.usgwarchives.net/la/sabine/history/byscie.txt (accessed February 14, 2023).

26. The mean interval was 7.3 miles, with a standard deviation of 3.5 miles, yielding a range of 3.8–10.8 miles, rounded to 4–11 miles. The median interval was 6.8 miles and the mode was 7 miles. Following the tracks, the distances were 7 miles from Rodessa Vivian; 8.2 miles to Oil City; 4.5 miles to Mooringsport; 8.2 miles to Blanchard; 9.3 miles to Bossier City; 8.3 miles to Forbing; 10 miles to

Frierson; 14 miles to Mansfield; 12 miles to Benson; 6.1 miles to Converse; 7 miles to Noble; 4.6 miles to Zwolle; 10.8 miles to Many; 5.3 miles to Fisher; 4 miles to Florien; 9.1 miles to Hornbeck; 6.6 miles to Anacoco; 9.5 miles to Leesville; 2.8 miles to New Llano; 12.9 miles to Neame; 3.8 miles to Rosepine; 3.3 miles to Ludington; 2.0 miles to DeRidder; 16.2 miles to Singer; 2.6 miles to Juanita; 6.5 miles to Oretta; 5.5 miles to DeQuincy; 4.9 miles to Perkins; 5.4 miles to Buhler; and 9 miles to Westlake. Analysis by author using Kansas City Southern Railway track maps and official state GIS data on community locations. See also "Frog Level and Rodessa History" historical plaque, https://www.hmdb.org/m.asp?m=128259 (accessed May 11, 2023).

27. Beyond this point, the KCS beat out the tram line in reaching Leesville first, which explains why the tram was later renamed the "Lake Charles & *Northern,*" dropping the reference to Leesville.

28. William Theodore Block Jr., "Early Sawmilling at Lake Charles, Louisiana," Calcasieu Parish—LAGen Web, http://theusgenweb.org/la/calcasieu/block/lakecharles.html (accessed February 16, 2023); Leeper, *Louisiana Place Names,* 151; Rand McNally Map of Louisiana Railroads (1896), courtesy of the Library of Congress.

29. Perrin, ed., *Southwest Louisiana,* 144; Millet, "Southwest Louisiana Enters the Railroad Age: 1880–1900," 176–177.

30. "Kinder: The Crossroads to Everywhere," interpretative sign in Kinder, Louisiana, https://www.hmdb.org/m.asp?m=201708 (accessed February 16, 2023); "About Us: The Town of Kinder," Town of Kinder: Crossroads to Everywhere, https://townofkinder.com/about-us (accessed February 16, 2023).

31. "Oberlin: A Blending of Cultures," interpretative sign in Oberlin, Louisiana, https://www.hmdb.org/m.asp?m=126071 (accessed February 16, 2023); Leeper, *Louisiana Place Names,* 179; "Oakdale Is After the Parish Seat," *New Orleans Item,* July 13, 1910.

32. *Beaumont Enterprise,* July 13, 1905, quoted in William T. Block, "Southwest Louisiana History Found in *Beaumont Enterprise,*" Southwest Louisiana, http://www.wtblock.com/wtblockjr/southwes.htm (accessed February 17, 2023); Fortier, *Louisiana—Comprising Sketches of Parishes, Towns, Events, Institutions, and Persons,* 2:268; "Town of Elizabeth," interpretative sign in Elizabeth, Louisiana, https://www.hmdb.org/m.asp?m=125179 (accessed February 18, 2023).

33. "History and Culture: History of the Kisatchie," U.S. Forest Service, https://www.fs.usda.gov/main/kisatchie/learning/history-culture (accessed February 17, 2023).

34. John Melish map of 1820, courtesy of the Library of Congress.

35. "Sugartown, One of the Oldest Settlements in Southwest Louisiana, Was Pioneer in Schools, Farming, Syrup Making, Tanning, and Highways," *The American Press,* July 4, 1924, as transcribed by the Louisiana Works Progress Administration, "Sugartown Louisiana and Its Residents, 1924" (McCormick-Beauregard Parish-Lake Charles section), https://louisianadigitallibrary.org/islandora/object/state-lwp%3A6622 (accessed February 18, 2023); Don McFatter, "History of Sugartown," presented in 1996, http://files.usgwarchives.net/la/beauregard/history/sugartown.txt (accessed February 18, 2023); "Old Campground," interpretative sign at Sugartown's Old Campground Cemetery, https://www.hmdb.org/m.asp?m=189246 (accessed February 18, 2023); "Sugartown," Beauregard Parish, http://www.beauregardtourism.com/sugartown.html (accessed February 17, 2023).

36. Mabell R. Kadlecek and Marion C. Bullard, *Louisiana's Kisatchie Hills: History, Tradition, Folklore* (Chelsea, Michigan: Book Crafters, 1994), 145–160.

37. For this reason, the name "Slabtown" was also applied to the settlement of Ringgold in the timber country of Bienville Parish. Ricky L. Sherrod and Annette Pierce Sherrod, *Plain Folk, Planters, and the Complexities of Southern Society: A Case Study of the Browns, Sherrods, Mannings, Sprowls, and Williamses of Nineteenth Century Northern Louisiana* (Nacogdoches, Texas: Stephen F. Austin State Univ. Press, 2014), 118–119.

38. Fortier, *Louisiana—Comprising Sketches of Parishes, Towns, Events, Institutions, and Persons,* 2:313–314; Blue Branch Cemetery Association, "Pitkin," historical overview, http://files.usgwarchives

.net/la/vernon/land/pitkin.txt (accessed February 18, 2023); "Pitkin," Vernon Parish Government, https://www.vernonparish.org/about-us/communities/pitkin (accessed February 18, 2023); Leeper, *Louisiana Place Names,* 192.

39. Will Price and Glenn Price, as cited in "History of Logansport," Town of Logansport, https://www.townoflogansport.com/logansport/history (accessed February 22, 2023); Texas Historical Commission, "Head of Navigation on the Sabine River: Belzora Landing," historical marker, https://atlas.thc.state.tx.us/Details/5423007705 (accessed February 22, 2023).

40. Raleigh A. Suarez, "The Sabine," in Davis, ed., *The Rivers and Bayous of Louisiana,* 78.

41. *Biographical and Historical Memoirs of Louisiana,* 2:42.

42. Seidemann, "Water and Power," 389–418.

43. Andy Crawford, "Ruby Anniversary: The Rocky History of Toledo Bend Reservoir's Construction," *Louisiana Sportsman,* https://www.louisianasportsman.com/fishing/ruby-anniversary / (accessed February 24, 2023).

44. Suarez, "The Sabine," in Davis, ed., *The Rivers and Bayous of Louisiana,* 79–80; Richard Campanella, "Sportsman's Paradise, or Paradise Lost? The Toledo Bend Reservoir," *64 Parishes* (Spring 2023): 58–61.

45. Bob Bowman, *The Gift of Las Sabinas: The History of the Sabine River Authority, 1949–1999* (Lufkin, Texas: Best of East Texas Publishers, 1999); Leeper, *Louisiana Place Names,* 248.

46. Sharon Kerr, "Building Toledo Bend Caused Controversy," *Beaumont Enterprise,* March 5, 2008, https://www.beaumontenterprise.com/jasper/article/Building-Toledo-Bend-caused-controversy -763036.php (accessed February 25, 2023).

47. Andy Crawford, "Ruby Anniversary: The Rocky History of Toledo Bend Reservoir's Construction," *Louisiana Sportsman,* https://www.louisianasportsman.com/fishing/ruby-anniversary/ (accessed February 24, 2023).

13. The Northern Hill Country

1. *Biographical and Historical Memoirs of Northwest Louisiana,* 104.

2. Nancy Maria Miller Surrey, *The Commerce of Louisiana During the French Régime, 1699–1763* (New York: Columbia Univ. Press, 1916), 82–83.

3. "History Pioneers of Webster Parish," publication and exhibits, Dorcheat Historical Museum, Minden, Louisiana, visited July 28, 2022.

4. Keumsoo Hong, "The Evolution of the Red River Valley Settlement System, 1714–1860" (Ph.D. diss., Louisiana State University, 1999), 147–148.

5. Patricia Barnwell, "History of Old Wire Road Is Traced," *Ruston Leader,* January 21, 1960; Wesley Harris, "Stagecoaches Once Ruled North Louisiana Travel," *Lincoln Parish Journal,* February 10, 2022, https://lincolnparishjournal.com/2022/02/10/stagecoaches-once-ruled-north-louisiana-travel/ (accessed October 14, 2022); "Old Wire Road," interpretative sign in Vienna, Louisiana, visited March 17, 2023.

6. The Caddo remained on the Brazos River until 1859, at which point federal authorities removed them to southwestern Oklahoma, where their descendants live today. Owen Lyon, "The Trail of the Caddo," *Arkansas Historical Quarterly* 11, no. 2 (Summer 1952): 128–129; Gudmestad, "Steamboats and the Removal of the Red River Raft," 392, 402–403.

7. Viola Carruth, *Caddo: 1,000: A History of the Shreveport Area from the Time of the Caddo Indians to the 1970s* (Shreveport, LA: Shreveport Magazine, 1970), 39.

8. Hong, "The Evolution of the Red River Valley Settlement System, 1714–1860," 368.

9. Carruth, *Caddo: 1,000,* 36.

10. Leeper, *Louisiana Place Names,* 117; Leeper, "Greenwood," March 13, 1966, in *Louisiana Places,* 116.

11. Fortier, *Louisiana—Comprising Sketches of Parishes, Towns, Events, Institutions, and Persons,* 1:481.

12. The villages appear on the Henry Schenck Tanner map of 1851, courtesy of the Library of Congress.

13. Clifton D. Cardin, *Bossier Parish History, 1843–1993: The First 150 Years* (Shreveport, LA: ImagePress, 1993), 48; Ann Middleton, "More Memories of Alden Bridge," Center for Regional Heritage Research, Stephen F. Austin State University, https://www.sfasu.edu/heritagecenter/7642.asp (accessed March 5, 2023).

14. Samuel J. Touchstone, *Bossier Parish History* (Princeton, LA: Folk-Life Books, 1989), 7.

15. J. W. Dorr, writing for the *New Orleans Crescent,* July 14, 1860, quoted in Cardin, *Bossier Parish History, 1843–1993,* 33.

16. Cardin, *Bossier Parish History, 1843–1993,* 107, 137–139.

17. Vickie Welborn, "State Doesn't Own Big Stretch of Bayou Dorcheat," *Houma Today,* June 15, 2010, https://www.houmatoday.com/story/entertainment/2010/06/15/state-doesnt-own-big-stretch-of-bayou-dorcheat/26918775007/ (accessed March 8, 2023).

18. From interpretative exhibits in the Dorcheat Historical Association Museum, Minden, Louisiana, visited July 28, 2022; Fortier, *Louisiana—Comprising Sketches of Parishes, Towns, Events, Institutions, and Persons,* 1:213.

19. National Register of Historic Places Nomination, "Downtown Minden Historic District, Webster Parish, LA" (Washington, D.C.: U.S. Department of the Interior, National Park Service, 1996), section 8, 1; Fortier, *Louisiana—Comprising Sketches of Parishes, Towns, Events, Institutions, and Persons,* 2:157; "History of Minden," City of Minden, Louisiana, https://www.mindenla.org/history/ (accessed March 8, 2023).

20. National Register of Historic Places Nomination, "Germantown" (Washington, D.C.: U.S. Department of the Interior, National Park Service, 1978).

21. Dorr, "A Tourist's Description of Louisiana in 1860," 1183.

22. Dorr, "A Tourist's Description of Louisiana in 1860," 1187.

23. Leeper, "Arcadia," December 24, 1961, in *Louisiana Places,* 14.

24. Leeper, "Athens," December 10, 1961, in *Louisiana Places,* 18.

25. Quoted in Marshall Scott Legan, "Railroad Sentiment in North Louisiana in the 1850s," *Louisiana History* 17, no. 2 (Spring 1976): 133; see also 125.

26. E. Dale Odom, "The Vicksburg, Shreveport and Texas: The Fortunes of a Scalawag Railroad," *Southwestern Social Science Quarterly* 44, no. 3 (December 1963): 277–285; "Map Showing the Route and Connections of the Mississippi Valley Railroad of Louisiana" (1882) and Rand McNally Company map of Louisiana (1896), both courtesy of the Library of Congress.

27. Leeper, *Louisiana Place Names,* 216; *Biographical and Historical Memoirs of Louisiana,* 1:242.

28. "West Hill" historic plaque, https://www.hmdb.org/m.asp?m=199038 (accessed March 13, 2023); Fortier, *Louisiana—Comprising Sketches of Parishes, Towns, Events, Institutions, and Persons,* 2:401.

29. Mildred Bernice Gallot, "Grambling State University: A History, 1901–1977" (Ph.D. diss., Louisiana State University, 1982), 149–164; Leeper, *Louisiana Place Names,* 114; "University History," Grambling State University, https://www.gram.edu/aboutus/history.php (accessed June 11, 2023).

30. Fortier, *Louisiana—Comprising Sketches of Parishes, Towns, Events, Institutions, and Persons,* 1:472–473.

31. Fortier, *Louisiana—Comprising Sketches of Parishes, Towns, Events, Institutions, and Persons,* 2:451.

32. "Yellow Pine: The Life and Death of a Lumber Town," anonymous paper written in 1997, distributed through "Yellow Pine History" section of Sibley, Louisiana website, https://www.sibleyla.com/ (accessed March 15, 2023).

33. Sherrod and Sherrod, *Plain Folk, Planters, and the Complexities of Southern Society,* 118–119.

34. Dr. Luther Longino, cited in "Yellow Pine: The Life and Death of a Lumber Town," anonymous paper written in 1997, distributed through "Yellow Pine History" section of Sibley, Louisiana website, https://www.sibleyla.com/ (accessed March 15, 2023).

35. *Jackson Parish, Louisiana* (Jonesboro, LA: Jackson Parish Chamber of Commerce, 1982), 34, 65.

36. Dorr, "A Tourist's Description of Louisiana in 1860," 1191; *Jackson Parish, Louisiana,* 34, 44–45; Fortier, *Louisiana—Comprising Sketches of Parishes, Towns, Events, Institutions, and Persons,* 1:601; "About Us: A Brief History of Jonesboro," Town of Jonesboro, https://www.jonesborola.net/about-us (accessed March 16, 2023).; "Shortlines: Tremont & Gulf Railway," https://hawkinsrails.net/shortlines/tg/tg.htm (accessed March 16, 2023); "A Look at Jackson Parish History," https://www.thenewsstar.com/story/news/local/2016/02/27/look-jackson-parish-history/80801044/ (accessed March 16, 2023); "The History of Jackson Parish—Founding of Jonesboro," *Jackson Parish Journal,* July 25, 2021, https://jacksonparishjournal.com/2021/07/25/the-history-of-jackson-parish-the-founding-of-jonesboro/ (accessed March 16, 2023).

37. Barthélémy Lafon, *Carte Générale du Territoire D'Orleans,* 1806; John Melish map of 1820, both courtesy of the Library of Congress.

38. Fortier, *Louisiana—Comprising Sketches of Parishes, Towns, Events, Institutions, and Persons,* 1:656–657; U.S. Environmental Protection Agency, "Superfund Record of Decision: American Creosote Works (Winnfield Plant), LA," EPA/ROD/R06-93/086 Report (Washington, D.C.: U.S. Environmental Protection Agency, April 1993), 15.

39. "Story of Winnfield from Civil War Days to Present Day," *Winnfield News-American,* November 5, 1948, http://files.usgwarchives.net/la/winn/history/hist1948.txt; "Winn Parish Boundary Lines Established Over 80 Years Ago," *Winnfield News-American,* September 9, 1938, http://files.usgwarchives.net/la/winn/history/ph1938.txt (accessed March 20, 2023).

40. Fortier, *Louisiana—Comprising Sketches of Parishes, Towns, Events, Institutions, and Persons,* 1:214.

41. "Junction City, Arkansas—Louisiana," historical plaque in Junction City, https://www.hmdb.org/m.asp?m=208815 (accessed March 12, 2023); Encyclopedia of Arkansas, "Junction City (Union County)," https://encyclopediaofarkansas.net/entries/junction-city-union-county-6139/ (accessed March 12, 2023); and other sources.

42. Statistical analysis by Richard Campanella, based on information in text and data in appendix; see final chapter for more synoptical analyses of Louisiana siting stories.

14. The Ouachita River Valley

1. Saucier, *Geomorphology and Quaternary Geologic History of the Lower Mississippi Valley,* 1:51; and other sources.

2. Louisiana Division of Archaeology, "Poverty Point," in *Discover Archaeology* (Louisiana Department of Culture, Recreation and Tourism, 2014), 4.

3. Information from Poverty Point exhibit at Louisiana State Museum, Baton Rouge, visited October 28, 2023.

4. Jon Gibson, *The Ancient Mounds of Poverty Point: Place of Rings* (Gainesville: Univ. Press of Florida Press, 2001).

5. Newton, *Louisiana: A Geographical Portrait,* 95.

6. Glen S. Greene, Ernest Russ Williams, Lorraine Heartfield, Mitchell Hillman, John R. Humble, and Dorothy Raney Anderson, *The Search for Fort Miro: A Colonial Spanish Fort in the Ouachita Valley* (Northeast Louisiana Archaeological Society, 1975), 5; Din, *Francisco Bouligny,* 92–93.

7. Samuel Dorris Dickinson, "Don Juan Filhiol at Écore à Fabri," *Arkansas Historical Quarterly* 46, no. 2 (Summer 1987): 133–155; Sylvester Breard, *Early History of Monroe* (Gretna, LA: Pelican, 2012), 56–58.

8. Gordon E. Harvey, *Historic Ouachita Parish: An Illustrated History* (Monroe, LA: Monroe Chamber of Commerce, 2007), 6.

9. Ernest Russ Williams, "Jean Baptiste Filhiol and the Founding of the Poste du Ouachita," in *North Louisiana: Essays on the Region and Its History,* vol. 1, *To 1865,* ed. B. H. Gilley (Ruston, LA: McGinty Trust Fund Publications, 1984), 18–21.

10. George Hunter, November 6, 1804, in John Francis McDermott and George Hunter, "The Western Journals of Dr. George Hunter, 1796–1805," *Transactions of the American Philosophical Society,* new series 53, no. 4 (1963): 87–88.

11. Harvey, *Historic Ouachita Parish,* 6–10; Breard, *Early History of Monroe,* 167–169.

12. Dorr, "A Tourist's Description of Louisiana in 1860," 1194.

13. Based on various maps and sources, including Lora Peppers, "Cottonport, Trenton Started West Monroe," *News Star,* June 15, 2016, https://www.thenewsstar.com/story/news/local/2016/06/15/cottonporttrenton-started-west-monroe/85607854/ (accessed August 22, 2023); historical plaque, "Trenton," in West Monroe, visited December 29, 2021; Harvey, *Historic Ouachita Parish.*

14. Based on John Melish map of 1820, Henry Schenck Tanner map of 1851, and J. H. Colton maps of 1855 and 1863, all courtesy of the Library of Congress.

15. Federal Writers' Project of the Works Progress Administration, *Louisiana—A Guide to the State,* ed. Harry Hansen (1941; reprint, New York: Hastings House, 1971 rev. ed.), 583–584.

16. Dorr, "A Tourist's Description of Louisiana in 1860," 1198.

17. Gilbert C. Din, "Spain's Immigration Policy in Louisiana and the American Penetration, 1792–1803," in Din, ed., *The Spanish Presence in Louisiana, 1763–1803* (Lafayette, LA: Center for Louisiana Studies, University of Southwestern Louisiana, 1996), 341–344.

18. Henry Schenck Tanner map of 1851, courtesy of the Library of Congress.

19. Federal Writers' Project of the Works Progress Administration, *Louisiana—A Guide to the State,* 584. "Railroads, 1915" map in Goins and Caldwell, eds., *Historical Atlas of Louisiana,* 68–69.

20. The name Logtown may have originated from an attempt by the Baron of Bastrop to purchase a cypress forest from Filhiol and build a sawmill, or it may have come from a timber operation by Filhiol or his descendants. Din, "Spain's Immigration Policy in Louisiana and the American Penetration, 1792–1803," 343.

21. National Register of Historic Places Nomination, "Logtown Plantation" (Washington, D.C.: U.S. Department of the Interior, National Park Service, 1980), 1–3; "History of Logtown Plantation," https://logtownestate.com/pages/history (accessed March 28, 2023); Breard, *Early History of Monroe,* 167.

22. H. Ted Woods, "Dan Humphries Settled Columbia Back in 1827," in Woods, ed., *Caldwell Parish in Slices* (Baton Rouge: Claitor's, 1972), 236–238.

23. Based on various cartographic sources, including Public Land Survey System maps (1840s) of the Louisiana Office of State Lands, Division of Administration; H. Ted Woods, "Caldwell Parish Is Created in 1838," in Woods, ed., *Caldwell Parish in Slices,* 5–6; historic plaque, "Ouachita River Steamboat Era, 1819–1927," https://www.hmdb.org/m.asp?m=120875 (accessed March 29, 2023).

24. H. Ted Woods, "New Kentucky Is First Post Office Established in Caldwell Parish," in Woods, ed., *Caldwell Parish in Slices,* 16–17; H. Ted Woods, "Railroad Almost By-Passed Columbia," in Woods, ed., *Caldwell Parish in Slices,* 58–60.

25. Leeper, *Louisiana Place Names,* 272.

26. Historical plaque, "Franklin Parish," https://www.hmdb.org/m.asp?m=51634 (accessed March 29, 2023).

27. Fortier, *Louisiana—Comprising Sketches of Parishes, Towns, Events, Institutions, and Persons,* 1:492–493; Leeper, *Louisiana Place Names,* 120; Helmuth Holtz, *Map of Louisiana & Arkansas* (1864), courtesy of the Library of Congress; "Harrisonburg, Louisiana," https://villageofharrisonburg.com/about-the-village/ (accessed April 1, 2023).

28. "An Act for the Purpose of Opening a Public Road from Vidalia, in the Parish of Concordia, to Harrisonburg, in the Parish of Catahoula," January 18, 1825, in *Acts Passed at the First Session of the Seventh Legislature of the State of Louisiana, 1824–1825* (New Orleans: M. Cruzat, 1825), 32–34.

29. Dorr, "A Tourist's Description of Louisiana in 1860," 1203–1205; John D. Winters, "The Ouachita-Black," in Davis, ed., *The Rivers and Bayous of Louisiana,* 26–28.

30. Megan C. Kassabaum, "Early Platforms, Early Plazas: Exploring the Precursors to Mississippian Mound-and-Plaza Centers," *Journal of Archaeological Research* 27, no. 2 (June 2019): 215.

31. George Hunter, October 23, 1804, George Hunter, November 6, 1804, in McDermott and Hunter, "The Western Journals of Dr. George Hunter, 1796–1805," 82.

32. Fortier, *Louisiana—Comprising Sketches of Parishes, Towns, Events, Institutions, and Persons,* 1:601; *Colton's Railroad Map of Part of the United States South of the 37th Parallel* (1883), courtesy of the Library of Congress.

33. An illustration from the 1860s showed that the ancient mounds stood high and dry even during the worst deluges. H. J. Lewis illustration in *Frank Leslie's Illustrated Newspaper,* circa 1860s, on display at Louisiana State Museum, Baton Rouge, visited October 28, 2023.

34. "Science Loses When Steam Shovel Wrecks Indian Mound," *Science News-Letter* 20, no. 550 (October 24, 1931): 271; Leeper, *Louisiana Place Names,* 134.

35. Signage throughout Jonesville, based on visit by author on July 1–3, 2023.

36. Gilbert Osofsky, "The Hebrew Emigrant Aid Society of the United States (1881–1883)," *Publications of the American Jewish Historical Society* 49, no. 3 (March 1960): 178; Breonne DeDecker, "Hidden Louisiana: The Socialist Jewish Commune of Sicily Island," *Antigravity Magazine* (May 2017), https://antigravitymagazine.com/column/hidden-louisiana-the-socialist-jewish-commune-of-sicily-island/ (accessed July 10, 2023).

37. Based on numerous maps and sources of the late 1800s and early 1900s, including the General Land Office map of 1876, the Colton Company map of 1882, the Rand McNally Company map of 1896, and the Map of Louisiana of 1902, courtesy of the Library of Congress and East Baton Rouge Library, as well as the "Railroads, 1915" map in Goins and Caldwell, eds., *Historical Atlas of Louisiana,* 68–69. Care must be taken in analyzing old railroad maps, as lines often changed names, and tracks and stations were sometimes plotted speculatively.

38. L. H. Taylor, "History of Castor Sulphur Springs Recounted," in Woods, ed., *Caldwell Parish in Slices,* 185–187.

15. The Upper Delta Country

1. R. T. Saucier, *Technical Report No. 3-757: Geological Investigation of the Boeuf-Tensas Basin—Lower Mississippi Valley* (Vicksburg, MS: U.S. Army Corps of Engineers Waterways Experiment Station, 1967); Fred B. Kniffen, *Louisiana: Its Land and People* (Baton Rouge: Louisiana State Univ. Press, 1968), 6; and other sources.

2. Randel Tom Cox, "A Geologist's Perspective on the Mississippi Delta," in *Defining the Delta: Multidisciplinary Perspectives on the Lower Mississippi River Delta,* ed. Janelle Collins (Fayetteville: Univ. of Arkansas Press, 2015), 11–12; Anka Muhlstein, *La Salle: Explorer of the North American Frontier* (Paris, France: Grasset and Fasquelle, 1992; trans. ed., New York: Arcade Publishing, 1992), 149.

3. The dubious distinction was computed by the U.S. Census Bureau in 1990, and came to public attention through a *Time Magazine* article by Jack E. White titled "The Poorest Place in America: Lake Providence's Poverty Is Extreme and, Despite Civil Rights Progress, Too Familiar in the South" (August 15, 1994). Since then, other places have qualified for the onerous superlative, but not because Lake Providence has done much better.

4. Sallie Benton Powell, "Lake Providence, La.," Works Progress Administration transcription

of 1928 history of Lake Providence in East Carroll Parish, in Ouachita Parish Public Library, Fifth District Works Progress Administration Collection.

5. Brasseaux, Conrad, and Robison, *The Courthouses of Louisiana,* 69; *Biographical and Historical Memoirs of Louisiana,* 1:225.

6. Fortier, *Louisiana—Comprising Sketches of Parishes, Towns, Events, Institutions, and Persons,* 2:32; National Register of Historic Places Inventory Nomination, "Lake Providence Historic District (Commercial)" (Washington, D.C.: U.S. Department of the Interior, National Park Service, 1979), 8–9.

7. Brasseaux, Conrad, and Robison, *The Courthouses of Louisiana,* 179–180.

8. Legan, "Railroad Sentiment in North Louisiana in the 1850s."

9. William M. Murphy, *Notes from the History of Madison Parish Louisiana* (Louisiana Polytechnic Institute Department of Printing, November 1927), as transcribed by Dick Sevier, https://sites.rootsweb.com/~lamadiso/articles/murphy.htm (accessed July 10, 2023); "Burning of Richmond," historical plaque, visited July 2, 2023. Note: Richmond today is a neighborhood in Tallulah across Roundaway Bayou, about two miles east of its original location. The historical site of Richmond was located at what is now Englewood, two miles south of Tallulah.

10. Yvonne Phillips, "Settlement Succession in the Tensas Basin" (Ph.D. diss., Louisiana State University, 1953), 113–115; "Map Showing the Route and Connections of the Mississippi Valley Railroad of Louisiana" (1882), courtesy of the Library of Congress; "Louisiana 1907," *Rand McNalley & Co.'s New Ideal State and County Survey and Atlas 1907,* courtesy of USGenWeb Archives; "Railroads, 1915" map in Goins and Caldwell, eds., *Historical Atlas of Louisiana,* 68–69.

11. "Mileage Tour—Lake Providence to Vidalia," 1937 field notes from anonymous researcher, Ouachita Parish Public Library, Fifth District Works Progress Administration Collection, courtesy of Louisiana Digital Library, https://louisianadigitallibrary.org/; "Roosevelt," historic plaque along Highway 65, visited July 2, 2023.

12. Phillips, "Settlement Succession in the Tensas Basin," 27–28.

13. Jeffrey Alan Owens, "The Burning of Lake St. Joseph," *Louisiana History* 32, no. 4 (Autumn 1991): 393–412.

14. "A Bit of Early History of Newellton," *Tensas Gazette,* July 10, 1936, as transcribed by Edith Ziegler for Tensas Parish History, USGENWEB Archives Project, http://files.usgwarchives.net/la/tensas/history/js000004.txt (accessed April 10, 2023); Leeper, *Louisiana Place Names,* 174.

15. Phillips, "Settlement Succession in the Tensas Basin," 32–35.

16. José Montero Marqués de Casa Mena de Pedro, *The Spanish in New Orleans and Louisiana* (Gretna, LA: Pelican, 2000), 141–142; *Biographical and Historical Memoirs of Louisiana,* 1:227; and other sources.

17. Phillips, "Settlement Succession in the Tensas Basin," 32 (footnote), 33.

18. Today, the historic Concordia Parish Courthouse Building sits just two blocks from the bridge to Natchez, and on its lawn is a granite monument marking the ferry landing and starting point of the Old Harrisonburg Road. "Natchez-Natchitoches Road/Harrisonburg Road," "Relocation of Vidalia, 1938–1939," monument and historic plaque in Vidalia, Louisiana, visited July 1, 2023.

19. Phillips, "Settlement Succession in the Tensas Basin," 34–35, 50.

20. National Register of Historic Places Nomination, "St. Joseph Historic District" (Washington, D.C.: U.S. Department of the Interior, National Park Service, 1980), 3; "St. Joseph," historical plaque in St. Joseph, Louisiana, https://www.hmdb.org/m.asp?m=119545 (accessed April 14, 2023).

21. Phillips, "Settlement Succession in the Tensas Basin," 85; Leeper, *Louisiana Place Names,* 262.

22. Marion Bragg, *Historic Names and Places on the Lower Mississippi River* (Vicksburg, MS: Mississippi River Commission, 1977), 181–182; "Weekly Packet, New Orleans-Natchez-Waterproof," *Daily Picayune,* November 4, 1841, 3.

23. Elaine Dundy, *Ferriday, Louisiana* (New York: Donald I. Fine, 1991), 58–59. Dozens of Louisiana railroad towns and mill towns arose similarly in this era.

24. Phillips, "Settlement Succession in the Tensas Basin," 116–117; Leeper, *Louisiana Place Names,* 96–97; John La Tourrette, "La Tourrette's Reference Map of the State of Louisiana" (New Orleans: John La Tourrette, 1848).

25. Dundy, *Ferriday, Louisiana,* inside flap.

Conclusion

1. German settlers of the 1720s did indeed form the villages of Hoffen, Marienthal, Augsburg, and Carlstein along La Côte des Allemands. But none of these villages survived, in name or place, and early German families eventually assimilated into Creole society and became part of the plantation economy preceding modern-day River Road communities. The four lost villages are not included in the analysis. John Hanno Deiler, *The Settlement of the German Coast of Louisiana and the Creoles of German Descent* (Philadelphia: American Germanica Press, 1909), 10–49; René Le Conte, "The Germans in Louisiana in the Eighteenth Century," trans. and ed. Glenn R. Conrad, *Louisiana History* 8, no. 1 (Winter 1967): 72–73.

2. It should be remembered that Spanish officials were not fully in control of Louisiana until the late 1760s and had largely relinquished the colony by 1802–1803. At least one settlement originating during Louisiana's Spanish dominion, Baton Rouge, owes its existence in part to British colonial activity.

3. Joseph C. G. Kennedy, *Population of the United States in 1860, Compiled from the Original Returns of the Eighth Census* (Washington, D.C.: Government Printing Office, 1864), 195. The entries for Louisiana included New Orleans (population 168,675); Donaldsonville (11,848); a likely erroneous entry for "St. Landry" as having 10,346 residents (which I excluded from the above calculations); Algiers (5,816, part of greater New Orleans); Baton Rouge (5,428); Jefferson (5,107, part of greater New Orleans); Shreveport (2,190); Carrollton (1,756, part of greater New Orleans); Plaquemine (1,663); Alexandria (1,461); Homer (1,451); Thibodeaux (1,380); Minden (1,146); Opelousas (786); Bayou Sara (540); Washington (536); Vermilionville (later Lafayette, 498); Bastrop (481); Pineville (393); Floyd (298); and Delhi (175). No other communities were listed, including Natchitoches, Monroe, Lake Charles, or Houma.

4. Kennedy, *Population of the United States in 1860,* 195, 373–396.

5. Lawrence N. Powell, citing his 2017 paper "You Are Who You Trade With: Why Antebellum St. Louis Industrialized and New Orleans Didn't," later published in *French St. Louis: Landscape, Contexts, and Legacy,* ed. Jay Gitlin, Robert Michael Morrissey, and Peter J. Kastor (Lincoln: Univ. of Nebraska Press, 2021).

6. I credit this phrase to historian Lawrence N. Powell, personal communications, March–April 2024.

7. Overview, Lawrason Act, Louisiana Revised Statutes, January 2019, https://app.lla.state.la.us/llala.nsf/BC353E94C499B01086257AB800697A27/$FILE/Lawrason%20Act%20FAQ.pdf (accessed November 8, 2023).

8. Richard Campanella, "Louisiana Cities and the Rank-Size Rule," *Louisiana Cultural Vistas* (Spring 2015): 66–67.

9. "Louisiana has to offer more miles of those great levelers of rail rates—navigable waterways—than any two other states combined," stated a 1917 publication in regard to the state's 4,794 miles of navigable rivers, bayous, and canals. D. D. Moore, ed., *Louisiana: A Text Book on the Industrial, Commercial, Financial, Agricultural, Live Stock, Produce, Lumber and Mineral Resources, and Advantages of a Great State* (New Orleans: Times-Picayune, 1917), 3.

10. Paraphrased from Hurd, *Principles of City Land Values,* 13–24.

Appendix

1. Identifying a primary and/or secondary rationale may be straightforward for most railroad and timber towns, but can be difficult for those many settlements with concurrent or complementary rationales. For example, did Bienville site New Orleans on account of a shortcut/portage, or as a port/landing? In the text, I emphasize the portage, because it directed Bienville's attention to one particular riverbank. But that portage had no intrinsic value; rather, it *added* value to what Bienville truly sought, which was a river port. So, in the appendix, I recorded "port/landing" as New Orleans's primary siting rationale, and shortcut/portage as the secondary rationale.

INDEX